THE MORMON QUESTION

STUDIES IN LEGAL HISTORY

Published by the University of North Carolina Press
in association with the American Society for Legal History

Thomas A. Green and Hendrik Hartog, editors

The Mormon Question

Polygamy and Constitutional Conflict in Nineteenth-Century America

SARAH BARRINGER GORDON

The University of North Carolina Press

Chapel Hill and London

The paper in this book meets the guidelines for permanence
and durability of the Committee on Production Guidelines
for Book Longevity of the Council on Library Resources.

Library of Congress Cataloging-in-Publication Data
Gordon, Sarah Barringer, 1955–
The Mormon question: polygamy and constitutional conflict
in nineteenth-century America / Sarah Barringer Gordon.
p. cm. — (Studies in legal history)
Includes bibliographical references and index.
ISBN 0-8078-2661-8 (alk. paper)
ISBN 0-8078-4987-1 (pbk.: alk. paper)
1. Freedom of religion—United States—History. 2. Church
and state—United States—History. 3. Polygamy—Utah—
History. I. Title. II. Series.
KF4783 G67   2002
342.73′0852—dc21
2001041472

06 05 04 03 02   5 4 3 2 1

Portions of Chapters 1, 2, and 5 were published, respectively, in
Sarah Barringer Gordon, " 'Our National Hearthstone': Anti-
polygamy Fiction and the Sentimental Campaign against Moral
Diversity in Antebellum America," *Yale Journal of Law and the
Humanities* 8 (Summer 1996): 295–350; "Blasphemy and the
Law of Religious Liberty in Nineteenth-Century America,"
American Quarterly 52, no. 4 (December 2000): 682–720; and
" 'The Liberty of Self-Degradation': Polygamy, Woman Suf-
frage, and Consent in Nineteenth-Century America," *Journal of
American History* 83 (December 1996): 815–47 (all reprinted by
permission).

Publication of this book has been aided by a generous grant
from the Legal History Consortium at the University of
Pennsylvania Law School.

TO NANCY SOUTHGATE,
who loved books

CONTENTS

CONTENTS

ILLUSTRATIONS

PREFACE

This book grows out of my journey into a dual scholarly commitment. My underlying (and gradually unfolding) inquiry is into conflicted loyalties, especially those that trap the believer between religious command and temporal authority. I first experienced this dilemma in my own education when I applied to graduate school. I was torn between divinity school and law school. Which should it be, divine Word or secular law? I assumed that these were separate and mutually exclusive. Little did I know.

Every law student learns in constitutional law classes that conflict between sovereigns is basic to all of constitutional history. Such conflicts have been—and continue to be—central also to the fields of social ethics and justice in the ministry. If few clerics or lawyers plan in advance to venture onto the field of conflict, many are drawn in willy-nilly. The pages of the Supreme Court Reports are full of hard-fought and deeply felt cases. I even argued one in my first-year Moot Court competition. It was wonderful. I wrestled with questions of separation of church and state, individual religious liberty, and even the definition of "religion." I felt I had at last found my calling—I would work with and study those who lived such conflicts.

Thanks to two understanding deans at Yale, I pursued simultaneous training in both religion and law. Symbolic of the luxury and the tension of pursuing such a vocation was the mile-long walk between divinity school and law school. There was a virtual barrier, somewhere on the slope (upward to religion or downward to law, depending on which way I was walking) of Prospect Street in New Haven. For several years, I led an apparently split life, disappearing into one or another intellectual and institutional universe, walking up and down the hill thousands of times in fair weather and foul (mostly foul). It made sense to me to study such conflicts from both sides of the divide. But often it was not easy. I was teased about "prayer breakfasts" in law school and outraged when expected to say "amen" to a professor's spontaneous prayer in Bible classes taught in the "div" school chapel. Conflicts between law and religion were everywhere, even in the life of a grad student.

There was more to my decision to write this book, however. The past is also a vital part of this story. This book is a work of American history. As a lawyer representing religious individuals and organizations in constitutional litigation, I became convinced that sustained and thoughtful work on law and religion—as opposed to visceral response to the latest crisis—was possible only in the exploration of past conflicts. And of course the lure of books and school and ideas was tempting beyond measure. Pulled by the world of history, eager to delve more deeply into conflicts than was possible as a practicing lawyer, I soon found myself pursuing doctoral work in legal and religious history, too.

This book unites the three fields of religion, law, and history. Many topics familiar to most Americans call upon this combination of knowledge. They include such diverse and fascinating movements as antislavery humanism in the nineteenth century, civil rights, school prayer, and debates over abortion in the twentieth. I took a road less traveled. My book tells the story of how marriage became a central social and spiritual issue of constitutional conflict in the second half of the nineteenth century.

My own intellectual history, and my ability to spend a decade writing this book, is a tale of the gift of education and professional training. I am grateful for the opportunity to reflect on the meaning of faith in the lives of people. The power of such faith infuses the story that follows and the lives of those who lived the conflict.

INTRODUCTION

Faith and the Contested Constitution

In the mid-nineteenth century, an extraordinary contest over religion and law took shape. The conflict began with the announcement in 1852 by Brigham Young, president and prophet of the Church of Jesus Christ of Latter-day Saints, popularly called Mormons. Young proclaimed that Mormons believed in and practiced polygamy—known to the faithful as the "celestial" law of plural marriage, or "Patriarchal Marriage," or simply "the Principle."[1] In 1890, however, the church formally announced that it would no longer counsel the Saints to disobey the laws of man by practicing polygamy. The public announcement of the intention to abandon all claims to legal right eventually (although with aftershocks that lasted into the twentieth century) satisfied the great majority of those who opposed polygamy (antipolygamists) that their goal had been achieved at last, and that American civilization had been saved from a potent and destructive "barbarism."[2]

What went on during the years between? As this book shows, the conflict over polygamy became the preoccupation of novelists, journalists, political cartoonists, and newspaper editors, clerics, lecturers, lobbyists, woman's rights activists, political theorists, missionaries, state and national politicians, criminal defendants and their families, constitutional and criminal defense lawyers, federal and territorial officials, presidents, and Supreme Court justices. This book is about their efforts to explain why the practice of polygamy in the Mormon territory (eventually state) of Utah and surrounding jurisdictions created a constitutional conflict over the meaning and scope of liberty and democracy in the United States. Vast quantities of ink and paper were invested in the project, and yield rich rewards. The "Mormon

THE

BOOK OF MORMON:

AN ACCOUNT WRITTEN BY THE HAND OF MOR-
MON, UPON PLATES TAKEN FROM
THE PLATES OF NEPHI.

Wherefore it is an abridgment of the Record of the People of Nephi; and also of the Lamanites; written to the Lamanites, which are a remnant of the House of Israel; and also to Jew and Gentile; written by way of commandment, and also by the spirit of Prophesy and of Revelation. Written, and sealed up, and hid up unto the LORD, that they might not be destroyed; to come forth by the gift and power of GOD unto the interpretation thereof; sealed by the hand of Moroni, and hid up unto the LORD, to come forth in due time by the way of Gentile; the interpretation thereof by the gift of GOD; an abridgment taken from the Book of Ether.

Also, which is a Record of the People of Jared, which were scattered at the time the LORD confounded the language of the people when they were building a tower to get to Heaven: which is to shew unto the remnant of the House of Israel how great things the LORD hath done for their fathers; and that they may know the covenants of the LORD, that they are not cast off forever; and also to the convincing of the Jew and Gentile that JESUS is the CHRIST, the ETERNAL GOD, manifesting Himself unto all nations. And now if there be fault, it be the mistake of men; wherefore condemn not the things of GOD, that ye may be found spotless at the judgment seat of CHRIST.

BY JOSEPH SMITH, JUNIOR,
AUTHOR AND PROPRIETOR.

PALMYRA:
PRINTED BY E. B. GRANDIN, FOR THE AUTHOR.

1830.

The title page of the first edition of the *Book of Mormon* (left). The Word of God revealed to Prophet Joseph Smith in these latter days, first published in 1830, began a journey of faith and constitutional conflict. Five decades later, a political cartoon in *The Judge* magazine (right) depicted a Mormon man defying the

AN UNSIGHTLY OBJECT--WHO WILL TAKE THE AXE AND HEW IT DOWN?

rest of the nation, holding women captive, and proclaiming his victory over a sheepish and ineffective national government. The journey from the birth of a new religion to constitutional struggle is the story of the Mormon Question in nineteenth-century America. Courtesy of Alfred Bush and Yale University Library.

Question," as many nineteenth-century Americans called it, posed fundamental questions about religion, marriage, and constitutional law. The national Constitution must not shield such immorality, those who opposed polygamy (antipolygamists) argued, or liberty would be fatally compromised. There *must* be a relationship between the structures of government created by the Constitution and the structures of Christian morality that made civilized life possible.[3]

The doubt that swirled about the moral nature of the Constitution, however, meant that such claims were always tinged by uncertainty. Real and significant differences about the core of sovereign authority in America propelled defenders of monogamy into untested constitutional theories, as they struggled to articulate how the national government could assume authority over marriage and faith in Utah. Most important, such arguments met with fierce resistance from Mormons.

The glory of the Constitution, according to Mormon theorists, was that its protection of religious liberty and local difference created the space through which the New Dispensation could enter. Nineteenth-century Mormons and their opponents agreed that marriage was central to religious faith and political order. Yet Mormons believed in a distinct and different moral order based on new divine revelation. To many Mormons, polygamy was the most difficult, and arguably the most exhilarating, of the revealed Word in these latter days. God, speaking through Prophet Joseph Smith, commanded Mormon men to marry more than one wife—to practice polygamy when called upon by faith and church authority to do so. The restoration of God's eternal law of marriage was a vital aspect of the new faith. It also brought Mormons into direct and prolonged conflict with the law of marriage in the rest of the nation. As one polygamist argued, the "whole superstructure" of government rested on divine authority exercised in marriage. From its starting point in Utah, the spread of latter-day faith and practice would remake government, cleansing society of the scourge of prostitution, and elevating all of humanity. A Mormon wife reflected on the struggle of the faithful, "It was the principle of plural marriage that we were trying to establish . . . and if we had established it, it would have been for the benefit of the whole human race, and the race will say so yet."[4]

These debates were not about a "place" for faith in law and government; rather, they revealed the fact that differing faiths, vital and hotly contested, involved the very cornerstones of government in nineteenth-century America. Then as now, the Constitution set such cornerstones. But the precise meaning of the Constitution, then as now, was painfully elusive. Both sides fought over the meaning of liberty and self-government in Utah, which remained a territory (and thus neither a state, nor quite a part of the national government) throughout the conflict over polygamy. As Mormons and their opponents learned through repeated battles, constitutional contests can consume a people's stamina as well as its interpretive skill and moral vision.

Both sides of the religious divide realized that a broad understanding of local autonomy preserved by the national Constitution was integral to the Mormons' ability to remake marriage and law for Utah. The relationship between national and state governments described in the Constitution, which constitutional lawyers and theorists call "federalism," mediates the degree of power the national government may claim over any one of its constituent parts. Principles of federalism changed over the course of the nineteenth century, although the basic structure of national and state governments remained the same. The Civil War determined first that states did not have the right to secede, and second that local governments did not have the right to maintain slavery. Beyond that, however, the power of local governments to resist federal intervention was staunchly maintained by many Americans (especially Southerners) and bitterly opposed by others (usually Northerners). Battles over polygamy recast and focused such constitutional debates in ways both new and familiar.

Mormons insisted that constitutional principles of federalism protected their right to govern themselves even as the states did, and to practice whatever religion seemed best to the majority of the inhabitants of the territory. The Mormons' claim to local sovereignty resonated with powerful strands of constitutional theory, as well as with the language of faith. Mormons drew on constitutional lessons that were key to the structures of federalism before the Civil War. They forced their opponents onto new ground; in reply, antipolygamists drew on the moral and legal reform that surrounded the conflict over slavery, and that supported a stronger and more authoritative central government. As they poured emotion and energy into constitutional argument, the contestants translated the conflict into a struggle between faiths for constitutional validity.

Driven by religious difference, Mormons and their opponents learned that faith had everything to do with government, and vice versa. Spiritual meaning and this-worldly power converged most poignantly in marriage. In monogamy (as in polygamy), husbands and wives blended faith with governance, obedience with power, spiritual growth with human sexuality. Commitment to one or the other form of marriage shaped public as well as private life. Participants in the conflict discovered that local sovereignty, democracy, consent, economic power, and wifely subordination all hinged on faith and its realization in marriage. As one vision flourished, it diminished the other; and the power to live in light of faith was proportionately realized or denied.

The conflict of faiths pitted the laws of God against the laws of man; believers on both sides learned that their Constitution was, perhaps, not theirs after all. The instability of constitutional claims and interpretation tortured and energized the combatants. Their struggle to capture and hold the Constitution provided a unifying field of conflict; antipolygamists and Mormon defenders of polygamy alike yearned for the dignity and validity that the defeat of their enemies would bring. To win would be to acquire constitutional legitimacy, and to prove that the opposition had betrayed the legacy that was enshrined in the constitutional text. The long and painful conflict over religious liberty, marriage, and law is the subject of this book, which tells the story of the Mormon Question and constitutional change in the nineteenth century.

Mormons and their opponents began their conflict in a legal world that was far different from the one they created. In 1830, when the Church of Jesus Christ of Latter-day Saints was founded in upstate New York, the federal government was weak and legal power was decentralized. The national Constitution, which occupies so much legal space in the early twenty-first century, was all but invisible in most Americans' day-to-day lives. If anything at all was clear about constitutional law in the new nation, moreover, it was that the constitutional amendments known as the Bill of Rights did not apply to the states. Freedom of religion, separation of church and state, freedom of speech, trial by jury, the prohibition of cruel and unusual punishment, unreasonable searches and seizures by government officials, all of these limited the power of the national government. But unlike the twentieth and twenty-first centuries, in which federal constitutional rights have been applied against state as well as federal government action, in the eighteenth and nineteenth centuries, states were immune from federal intervention in crucial areas of civil liberties. Confirming earlier cases, the U.S. Supreme Court held in 1845 that the First Amendment, which addresses the "free exercise" of religion as well as separation of church and state, did not limit the rights of states to govern within their borders.[5]

The establishment clause, for example, as the provision of the First Amendment that prohibits Congress from enacting legislation "respecting an establishment of religion" is called by constitutional lawyers, prevented the federal government from establishing a given denomination as the official federal church. It also protected the established religions in six of the original thirteen states from federal interference. Thus it is a mistake to assume that the national Constitution guaranteed the separation of church and state or religious liberty to all citizens from its inception: "[T]hat is left," held the Supreme Court, "to the state constitutions and laws." There had been momentous and important changes in law and religion by the 1830s, to be sure, but it was not the federal Constitution that mattered.[6]

That constitutional world was both essential to the conflict over polygamy that followed and irrevocably changed by it. When Mormonism appeared on the crowded and ebullient religious scene in 1830, the constitutional law of religion in many states was already well developed. Many of the legal doctrines that were later deployed in cases dealing with Mormon polygamy were developed in decisions by state courts in the early national period. Americans valorized their national Constitution, but it was in state courts and legislative assemblies that they first fought out basic questions of civil liberties.

Disestablishment, or the separation of institutions of religion from institutions of government, had been a new and potentially upsetting idea in the late eighteenth century. But the American colonies, and then the new states, especially in the mid-Atlantic region, were as diverse religiously as they were ethnically. Pennsylvania, just to give one example, was home to English Quakers, Scotch-Irish Presbyterians, German Moravians, and many more. In the new nation, the separation of church and state formally began in Virginia with the enactment of Thomas Jefferson's Bill for the Establishment of Religious Freedom in 1785. Jefferson's bill was not motivated by the conviction that religious belief would flourish in a disestablished state; instead, the skeptical Jefferson hoped to purge Virginia politics of religious influence. Religious diversity affected politics as well as worship in Virginia, however; Baptists and other dissenters were crucial to the enactment of the bill, as they joined forces with Jefferson and elite rationalists to defeat the Anglican establishment.[7]

Six states retained establishments into the national period, though they generally were weak and underfinanced. Other states either followed Virginia's lead or had never had a formal establishment. Even those states that maintained a formal establishment soon found that religious diversity and republican government undermined its value to the holders of the privilege. By the second quarter of the nineteenth century, only Massachusetts maintained an establishment, and it, too, was in crisis. Following the lead of other states, the Supreme Judicial Court in 1820 held that the majority of voters (rather than only those with the most impeccable religious credentials) could decide whom to employ as their minister. Disestablishment eventually followed this decision. Embracing democratic rule for established faiths, state court judges also implicitly attacked nondemocratic theologies. In the early Republic, Roman Catholicism was the primary object of such attacks. American judges, by convincing themselves that democratic institutions were essential to religious as well as secular governance, allied themselves with a fundamentally Protestant conception of religious liberty. Local decision-making, majority rule, and a minister's accountability to his congregation rather than to a remote and hierarchical (read Roman) authority all distinguished Protestantism in American "nativist" theory from foreign, "papist" Romanism. Thus in a constitutional world defined in part by anti-Catholicism, separation of church and state took root and flourished.[8]

The law of religious liberty also dovetailed comfortably with Protestantism. As one eminent New York judge put it, religious freedom was bounded by majority rule in much the same way that establishments were. The "moral discipline" created by the "people of this state" reflected their "profess[ion of] the general doctrines of christianity, as the rule of their faith and practice." The great majority of the people were Christians, and the law mirrored their preferences. An argument that religious liberty should protect anything other than "general [Protestant] Christianity" was thus an attempt to shield undemocratic beliefs and practices, confusing the abuse of liberty with its exercise. Disestablishment and constitutional protections of religious liberty in the states may have unsettled centuries of English legal tradition, but by the 1830s, American jurists recrafted links between democracy and "general" Protestantism, reassuring themselves that their government was neither heathen nor sectarian.[9]

That was, briefly described, the constitutional world in which Mormons sought protection for themselves and their practices. Like many Americans, most Mormon leaders in the early period had only the sketchiest idea of the relationship between the state and federal governments. Mormons also did not have a clear understanding of state constitutional law. They had a profound admiration for the federal Constitution, and they believed that its provisions were divinely inspired—there to safeguard them against the ravages of mobs that tarred and feathered their prophet, harassed their missionaries, pillaged their fields, and even murdered women and children in the 1830s and 1840s. They were amazed and mortified that the Constitution failed to protect them or to avenge their suffering at the hands of

MASSACRE OF MORMONS AT HAUN'S MILL.

In 1838, seventeen Mormon men and two boys were killed in a brutal massacre in Missouri. The survivors were outraged to learn that the federal government could neither offer them protection against further persecutions nor punish the state officials who countenanced the violence. Courtesy of The Huntington Library, San Marino, Calif.

local populations. Principles of federalism, Mormons found to their chagrin, meant that they had no claim to national protection. As a concept, federalism, like many abstract legal doctrines, is the stuff of learned and dry theorizing. On the ground, as Mormons learned from bitter experience, questions of states' rights and the limits of federal power can make all the difference.[10]

As they absorbed this painful lesson in federalism, the Saints eventually turned it to their advantage. After they fled westward in the late 1840s, Mormon leaders claimed that the same principles that left them exposed to the vicissitudes of local majority rule in the states, dictated that they had the same rights to self-governance in their own jurisdiction—the Territory of Utah, which was admitted into the union as part of the famous Compromise of 1850. And yet Utah was a territory, and thus neither a state nor entirely under federal control. Territories occupied an ambiguous and changeable place in the legal order, for although they clearly were not states (yet), they also were presumed to have the power to become states. Territories were subject to federal organization as political entities. But it was not clear how much of the states' power to govern themselves they acquired after organization but before statehood. Advocates of states' rights fre-

Tarred and feathered.

Violence against Mormons included attacks on the prophet himself, shown here as the victim of the painful and humiliating practice of tarring and feathering at the hands of an Illinois mob. From T. B. H. Stenhouse, *Rocky Mountain Saints*. Courtesy of The Huntington Library, San Marino, Calif.

quently argued in favor of local sovereignty for territories; the existence of slavery and polygamy in the territories prompted others to rethink the virtues of localism. Antipolygamists in particular struggled to cope with what they considered a betrayal of fundamental constitutional principle, applicable to all jurisdictions through "general Christianity."

To most political, religious, and legal theorists of post-Revolutionary America, Christian faith was indispensable to the survival of the new nation. Without the authority of God, insisted outgoing president George Washington in his farewell address in 1796, the less potent commands of earthly sovereigns could not ensure the obedience of citizens. "[W]here is the security for property, for reputation, for life," Washington queried, without "religious principle" at the back of public morality and patriotism? Washington assumed that "[w]ith slight shades of difference," Americans shared the "same Religeon." This assumption was soon challenged by the appearance of new faiths. As many Americans learned to their chagrin, even Christian belief was ungovernable in a land of such diversity and size. Religious enthusiasm led new believers in new directions, often onto divergent political and spiritual paths.[11]

Mormonism was one such new direction. However different from most Christian expression in the early nineteenth century, Mormonism was integrally connected to the broader American religious experience. This relationship would have been vehemently denied both by polygamists and by their foes. Nonetheless, the religious fervor of Mormons and Mormonism was an example of the vigor of American religious experience. Both pro- and antipolygamists shared a deep sense of religious mission and of the cosmic significance of the American experiment. Yet, personal testimony and action reflecting the experience of God's love and authority—most aptly summarized in the phrase "religious witness"—led believers in radically different and conflicting directions. Their divisions were painful in part because each side shared a fundamental conviction that it had exclusive access to the true American faith.[12]

Most antipolygamists were so alarmed by the Mormons that they refused to concede even that latter-day faith was itself Christian. For their part, the Latter-day Saints condemned the religious and social confusion, the "war of words" they saw everywhere around them. The Saints insisted theirs was the true Christian church, that the Protestants who opposed them were apostates, and the Catholic Church, the "Mother of Harlots." Mormons rejected the heresies and hypocrisies of the rest of the Christian world, and embraced a new sense of sacred space and time. Plural marriage, evidence of profound commitment and sacrifice to those within the faith, also communicated defiance of traditional Christian precepts to the rest of the country.[13]

In some senses, latter-day revelation and practices were indeed so distinct from other forms of Christianity that it is valid to call Mormonism a new religion. Religious historian Jan Shipps has cogently argued that Mormonism in the nineteenth century brought believers out of one faith and into a new one—a distinct religion, emerging out of but different from Christianity. As this book emphasizes, latter-day faith was also deeply related to American Protestantism and was frequently opposed with tools that had been deployed against Catholicism. If nineteenth-century Mormonism was a new, post-Christian dispensation, it was also developed and defended in American space and time. The Mormon Question was riveting and

Popular author Maria Ward depicted in her *Female Life among the Mormons* a "Mormon meeting" that closely resembled images of other Christian revivals along the frontier. Courtesy of Oberlin College Library.

different in part because Mormonism shared so much with other forms of religious witness.[14]

The conflict over polygamy forces us to reassess the strength of national legal and political movements after the Civil War and to appreciate the role of faith in nineteenth-century legal interpretation and political culture. The breadth of issues both sides addressed is astounding—religion, sexuality, slavery, moral relativism, freedom, consent, democracy, women's rights. The conflict included disputes over the relationship of political legitimacy to private structures of governance and state control over marriage, as well as the moral meaning of religious liberty and separation of church and state, all issues that have dogged lawyers and constitutional theorists for a century and more. By recovering important constitutional debates and legal developments, this book begins to explain why such issues provoke tangled and enduring questions. Legal scholars and constitutional historians have focused on the abolition of slavery, the failure of

INTRODUCTION

This detail from an antipolygamy cartoon from *The Daily Graphic* in the early 1880s depicted Mormonism as a pirate, complete with captive women tied to his belt and a dagger labeled "Defiance." Courtesy of Yale University Library.

Reconstruction, and the jurisprudence of race, all important topics but not capable of yielding an understanding of the role of religion in the development of constitutional law and federal power. They have neglected slavery's "twin relic of barbarism," as contemporary Republicans called polygamy, missing the conflict over religion that remade legal history and constitutional law in the second half of the nineteenth century.

Attention to the conflict, moreover, reveals a history at odds with shopworn stories of the "rise of religious liberty" in the United States. According to these stories, religious diversity and freedom grew naturally over the course of American history. Other old chestnuts include

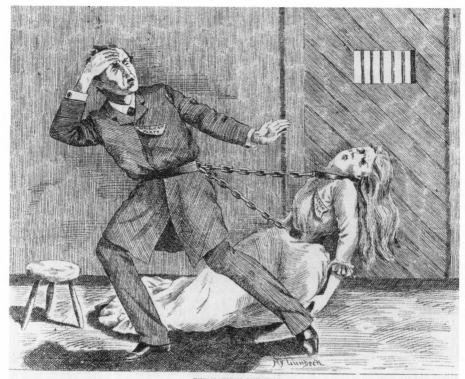

THE MORMON QUESTION.
LET THE TERRIBLE RESPONSIBILITY BE CHAINED TO THE REAL CRIMINAL.

Antipolygamists urged national politicians to take responsibility for what they argued was the enslavement of women in Utah. Republicans responded by enacting federal legislation to criminalize polygamy and eventually to dismantle the power and property of the Mormon Church itself. From *The Daily Graphic*, 22 October 1883. Courtesy of Yale University Library.

theories that questions of marriage and family did not trouble the federal government before the privacy cases of the 1960s and 1970s, and that the abandonment of Reconstruction in the South spelled the end of federal moral oversight, at least for the duration of the nineteenth century. My research has led me to qualify such theories, as I probed the significant restrictions on religious difference imposed by the national government. The campaign against polygamy created a second reconstruction in the West as the national government forcibly retooled marriage in Utah in the late nineteenth century.[15]

The Mormon Question also adds tone and texture to historical studies of the "Christian nation" that jurists and clerics hoped was the nineteenth-century United States. As the struggle between Mormons and their opponents shows, the religious nature of the nation was in substantial doubt until the very end of the century. Even then, anti-polygamists' victory was expressed in explicitly secular terms. The Supreme Court protected the constitutional vision of American Protestants by holding that religious belief was not a valid criterion for challenging legal mandates; new faith could not validate a new and different legal order. Mormons protested that this was a vapid understanding of religious liberty, but the unpopularity of the Latter-day Saints and their faith obscured the vulnerability that such decisions created for all faiths. Thus the battle over religion and law, and the constitutional triumph of antipolygamy, indirectly and implicitly undermined the constitutional power of antipolygamists, even as it eviscerated the constitutional claims of Mormons.[16]

The courage, tenacity, and conviction of both sides impressed me throughout my research and writing on the Mormon Question. Mormons, and their church, lost the battle for a religiously determined legal order. The defeat was wrenching, but the battle was also exhilarating and productive of important victories. As the Mormon Question roiled through the nation, the Saints and their opponents retooled the constitutional landscape. The struggle for constitutional recognition and protection was fast paced and tellingly argued. It finally defined the basic and still valid federal law of church and state. The story is rich and intriguing. Contestants left voluminous and important records of their conflict. More than a century later, the power of their competing convictions leaps off the page, drawing us in and leading us on to the edge of the spiritual and constitutional precipice they confronted.

PART ONE

The Laws of God and
the Laws of Man

CHAPTER I

The Power of the Word(s)

The conflict began with religious faith. Founded in 1830, the same year as the first publication of its new scripture, the *Book of Mormon*, the Church of Jesus Christ of Latter-day Saints quickly acquired passionate adherents. Joseph Smith, the sect's founder, prophet, and first president, translated the "golden plates," which he reported were revealed to him by an angel. Smith was a visionary who had a reputation in upstate New York as a counterfeiter, fortune-teller, and treasure hunter. His inspiration forever changed his world and drew to his church a following whose faith was tested by the scorn and persecution of outsiders.[1]

Mormonism was born in a culture saturated with religious messages. The Second Great Awakening, as the religious revivals of the late eighteenth and early nineteenth centuries are called, burned through layers of apathy and confusion after the Revolution. The conviction that faith was essential to individual salvation, political freedom, stability, and prosperity traveled across Protestant America in the early Republic, affecting legal and political thought as well as popular culture. Mormons were schooled in the language as well as the practices of religious commitment. In the conflict that followed, both Mormons and their opponents marshaled the techniques of popular persuasion. They understood that effective religious expression was the key to broad appeal, and ultimately to political power.

Mormons were part of this broader religious revival, but they also rejected many parts of mid-nineteenth-century American culture. The decision to become a Mormon was also a commitment to step out of the profane world and into a new and powerful spiritual realm. The Saints rededicated themselves to authority and purity in light of

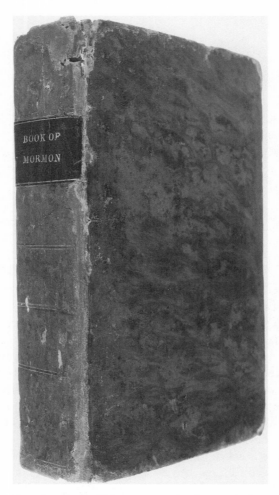

Published in 1830, the *Book of Mormon* contained an entirely new revelation, about and for the New World. Courtesy of Alfred Bush.

latter-day revelation. By the time polygamy became a topic of national attention in the early 1850s, Mormonism was two decades old. The faith was fast growing and structurally and theologically complex. The early church combined innovative methods of religious expression with the extraordinary charisma and inspiration of Joseph Smith. Like other religious Americans, Smith, too, believed in the power of language. He used words, rather than some other weapon, to express his vision. Smith countered what he called the Christians' apostasy with a new Word. The *Book of Mormon*, an elaborate account of the place of the New World in the history of the universe, provided a concrete example of divine intervention in the lives of Americans and the promise of the Second Coming. Smith claimed to have translated plates of pure gold that predated biblical manuscripts and that were untainted by mortal scribes. By contrast, he charged, the Bible had been corrupted while sequestered by the Catholic Church "from the year AD 46 to 1400." Telling a new and intricate history of two families who fled to the New World centuries before the birth of Jesus, the *Book of Mormon* resonated with the desire to unite American history with religious truth.[2]

Mormonism also embraced other revelations that supplemented and elaborated on the founding text. God spoke to Joseph Smith through the golden plates, and also with direct communication. The "latter days" of the nineteenth century truly were filled with the wonderful power of God's words. New revelation assured the faithful that this was indeed the one true church, and that the New Dispensation had been delivered to Americans in the New World. The old faiths, constricted and corroded by centuries of corruption, could not match the texts or the commitment of the Saints.

Through ongoing revelation and always in the midst of external pressure as well as internal inspiration, Smith instituted a graduated system of authority within the new sect, erecting a hierarchy on top of a democratic priesthood composed of all men. He envisioned a communal ethic for the faithful—they were to act as one, because they followed divine command through God's prophet, Joseph Smith. His charisma, and the power of his message, catapulted Smith into national fame. His latter-day church made extraordinary gains almost from the moment of its birth. The fluidity of the early church should not be confused with indirection. Instead, Smith's continuing inspiration knit together belief and practice in ways that still guide the lives of millions of Mormons. Mormonism created for its followers a new structure for faith, and a new sense of cosmic history.[3]

The new covenant between God and the Latter-day Saints changed theology and the order of the universe, as well as the Word. Mormons believed that God was a material being, who progressed from manhood to godhood through gradual stages of celestial life; that procreativity continued in multiple celestial kingdoms as on earth; that Jesus was sired by a physical act; and that he appeared in the New World as well as the Old. The *Book of Mormon* and Smith's ongoing revelations persuaded Mormons that the new Zion, the site of the Millennium, would be in North America, where the faithful gathered. Multiple worlds and multiple layers of revelation enveloped the Saints in the sense of wondrous possibility for progress in heaven as on earth. Continuous revelation, combined with the conviction that transcendent beings are themselves physical, allowed Mormons to identify this world (and themselves) with the celestial kingdoms of latter-day revelation. To remake their lives and their society in light of God's law was the thrilling challenge of the New Dispensation. "Eternal progression" toward godhood was the goal of Mormon life and ritual. The demands might be heavy, but the prospect was exhilarating beyond all measure.[4]

Polygamy was not one of the original tenets of the faith. The official association of polygamy and Mormonism is dated to the "Revelation on Celestial Marriage" received by Smith in 1843, the year before his death. Rumors at the time, and evidence of experimentation disclosed by subsequent research, date the practice considerably earlier than 1843, however. Smith dictated the document to his secretary after his marriage to a young woman who had been living with his family. The extraordinary difficulty of accepting such a revelation was apparent even in the prophet's household. Joseph's first wife, Emma, declared after Smith's death that she had never consented to the match, and her children denied it had taken place.[5]

The revelation proclaimed that the marriage of one man to more than one woman was "justified" by the example of Abraham. In these latter days, the heirs of Abraham were once again commanded to work "for their exaltation in the eternal worlds" (that is, the stages of heaven) by siring "the souls of men." Men called upon to enter the celestial principle were thus sanctified in their union with additional "virgins," in the interest of procreation by righteous patriarchs as of old. A wife's consent was required for her husband to take additional wives, but wives who for selfish reasons refused to consent to their husbands' polygamy would be "damned." The new covenant of celestial marriage celebrated on earth would endure for eternity, governing relations in heaven as in life, and dictating the degree of exaltation achieved in the afterlife. Only marriages celebrated in accord with the revelation would endure after death, and "whatsoever things" that did not conform to God's Words "shall be shaken and destroyed." Phrased in terms of "the law which was appointed . . . before the foundation of the world," the revelation asserted control over marriage for church members, in the interest of their salvation and as an essential prerequisite to achievement of the kingdom of God.[6]

Through this combination of legal exceptionalism (the assertion that Mormons were not subject to the law of marriage that governed the rest of the country) and state-building (the projected construction of a "kingdom" based on an alternative structure of private governance), Smith also reinterpreted the political authority of religion. Especially in the series of revelations received shortly before Smith's death, Mormon metaphysics and political theory reestablished the cords of power that explicitly tied church and state. Smith, for example, had himself crowned "king" and became a candidate for president in 1844; his closest counselors also held the highest political offices of the Mormon settlement in Nauvoo, Illinois. In the rest of the country, the cords linking church and state had painfully (and productively, according to most Americans) been cut over the past half century. Even more poignant to outsiders, Mormon leaders were themselves polygamists, tying political power to plural marriage. The sweep of the Mormons' assertion of religious authority over politics and law would become apparent in future decades, as the Saints struggled to defend their practice and to explain to themselves why the defense was fundamental to the integrity of their faith.[7]

At the time of the revelation in 1843, and for almost ten years afterward, polygamy remained secret, revealed to a few trusted church leaders and the women who married Smith and his closest advisers. In public, Smith, before his death, and other Mormon leaders after Smith's martyrdom, denied rumors of plural marriage. Missionaries in Europe, for example, published tracts denying polygamy and quoting passages from the *Book of Mormon* that condemned the taking of more than one wife. Polygamy remained only one of many rumors about Mormons and their alleged iniquities.[8]

The "Revelation on Celestial Marriage," which described the law and established that celestial marriage was essential for the faithful, is, of course, the single most important text in the conflict between Mormons and their opponents. Polygamy shocked and offended those outside the faith; and it was not readily accepted by many Mormons when they first learned of "the Principle" of plural marriage. Yet the Saints' embrace and defense of polygamy makes sense only in light of the role of revelation and the promise of exaltation in all aspects of the faith. Joseph Smith galvanized his followers into profound expressions of faith and commitment to practice. Plural marriage was evidence of obedience to God's law of celestial marriage and the hope of eternal progression through stages of heaven to eventual godhood. The sacrifice of deeply ingrained convictions in this life in return for rewards in the celestial worlds to come created a tangible tie between acceptance of the most difficult and controversial of all the prophet's tests here on earth, and glory in the afterlife. Crystalliz-

In the early 1840s, "Lieutenant-General" Joseph Smith formed the "Nauvoo Legion," an organization that was viewed by those outside the faith with considerable suspicion. Courtesy of Princeton University Library.

ing political, legal, and sexual commitments in the service of the faith, polygamy transformed ordinary tasks into spiritual exercises.[9]

In Ohio, Missouri, and Illinois, neighbors who initially welcomed the Mormons soon became their enemies. By the 1840s, Mormons maximized their political and economic strength by bloc voting, forming a private militia, and dealing exclusively with approved merchants. These activities, combined with rumors of sexual irregularities, Mor-

The murder of Joseph Smith has become a central event in Mormon religious history. The murder of Smith, who was ostensibly under the protection of state officials, confirmed for many Mormons that persecution was all they could expect from the states. Courtesy of Princeton University Library.

mons' aggressive proselytizing, and their apparently unquestioning obedience to Smith, made Mormon settlements unpopular with nearby residents. Mormons were derided, harassed, and sometimes killed. After Smith ordered a printing press in Nauvoo destroyed when its owner published a story critical of his policies, he was arrested by Illinois law enforcement officials. Despite promises by state officers to protect him, Smith was murdered by a mob of anti-Mormons who attacked the jail in June of 1844.[10]

After Smith's martyrdom, faithful members of the church migrated in 1847 to the Great Salt Lake Basin with their new leader, Brigham Young. One of the earliest converts to the faith, the energetic Young led the church westward and onward. He consolidated the authority of the faith and cemented the hierarchical church organization that administered to the spiritual and material needs of the faithful. Young's authority and skill ordered their lives, their settlement patterns, and even their style of dress. The trek westward was remarkable both for its organization and its destination—an arid, remote, and forbidding area that at the time belonged to Mexico and could only be reached by an arduous trip across plains, deserts, and mountains. The migration was motivated by the desire to find the new Zion as well as to avoid persecution.[11]

Mormons had good reason to choose the territory of the Great Basin. They needed isolation to ensure peace for their members. They also needed space, for church membership grew exponentially throughout the nineteenth century. Through early and constant missionary work, and through an organization known as the Perpetual Emigrating Fund (a revolving fund that financed the migration of converts to Zion), the flow of immigrants swelled the Mormon population first in Utah, and eventually in Arizona, Idaho, and California.[12]

After the Mormon exodus westward in the late 1840s, Brigham Young and other leaders relaxed their restrictions on polygamy, as they settled in to build the political kingdom. The early settlement of Utah was orderly, successful, and, with notable exceptions, peaceful. The authority and inspiration of the faith, and the obedience of the faithful, accomplished in Utah what other Americans yearned for—security, unity, trust in their community. As Mormons pointed out to their detractors, theirs was the faith that "made the desert bloom as the rose." They petitioned the national government for admission as the state of Deseret in 1849, with borders far exceeding the current boundaries of Utah.[13]

The Territory of Utah was organized by Congress in 1850, however, temporarily dashing but by no means destroying the quest for legal and political autonomy. One of the first acts of the Mormon-controlled territorial legislature was to grant the church corporate status, awarding it the absolute legal right to govern the marriages of members. The act also empowered the church corporation to acquire and control unlimited amounts of property, both real (land) and personal (money and goods). These extraordinary legal powers were unlike those granted to church corporations in the States. Many jurisdictions strictly limited the amount of property a church could acquire; none provided that the decisions of the church with regard to marriage "could not be legally questioned," as did the Utah statute.[14]

The legal powers of the church were matched by the political power of its leaders. Political offices frequently were filled by high-ranking church officials, whose authority was based on their faith in the New Dispensation. Brigham Young, for example, was the first governor of the territory. The Saints' confidence grew as their kingdom prospered. For the first time, Mormons constituted a political majority; their leaders were patriarchs openly proud of their several wives and many children. The reality of plural marriage became ever more difficult to deny. Travelers passing through Salt Lake reported that Mormon men flaunted their "plural" wives. At a special conference in 1852, the church acknowledged what had long been rumored. Elder Orson Pratt read the 1843 revelation aloud and delivered a lengthy sermon on the religious and social superiority of polygamy.[15]

The practice of plural marriage required self-discipline, especially for women. Brigham Young sermonized on the topic frequently in the 1850s, exhorting women to bear their burdens cheerfully. He even challenged his own wives to "round up their shoulders to endure the afflictions of this world and live their religion, or . . . leave." Especially during the 1850s, Young's fiery sermons goaded faithful men to marry multiple wives, and faithful women to encourage their husbands' polygamy. Such sermons were widely circulated in the East and reappeared for decades as evidence of Mormon perfidy. Yet the demands of polygamy were designed for the leaders of the faith; plural marriage was never the only or even the most common form of marriage within Mormonism. Polygamy was considered the most exalted and exemplary marital structure, to be practiced by those whose dedication and sacrifice qualified them as leaders in these latter days. Only true Saints could practice plurality in all purity and rectitude.[16]

Mormon leaders practiced polygamy for at least a half century. Plural marriage frequently became synonymous with spiritual (and often temporal) success in Mormon Utah. Through its leaders, the church dominated the economic life of the territory, as well as its spiritual and political establishments. Within a decade of the Mormons' arrival in the Great Basin Kingdom, church leaders controlled valuable watercourses, forested canyons, and grazing pastures, as well as a growing structure of manufactures and interlocking directorates. The relationship between religion and market power in territorial Utah was deep and abiding. Church leaders were polygamists and industrial, financial, and agricultural leaders, as well as political figures. This fusion of religious, economic, and political power was key to building the new Zion—the kingdom of God as envisioned by Mormon doctrine. It was also vital to the opposition that devastated the kingdom and its patriarchs in the latter half of the nineteenth century.[17]

The rest of the country was stunned by the news from Utah in 1852. Yet the religious world into which the Mormons dropped their bombshell was neither stable nor impermeable. Nor was the logic of Mormon claims to absolute control over the marital structure of the "kingdom of God" in Utah unprecedented or un-Christian. Polygamy had been bruited about on the fringes of Protestantism for centuries before the Mormon embrace of the "Patriarchal Principle." The Reformation in Europe had spawned several arguments in favor of recreating the marital structure of the Old Testament as a means of recovering genuine Christian primitivism. Americans, too, were intrigued by such biblical primitivism. "Spiritual wifery" was a concept well known outside Utah.[18]

In early-nineteenth-century America, the relationship between religious and sexual fervor was especially clearly marked. New religious movements sprouted like mushrooms in the fertile soil of post-Revolutionary instability. Often, they turned their spiritual enthusiasm to sexual innovation. The notorious Matthias combined prophecy and spiritual wifery in a tantalizingly dangerous mix in the 1830s. Jacob Cochran in Maine indulged in reenactments of the creation myth combined with sexual prowess. Oneida Perfectionists practiced group marriage and selective breeding. Shakers blended ecstatic worship with total celibacy.[19]

Mormon theology and sexual practice were thus innovative expressions of a dissenting tradition that probed the boundaries of authority and tolerance in post-Revolutionary America. Mormons were not the first dissenters to challenge traditional structures. Nor were they the only group to explore the connections between marriage and politics. But the Saints were the largest, the most powerful, and the best organized. They also had their own jurisdiction, Utah Territory. Mormons illustrated both the power and the instability of religious innovation in the young nation.

More than any other single group, Mormons tested and exposed the uncertainty and insecurity of liberty. Particularly unsettling were Mormon arguments based on the claim to an alternative, divine authority. Mormon believers found new security in their new faith. Historians have studied the erosion of stable hierarchies in social and political life in the early Republic, the "democratization" of private and public governance that characterized American freedom. Insecurity and anxiety were frequently the flip side of change and mobility. Spiritual security appealed to Americans as other forms of authority and predictability slipped away.[20]

Even as traditional lines of authority frayed at the end of the eighteenth century, however, others hardened and flourished. Slavery, especially, stands as the sine qua non of authoritarian power in the early Republic. The growth of slavery and the increasing intolerance of slave codes in the early-nineteenth-century South, and in the West by the middle decades of the century, qualify claims that democracy or equality was truly "characteristic" of America in the antebellum years. Yet by the time Mormons announced their practice of polygamy in the early 1850s, slavery, too, had become a "question." The excess of authority, like its absence, plagued Americans as they wrestled with growth and instability.[21]

Mormons, convinced that the New Dispensation had created a new order that would usher in the Millennium, embraced authority, patriarchy, certainty. In so doing, they challenged those around them to explain how such a faith could be inconsistent with religious freedom, and why liberty, marriage, and government depended on Christian monogamy. Mormonism, like slavery, became a "question." Antipolygamists could not, of course, summon new revelation to counteract latter-day claims. Instead, they worked with another form of text. They appealed in ways that abolitionists and other reformers had taught them were effective. They told stories.[22]

Popular novelist Metta Victor explained to her readers in 1856 that monogamous marriage was essential to "the spirit and intent of that Constitution which is to perpetuate the republic, and render it, in truth, the refuge for the oppressed, the *home* of liberty." It was a big claim, but one that antipolygamists in the 1850s made repeatedly. To Victor and other early antipolygamists, true marriage as the source of liberty for husbands and wives was a touchstone, the faithful *home* around which the Constitution revolved. Popular literature—novels, short stories, newspaper exposés—created the initial rhetoric. Middle-class women authors in the East, never themselves directly threatened by Mormons or polygamy, imagined the pain and humiliation that polygamy inflicted upon women. The authors themselves are obscure—popular in the nineteenth century but by now long forgotten. Yet the stamp of these writers endured for decades, even as antipolygamy activity expanded from literature to political and legal organizing.[23]

Four novels written in the mid-1850s were the nucleus of the first wave of propaganda. Metta Victor's *Mormon Wives*, Maria Ward's *Female Life among the Mormons*, Orvilla Belisle's *Mormonism Unveiled*, and Alfreda Eva Bell's *Boadicea* were the genre's cornerstones. Almost 100 novels and many hundreds of magazine and newspaper stories (including the first Sherlock Holmes story, *A Study in Scarlet*, published in 1887) built on the market for antipolygamy fiction over the next half century. The work of these popular writers captured the drama of the conflict, painting vivid pictures of the disintegration of marriages in a far western territory. Stories of blushing brides whose hopes were dashed by a husband's self-indulgence under the mantle of "religious difference" made thrilling and disturbing reading. These early works all placed ordinary women in extraordinarily difficult circumstances, challenging them to suffer with sanctity, and to (re)construct the "home of liberty."

Novels, especially, connected questions of constitutional meanings and the limits of freedom, on the one hand, to religious dissent and marriage, on the other. The power of fiction was as disturbing to Mormon leaders as it was appealing to antipolygamist authors. Brigham Young warned that novels were "falsehoods got up expressly to excite the minds of youth"; other leaders condemned fiction for distracting readers from "the plain truth" and "real life as it exists." The "startling and thrilling dramas" of Mormon history, argued one Mormon writer, was the proper focus of literature. The very different dramatic histories in antipolygamy fiction grated against the Mormon injunction to accept the "realities of life" rather than the "warp[ing] the imagination" and "pining and fretting." As historians of Mormonism quite correctly point out, moreover, antipolygamy novels often had little basis in fact. But the fact that they were "wrong" does not mean they were ineffective. Although Metta Victor probably knew little about the real experience of women in Utah, the world she described reveals the assumptions and strategies the antipolygamists employed.[24]

In the 1850s, fiction was a valuable tool for bringing home to readers the fear of betrayal and spiritual desolation that novelists claimed were the consequences of polygamy. Antipolygamy novelists used stories about marriage, religion, and westward migration as their medium of persuasion. These works were designed to arouse sympathy, and ultimately to inspire activism for legal change. Popular writers explored the Constitution and its meaning in everyday life; they challenged legislators and jurists to create a legal system that mirrored the emotional and spiritual truths they insisted were the basis of all valid government. As Metta Victor put it, antipolygamy stories taught the reader that "whatever corrupts [the] moral, intellectual, and physical well-being [of the people] is inimical to the well-being of society, to the State, to the whole country." The welfare of the country, claimed Victor, depended on Christian monogamy and its attendant protection of women in marriage. The Constitution, she argued, was infused with the Christian faith of its founders. There *must* be a way to answer the Mormon Question, early antipolygamists reasoned, and thus to save the Constitution from its abuse at the hands of heretics and zealots. Otherwise, liberty itself would perish.

Mormons exploited the freedom to believe, antipolygamists insisted, confusing it with license to indulge themselves in the name of a spurious religion.

Metta Victor and other early antipolygamists relied on the national Constitution to shield them from the power of latter-day revelation and practice. Their belief in the power of the Constitution gave antipolygamists a solution to the dilemma of Mormon Utah; and yet their understanding of constitutional structures and principles was no more expert than the Mormons' had been only a decade earlier. But their appeal was far wider and more grounded in the emotional logic of Americans' vision of religious liberty and the importance of marriage.[25]

The moral compass of the state, as antipolygamist novelists described it, rested on the private relations of husband and wife, and the spiritual benefit of their mutual support and trust. In this light, marriage connected religion to the state by creating in each household a sanctified system of mutual governance based on conjugal love. The abuse of this system resulted in suffering, violence, even death. Such were the painful truths that these novelists invited their readers to experience. Polygamy betrayed the emotional structure of marriage through a system that actually promoted adultery, they argued. Mormonism sucked in innocent people from the rest of the country, they charged, dragging them downward as they migrated westward.

The plot of Metta Victor's novel illustrated the dramatic core of antipolygamy fiction. Margaret Wilde, the heroine of *Mormon Wives*, died in Utah, far from her native New England soil. Her will to live was sapped by her husband, Richard, who "dared to trample the heart of a woman under his foot." Lured by promises of wealth and power to convert to Mormonism and to emigrate with his bride, Richard succumbed to polygamy after two years in Utah. The other woman was Sarah Irving, Margaret's childhood friend. Sarah, assuaging her conscience with "free love" pamphlets that argued that monogamy was contrary to man's primitive nature, followed the newlyweds to Utah and became Richard's second wife. Margaret developed a brain fever when she learned of the betrayal, but she forgave her killers before her death, begging only that Richard remain true to Sarah. Richard, however, had taken a third wife that morning. Sarah was devastated by his duplicity as well as by her own role in Margaret's death. Reborn as a Christian penitent, Sarah vowed on Margaret's grave to devote herself to a life of antipolygamy activism: "Always, always, my voice shall rise in defense of one love, constant through life, and faithful in death—one home—one father and mother for the children—one joy on earth—one hope in heaven."[26]

Victor's book sold some 40,000 copies during the 1850s alone. The plot of *Mormon Wives* blended the central story of betrayal with themes of sexual and domestic abuse common to nineteenth-century reform fiction. Antipolygamy novels described a shared nightmare— the perversion of liberty and the corruption of religion by those who turned the Christian sanctity of marriage to selfish purposes. Along with Orvilla Belisle, Maria Ward, and Alfreda Bell, Victor created and satisfied a significant market for antipolygamy fiction. Their imagined world of polygamy (in which marriage disintegrated, women suffered, husbands called themselves priests, and legal order evaporated) resonated with Eastern audiences. Although for the most part we cannot recover the thoughts and reactions of readers, or even know how many men and women read these novels, we can surmise that stories of hopes dashed and wives lost were invigorating and inspiring. As one young reader put it upon finishing Cornelia Paddock's *The Fate of Madame La Tour* in the early 1880s: "Resolved: If I should ever become a statesman, I will dedicate myself to exterminating this curse. Signed, A Reader."[27]

Antipolygamy novels sold well for decades. Edition after edition of Maria Ward's *Female Life among the Mormons*, for example, were issued from 1855 until the final version was published in 1913. The same stories appeared in countless guises and formats. Predictable patterns, the "inevitability" of "murders, seductions, thefts and all manner of iniquity" in a polygamous society, were precisely what made these novels so persuasive for readers. Recognizable characters and plots were emotionally effective for audiences schooled in Christian reform. The appeal to the pain of the reader fostered empathy with the victim. In this way, antipolygamist writers created a new story in which the reader's own marriage was threatened by the existence of polygamy. Just as Harriet Beecher Stowe's novel *Uncle Tom's Cabin* transformed sympathetic readers into emotional activists against slavery, the blueprint for legal reform to prohibit polygamy arguably was complete in the novels themselves.[28]

Betrayal lay at the heart of antipolygamists' fears. They saw spiritual, marital, and political danger in polygamy, which they condemned as a breach of the trust essential to marriages (and republics). The novelists rallied to the defense of monogamy and, as they saw it, true religious liberty and constitutional rectitude. To combat the abuse of trust, they, too, drew on the lessons of religious feeling and communication that sustained and invigorated faith in the early Republic. Stories connected storytellers and listeners in emotional response to moving tales. As one minister put it, "Never [did his parishioners] love one another so well as when they witness the outpouring of each other's hearts in prayer," entering into the "warm and overpowering feelings" of sympathetic identification. The power of sympathy and the energy unleashed by emotional outrage were antipolygamy novelists' stock in trade. The spiritual danger they described was all too understandable because the people involved were so typical, and so vulnerable.[29]

When novelists depicted the emotional and spiritual consequences of polygamy, they also connected the efficacy of individual faith to constitutional structures. Only Christian monogamy, they insisted, could construct and then protect the "home of liberty" envisioned by the Constitution. The connective threads spun in antipolygamy novels were new (and proved to be enduring) ways of illustrating the perceived danger of polygamy. They also created a call to action, drawing strength from related endeavors. Antipolygamists, like their Mormon counterparts, were part of a world already galvanized by the power and perils of religious storytelling in a disestablished country.

Such strategies validated the stories of those (white women, enslaved women and men, and children) whose voices were quite literally not heard before the emergence of liberal Protestant storytelling. This impulse to hear the tales of sympathetic (or just plain pathetic) speakers implicitly rejected theological rigor in favor of more visceral forms of communication. Antipolygamy novels frequently were as superficial in their examination of Christian doctrine and practice as they were in their investigation of Mormonism. One novelist described a burial scene in which a surviving woman read "beautiful" (but unspecified) prayers over the grave of a woman who died of a broken heart on the long trip to Utah. She appealed instead to emotion, and sympathy. Her prayer service was vague, but indubitably Protestant. Like other antipolygamists, novelists connected Mormonism to other non-Protestant faiths, drawing on popular prejudice to argue that any radical departure from Protestantism would corrode true liberty.

Antipolygamist writers reframed the traditional American condemnation of formal ties between church and state. To drive home the dangers they believed flowed from excesses of clerical power, they focused on the political power of the Mormon priesthood. Drawing on decades of anti-Catholic feeling in America, for example, Orvilla Belisle compared Joseph Smith to the pope, claiming that both held their followers in abject poverty and ignorance. More often, popular writers treated Mormons as boorish tyrants, unrelated to other Christians, unique in their self-indulgence and spiritual chicanery. Maria Ward's *Female Life among the Mormons* was direct and explicit. Her novel, which told the story of a young bride whose experiences on the trip to Utah and in the territory itself finally persuaded her that to escape dressed as an Indian was preferable to continued "life among the Mormons," included many vignettes designed to illustrate the dangers of polygamy. In one story, a lecherous old man purchased two young women from their father for two horses and a cow. He explained: "Polygamy, as I take it, is the legitimate offspring of the union of Church and State. The Church is more . . . tender of the interests of believers, than the State, when divorced from her, could ever be." Plural marriage, he claimed, was "the chiefest of our blessings, . . . that will be what the heathen will attempt to root out and destroy."[30]

Although the "union of church and state" was a frequent target of antipolygamy theory, confusion about the precise relationship of church and state continued. Massachusetts was the last state formally to "disestablish" in 1833, but Bible reading in the public schools, challenges to Sunday delivery of the mail, and most divisively the legal protection of slavery all linked questions of politics and religion. In one sense, therefore, antipolygamy was a valuable arena for debate about the meaning and value of separation of church and state. To early antipolygamists, the purported evils of an established church were easily spotted in Utah, especially in Mormons' legal claim to practice "celestial marriage" and in the political power of the polygamists. Antipolygamist authors argued that polygamy (and Mormonism) were dependent on theocracy. As a Mormon leader in Ward's novel put it, polygamy could be protected only by a legal order in which priests made laws: "Mormonism can only flourish as a theocracy; but so long as the head of the church makes the laws we are safe." When religious leaders wielded such political power, and based legislation and political favors on personal revelation, the antipolygamists charged, then the laws of God (and the Constitution) were betrayed by the laws of man.[31]

If the informal, home-based religion of spiritual union in marriage was the true source of the faith and virtue essential to republican government, the argument went, then any formal empowerment of religion (or religious leaders) was in fact the degradation of religion, and of marriage. Ultimately, the Constitution itself would be compromised. Utah, in this view, was not only overgoverned (by an interventionist priesthood) but also undergoverned (by the absence of protective legislation for marriage). The evaporation of legal order, antipolygamy novelists insisted, was the consequence of the political power held by Mormon leaders. The simultaneous existence of theocracy and anarchy seemed predictable to antipolygamists. Mormonism, which placed priests in charge of legislatures and in charge of households, they charged, had gotten the source of valid government wrong. By undermining the distinctions between church and state, and between church and home, Mormons jeopardized all three. Their error led them into fundamental mistakes of belief and practice, of which polygamy was the most egregious and the most telling. Brigham Young, Orvilla Belisle charged, tyrannized Utah, where the entire legislature was composed of his "creatures," and did his bidding. There, homes, which should have been "sacred retreats" from oppression, were denied the "peculiar sanctity" unique to Christian homes. Instead, only some households were venerated, as Young and other leaders cast "the burdens upon the labourers, to wring from them the means to support" their "largely stocked harems."[32]

Mormons were not the first to confuse religious freedom with sexual license, according to antipolygamists. Metta Victor described Sarah Irving's temptation as a product of "free love" pamphlets that assured her marriage was not sacred. With the aid of tracts on "Psychological Twinships" and "Passional Attractions," Sarah convinced herself that her own desires, rather than any Christian inhibitions, were the appropriate guide for action. Richard Wilde created the opportunity for betrayal by converting to Mormonism; Sarah completed the betrayal by indulging herself in another heresy—free love. By constructing an alliance between polygamy and free love, antipolygamists were able to show how distinct and rival forms of dissent produced identical threats. Sexual indulgence flowed from heretical faith, Metta Victor claimed, and flourished in an overheated atmosphere of freedom that created room for license as well as liberty. Free thought and Mormonism, Stephen Pearl Andrews (famous for his advocacy of free love and easy divorce) and Brigham Young, however "fair and proper [their] language," Victor wrote, "have cursed the ground with thistles and thorns, instead of blessing it with the lilies and roses of purity and love." The danger lurked in the misapprehension that the Constitution shielded all manner of iniquity.[33]

Danger also lurked in the power of persuasive language. The "glory and fascination of genius" cloaked evil as well as good, Victor lamented, tempting the weak or the trusting with fine phrases and flattery, "blighting the[ir victims] eternally." Even "elegant, refined" men could be seduced in the "murky lake" of religious error, wrote Orvilla Belisle in her novel *Mormonism Unveiled*. Belisle's heroine,

The frontispiece of Orvilla Belisle's *Mormonism Unveiled* showed Brigham Young making advances to an affronted (and unprotected) young woman. Courtesy of Yale University Library.

Margaret, died of shock when her husband brought a second wife into her house and made love to the interloper in the very next room. The betrayal was accomplished under the influence of "unhallowed tenets" and "mystic vapours" that the prophet whispered in the ears of his followers, leading them to "perjure [their] souls." The instability of religious words and ideas was manifest in Joseph Smith's success, Belisle implied. Antipolygamists thus drew on the painful lesson that as dramatic portraits of religious experience acquired pride of place, new venues for dissent also mushroomed. With legal constraints protecting the content and structure of faith removed, religious fervor nurtured a fruitful environment for dangerous words and ideas to reverberate through the hearts and minds of Americans. Antipolygamists tapped into insecurities that plagued nineteenth-century Americans, who both gloried in and feared the emotional power of words.[34]

A religious language of emotion—pulsating senses and palpitating hearts—was all too easily perverted by the licentious. The human body, as the historian Robert Abzug has pointed out, had become in many evangelical Protestants' eyes a physiological companion to the Bible by midcentury, and the cultivation of healthy bodies had become a means of embodying the Word. At the same time, however, the relationship of the body to words of less elevated origins was also called into question. Thus the ties between sexual morality and Christian belief acquired new urgency. "The fanatic is of logical necessity either an ascetic or a sensualist," one antipolygamist concluded, arguing that polygamy and celibacy were actually cut from the same cloth. "He either gives full rein to his baser propensities under the specious name of 'Christian liberty,' or with a little more conscientiousness, swings to the opposite extreme and forbids those innocent gratifications prompted by nature and permitted by God."[35]

The exquisite tension spawned by emotional arousal and its containment within the boundaries of Christian morality (the constant reference to sensation and intimacy, on the one hand, and the discipline of sexual restraint, on the other) created a delicate balance. Temptation lurked at the edges of such arousal. It also intensified interest in stories of orgies and their licentious participants. Exploring the sensual excesses of dissidents, sensational writers and lecturers satisfied the urge to probe and expose the sexual consequences of religious lapse. Antipolygamists fed the flames, dwelling on "the modern Sodom, . . . where women are forcibly seized and imprisoned in a harem, and where a bashaw's passions are under more restraint than during the reign of Mormonism." Reflecting on the connection between all forms of sexual indulgence, Metta Victor claimed that "yielding to a belief in [free love]" was the first step into Mormonism, for both deluded their followers that "lust was love."[36]

To its opponents, polygamy united the specter of sexual indulgence with religious difference. The Mormons exemplified the dangers of licentiousness in a land of liberty. That antipolygamists turned to law and legal concepts for answers to these dangers was predictable, if freighted with difficulty and uncertainty. Christians had learned to exploit the strategic power of law in earlier battles against other dissenters.

By the time the *Book of Mormon* was published in 1830, the emotional outpouring of religious expression had eroded the credibility of eighteenth-century deism and secularism that were frequently associated with the Enlightenment. But in the opening years of the nineteenth century, evangelical Christians and their more orthodox counterparts saw themselves battling the forces of unbelief, led by the "arch-infidel, the Virginia Voltaire" Thomas Jefferson, with Thomas Paine ("that filthy little atheist") as second in command. Sermons and tracts on the "Triumph of Infidelity" and the "Dangers of our Country" were delivered as exposés of a small but articulate tradition of free thought in America. And although "infidelity" (originally a theological, rather than a marital or sexual term) was less prevalent than its opponents claimed, skepticism was nonetheless the visible wing of a more broadly based anticlericalism. Deeply suspicious of a conspiratorial "evangelical juggernaut," for example, Jefferson refused while he was president to follow the federalist tradition of proclaiming fast and thanksgiving days.[37]

Fanny Wright, known as the "Red Harlot of Infidelity," was even more outspoken. She combined religious free thought with a philosophy of "free love," opposing marriage and its restrictions. Wright embodied sexual as well as religious danger, a challenge to the rights of husbands and the very law of marriage. Her enemies called her a "voluptuous priestess of licentiousness" and linked "Fanny Wrightism" with the "dissolution" and infidelity that precipitated the French Revolution. The political dangers of religious skepticism, argued defenders of Christianity, were proven by the ideas that led to the Reign of Terror in France in the 1790s. Popular criticism of Wright frequently focused on the special evils associated with women who abandoned traditional faith and launched themselves into experimental sexual practices.[38]

The tools believing Christians used against freethinkers were effective and adaptable. Many of the arguments made in attacks on Jefferson and Fanny Wright were recycled for use by antipolygamists, who insisted that polygamy and infidelity were related abuses. Sexual experimentations, whether in free love or Mormon guise, argued Metta Victor, betrayed the essence of true liberty. Only Christian restraint, she insisted, would preserve the structures of freedom that maintained the "*home* of liberty." Religious freedom and free thought or polygamy were, from this perspective, opposite ends of the moral spectrum, the former a component of liberty, the latter manifestations of licentiousness. To explain how Frances Wright and Brigham Young posed parallel threats to religious liberty, antipolygamists at midcentury drew heavily on moral theory. God's moral law made such aberrations disgusting; spiritual weakness among men allowed error to flourish in the crevices of religious freedom.

Indeed, by midcentury the identification of Protestantism and morality was so close that the space between the two was gossamer thin. As the historian James Turner put it, although "[m]oral law still came from God, . . . finding it out became a matter of observation and reason." Such moral laws were hardly the mystical result of an incomprehensible God's will but reliable precepts for navigation through life. The popular campaign against infidelity, which had been undertaken as a defense of Christianity against the noxious corruptions of atheism, agnosticism, or even humanism, was finally fought not on theological or doctrinal grounds but on grounds of law and popular morality, especially sexual and marital propriety. And there it was won.[39]

Antipolygamists in the 1850s claimed that Mormons posed a parallel and even more deadly threat to Christian liberty than their freethinking predecessors. Historians Michael Quinn and John Brooke have argued, however, that early Mormonism had less in common with Enlightenment rationalism than with the traditions of magic that flickered at the edges of Protestant society throughout the colonial and early national periods. Yet to the opponents of Mormonism, latter-day precepts had much in common with the dangers of infidelity. Both Mormons and infidels, they charged, gave in to their passions, covering base self-indulgence with fraudulent arguments about "religious freedom." So, no sooner was free thought vanquished, antipolygamists claimed, than a new threat to religious and sexual authority appeared, this time from the poor and "superstitious" rather than the rich and secular.[40]

Antipolygamists at midcentury drew strength and substance from the legal campaigns waged against prior dissidents. Infidels had prepared the ground, illustrating the potential for religious liberty to degenerate into sexual licentiousness and to erode marriage. As the Reverend Samuel Gridley Howe put it in his call for the ostracism of freethinker Abner Kneeland in 1834, doctrines that "deny the sanctity of the marriage contract; . . . give full play to licentious indulgence, and shew the young how to avoid its natural penalties." He called upon all good Christians "to unite; ay, to *unite* in defence of the morals, the laws, and the order of society." If they did not, the "dreadful under-current, which is sapping the very foundation of the social edifice," charged Howe, would seduce wives from their husbands and divide the property of the rich among the poor. The threat to marriage from "infidel authors" of pamphlets "abound[ed] with blasphemy, ribaldry, and obscenity." Mormons and freethinkers could hardly have been more different, yet they both tapped into antipolygamists' fears that marriage was threatened from all sides.[41]

To protect marriage, mid-nineteenth-century novelists in general, and antipolygamists in particular, ratcheted up the importance of household relationships to the point where they became the key to national survival or doom. In their best-selling advice book *The American Woman's Home*, for example, popular writers Harriet Beecher Stowe and her sister Catharine Beecher blended family, church, and home in the person of the housewife. The glue that held the whole structure together was sacred emotion—love of a husband for his wife, love of children for their mother, and the returning love for them all from a devoted woman, whose spiritual wisdom made her God's representative in the family. The family home truly became a "sacred circle," as Metta Victor put it, the wife, its guardian angel. Together, husbands and wives found God in conjugal love. In these terms, adultery acquired heightened importance and visibility, not only as a violation of a direct and ancient commandment but as an act of sacrilege—a violation of the incarnation of union with God in the person of the spouse. The mix was a heady one. Marriage in these books was both the apogee of human potential and unbearably fragile; exposed, as Victor said, to "chance and change."[42]

The challenge, then, was to create a legal structure that mirrored the moral and spiritual structure of marriage. The authors who championed legal reform, and the readers who made their work popular, had a powerful vision. They called on the federal government to intervene to protect "true" marriage in Utah. Antipolygamists did not trust the rest of the nation to sense the danger to its own spiritual and moral welfare. For they maintained not only that Mormons in territorial Utah were relevant to the rest of the nation but that their claim to redefine the law of marriage exposed the fundamental weakness of liberty. If liberty included the right to differ on moral questions of vital importance such as polygamy, then morality itself was subject to diverse interpretations in the name of "liberty."

Moral difference in a federal system implied actual legal difference across space, across religions, and across marriages. Polygamy was the outer edge of such difference in the nineteenth century, but antipolygamy novelists understood that the liberty to differ could mean radical instability. The weakness in the system exposed by Mormon polygamy, they argued, could topple the whole structure. In the wrong hands, precious liberties were perverted into justifications for licentiousness. Inherent in such arguments was a profound, if not technically expert, critique of the concept of states as "laboratories" for social experimentation and moral difference. As antipolygamy novelists saw it, any system that placed polygamous priests in charge of government as well as religion had made a fatal mistake. Maria

HUBERT WITH THE MORMON WOMEN LEAVES BOADICEA.

The pain of her husband's betrayal was compounded for the heroine Boadicea (from Alfreda Eva Bell's *Boadicea; The Mormon Wife. Life Scenes in Utah*) by the willing participation of other women in the system of polygamy. Courtesy of Princeton University Library.

Ward, for example, condemned the system that would allow the Mormons to establish "a social system founded on radically different principles" from those of the rest of the country. By traveling westward to the Great Basin, Mormons had eluded the moral oversight of "neighboring communities . . . whose influence might retard their growth," Ward argued. She called upon the rest of the country to exercise such moral oversight, insisting that physical distance should not excuse moral difference.[43]

Exposure to unheralded dangers through migration to new and possibly uncharted legal terrains was a theme that pervaded antipolygamy novels. Ward's *Female Life among the Mormons*, for example, gradually exposed the "truth" about Mormonism as Mrs. Ward, the narrator, traveled westward. The knowledge did not kill her; she took the only other avenue open to virtuous women in Utah—she escaped. But her life was forever changed; her tale of "Truth Stranger than Fiction" was an emotional journey for the reader, a story designed to provoke commitment to prevent such descents into misery for others. Women, Ward claimed, were relegated to ever more marginal and degraded positions as they traveled deeper into Mormon territory: "As the principles of Mormonism developed, it became evident that the females were to be regarded as an inferior order of beings. One by one the rights to which they had been accustomed, as well as the courtesies generally conceded to them, were taken away."[44]

The journey into a different moral place challenged migrants to resist or adjust. In popular fiction, the challenge was felt most directly by women, whose spiritual and material circumstances were altered so drastically in new surroundings. Antipolygamy novelists maintained that women were more likely than men to hold fast to universal truths in the face of local deviance. Faced with polygamy, women in these stories met with one of two fates: the virtuous suffered, even died, the weak descended into viciousness and vulgarity. In antipolygamy fiction, first wives overwhelmingly fell into the former category. The fatal blow was administered by a callous husband, who brought home a second wife. Ward, for example, gave the flavor of the deadly consequences: Mrs. Murray learned that her husband had taken a second wife. Shortly thereafter, her children sickened and died of dysentery. She called Mrs. Ward to her deathbed:

> "You have sympathized with me in my great affliction; once I believed in Mormonism. . . . But the estrangement of my husband opened my eyes, and . . . I knew . . . that a belief which sanctioned such sinful practices, must be of the Evil One. . . ."
>
> "You weary yourself, Mrs. Murray," I said; "here, take this," and I administered a pleasant cordial. . . . I saw that she was sinking rapidly.
>
> "Joy! Joy!" she said. "I go."[45]

Such melodramatic scenes occurred throughout the genre. The deaths of broken-hearted wives were never for naught, even if their redemptive effect was not immediately apparent. Margaret Wilde's death in *Mormon Wives*, for example, converted Sarah Irving to a life of antipolygamy activism. Death, in this sense, was not defeat but a Christian exercise in reformation. By dying, Margaret forever escaped the power of her husband to harm her further. She also provided a compelling example to those left behind of the price paid by women for abandoning Christianity. Margaret was the real victor, although she died to win her point.[46]

Second wives rarely received such sympathetic treatment. Single women were frequently depicted as complicit in the tragedy. The potential for real moral difference between women was among the most nagging and relentless of the problems that plagued popular fiction. The glorification of the household and its "guardian angel" was undermined by the presence of women whose morals defied the claim that women were by nature monogamous. The infidel Fanny Wright had proved earlier in the century that women could be tempted away from the "home of liberty." Novelist Maria Ward described one aspiring Mormon wife as a "coquette," who was in part culpable "for the continuation of polygamy, because [she] preferred a rich man, with a dozen wives, to a poor one without any, and, though repentance must inevitably ensue, it would be too late." First wives were terrorized by such jades, who usurped wifely authority and destroyed "all domestic peace . . . and all household affection." The bitterness of betrayal by another woman, as Margaret Wilde discovered, was spiritually devastating in the deepest sense. "Women of genius, who . . . polluted the gifts which God had graciously bestowed on them," Victor maintained, alluding to Fanny Wright's free-love doctrines in particular, had shown how duplicity could lurk within women's hearts and infect those they touched. The corruption of women was the most deadly, antipolygamy novelists claimed, because the "true mission of woman" was so fatally compromised from within: "It [was] as if angels, who have pure vessels of incense, breathing fragrance and delight upon all who approached, should fill them up with the fires and flames of the lower world, and tempt other spirits to taste, unawares, of the draughts which blight them eternally." The potential for betrayal by other women was worst of all.[47]

But in antipolygamy fiction most women instinctively shunned polygamy. Fundamentally, the stories implied, women could not be morally different from one another—they all shared an innate spiritual sense that revolted at polygamy. How, then, could one explain the presence of thousands of women in Mormonism in the first place? How could they accede to their own degradation? Novelists agreed that women whose husbands converted to Mormonism had little choice but to follow them to Utah, both because one of the qualities that all women shared was a deep desire to obey their husbands, and especially since polygamy was concealed until escape was out of the question. But what about those unmarried women who converted, and those who remained despite plural marriage?[48]

Maria Ward gave two explanations, both of which were widely advanced in subsequent novels and magazine literature. The first described how single women were recruited, and the second focused on the apparent acquiescence of women in Utah. Ellen, a young Englishwoman, explained to Mrs. Ward her presence in Salt Lake. Ellen's description of her seduction illustrated the first category. Joseph Smith used the hypnotic power of "ANIMAL MAGNETISM": "His pres-

According to antipolygamy novelists, Mormon prophet Joseph Smith combined great physical charm with hypnotic powers and boundless sexual appetite. Courtesy of The Huntington Library, San Marino, Calif.

ence was of the basilisk. He exerted a mystical magical influence over me—a sort of sorcery that deprived me of the unrestricted exercise of free will. It never entered into my brain that he could cherish impure motives . . . could seek the gratification of lawless passions. No friendly voice was near to warn me, and I fell."[49]

Once the women were in Utah, a less mystical power kept them docile, the novelists charged. The great difficulty of escape, and the brutality of retaliations against dissent, prevented women from voicing their opinions. Ward argued that "[t]he most . . . that a woman can do, is to conform to her circumstances, and be satisfied with her lot. Who would complain, when conscious that the complaint would only make matters worse?" According to one of Ward's most fruitful "informants," wives were confined in cellars for revealing any information "that can have a tendency to bring the institution of polygamy into disrepute." One wife threatened to run away if her husband brought home a second wife. He was not impressed: "No, madam, you won't [leave]. Among the Mormons, husbands are lords. They have the privilege of punishing disobedient wives, and enforcing their homage." Ward accused the Mormons of instituting a "Lynch law," of which "women were mostly the victims" for daring to "expose the weakness or sensuality of an elder." Polygamy provided the justification for the abuse of women in all sorts of ways, charged Maria Ward. Wives, she said, were trapped in Utah.[50]

Popular novelists also explained why men participated in the system. Ward, for example, attributed polygamy to men's natural "passion for variety." Betrayal and adultery, so the argument went, were already lurking in men's nature; Mormonism elevated such base inclinations to religious precept. The polygamist's acceptance of moral difference, antipolygamists claimed, was deeply connected to his appetite for sexual variety in violation of Christian norms. The legalization of such a "double standard" for men spelled the end of all affection, they charged, and eventually of all law. The same wife in Ward's novel who described the punishments inflicted on dissenting wives explained that her husband had no love for her: "He is for ever smitten with new faces; and that is the abomination of polygamy. Men are naturally inclined to variety, but habit, public opinion, everything, tends to restrain that inclination, in most communities. Among us, however, polygamy gratifies and encourages it." Sexual betrayal, antipolygamists declared, was institutionalized in Utah.[51]

Connected to the theme of betrayal was the claim that greed—for money and power, as well as women—motivated men's conversion to Mormonism. In Metta Victor's *Mormon Wives*, for example, Margaret Wilde's faithless husband, Richard, sought easy wealth. Attempting to persuade Margaret to join him in converting to Mormonism, Richard "painted their future success and prosperity in almost too glowing terms; for Margaret apprehended that his mind was more captivated by the projected splendor of their worldly enterprises, than by their religion."[52]

In her novel *Mormonism Unveiled*, Orvilla Belisle claimed that Mormon converts were failed men, foolish or even criminal. Belisle argued that these were the very people whose ability to follow strange new religions should be circumscribed. Self-indulgence, claimed Belisle, eroded all restraint. Mormon men, she said, were "steeped in crime." Mormon husbands were freed from the marital rules that protected women; and thus all other rules crumbled, too. They were not troubled by adultery or other misdeeds, Belisle claimed, because Mormon leaders assured them that no crime could undermine the power of a Mormon baptism: " 'If you have murdered all your days, . . . you would arise at the resurrection and your spirit be restored to your body, because you have received the baptism which cleanseth from sin. A Mormon can no more be lost than a [non-Mormon] unbaptized saved.' " Maria Ward also condemned Mormonism's appeal to outcasts: " 'The way of the truth is so plain,' said [Joseph] Smith, 'that a fool can point it out just as well as anybody. Let those who are considered fools by their neighbors and relations come to us—we will make them kings and priests.' And certainly a multitude of fools accepted the invitation." Mormonism, Ward claimed, appealed to "thieves, cut-throats and swindlers," whose conversion brought them "riches, honors, and all the wives [they] wish for in this world, and in the next, life everlasting." By claiming that men who converted to Mormonism were already weak or even criminal, anti-polygamist novelists implied that their faith did not deserve the legal or political deference accorded to most men.[53]

Because the familiar restraints of class structure were removed in the West, antipolygamists insisted, moreover, Mormonism ensnared men who wished to rise above their origins and to reap material rewards beyond their due. But the real danger, apparent from the beginning to the heroine of *Mormonism Unveiled*, was that instead of raising themselves, Mormons would drag most people down. Novelists depicted converts lured by promises of wealth as being exploited by the polygamous Mormon elite. Orvilla Belisle even accused Joseph Smith of being motivated by a "leveling" desire. In her view, such religious diversity threatened structures of economic difference that were essential to the well-being of all. The consequence would divide society into rich and poor, with a few men enjoying luxury at the expense of all women and most men: "[In Utah] with thirty thousand subjects, [Brigham Young] reigned supreme autocrat, holding the wealth, labor, liberty and lives of his followers at his mercy, which was swayed by the passions that held him in bondage, and whose slave he had become." The circularity of this argument, the claim that inequality would be increased by the failure to observe the structures of inequality already in place, was ignored by those who feared the disruptions that religious and geographic mobility brought.[54]

More ominous still, foreigners recruited in the slums of Liverpool and Copenhagen with promises of great reward for little labor came to Utah in droves. Belisle, for example, claimed that "[immigrants] with no other naturalization than that of a Mormon baptism, being permitted to vote, . . . were even admitted into the Legislative body to make laws to govern free-born Americans." In her novel, Metta Victor described a boatload of converts newly arrived from Liverpool: "They all belong to the lower, almost to the lowest classes of society. . . . Their countenances were imbruted with ignorance and dirt—not the material dirt of a sea voyage, but the moral dirt of a life of imbecility and indolence. The Apostles of Joe Smith and Brigham Young found them an easy prey, although, as our reporter was told, they were quite above the average of Mormon respectability."[55]

In *Boadicea*, Alfreda Eva Bell graphically probed the violence by men that she argued was the consequence of polygamy and its attendant vices of tyranny, self-indulgence, and lawlessness. Mary Maxwell, an escaped wife of Bernard Yale (a pseudonym for Brigham Young) was on the verge of giving birth when Yale found her in Boadicea's home:

"Will you go with me?" asked he.
"No," answered the dying woman.
"Then you are done for," said Yale; and deliberately, before my very eyes, in spite of my wild screams for his mercy, he fired at her, and scattered her brains over the floor. I fell down in a death-like swoon.

Such sensationalism and graphic violence catered to audiences whose humanitarian sensibilities by the 1850s had become increasingly jaded. Ever more vividly detailed violence was the key to arousing awareness of the danger to the household and its analogue, the nation.[56]

The antipolygamists' description of society riven by a much-married male aristocracy at one end and oppressed wives and poor men at the other and their emphasis on the licentiousness and violence of polygamous husbands, and the death of those wronged by an abusive system, point to a connection that popular authors drew early and often. Polygamy, they claimed, was a form of slavery. Alfreda Eva Bell, for example, insisted that women in Utah "are in fact white slaves; are required to do all the most servile drudgery; are painfully impressed with their utter inferiority, in divers ways and at all seasons; and are frequently . . . subjected to personal violence and . . . corporeal punishment." Like Southern slaveholders, Bell insisted, Mormon men bought and sold women—even their own daughters—and were "to the last degree demoralized, effeminate, and lazy." Maria Ward maintained that surveillance in Utah was fully as "cruel and remorseless"

A MORMON FAMILY.

Violence, argued antipolygamy novelists, was endemic in Mormon families. From Bell, *Boadicea, the Mormon Wife.* Courtesy of Princeton University Library.

as the "bloodhounds" who tracked "runaway slave[s]." Ward even claimed she had seen "[Mormon prophet Joseph Smith] sitting lazily on the door-stone, basking in the sun, while [two of his wives] were at work in the neighboring corn field." The analogy to slavery drove home the threat of regional differences to concepts of liberty and freedom.[57]

The comparison of polygamy to slavery also highlighted the role of law in perpetuating both systems. Especially galling to popular novelists was the absence of an established legal system that protected wives. Like the abolitionists, antipolygamists claimed that the inability of wives in Utah to seek legal protection transformed white women into slaves. Such rhetoric is especially evident in the work of Maria Ward. "Had injured wives possessed the chance of redress by law, or even the opportunity of flying from the scene of such licentious habits," she wrote, "polygamy, even in its infancy, would have received a death-blow; but these, the ones most interested in its suppression, and upon whom fell the burdens of its intolerable evils, were constrained to abide by it, and, in most cases, without murmur or complaint."[58] Legal power, Metta Victor argued, had been vested in "those who made their own laws to suit their own purposes, who brought strange doctrines out of the depths of their own foul imaginations and called them revelations." Although Mormon men pretended to follow the dictates of God, the novelists wrote, they actually indulged their own proclivities—the laws of men. The corruption of God's law was ensured by toleration of moral difference, by the priesthood's domination of statecraft in Utah, and by self-deception mixed with outright fraud. The novelists understood that Mormons claimed a legal foundation for polygamy and that it would require positive legal action to destroy it.[59]

Polygamy's connection to slavery in popular thought provided a blueprint for legal action, based on an appeal to the emotional suffering created by a system of oppression. If suffering was essential to empathic identification with women in Utah, the right of the sufferer to legally challenge the authority of the tyrant was the prerequisite for antipolygamists' activism. Abolitionists made the logic of such appeals compelling. The popularity of Harriet Beecher Stowe's *Uncle Tom's Cabin* was not lost on antipolygamists, who capitalized on the sympathy generated by antislavery fiction. Stowe, too, recognized the connection, arguing that emptying the "slave pens" of the South was precedent for action against polygamy in Utah.[60]

That brings us directly to an issue that saturated the history of antipolygamy over the next four decades: the role of legislation, and its enforcement in the courts, in bringing a dissenting religious and social system into line with the rest of the country. Antipolygamist authors of the 1850s advocated stringent federal oversight of territorial lands, clear and readily enforceable laws, and unequivocal punishment of wrongdoers, not only to protect monogamy in Utah but also to send a message about the political value of Christian marriage to the rest of the nation. They argued for the creation of new legal authority to protect the "home of liberty" against incursions into the union of husband and wife. For what gave marriage its sanctity was the trust and exclusivity that were its spiritual and political essence, long after the flush of physical passion had subsided.

It would be an exaggeration to assert that popular authors had a detailed understanding of constitutional law or how federal enforcement of antipolygamy legislation would or could be carried out. What these writers explored at length and in depth was the nature of spiritual union between spouses, and the relationship between legal power and marital structure.[61]

Even under the best of circumstances, these authors implied, marriage entailed a sacrifice of the self, a sanctified submersion in the other as a prerequisite to the creation of a "home of liberty." In polygamy, the abuse of marriage was felt immediately by women, but men were also vulnerable. Margaret Wilde's husband's sudden and powerful (if temporary) contrition at her death, for example, conveyed to readers that even men caught in the snares of polygamy knew in their heart of hearts that they had betrayed their wives. The sacrifice of self essential to the meaning of marriage was thus exploited and ultimately undermined by plurality, according to antipolygamists. Marriage itself would not survive long, and with its collapse would come the disintegration of civilization. The immediate solution to the problem of plural marriage was death or dissolution through escape. The long-term solution was legal reform.[62]

Mormons, Maria Ward claimed, had escaped the ambit of the "laws of the land" by their move westward. The Territory of Utah provided the space and power for Mormons to create a legal system in their own interest, antipolygamists charged. In Ward's novel, a fictive Brigham Young bragged to a beautiful young woman of his power to make whatever laws he wished: "Laws of the land! now that is too good—laws of the land! indeed, what laws of the land are there, but my will? what State? what government has power or authority? No! my beauty. . . . Here I do as I please with my own. I consider myself amenable to no law, but the code of Mormon, and that places all authority in my hands." To antipolygamists, the notion that law could be created by one man, that the sovereign could not step in to protect marriage, meant that legal authority itself could not survive.[63]

It was a small step from the lawless abuse of wives, antipolygamists believed, to loss of respect for all law. Orvilla Belisle claimed that Mormons stole grain, horses, and merchandise as readily as they did daughters and sisters. Rape, kidnapping, and even murder were sanctioned by Mormonism, she maintained. Because Mormons had attempted to separate vice from crime by claiming virtue for what everyone knew to be a vice, novelists insisted, they had started down the slippery slope to lawlessness, even while preserving a veneer of order. Belisle's heroine, raised in the bosom of civilization, saw through Mormon claims to be law-abiding: "[Margaret] knew vice under no other name than crime, every grade of which she had been taught to abhor and call by its right name, lest in softening it she apologized for the act by misnaming the criminal."[64]

The connection between polygamy and crime also revealed the dangers of regional difference, most poignantly evident in defenses of local customs such as slavery, these authors argued. They probed the similarities between the South's defense of its "peculiar domestic institution" and the defense of polygamy in Utah. In *Mormonism Unveiled*, for example, Orvilla Belisle described a Mormon missionary attempting to seduce an English girl. When the young woman demurred that polygamy was illegal, the missionary replied that in America there was no single legal code: "The Union is made up of distinct States; . . . and whatever laws the people of any one State construct for their own government, the other States have no right to interfere with; therefore, it is not necessary for the whole Union to give their assent to any custom to make it legal, or to have custom sanction it; if one State sanctions it within her territory, it is both legal and right."[65]

This was a reprise (and critique) of the territorial sovereignty argument current among many Democrats in the 1850s, which attempted to remove slavery from debate at the national level. Stephen Douglas, Democratic senator from Illinois and Abraham Lincoln's chief rival, is commonly associated with the claim that local self-determination should allow voters to decide basic questions of domestic governance. Territorial sovereignty would dictate that slavery (and polygamy, according to Republican polemics) was not a question for national debate or resolution. But territorial sovereignty in matters of moral and spiritual welfare was anathema to antipolygamists, as it was to abolitionists. The moral code that protected democratic processes was imperiled, in this view, by toleration of abuse in the name of localism. Such "squatter sovereignty," argued Metta Victor, violated the constitutional design of the Union. "Reject [polygamy], and we accomplish the first step in a reform which shall restore our country to its once proud purity. . . . Under its laws we ought to be the best, the purest, the wisest, the bravest people on earth; and this we shall be are we but true to the first principles laid down by our Revolutionary fathers— the nobility of man." Thus antipolygamists argued that local difference and local control were in fact contrary to the design of the Constitution because they allowed Mormons to claim protection for polygamy.[66]

The humanitarian connection to slavery also provided a blueprint for constitutional-rights consciousness. Antipolygamists embraced the theory that marriage was not only a component of human happiness but of the Constitution itself. The right to emotional and spiritual fulfillment, conceived as the "spirit and intent of th[e] Constitution," they argued, was integral to the novelists' claim that polygamy entailed an illegitimate exercise of authority.[67]

Depicting Mormon polygamy as not just unconstitutional but anticonstitutional stirred the emotions. Constitutional-rights rhetoric in this vein called for "destabilization," as one scholar put it in a related context, "of the settled rights of those who oppressed [plural wives and slaves]." The logic of such constitutionalism rested on a theory of human nature and constitutional rights as being constant with the natural law of God. Conversely, this logic dictated that oppressive structures of authority (such as polygamy and slavery) should be subject to destruction, since it was the government's positive moral obligation to protect constitutional rights and rights bearers. Antipolygamists implied that anything less would betray the constitutional order. Failure to act would corrupt and corrode not only those who practiced Mormon polygamy but also the broader government that failed to intervene.[68]

By opting for a moral focus for law reform, antipolygamists in the 1850s implied that legal structures mirrored religious truth (or error) and that legislation was the means of recovering moral authority. They called unequivocally for federal intervention in Utah. The appeal of such calls was felt widely, in part because the appeal did not require those outside Utah to change their own lives.

Although they entreated federal politicians to protect "otherwise helpless" women in Utah, the novelists were careful not to directly challenge legislators' views of themselves as husbands or their relationships with their wives. Metta Victor, for example, asked legislators only to recognize the rights of women in the home. State intervention, it was argued, could adequately protect marriage against betrayal. In other words, they argued for the moral evaluation of marriage by insisting that most marriages would not be subject to scrutiny. They appealed instead to legislators' obligation to protect and cherish their wives as autonomous beings, whose support provided their husbands with spiritual, emotional, and moral security. While men might technically have the legal power to tyrannize their wives, they claimed, monogamous men were restrained by the very structure of marriage.[69]

Antipolygamists recognized that the existence of Mormon men who refused to acknowledge this moral vision created a powerful argument for reform. They also proposed interventions that could be enacted by legislators in Washington without seeming to affect their own lives. Denying men's power to engage in polygamy legally could be reasonably understood as a reinforcement of husbands' power in valid marriages. The appeal itself reaffirmed both the power of men in law and the power of husbands in marriage. Legislative action, like husbands' restraint, was an act of grace, a gift of reform by thoughtful men—a reaffirmation of the validity of the system rather than a fundamental reworking of it.[70]

Popular novelists thus indirectly provided legislators with a means of distancing the rumblings of woman's rights activists in the East. Marriage and the prerogatives of husbands were deeply contested by midcentury. Into waters stirred by abolitionism, utopianism, evangelicalism, and other powerful and often spiritually driven reforms in the 1830s and 1840s, woman's rights activism poured more turmoil. Many woman's rights advocates in the 1850s drew their inspiration from abolitionism. Quaker abolitionist Angelina Grimké's investigation of the disabilities of the slave, for example, led her to the realization that married women endured many of the same handicaps and suffered from similar legal invisibility. Feminist abolitionists, while a small minority even within the abolitionist community, made telling arguments about the uncanny resemblance of the laws of marriage and slavery that threatened to unsettle all of society.[71]

Woman's rights theorists attacked the unequal laws of marriage, especially the legal doctrine of coverture or considering husband and wife as a single legal entity, arguing instead for equality and equity in the distribution of marital power. Many of their criticisms mirrored earlier critiques made by freethinkers and other religious dissidents. Defenders of Christian monogamy, disturbed by the rhetoric of equality, bitterly opposed woman's rights notions. "The sanctity of the home and the security of the marriage bed," as one lawyer put it in a famous murder trial, was threatened by the "equality of our social condition." The law of marriage had been infected by rights talk. The rhetoric of woman's rights, as well as married women's property acts and judicial decisions awarding child custody to wives in divorce suits, may have had more symbolic than actual importance in the lives of husbands and wives before the Civil War. Yet they excited fear of women's dissatisfaction with marriage.[72]

But most antipolygamists made a counterargument, claiming that Mormon polygamy demonstrated that traditional marriage protected and respected women. The popular appeal of antipolygamy gave legislators a convenient out—here was a form of marriage that *truly* replicated "slavery" for white women. By enacting laws to prohibit the "enslavement of women in Utah," congressmen could deflect attention from domestic relations in their own states and direct it toward a rebellious territory. In this sense, Utah became a handy foil.[73]

And yet all marriages, even those protected by the law of monogamy, were painfully vulnerable to betrayal. Antipolygamy novelists condemned that vulnerability in the 1850s, even as they claimed that polygamy was a disastrous exploitation of it. Legal reform would both reaffirm the existing order and codify the political importance of marriage as the central site of Christian virtue. Popular novels allowed readers to appreciate the moral and emotional power of the argument for law reform, to internalize the threat to marriage, and to condemn polygamy.[74]

CHAPTER 2

The Twin Relic of Barbarism

Debate over polygamy was key to the formation of the third-party system in the 1850s. At the first Republican national convention in 1856, the new party adopted a radical, reformist platform. Included was an explicit connection between polygamy and slavery—a call for the abolition of the "twin relics of barbarism" in the territories. The platform, platitudinous and multilayered, as all such texts are, contained the kernel of a new, national politics of race, gender, and progress. Republicans broadcast to the country their commitment to humanitarian reform of the nation's two "peculiar domestic institutions."[1]

The connection between polygamy and slavery was deep and abiding in political thought across the North. Its usefulness as a partisan tool waxed as Republican reformers made the two domestic-relations issues peculiarly their own. Historians of Mormonism are familiar with the 1856 Republican Party platform; many political historians, however, miss the point that bears emphasizing here. Slavery had long been a yawning, frightening problem for Americans. The disintegration of the Whig Party in the early 1850s and the growth of slavery in the new western territories brought slavery, questions of freedom, and local sovereignty to the forefront of national politics. Antislavery was the immediate conduit for the unification of such diverse elements into a new party system. Antipolygamy was the essential partner of antislavery theory, however, because in 1856 it was far less controversial to condemn Mormon patriarchs in Congress than to condemn slaveowning patriarchs. Republicans capitalized on the popular identification of polygamy and slavery. They called both the "twin relics of barbarism."[2]

The phrase has many possible meanings. "Relic" conveys a sense of

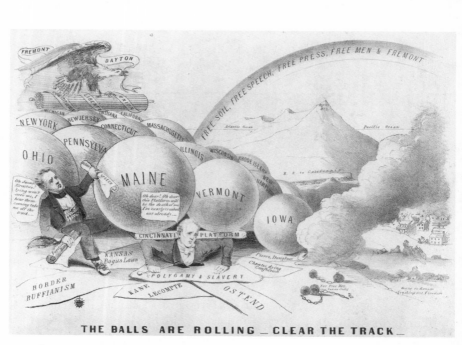

THE BALLS ARE ROLLING — CLEAR THE TRACK—

This Currier & Ives lithograph commemorating the 1856 Republican Party platform and its antipolygamy and antislavery provision depicts President James Buchanan as bowled over by Republican forces. Courtesy of Library of Congress.

anachronism, a useless (even harmful) vestige of a bygone age, vigorous perhaps in its day, but decrepit, backward in modern times. The "twin relic" label implied kinship, as well as the moral despicability of both peculiar domestic relations. "Barbarism" also carried a host of possible interpretations freighted with cruelty, savagery, animalism. In nineteenth-century American thought barbarism occupied a special, un-Christian place. It constituted the inversion of progress, a Manichean counterweight to its successor, civilization. Native cultures and their "savage" customs made barbarism more than an abstract concept for most Americans. Popular fear of "Indian barbarisms" fed insecurities about the vulnerability of civilization, especially private relations of property and marriage, which were the cornerstones of civilized societies.

The identification of civilization with Christianity was deep and widespread; for many theorists and politicians in the nineteenth century, civilization was founded on a basic commitment to Christianity. The party that identified itself successfully as the protector of Christian civilization (and the vanquisher of barbarism) thus acquired significant spiritual as well as political advantage. As Republicans learned quickly, the identification of slavery with Mormon polygamy allowed opponents of both to claim that the patriarchs of Utah and those of the slaveholding states and territories violated Christian mandates. The political salience of antipolygamy was thus linked inextricably to Christian abolitionism. And although it was easier to condemn polygamy than to condemn slavery, action against polygamy was understood by all concerned as an opening wedge in the protective shield around states' rights, and the South's "peculiar domestic institution." The relationship between Christian humanitarianism, antislavery, and antipolygamy galvanized all three. By 1860, antipolygamy so overwhelmed other forms of political anti-Mormonism that it subsumed them almost entirely. Republican politicians hammered home the relationship between Christianity and legal reform.[3]

Thomas Nelson, a pro-Union representative from Tennessee, for example, urged passage of antipolygamy legislation in 1860. He declared that the Christian duty of legislators was to recognize "woman as the highest, last and greatest blessing [given by God] to man. . . . It was designed that she should give her whole heart in exchange for the undivided affection of man, and become his partner in lawful marriage. Enthroned in the domestic circle, she becomes our refuge amidst the storms and conflicts of life, and sheds a halo of happiness around the joys of home." The "law of God" required congressmen, Nelson argued, to avenge "the insult [of polygamy] to our own wives and our own daughters, and the wives and daughters of our constituents" by prohibiting polygamy in the territories of the United States. The constitutionality of reform was a more difficult question.[4]

Translating the "insult" of polygamy into federal legislation proved extraordinarily difficult, however. Controversy over federal power to legislate the structure of "domestic relations" in the territories tore into Congress in the 1850s. Domestic relations was a legal category that in the nineteenth century included the law of master and servant as well as the law of husband and wife; it described slavery as well as polygamy. No topic could have been more incendiary or divisive. The emotional and spiritual appeal of antipolygamy rhetoric energized Republicans, not least because the same appeal infuriated Democrats. The connections between slavery and polygamy in political and constitutional debates meant that claims of authority over the law of marriage fed into battles over the law of slavery. The "twin relics of barbarism" platform in 1856 rendered popular antipolygamy in explicitly political terms, connecting patriarchy (in the South as well as in Utah) to barbarism, and voluntarism (in labor as in marriage) to civilization. Republicans clothed popular antipolygamy in partisan fabric.[5]

The emotional volume of the debates escalated quickly, as proslavery Democrats reacted to the condemnation of slavery inherent in Republican rhetoric. Southerners understood that the broad appeal of antipolygamy outside Utah created the potential for the expansion of federal power, and thus for an opening wedge into interference with slavery. Unpalatable comparisons between polygamy and slavery compelled many Democrats to defend both against federal interference, even as they railed against the speciousness of the comparison.

The polemical appeal of the "twin relics" label, as Democrats never tired of pointing out, obscured the substantial constitutional barriers to antipolygamy legislation. The extension of federal power over domestic relations in Utah would take the national government into new territory, an area that had previously been understood as subject to local governance. They warned against allowing emotion to overwhelm federalism, even as they vehemently condemned any suggestion that expansion of federal power was possible.

To Democrats, the restructuring of government contemplated by Republicans was far more dangerous than the practice of polygamy by Mormons in Utah. Talk of the barbarism of polygamy, of moral stewardship of the territories, was anathema especially to Southerners. Democrats also used the language of tyranny and oppression to describe the political objectives of their opponents. They charged that the Republicans' deceptively appealing agenda was a surreptitious expansion of federal authority in the name of civilization. That way lay tyranny of the kind long feared by Americans: the erosion of the rights of states to protect their citizens and to govern themselves in ways that only local government could accommodate. Southerners heard the veiled threat to slavery in such proposals. "If there is power in Congress to inspect the morals of a nascent political community, and of its own autocratic will to decree this and prohibit that," queried Representative Lawrence Keitt of South Carolina in a speech condemning proposed antipolygamy legislation, "may they not declare slaveholding a crime? To allow this power is to consolidate the Government."[6]

The turbulence of the late 1850s swirled in Utah as it did throughout the rest of the nation. In 1856 and 1857, Mormon Utah experienced a searing religious revival. The "Reformation," as it is commonly termed, entailed a massive (re)commitment by the faithful, who examined their own lives and those of their fellows and found them wanting. As one Mormon put it in early 1857, "Misdeeds are not only publicly denounced, but the doers and their misdeeds are named

Brigham Young in the 1850s was both the governor of Utah Territory and the president and prophet of the Mormon Church. His fiery sermons and apparent power to command his followers convinced national politicians that Mormons were in a state of rebellion. Courtesy of Princeton University Library.

before the public congregations. The arrows of the Almighty are with President [Brigham Young]. The terrors of the Lord are upon them, and are coming upon the people."[7]

The Reformation increased Mormons' moral isolation from the rest of the country. Mormon sermons grew hyperbolic, some even including topics such as the infamous doctrine of "blood atonement" (or the theory that only the shedding of the sinner's blood could atone for some sins), predictions of victory over the forces of Babylon (that is, the rest of the nation), and even killing of non-Mormons. Inflamed rhetoric in turn encouraged acts of insubordination against officials sent by Washington to govern Utah Territory. One federal judge who challenged Mormon officials saw his office "raided" and court records confiscated and presumably burned. Another federal agent left the territory shortly after lecturing the Mormons on their moral laxness, claiming that his life had been threatened.[8]

President James Buchanan understood the potential political value of reducing tensions by deflecting attention from slavery and promoting union by meeting rebellion with immediate federal reprisal. For the feverish atmosphere in Utah was matched by a different but no less ominous sense of sinfulness and retribution elsewhere. "Bleeding Kansas" exploded under the strain of trying to maintain popular sovereignty without popular agreement on the vital question of slavery within the territory. The combination of the Reformation in Utah and the bloodshed in Kansas enticed desperate Democratic politicians to hope that a lesson imposed on Utah would send a message to the rest of the nation. Equally important, Democrats began to feel that by quelling insubordination in Utah, they could distance themselves from the more unsettling aspects of the notion that "domestic" government should be left to local majorities. Polygamy, at least, would no longer be paired with slavery in Republican rhetoric.[9]

One of the most obvious uses of the "twin relics" label was an attack on Northern Democracy's most powerful theorist—Stephen Douglas of Illinois. Among other things, Douglas was charged with being inordinately fond of Mormons, a group still hated by many Illinois residents, who remembered the Mormon settlement there with bitterness. Aware of the political costs of the identification of polygamy with slavery, Douglas claimed in a speech in 1857 that his pet doctrine of local sovereignty no more supported Mormonism than it did any other kind of rebelliousness. He declared himself convinced that the Mormons in Utah were in a state of rebellion that merited swift and sure punishment. Intervention in Utah would show Republicans (and reassure Democrats) that protecting slavery did not mean countenancing polygamy.[10]

The Mormon War of 1857 illustrates how the local tradition of anti-Mormonism that flourished in the 1840s was replaced by a national antipolygamy ethic by the late 1850s. Before his murder, Joseph Smith had importuned the federal government to intervene in the states, only to be dismissed by federal officials who advised the Mormons to look to the states for protection. But by 1857, the Mormon Question had become national, fueled by polygamy and the political power to protect it that arguably went with territorial sovereignty. Eager to deflect attention from slavery, Buchanan credited claims of Mormon treason made by former territorial officials and Mormon apostates.

BRIGHAM YOUNG AND HIS WIVES REVIEWING THE MORMON LEGION.

Novelist Maria Ward, in a late-1850s edition of *Female Life among the Mormons*, imagined that Brigham Young commanded a well armed and drilled army. Courtesy of Oberlin College Library.

The potential windfall from a confrontation in Utah prompted him to dispatch one-sixth of all federal troops there in late 1857. As a military tactic, Buchanan's timing was off—it was too late in the season to send an army over the Rocky Mountains. The army foundered in the snow and with it Buchanan's hopes for swift action against upstarts in the West. Congress eventually refused to fund the expedition.[11]

The combative rhetoric and millennial hopes of Mormon leaders also fizzled, however. As one historian put it, by early 1858 Young had modified his tone to sound more like "an extreme states'-righter . . . than a ruler of an independent country." A truce negotiated in 1858 was hardly the final resolution of the conflict, but it did avoid bloodshed then and for decades to come. Fort Douglas, established in the hills above Salt Lake with a few well-placed cannon, became an effective deterrent against both armed resistance on the part of the

Mormons and armed interference from the East on the part of anti-Mormons. Instead, the conflict flowed into political channels—Brigham Young embraced the language of states' rights and popular sovereignty and tried to gain admission for Utah as a state. Republicans capitalized on the predictable connections between such talk and slavery.[12]

Southern Democrats, wedded to the principle that liberty resided in the democratic commitment to freedom from dictation from the center, clearly saw the moral (and spiritual) precedent in Republicans' proposed antipolygamy legislation. By 1860, it was impossible to talk about Utah without provoking Southerners to immediate defense of slavery. "The invariable law of political development," argued one senator, would be to reduce the states to "mere subordinate and dependent corporations." The national government would deploy the "equivocal subterfuges of party platforms" (that is, the "twin relics" analogy of polygamy to slavery) to disguise the unprecedented expansion of federal power inherent in the antipolygamy legislation. Imbuing the federal government with powers of moral evaluation, Southerners claimed, was the repudiation of the "long-settled principle of non-interference . . . but one short step further [would] apply the doctrine to that other of the 'twin relics of barbarism,' " a warning to all the "slave protectionists of this [Democratic] side of the House."[13]

Southerners also warned Republicans that antipolygamy legislation would be ineffective because Mormons would not heed commands from Washington. Republicans replied that they contemplated enforcing the law. Arguments about the ineffectiveness of humanitarian reforms were typical of slaveholding patriarchs, Republicans charged. As it turned out, Democrats were right about the failure of antipolygamy legislation as conceived by Republicans in the 1850s. For their part, Republicans relied heavily on the hortatory aspects of law. They stressed the moral message of criminal prohibition rather than its practical implications. They also made much of Democrats' implicit defense of polygamy.[14]

Indeed, the 1860 presidential campaign only hardened the party divisions on the polygamy question. Lincoln and his supporters taunted Douglas with advocating immorality through the doctrine of popular sovereignty, "which permit[s] the people to do as they please, and sanctions, not only slavery, but polygamy, piracy, and whatever else is revolting and monstrous." As they pieced together proposals for instituting the moral stewardship of the territories, Republicans drew on the traditional relationship that they believed existed between

Christian faith and the state legal systems. They argued for the moral rehabilitation of Utah through the imposition of a legal system that respected the Christian mandates for monogamous marriage and disestablishment of religion. They were convinced legal reform was the only way to protect the rights of all citizens of Utah. Crucial to such arguments was the assumption that voluntarism (free will) was as central to marriage as to religious life. Yet, until Southerners left the Union in 1861, action on the twin relic was stalled by proslavery interests, to whom voluntarism in domestic relations spelled the end of the world they knew.[15]

For the most part, therefore, Republicans spoke among themselves and for their own edification, gathering momentum for the fight against polygamy in the territories. Reform in the interest of traditional Christian principles had substantial appeal to Republicans who were also committed to reform of another sort—the abolition of slavery. But the battles over polygamy (unlike those over slavery) were fought throughout in political and legal, rather than military, terms.

To explore the political development of antipolygamy in the Civil Wars years is to grapple with Republicans' embrace of the power and possibility of reform. With newfound authority and moral passion, Republicans reconstructed constitutional theory to allow the expansion of federal power at the expense of local sovereignty, and the adapting of state law to federal legal structures.

Justin Morrill, a young congressman from Vermont, was a prominent spokesman of this reformist wing of the Republican political coalition and eventually put his name to the first important antipolygamy bill. Morrill assumed that meaningful consent by women was by definition lacking in all polygamous marriages. He claimed that the voluntarism essential to freedom had been violated by Mormon polygamists. In 1857, in one of his first and most important antipolygamy speeches, Morrill stressed that the question of the Mormons' peculiar institution "seems to acquire greater gravity in each successive year." He connected the issue of polygamy to that of slavery, arguing among other things that the Mormons in Utah, who believed that "bondage [and] polygamy are Bible doctrines," had imported black servants and enslaved Indians. Worst of all, they reduced white women to the level of beasts, "mak[ing] woman no longer an equal and man the tyrant, . . . tear[ing] the endearing passion of love from the heart, and install[ing] in its place the rage of jealousy; . . . and degrad[ing] her to the level of a mere animal." Polygamy, in his analysis, guaranteed women's suffering and thereby created a mandate for their rescue.[16]

Justin Morrill, Republican of Vermont, served first in the House then in the Senate for more than four decades. Morrill was a dedicated abolitionist as well as an antipolygamist. Courtesy of Cornell University Library.

Advocating legal reform based on sympathy for women whose lives were (in theory, at least) made miserable by a system that mandated their suffering had a strong humanitarian flavor. The Republicans' condemnation of a "barbarism revolting to the civilized world," the foundation of cruelty upon which the flogging of the slave's back or of the Mormon woman's soul was based, called for action. Morrill dwelled on this suffering, pointing to Utah as a place of systematic misery for women: "To suppose that polygamy conduces to happiness is to suppose a total subversion of woman's nature. . . . The little home, which ought to be her throne and her empire, is lost to her. They are jealously watched, and dreadfully abused if they are seen to show, by even so much as a glance, that they are unhappy. But the long and anxious countenances of the 'mothers of Israel' proclaim too plainly their entire misery." Polygamy, charged Morrill, existed in Utah "in its most disgusting form, including in its slimy folds sisters, mothers, and daughters," whose lives were devastated by "cruelty and loathsomeness." Establishing the "entire misery" of wives in Utah did not by itself solve the problem for legislators, however. Two vital steps remained: the assumption of responsibility over the domestic relations of a remote territory and the conviction that reform was, in fact, achievable.[17]

By the late 1850s, Republicans were convinced of both. Utah's status as a territory provided the opportunity to explore and expand federal power, because territories were technically subject to federal control. And yet everybody knew that domestic relations were matters of local constitutional practice. To intervene in such questions was not only to violate a cultural expectation but also to satisfy the popular desire to vindicate the local practice of all jurisdictions but Utah. Republicans cast around for suitable theories to justify intervention. As Daniel Gooch of Massachusetts put it in 1860, "[W]e should adopt the same policy that a judicious parent pursues with reference to this child. He permits the child to regulate and govern his own conduct so long as he applies wholesome and salutary rules to himself; but when he fails to do that, the parent again resumes the exercise of control over his own offspring." According to Republican sponsors of anti-polygamy legislation, the national government should educate its wayward territory in the lessons of citizenship and the essential private structures for republicanism. Only when the legal structure of Utah had matured to include the freedom of choice that inhered in religious liberty and monogamy would it be ready to resume its own self-governance.[18]

Long before the federal government grappled with Mormon polygamy, state courts and lawyers confronted tangled questions about the relationship of the law of marriage to the security of the post-Revolutionary nation. They also tackled questions of the limits of religious liberty and the meaning of disestablishment (or establishment). Republicans' arguments for reform in Utah drew on earlier debates about the relationship of Christianity to the common law, and the common law to monogamy. These had been topics of pro-found concern to jurists and political theorists of antebellum America from James Kent, to Joseph Story, to Francis Lieber. Antipolygamists were able to select material from the storehouse of earlier law and commentary, focusing especially on the nature of limits on liberty imposed by state courts. They worked in state legal traditions that melded common law with constitutional concepts. They drew on doctrines that integrated faith and legal structure, blending Christian precepts with secular law.

Antebellum constitutional lawyers knew well that American juris-dictions harmonized the English assumption of the essential Chris-tianity of the common law with the American state tradition of re-ligious liberty. However loudly American statesmen might proclaim the absolute religious liberty of their country, Christianity was pro-tected by a hedgerow of legal structures by midcentury, especially in family law. As Thomas Cooley of the Michigan Supreme Court sum-marized the state of the law in his landmark treatise *Constitutional Limitations,* Christianity was part of state common-law jurisprudence "for certain purposes," primarily "those which relate to the family and social relations," including the permanence of marriage, the prohibi-tion of polygamy, and the support due from a husband to his wife. And, of course, for the related purpose of the punishment of blas-phemy, and the lesser included offenses of obscenity and pornogra-phy. The constitutional law of the states provided antipolygamists with a corpus of case law that connected individual faith, sexual propriety, and political stability, describing the bounds of religious liberty in terms of a common law that was both sturdily Christian, and exquisitely American.[19]

Mormon plural marriage fell plumb into the overlapping circles that faith and law drew around marriage in nineteenth-century legal doctrine. Polygamy challenged both the Christian concept of marital unity and the related common-law concept of coverture, which de-fined married women's legal status. From the biblical injunction that a man and woman were translated by their marriage into "one flesh," common lawyers drew the principle that husband and wife were one legal person (represented by the husband; the legal existence of the wife suspended—or "covered"—by his authority for the duration of the marriage). The classic statement is Blackstone's, in his *Commen-taries on the Common Law,* first published in 1765 and profoundly influential in American law and jurisprudence throughout the nine-teenth century. "By Marriage," wrote Blackstone, "the husband and wife are one person in law [citing Leviticus 1:6]. . . . Upon this princi-ple, of an union of person in husband and wife, depend almost all the legal rights, duties, and disabilities, that either of them acquire by the marriage." The idea of a multiplicity in such unity (that is, of a husband who became one with more than one wife at the same time) drew shocked and affronted responses from those versed in law. Coverture presumed that a wife was, in legal theory, not a separate person. Her husband's union with another woman in precisely the same relationship would explode the fiction of perfect unity, replacing it with multiplicity and tumbling the intricate structure built on the fantasy.[20]

Yet as antipolygamists knew, by the mid-nineteenth century the law of coverture was in substantial disarray. The distribution of power within marital relationships was amended in some states by married women's property acts and earnings statutes, which allowed wives to keep and even to manage their own property during the tenure of a marriage. This shift in law blended with an increasingly accepted (even required) degree of choice in a marital partner (that is, the idea that love should precede, rather than follow, the celebration of a marriage and that love was only truly present when given by a self with the theoretical power to withhold the gift).[21]

The steely-eyed patriarchy of many traditional aspects of the common law of coverture (such as the husband's absolute control of the wife's property, and his power over her person) traveled uneasily alongside the romantic desire of husbands to be assured of their wives' love as the key to their own happiness. The legitimate uses of overt power, especially in the face of a wife's humiliation, seemed fewer and fewer. Romantic sympathy between husbands and wives weakened patriarchal structures, even as it (in theory, at least) brought husbands and wives closer physically and spiritually than they had ever been. In this sense, the "sacrament" of marriage was inherent in the mystical union of the couple through their love rather than merely in the exchange of vows. The profound religious significance of human love, as the historian Karen Lystra has aptly pointed out, was not generally a substitute for Christian faith in the nineteenth century. Instead, conjugal love functioned as a new incarnation of faith, absorbing some of the basic focus, language, and structure of religious institutions, as men and women found God in each other through their marriage.[22]

The harsher rules of coverture grated against this vision of earthly bliss in marriage. The biblical concept of a physical union—perfect identification of husband and wife through their love—acquired new luster in romantic love, however. The metaphor of "one flesh," while it arguably no longer justified the raw invocation of power to control or discipline wives, retained cultural currency, and even increased in religious significance as husbands and wives discovered spiritual meaning in their romantic selves. The popular antipolygamy novels and the common law comfortably reinforced one another in this respect, as both dwelled on the spiritual union possible only in marriage.[23]

The romantic premises of such immersion in the beloved other were based first on its voluntary nature, and second on its exclusivity. The trust essential to this emotional investment in marriage required both legal protection and the conviction of a spiritual mandate for such indulgence ("one flesh"). Rescuing the common law from an ingrained patriarchy, defenders of the metaphor of marital unity described it as the codification of conjugal love and companionship. Thus the common (human) law reflected the biblical (divine) law of marriage, proving once again the harmony of Christianity and the practical wisdom of the common law, much to the satisfaction of legal commentators. As antipolygamist Thomas Nelson put it: "The law of God is the only unerring and unvarying standard of right and wrong. . . . But it requires no blind or slavish submission on our part to believe, what the evidence of centuries as well as the observation of enlightened man has established, that the very highest degree of wisdom was displayed in the restriction, from the beginning of the world, of the marriage relation to two persons only."[24]

Polygamy, as legal commentators stressed by way of contrast, had "always" been a crime in common law. Mormons glorified the transgression of what the influential treatise writer and judge James Kent called the "direct and serious prohibition of polygamy . . . founded on the precepts of Christianity, and the laws of our social nature, and . . . supported by the sense and practice of the civilized nations of Europe." Thus congressional antipolygamists in the 1860s tapped into a deep and religiously based common-law tradition when they argued that true marriage was, by definition, monogamous. They asserted that polygamy was contrary to the legal text of marriage, even as sentimental novelists in the 1850s maintained that polygamy violated its emotional text. The monogamy that they contrasted to Mormon polygamy, in their perspective, was the product of God's common law of love, the location of spirituality in the home, embodying the biblical injunction for union in a kinder, gentler version of coverture.[25]

The common law and its protection of Christian marriage also provided the tools for the argument that Congress was not required to "tamely submit to any burlesque, outrage, or indecency which artful men may seek to hide under the name of religion!" As Justin Morrill understood it, the most expansive interpretation of religious freedom "could not be understood to license crimes punishable at common law." The common law, he argued, described the freedom protected by constitutional law. The boundaries of religious liberty and the common law were mutually self-referential; both, as the antebellum law of religious liberty in the states made clear, were based on Christian moral truth. In congressional antipolygamists' eyes, the Mormons claimed the protection of the Constitution for a practice that was outside its scope—that is, polygamy—even as they violated the American mandate for separation of church and state by empowering their church to control lives and law in Utah Territory.[26]

Many antipolygamists argued that the existence of polygamy was explained (and polygamists were shielded) by the legal power granted with the incorporation of the Mormon Church, and the extraordinary property rights and internal control over the marriage of members that the territorial assembly ceded to the church corporation. The legal powers of the church effectively "established" the Mormon faith as the official church of the territory, they claimed, all to protect and perpetuate polygamy. For example, Justin Morrill charged that "polygamy is now attempted to be hedged in and barricaded by law in the very citadel of the church," proving that the church corporation had twisted constitutional liberty into an untenable moral abomination. If Congress itself was forbidden to establish a church, queried Morrill, how could a territory, itself the creature of Congress, create "an insolent and all-grasping power" dedicated to the "foul abomination of spiritual wifery"?[27]

Antipolygamists could embrace disestablishment and apply the concept against the powers of the Mormon Church corporation because by midcentury legal theorists had made it clear that to be a good, Christian American was also to believe deeply in separation of church and state. Republicans capitalized on the laws of the states, importing legal concepts developed in local jurisdictions and applying them against Utah. In this way, they assured themselves that they were not really creating "new" law at all but simply requiring the Mormons to observe rules and limits that other Americans followed. Their advocacy of the expansion of federal control was thus cloaked in the comforting familiarity of the law they proposed to deploy against a resistant local population. Customs observed in all the states, they insisted, were themselves the product of local (yet also universal) wisdom. Allowing Utah to create its own very different law would upset the security of those customs everywhere.[28]

To control the economic and political power of the Mormon Church, antipolygamists drew on the precedent of mortmain laws (legislatively imposed limits on the amount of property owned by a church corporation) across the country and in English history. Drawing on legal traditions that traced their roots back to the Protestant Reformation, antipolygamists advocated limits on the amount of real property the Mormon Church could acquire as a means of controlling "ecclesiastical domination." They charged the church and its leaders with monopolizing the land and resources of the territory, subjecting the citizens of Utah to "priestcraft," just as Catholic priests in England had exploited the poor before the Henrican Reformation.[29]

It is worth emphasizing here that antipolygamist congressmen, while acting on explicitly religious principles, also used traditional secular methods. They drafted mortmain statutes (which were themselves pointedly anticlerical and anti-Catholic, at least in origin) to create new boundaries between church and state for Utah Territory. In part, then, the tradition of disestablishment (the hobbling of institutional power in the interests of the flourishing of dissenting— read Protestant—religious voices) was deployed to preserve the moral structures of the religious mainstream. Antipolygamist Republicans imposed their religious and legal values on Utah, claiming that in doing so they were protecting true liberty. In their eyes, religious liberty could not be deployed validly to enhance the legal and political power of any religious institution. Such power, they came to believe, was itself un-Christian, because it entailed an inherent erosion of the freedom of will essential to true Christian belief (that is, Protestant belief). By folding the separation of church and state into Christianity, and this "disestablished" Christianity into the expansion of federal power, theorists adapted to American jurisdictions a conception of religion that was at once popular and powerful yet also yoked to republicanism, democracy, and lack of a formal political voice.

This paradoxical relationship—the flourishing of vibrant popular religious politics in an avowedly secular republic—had also been vital to disestablishment at the state level. As Alexis de Tocqueville noticed in the 1830s, the public influence of religion in America was undeniable, despite the purported secular rationality of the government. The ubiquity of profound religious faith, and the informal political influence of religious thought, Tocqueville mused, were inversely related to their lack of formal political power. The incorporation of democratic principles into the polity or rule of established faiths presaged disestablishment in the states. It also provided a working theory of democratic limitations on religious dissent.[30]

Democracy infected the law of religious establishments as state court judges and constitution-drafting conventions put their imprimatur on the Protestant forms of church polity they knew and valued most. In contrast to their understanding of Catholic hierarchy and papal control, liberal American Protestants presumed (and imposed where they had the power to do so) that democratic denominations were the standard for right-thinking Christians. In *Baker v. Fales*, for example, the Massachusetts Supreme Judicial Court held in 1820 that the Unitarian majority of the Dedham parish (that is, the voters in the town) could validly call a Unitarian to the tax-supported town ministry over the objections of the covenanted, Congregational members of the church. In response, orthodox Congregationalists joined more liberal Protestant denominations in embracing separation as a means of preserving control over church policies. Disestablishment was finally achieved in 1833. Although dissolution of religious establishments cut institutional ties, individual responsibility for deferring to the Christian sensibilities of the majority remained intact, as the prosecution of freethinker Abner Kneeland for blasphemy in Massachusetts in 1834 clearly demonstrated. The brief interval between disestablishment and the prosecution of a notorious dissident only a year later telegraphed the lesson to citizens. In Massachusetts, as other antebellum states' laws had already made clear, the separation of church and state was explicitly paired with the understanding that religious liberty did not include the protection of anti-Christian actions. These lessons were later deployed against Mormons, as they had been against freethinkers in the earlier period.[31]

Principles of popular sovereignty sustained the punishment of obstreperous dissenters, just as the same principles had defined religious establishments. The troubling boundaries between liberty and license were probed and tested by religious dissidents in the early Republic, challenging jurists and legal theorists to construct a positive legal distinction. The result was an American law of blasphemy that highlights the legal meaning of religious liberty in the early nineteenth century, and the relationship of that liberty to democracy. The power of religious expression in the early Republic galvanized the legal structure of the new American states as well as the spiritual lives of believing Christians. The instability of the boundaries between church and state in the decades after the Revolution provided an invaluable opportunity for lawyers and politicians to reweave the legal fabric in an American design.

The story began in 1811, when James Kent, chief justice of the Court of Appeals of New York, upheld the conviction of John Ruggles for "wickedly, maliciously and blasphemously" uttering the words "*Jesus Christ* was a bastard, and his mother must be a whore." The jury that heard Ruggles's case concluded that "these words were uttered in a wanton manner, and, as they evidently import, with a wicked and malicious disposition, and not in a serious discussion upon any controverted point in religion." By the late eighteenth century, such "contumelious reproaches or profane ridicule of Christ or Holy Scripture" were treated in England as common-law crimes, because "whatever strikes at the root of christianity, tends manifestly to the dissolution of civil government." Seizing on the obvious distinction between the union of church and state in England and the provisions of New York's constitution allowing "free toleration to all religions and all kinds of worship," Ruggles's lawyer had argued that "*christianity* did not make a part of the common law of this state." How could an offense against Christianity be made the subject of criminal penalties (in this case, a common-law rather than a statutory offense), if Christianity had no legal status—if there were no establishment to defend, and all religions were freely tolerated?[32]

Kent's answer to this question relied on what he called "moral discipline, and . . . those principles of virtue, which help to bind society together." Such society, created by the "people of this state," was indelibly stamped with their essential Christianity. The offense, then, was not against any religious establishment but against the earthly sovereign—the people of New York, whose sensibilities had been offended by the blasphemer. Using the people as his sovereign touchstone, Kent explained why Ruggles must be punished. He also explained why "attacks upon the religion of *Mahomet* or of the grand *Lama*" were not within the purview of American law "for this plain reason, that the case assumes that we are a christian people, and the morality of the country is deeply engrafted upon christianity, and not upon the doctrines or worship of those impostors." Every European country (with what Kent called "a single and monitory case excepted"—surely revolutionary France) maintained a watchful eye over public morals, punishing "[t]hings which corrupt moral sentiment, as obscene actions, prints[,] and writings, and even gross instances of seduction, have, upon the same principle, been held indictable; and shall we form an exception in these particulars to the rest of the civilized world?" The regrettable existence of savage tribes, barbarity among nations or in individuals close to home, Kent stressed, did not undermine the essentially Christian morality of the American people. "Christianity, in its enlarged sense," Kent held, "is not unknown to our law."[33]

This "religion in general," the basis of "public decency," remained central to the concept of religious liberty, as distinguished in the New York Constitution (and in common sense, as Kent and other jurists argued) from "acts of licentiousness, or . . . practices inconsistent with the peace and safety of this state." Such a generalized Christianity was already protected by the laws of the state of New York, Kent emphasized, born out by the *statute for preventing immorality*," which consecrated Sunday as "holy time," as well as by the apparatus for determining truth in the legal system. Failure to punish blasphemy would undermine the integrity of oaths, required by statute to be based on "laying the hand on and kissing the gospels." Vilification of the Gospels was in this sense an attack on the moral foundation of law. By punishing an agitator such as Ruggles, Kent maintained, he was protecting constitutional liberty.[34]

The punishment inflicted upon blasphemers was not imposed by any particular belief as judges explained it, therefore, but the consequence of deliberate and provocative "defiance to all public order, [the] disregard of all decency, [with] contumelious reproaches, scoffing at and reviling that which is certainly the religion of the country." They paired the punishment of such defiance and indecency with accolades for religious "opinion, whatever it may be, and free and decent discussion on any religious subject." "Decent" and "serious" discussions were protected by constitutional provisions for freedom of conscience and worship. However, the vilification of religion "with malicious and blasphemous contempt" was an "abuse" of the right of religious liberty. Belief, then, was absolutely free; but when conscience spilled over into action (blasphemy was in this sense a "speech act"), then the sensibilities of the people were entitled to protection against the actor.[35]

The popularity of the *Ruggles* decision grew over time. Evangelicals embraced the opinion as proof of the essential Christianity of the Republic. And other courts followed. As the Supreme Court of Pennsylvania put it in 1824, "General Christianity [is] the cement of civil union, and the essential support of legislation." In this view, the common-law and legal protection of Christian truths together functioned as the essence of democracy, a translation of the will of the people into legal language. Both were tied to the common sense of the people and created a framework whose subtext was the protection and invigoration of faith. Antipolygamists grew up with state laws of religious liberty that assumed the essential (Protestant) Christianity of their legal systems and the people they governed.[36]

This symmetrical legal edifice could not be constructed without opposition. Resistance to judicial power, and claims that judicial invocation of the common law was essentially foreign and undemocratic, propelled the "codification" movement of the first half of the nineteenth century. Many Americans, Jeffersonian Democrats especially, were concerned that judicial power usurped the legitimate authority of elected representatives of the people. They advocated the codification of laws, incorporating legal doctrines into state statutes to limit the power of the judiciary to draw on an undemocratic, judge-made "common-law" heritage. The broad popularity of decisions such as *Ruggles*, however, and the sense that the de facto establishment of "general" Christianity was consistent with good order, community welfare, and popular sentiment, helped disarm critics of common-law jurisprudence. The "Americanization" of English common-law doctrine in cases such as *Ruggles* domesticated and democratized otherwise disturbingly amorphous judge-made law.[37]

Mormons also opposed the common law and refused to follow the practice of "receiving" the common law into territorial law. The territorial legislature explicitly declared that the common law was to have no effect in Utah courts. Utah was the only American jurisdiction to reject the common law outright; the relationship between Protestant Christianity, the common law, and monogamy troubled Mormon leaders. In this sense, Mormons were part of a tradition of resistance to a religiously orthodox common law. Yet by the time Mormons declared their resistance to the common law, its popularity in the rest of the country had rebounded, particularly in cases involving religion. Mormons' rejection of the common law reconfirmed their opponents' commitment to it, and their conviction of its integral relation to civilization and Christianity. Indeed, Mormons played into a lingering sense in the rest of the country that opposition to the common law was tantamount to rejection of Christianity, and an embrace of atheism and political rebellion.[38]

Thomas Jefferson had been the central opponent in the legal debate, as he was in the religious campaign against infidelity discussed at length in Chapter 1. Alarmed by the growing agreement between popular religious sensibilities and legal doctrine, Jefferson charged in 1824 that "the judges have usurped" the legislative powers "in their repeated decision, that Christianity is a part of the common law." From such misguided statements, Jefferson argued, English judges had derived "authority for burning witches" and "all blasphemy and profaneness," and their American counterparts "have piously avoided lifting the veil under which [the mistake] was shrouded." Concerned that federal courts would hold that Christianity was part of the national common law, Jefferson argued that that way lay persecution. Although never a widespread conviction, Jefferson's charge nonetheless struck at the heart of concerns about the use of law to punish harmless differences among Christians.[39]

The indictment of one Thomas Jefferson Chandler for blasphemy in 1836 provided Chief Justice John Clayton of the Supreme Court of Delaware with the opportunity to refute the first Thomas Jefferson. Liberty as well as morality and social order, Clayton insisted, were dependent on legal protection against the denigration of the religion of the people of the country. "The tears and blood of revolutionary France during that reign of terror, when infidelity triumphed and the abrogation of the christian faith was succeeded by the worship of the goddess of reason," demonstrated this. The cautionary lesson of France, in this view, proved that "without [the Christian] religion no nation has ever yet continued free." Jefferson's sympathy for French radicals, according to his foes, colored his anti–common law campaign with the aura of atheism and blasphemy. Supreme Court justice Joseph Story also challenged Jefferson. An eminent treatise-writer in his own right, Story condemned Jefferson's argument as an attempt "to contradict all history" and common sense. In Story's analysis, the national union, as well as state governments, liberty, and social order, were all dependent on Christian principles of freedom and order, memorialized and applied through common law and positive statute.[40]

Yet Story and Clayton were as far from endorsing a formal union of church and state as they were from advocating a separation of religious principles from government. By embracing a particular version of democratic theory, Story and other American jurists could embrace a vigorous disestablishmentarianism without endorsing the secularism of Jeffersonian legal theory. Such secularism was not common at any level of legal or political theory by the mid-nineteenth century. Jeffersonian skepticism, however influential it became in the twentieth century, did not describe either positive law or abstract legal theory in the nineteenth. "[T]o exclude all rivalry among Christian sects," Story maintained, was the essential goal of toleration. But to leap from such an institutional disentanglement, as Jefferson did, to a duty to "countenance, much less to advance mohametanism, or Judaism, or infidelity, by prostrating Christianity" was to confuse respect for individual conscience with an inability to protect the state from the active erosion of public and private virtue. Jefferson would expose the Republic to the perversion of liberty into license, provoking "universal disapprobation, if not universal indignation."[41]

As jurists reconfigured the relationship of religion to American law and government, therefore, disestablishment itself became a Christian concept. Liberty of conscience and its corollary, uncoerced belief, were central to Protestantism as they were to free will as a political matter. By disestablishing religion, Americans congratulated themselves that they created a place for truly voluntary faith. Liberal Protestants, and liberal jurisprudes, boasted that America was an extraordinarily "Christian" nation by the 1840s. So persuasive was this vision of the proper relationship between law and religion that by the late 1830s, Chief Judge Lemuel Shaw of the Supreme Judicial Court of Massachusetts, sustaining the conviction of Abner Kneeland, explained that a statute prohibiting blasphemy was "not intended to prevent or restrain the formation of any opinions or the profession of any religious sentiments whatever, but to restrain and punish acts which have a tendency to disturb the public peace." The duty of the Christian patriot, then, was to inhabit and protect the space between institutional church tyranny, on the one hand, and anarchical anti-Christianity, on the other.[42]

Equally useful for antipolygamists was the Christian humanism that connected religious belief to good government. Lyman Beecher, for example, called the Bible "a Code of Laws" that articulated the "laws of a moral government." Radical abolitionist William Lloyd Garrison maintained that the Bible was the only statute book he needed. Such identification of law and morality with Christianity yoked law (and, by implication, legislators and judges) to the practical implementation of God's moral law on earth. The sacred mission of secular government was, in this view, important indeed. God's will required immersion in the world; good government became identical to the will of God. This formula infused political dissent with the distinctive odor of anti-Christianity, and vice versa. As the Supreme Court of Pennsylvania put it, "No free government now exists in the world, unless where Christianity is acknowledged, and is the religion of the country. So far from Christianity . . . being part of the machinery necessary to despotism, the reverse is the fact."[43]

Attacks on the "laws of a moral government" themselves frequently had sexual overtones, either through the use of profane language or by the advocacy of sexual experimentation of one kind or another. All too predictably, the "license" punished by blasphemy prosecutions spilled over into areas of sexual discipline mandated by Christian Scripture. The furrow connecting marital or sexual deviance and religious dissent had been well plowed by freethinkers as well as by less intellectually sophisticated dissidents. In the eyes of her opponents, radical theorist Fanny Wright, whose free-love philosophy was deeply connected to her religious free thought as discussed in Chapter 1, was the classic example of how religious and sexual restraint were mutually dependent. In law, jurists held that blasphemy, if allowed to proceed unchecked, would foster "impiety and profanity, . . . and [lead to] the worship of the Goddess of Reason . . . in the person of a naked prostitute." The Mormons provided an even more pointed example. Mormon theory and practice forced legal theorists to be explicit about the relationship between Protestant belief and social structures, and to adapt the law of religious freedom to suit new circumstances.[44]

For the first time in issues involving law and religion, the constitution in question was federal. Not only were the stakes arguably raised by the national (versus state) forum, but the contours of the challenge were enlarged and reconfigured in a more profound, more organized form of dissent. The Latter-day Saints, more effectively than other contemporary utopian sects or earlier freethinkers, achieved a degree of independence and influence that demanded attention. They also occupied a space—a territory—that hovered between state sovereignty and dependency on the national government. In such ambiguous legal territory, Mormons constructed a vigorous political and legal system based on a dissenting religious system.

Antipolygamists responded in ways that united the humanitarian sensibilities of Protestant reformers with the conviction that the political system of the Northern states (disestablishment, monogamy, free labor, common law) was the incarnation of ecumenical Christian humanism. There was a vital difference between disestablishment in the states and the religion clauses of the First Amendment, however. The former restructured the relationship between church and state in a given region, while everybody knew that the latter was a formal statement of the federal government's lack of power to interfere in those very relations at the state or local level.[45]

It wasn't until 1947 that the constitutional distinction between local and national disestablishment formally evaporated. The Supreme Court finally homogenized the constitutional law of religion through "incorporation" (the judicial doctrine that the Fourteenth Amendment broadened the application of many of the provisions of the Bill of Rights to be as binding on the states as on the federal government). But a popular constitutional culture that presumed separation of church and state was hardly new. Disestablishment was a practice, but not a rule, nationwide by 1850. Only in opposition to Mormon Utah did Americans discover that separation of church and state was a fundamental component of all republican government. Thus, many antipolygamists argued, a territory's capacity to *become* a state rested on conformity to this constitutional practice. This was not federal "incorporation," precisely, but neither did this position represent the full-blown localism envisioned by proponents of the Bill of Rights.[46]

In 1789, and on into the nineteenth century, the religion clauses were part of the vocabulary of states' rights. The states maintained a sense of independent control over the religious life of their inhabitants, reflected by the various state establishments as well as by the trend toward disestablishment. Freedom from official intervention in and support for religious interests was a "gift" of state governments, a political decision rather than a command imposed from above. Those states that maintained their religious establishments, ranging from as vague an endorsement as South Carolina's statement that the "Christian Protestant religion . . . is hereby deemed . . . the established religion of this State" to Connecticut's Congregationalism, succumbed one by one to prevailing political winds, amending their constitutions and throwing distraught ministers onto the mercy of their parishioners. Several states also included explicit prohibitions on officeholding by clerics. Yet in the states the decision to disestablish or limit the privilege of elective office was internal and political, rather than an externally imposed criterion of constitutional legitimacy.[47]

This tradition of local power traveled alongside an increasingly powerful assumption that separation of church and state was characteristic of American liberty everywhere. By the 1860s, disestablishment had assumed so fundamental a stature in the constellation of American liberties that the existence of a church with formal political power (and the high office held by church leaders in the territorial government) in Utah seemed to fly in the face of American constitutionalism. The Reverend Jesse Peck, for example, in his 1868 book *History of the Great Republic*, explained that true, Christian liberty in America resided in "emancipation from the fetters of priest-craft." The "political importance of th[e] great [Mormon] fraud" in Utah, Peck insisted, violated the legacy of "American independence," which for the first time in the history of the world created a system of "living justice" and "soul-liberty." Drawing upon such allegories of the founding, Republicans told themselves that to cleanse Utah of ecclesiastical domination was to bestow upon its inhabitants the blessings of liberty. Americans in Utah would then be truly free, despite their stubborn adherence to (or, as antipolygamists claimed, fear of) Mormon tyranny.[48]

The mandate for separation of church and state, and the theory of Protestant "soul-liberty" that underlay it, profoundly influenced the humanists whose natural political home was the Republican Party, as well as more conservative politicians. Their fundamental agreement on the essential virtues of disestablishment became, ironically, a device for taming the dangerous challenge to all temporal authority inherent in the higher-law arguments of Christian humanitarians. By the 1850s, extraconstitutional arguments for the illegality of slavery, based for the most part on religious conviction, proliferated. Radical abolitionist William Lloyd Garrison actually burned a copy of the Constitution on Boston Common in 1854, a dramatic gesture designed to show his contempt for a proslavery document, a "covenant with death," as he put it. New York Whig (and future Republican) William Seward openly challenged the legality of slavery in Congress during the debates over the Compromise of 1850, invoking a "higher law than the Constitution"—the law of God. His claim resonated with many people in the upper North. They, too, believed that a higher law condemned slavery as sinful and that moral regeneration was essential to the nation as a whole. This was dangerous talk; there was no controlling such supraconstitutional appeals to divine law.[49]

Antipolygamists drew strength from the higher-law argument, but they also reined it in, reconfiguring the relationship of the Constitution to Protestant faith, and to local difference. The process was complex and involved the shift to an active reformist constitutionalism as well as the realignment of the relationship of church and state. By the late 1850s, Republicans in Congress deployed antipolygamist rhetoric as a tool for the Christianization of the American Constitution. As they did so, Republicans renegotiated the boundaries between statecraft and moral theory, recycling the lessons of disestablishment in the states into federal law. In the antipolygamy era, the Constitution acquired a Protestant core.

To their opponents, Mormons were themselves a convenient illustration of the problem of an extraconstitutional higher law: they, too, claimed access to a higher law, a law that authorized multiple wives for righteous men. Such use of the rhetoric of higher law made Northern politicians squirm, hoisting them on their own petard, as it were. Justin Morrill insisted, for example, that the claim that religious liberty should include polygamy subverted the Constitution to a "pretence" of religion, twisting it impossibly to oppose true "Christianity" as well as "the republican form of government." Early Republicans realigned higher-law arguments, "reconstituting" the relationship of human law and morality. Abraham Lincoln and Salmon Chase, for example, were committed to a union of morality and constitutionality. They recrafted the higher-law claims of antislavery activists into a constitutional theory, incorporating God's law into the Constitution as a means of salvaging its essential moral character. In antipolygamy rhetoric, the mutually reinforcing relationship between Protestant moral theory and constitutional interpretation assumed center stage.[50]

A vital part of this moral invigoration of constitutional theory was the rediscovery of the Declaration of Independence as both an antislavery and an antipolygamy document. Abolitionists claimed the Declaration as the moral heart of the Revolution, the "fundamental idea [of freedom for all] to unfold and develop." This moral cornerstone, according to humanitarian theorists, yoked "the Bible and the Declaration of Independence [together as] the two-edged sword with which we shall slay the monster [of slavery]." This Christian mandate included not only the decision to rebel against tyranny, Republicans insisted, but also a fundamental commitment to respect God's law that was born of the rebellion against England. As Thomas Nelson put it in an antipolygamy speech in 1860, "[O]ur fathers, in the days of the Revolution, were not afraid or ashamed to acknowledge that the Almighty hand led them in that fearful and unequal struggle, and enabled them to establish the best and greatest Government that has ever existed. . . . Let us endeavor to cherish and preserve it in the same spirit in which they were led to establish it. . . . We will yet endeavor . . . to show our abhorrence of institutions that are not authorized by the Constitution . . ., and that are contrary to the laws of the Being who created us."[51]

Antipolygamy legislation was one of the earliest national strategies for domesticating the higher-law rhetoric of the antislavery movement. As Justin Morrill himself put it, constitutional formalism of the sort that protected peculiar domestic institutions was too specious for Northern tastes: "[W]e are told, because our constitution declares that 'Congress shall make no law respecting an establishment of religion, or prohibiting the free exercise thereof,' that we must tamely submit" to "artful" claims that outrageous practices (i.e., polygamy) are protected by the religion clauses of the First Amendment.[52]

In the place of such semantic "artfulness," antipolygamists promoted criminal legislation to protect the "true" higher law. "In prohibiting polygamy," argued Thomas Nelson "we shall act only 'in subordination to the great Lawgiver, transcribing and publishing His precepts.' He has said, 'Thou shalt not commit adultery.' He has authorized marriage alone with one person at the same time, and when the relation is extended further against His law, it becomes adulterous." The Old Testament may have "tolerated" polygamy, Nelson conceded, but the moral growth that was marked with "the advent of our Saviour" meant that the law was adapted to "society, in its different stages, according to [God's] own pleasure." Republicans, under the leadership of the new Abraham, had little patience for the exceptionalism claimed by Latter-day Saints. In language familiar to students of the antebellum state law of religious freedom, they argued that the Constitution protected the religious liberties of beliefs "founded upon the precepts of the Bible," preventing interdenominational competition between Christians. But "surely [the framers of the Constitution] never intended that the wild vagaries of the Hindoo or the ridiculous mummeries of the Hottentot should be ennobled by [the] honored and sacred name [of religion]."[53]

In its bare essentials, such a position amounted to a claim that all faiths were to be disestablished, while the free exercise clause protected only accepted Christian beliefs and practice, and not barbaric "mummeries." Political theorist Francis Lieber, for example, argued that monogamy was so fundamental a criterion of civilization that to pretend Mormon polygamy was just another question of localism was to ignore "our being moral entities [a]s a pre-existing condition of the idea of law." The theory that the Constitution set no moral limits on localism, Lieber maintained, flew in the face of "good faith, statesmanship and . . . sound morality in general." Utah's ambiguous place in the Union triggered the legislator's duty to investigate the condition of any applicant for its admission as a state, he asserted, to determine whether the admission would undermine the peace and safety of all. Lieber explained why polygamy was so dangerous. After all, polygamy led to "the patriarchal principle, and which, when applied to large communities, fetters the people in stationary despotism, while that principle cannot exist long in monogamy." Factored into this condemnation of patriarchal despotism, of course, was its inescapable connection to slavery.[54]

By 1862, when the Morrill Act for the Suppression of Polygamy received the overwhelming endorsement of the Republican dominated Congress, "patriarchal despotism" described the enemy. With Southerners gone, and war with the defenders of slavery eroding tolerance of moral difference, Republicans at last achieved the integration of law and faith. Morrill's restructuring of the law of religion and marriage in Utah was sweeping, although by no means lengthy. The statute consisted of three sections, each one designed to attack a distinct component of the Mormon-controlled legal system in Utah. The Morrill Act outlawed bigamy in the territories, providing for a prison sentence of up to five years and a fine of $500; annulled the Utah territorial legislature's incorporation of the Church of Jesus Christ of Latter-day Saints; and prohibited any religious organization from owning real estate valued at more than $50,000. The federal government had never before assumed such supervisory power over structures of private authority. The Morrill Act was unprecedented, especially in light of the majority opinion in the *Dred Scott* case, which only five years before had invalidated attempts to ban slavery from territories north of the Mason-Dixon line. As Southerners had feared (and many Northerners hoped), federal legislation on marriage was a prelude to action against slavery. Three months later, Lincoln resolved that slaves in the Confederacy should be emancipated at the first opportune moment.[55]

In its breadth and uncompromising restructuring of Utah's marital and religious corporation law, the Morrill Act was in effect a second disestablishment in the territories. The federal government directed a fundamental reordering of a society based explicitly and unabashedly on religious law to one based on the humanitarian impulses of a competing legal system and its silent yet potent Protestant subtext. The defense of "true" religion against the laws of man was an essential element of the antipolygamy campaign in general. By the 1860s, the defense mechanism of choice was the formal disempowerment of religion as a constitutive legal force in Utah. Republican antipolyga-mists believed they were participating in the elimination of state-supported barbarisms. They also believed that the secular law conformed in essentials with Christian mandates, the wisdom of which were revealed in everyday life.

Theirs was a grand vision. Reformers were committed to the release of fetters on human progress, to the onward march of civilization through the purification of marriage to protect and promote freedom, democracy, and equality—all in a constitutional system that integrated Christianity and political liberty. This vision, of course, bypassed the territorial structure altogether, sending to the states the indirect message that the domestic relations sanctioned by local governments were of considerable interest to the national government. If polygamy meant that Utah was by definition disqualified from those places eligible to become states, then perhaps, as Southern Democrats had predicted before the outbreak of war, the practices of states within their borders would also be of interest to the national government. Such a message, even sent via the criminalization of polygamy in the territories, was disquieting to those who were committed to the protection of local sovereignty.[56]

In the very act of disestablishing the Mormon Church in Utah, moreover, Republicans brought into being a new, indirect form of establishment. In a handy coincidence of doctrine and inclination, they understood themselves to be protecting religious truth against corruption, for they believed that formal separation of religion from government was the key to the expansion of Protestant Christianity. Without the protection afforded by establishment, Morrill and other Republicans were convinced, the Mormon Church would be revealed in all its moral weakness. Protestant faiths, by contrast, would gain strength. Even Mormons in Utah would learn what the virtues of humanitarian sensibility demonstrated to all Americans: namely, that constitutional liberty and Protestantism were mutually dependent. Republicans believed that the apparent strength of Mormonism rested not on the genuine faith that was so central to Americans' "soul-liberty" but on the fear produced by tyranny. The confidence they placed in legal reform to bring about the decline of Mormonism, however, was misplaced.

Despite the groundswell of political support for the bill, and the fascinating implications of its passage, the Morrill Act was not an effective means of dismantling polygamy in Utah. Nor did it ensure that the Mormon Church would cease to influence the course of politics in the territory, or to acquire property. The act was unenforceable: no grand jury of their peers would indict Mormon leaders for obeying the commands of their religion. Throughout the Civil War and beyond, the Morrill Act went untried. The act was a statement of principle from the central government stalled by the reality of resistance at the local level. As a judiciary committee report lamented five years after polygamy was outlawed, the Morrill Act was a "dead letter." Mormon leaders even petitioned for repeal of the statute in 1867, claiming that its inefficacy had been conclusively demonstrated by the absence of convictions. Antipolygamists in Washington learned quickly that the moral outrage of humanitarian reformers was ineffective against the tenacity of the Mormon faithful. In fact, their condemnation invigorated Mormon resistance.[57]

CHAPTER 3

The Logic of Resistance

Resistance to the laws of man galvanized the Saints in Utah. The virulence of attacks from outside (and, especially after the completion of the transcontinental railroad in 1869, from non-Mormons within) Utah were met and matched by Mormons. Many antipolygamists assumed that there could be no argument in favor of polygamy; certainly they believed that hypocrisy was the fundamental truth behind Mormon plural marriage. They did not anticipate the power and religious conviction of Mormon resistance, or the ability of Mormon leaders to articulate positive cultural and legal arguments in favor of polygamy. Only by focusing on Mormons' arguments *for* polygamy as well as those made against it does the length and breadth of the debate *over* polygamy make sense.

The Saints defended polygamy as a positive religious command, which they had designated "the Principle," and attacked monogamy as evil and unnatural. They offered their own theories of male and female sexual nature and eugenically focused claims that the children of polygamous marriages were physically superior. They also derided the hypocrisy of profligate opponents, calling themselves honest and forthright polygamists, and made arguments based on biblical mandates for polygamy as well as the power of the New Dispensation. Defending the Principle, Mormons constructed what one scholar has called a "denigration of the monogamous ethic."[1]

Mormon theorists also developed and deployed complex legal strategies and constitutional arguments. They used a range of tactics from passive resistance to the enforcement of federal antipolygamy legislation, to litigation of test cases, and eventually to subornation

THE PIONEERS.

The trek westward defined for Mormons a journey into a new constitutional space, sustaining their claims to self-government and creating a mandate for resistance. From T. B. H. Stenhouse, *Rocky Mountain Saints*. Courtesy of The Huntington Library, San Marino, Calif.

of perjury. Such strategies, tied to deft and tenacious political maneuvering toward the unwavering goal of statehood for Utah, bought Mormons valuable time to settle Utah and to cement the structure of polygamous practice (and legal and political control of the territory by church leaders). Delay also allowed Mormon politicians, notably territorial representative George Q. Cannon, the latitude to exploit political shifts and partisan enmities in Washington. The prospect of statehood, and thus local sovereignty over domestic relations, retained significant muscle in the second half of the nineteenth century, even if slavery and secession were no longer elements of that sovereignty. Cannon and other leaders understood that the ambiguity of their right to local control would evaporate if Utah were a state. They fought to escape the limitations of territorial status, even as they also claimed that they *already* had the constitutional right to structure domestic relations in whatever way the majority of the population saw fit.

Mormons argued for their right to be different (and separate), to follow God's law, and to build the political kingdom in these latter days in a federal republic that claimed to tolerate religious difference. Constitutional claims were as central to Mormon defense of the Principle as to antipolygamists' assaults on the "twin relic of barbarism."

The Mormons' strategy was offensive as well as defensive, socially and politically astute, and legally sophisticated.[2]

The logic of Mormon resistance was developed and focused in response to antipolygamists' attacks, but it also drew on experiences of persecution over several decades. The stakes grew in the Civil War era, especially after the Morrill Act labeled plural marriage a crime in 1862. Throughout the half century of more or less openly propolygamy politics, Mormon leaders adopted a multilayered approach. Their tactics were directed at developing and maintaining an internal mandate for resistance as well as at non-Mormons outside Utah. They had need of both sorts of strategy, for the pressure on the church and its members grew over time. The leaders of the church were hunted by territorial officials none too solicitous of the dignity of patriarchs, or of the honorable women whose dedication to the Principle elevated them above the jealousies and resentments of petty womanhood.[3]

The insults, and the high-handed moral condemnation that accompanied them, compounded Mormons' own sense of betrayal at the lack of tolerance that greeted their restoration of the only true Christianity in the New World. The Saints fled to and then tamed a wild and barren region, constructed a government, and built an economy from the ground up. They were loyal Americans, believers in the constitution and the liberties it protected. And still they were derided and abused; their faith attacked as heresy, and their marriages as immoral.[4]

During the "polygamy era," the embattled faithful struggled to maintain a sense of purpose and unity, as well as to strike a blow against the enemies of Zion. The development of a full-fledged alternative ethic of plural marriage required Mormon husbands and wives not only to live their faith in times of profound stress and dislocation but to join in active opposition, resistance, and obfuscation, if necessary, in the interests of preserving the Principle. For decades, leaders counseled the evasion of what they considered unconstitutional (and sometimes even diabolical) emanations from Congress.

In many senses, the "blessings of the Abrahamic household" the defenders of polygamy described formed an inverted image of companionate monogamy. Like their opponents, Mormons were committed to family life as the key to the stability and morality of the state. They, too, believed in the relationship of marriage to faith, and the origins of truth in revelation. The conclusions they drew from their investigations of such questions, however, convinced Mormons that genuine Christian practice, human nature, and divine law all demonstrated the fundamental corruption of monogamist systems.

The Apostle Orson Pratt.

Theologian Orson Pratt defended plural marriage as religiously and socially superior to monogamy. Courtesy of The Huntington Library, San Marino, Calif.

This corruption infected the profligate states, where monogamy and hypocrisy flourished. Mormons were as likely as their antipolygamist opponents to draw on contemporary political and social theory, claiming frequently that the very arguments deployed by their enemies proved the essential superiority of latter-day faith and practice. The prevalence of polygamy as a marital system around the globe, argued Mormon theorist Orson Pratt, for example, proved that it was both natural and civilized. Pratt also attacked the romantic sensibility so central to antipolygamy fiction, dismissing "novels" as immersed in a selfish and "irresistible" vision of love that interfered with the dedication to righteous living essential to all Saints.[5]

As attacks from non-Mormons escalated, Mormons piled ever greater freight onto the claim that polygamy was the central tenet of the New Dispensation. Patriarchal marriage was the "keystone of our faith," argued the church newspaper, inseparable from every other aspect of latter-day sainthood. According to Mormon theory, the centrality of polygamy dictated that it fell within the protection of difference contemplated by American federalism and by the religion clauses of the First Amendment.[6]

Polygamy frequently provided a rallying point for demonstrations of loyalty to the cause; it also required significant discipline as a system. Even as it was the central symbol of Mormon dissent to the outside world, polygamy was also the catalyst for much dissension within. Apostates were a constant danger, exposing painful secrets and frequently exaggerating and distorting instances of high-handed control (or outright violence) by Brigham Young or other Mormon leaders. For their part, dissenters often justified their own apostasy by claiming that their faith had been procured by deceit in the first place. John Bennett's serialized exposé of Joseph Smith's sexual experiments in Nauvoo in the 1840s, for example, carried an aura of authenticity because of Bennett's stature within the church itself prior to his defection. Equally damaging were those who claimed to remain within the faith but were critical of its leaders. Joseph Smith's own son, for example, led the splinter groups that eventually merged into the Reorganized Church of Jesus Christ of Latter Day Saints in 1860. From the end of the Civil War through the early twentieth century, followers of the reorganized church nipped at the heels of the main, Utah church by providing critical testimony about what they claimed was the hypocrisy of Mormon leaders at congressional hearings. Last but not least, the self-styled "New Movement," which lasted from 1868 through the early 1880s, attracted prosperous English converts in Utah whose entrepreneurial ambitions were frustrated by the leadership's control of Utah's economy. Both groups denied the centrality and the viability of polygamy in latter-day faith. Frequently, they had the ears of Eastern politicians and newspaper editors despite the efforts of Mormons from Utah to discredit their testimony.[7]

Thus, the main church constantly faced internal as well as external opposition, as its leaders labored to construct a vision in which a polygamous minority occupied a respectable (that is, not sexually profligate) and politically distinct position within the federal union. These efforts created tension, and there were frequent outbreaks of anger and frustration at the lack of understanding and acceptance that greeted Zion's representatives outside Utah. Such prejudice was exacerbated by the general lack of interest in learning from Mormons themselves about their lives and their faith. Added into the mix were Mormon leaders' predictions of an apocalypse that awaited the unregenerate and the certain triumph of the forces of Zion, despite present reverses. Indeed, opposition often fueled the drive for victory, for never had the path of righteousness been easy or smooth. Mormons in the 1850s and 1860s pleaded for acceptance as equals in a tolerant federal republic, and in the next breath asserted their essential superiority and fundamental separateness and concomitant disdain for all who spurned the New Dispensation. At the onset of the Civil War, Brigham Young prophesied that North and South would destroy each other. The Latter-day Saints, whose existence outside the Union would protect them from the coming implosion, would fill the vacuum. As one Mormon leader put it, "[T]he day will come when the United States government, and all others, will be uprooted, and the kingdoms of this world will be united in one, and the kingdom of our God will govern the whole earth."[8]

The Saints claimed both the right to be tolerated and the right to engage in a form of governance that arguably was intolerant—and at its most extreme, inconsistent with the very continuity of the American nation. Thus if antipolygamists claimed perfect toleration while punishing dissenting faiths, Mormon polygamists were caught in a contradiction of equal magnitude. The imperial ambitions of Mormon leaders in this period contemplated the end of the federal republic and its replacement by the kingdom of God. Mormons in the Civil War era proclaimed their fundamental loyalty to the federal Constitution as an inspired and freedom-producing document. Like many other Americans, Mormons believed that the Constitution vindicated their own hopes and dreams. They sidestepped the ambiguity and sometimes contradictory nature of the document. The Constitution was only a precursor, Mormon leaders declared, preparation for a greater and divinely mandated state of Saints, with Jesus as king. Mormons valued the Constitution for creating the freedom through which the divine incursion could enter and rescue the world from the apostasy that had plagued Christianity since its early Roman days. The Constitution was designed by God, according to Mormon theologian Orson Pratt, "to suit the people and circumstances in which they were placed, until they were prepared to receive a more perfect [government]"; that is, a theocracy. To usher in the kingdom of God and the millennial rule of Christ, Mormons believed, they must first remake the government of mortals. Only by reuniting religion and government in light of latter-day revelation, argued the Saints, could Americans recover from the moral degradation that characterized the Christian world. In a truly righteous state the union of faith and government would reflect the perfect sovereignty of God, ushering in the Millennium and the salvation of the world.[9]

The restoration of all things, according to Mormon doctrine, depended on the progressive cleansing of society and the enforcement of the fundamental law of the Old Testament of moral purity. By the mid-1850s, Mormon leaders developed powerful arguments about the relationship of polygamy to American law. As territorial chaplain Parley Pratt put it in an address to the legislature in 1856, "[M]oral and social affections and institutions are the very foundation of all government, whether of family, church, or state. If these are perverted, or founded in error, the whole superstructure is radically wrong, and will contain within itself the seeds of its own decay and dissolution." Monogamy, according to Pratt, was the essence of corruption in contemporary society, dooming America to destruction for violation of God's law of marriage. This was proven not only by the revelation on celestial marriage but by the Old Testament itself. "[Thus by example of the polygamous biblical patriarchs and their favor in the eyes of God] the matter is set for ever at rest," ran one typical argument. "[P]olygamy is included in the ordinance of marriage, and in the everlasting covenant and laws of God: ... under proper regulations, it is an institution holy, just, virtuous, pure, and, in the estimation of God, abundantly calculated to bless, preserve, and multiply a nation."[10]

This biblical mandate was, in Mormon eyes, fully consistent with constitutional law. Parley Pratt, pursuing the argument further than most, maintained that the common law itself was propolygamy. Christianity was part of the common law, he observed, and the Old Testament and polygamy were the foundations of Christianity. Further, the Constitution itself protected religious liberty and must include protection of all Christian doctrines—especially polygamy. From this perspective, the Constitution contained a mandate for polygamy. Laws prohibiting plural marriage were evidence of corruption in constitutional interpretation and enforcement. "[T]he laws of some of our States, which recognize polygamy as a crime," argued Pratt, were contrary to Scripture and the Constitution. The only defensible course for all jurisdictions would be to restore the law of God—establish and protect the holy law of marriage by restoring polygamy (and by punishing adultery and fornication with death). Only thus could the "vile abominations" of monogamy ("whoredoms, intrigues, seductions, wretched and lonely single life, hatred, envy, jealousy, infanticide, illegitimacy, disease and death") be forever banished from the land, preparing it for the millennial rule of Christ. Virtue in marriage, in other words, was the essential prerequisite for all righteous government. Such virtue was to be found especially in polygamy—the governance of the household according to patriarchal principles.[11]

In the 1850s, the force of this argument was directed within the kingdom, as well as without. Polygamy, especially as it was defended in territorial Utah, was urged on Mormons with a vehemence that convinced outsiders that plural marriage could not be a matter of real choice. In its most extreme formulation, men were assured not only that their degree of exaltation in the afterlife was enhanced by having several wives but also that their very membership in the church depended on plural marriage. Women were told that their refusal to consent to their husbands' plural marriage would condemn them both in this world and the next. As theologian Orson Pratt put it in the first public address on celestial marriage in 1852, rejection of the patriarchal order was a rejection of religious truth. Such obduracy had commensurately severe consequences: "[W]here there is great knowledge unfolded for the exaltation, glory, and happiness of the sons and daughters of God, if they close up their hearts, if they reject the testimony of His word, and will not give heed to the principles He has ordained for their good, they are worthy of damnation, and the Lord has said they shall be damned." Theoretically, refusal to practice the Principle was cause for excommunication. And polygamy was tied not only to personal exaltation in the celestial kingdoms but also to the earthly Millennium—the coming of Jesus to preside as king over the perfected race of men produced by vigorous and virtuous polygamists. The salvation of the world (not to mention individual followers of the Principle) depended directly on the sacrifice of the fathers and mothers of Israel.[12]

Polygamy was frequently a precursor to political responsibility and economic advancement for men, as well as increased stature in the church. As one Mormon put it, "[A] man obeying a lower law [monogamy] is not qualified to preside over those who keep a higher law [polygamy]." For wives, the reflected glory of their husbands' accomplishment was the gauge of their own future reward. For both husbands and wives, bearing up gracefully under the difficulties and moral discipline of life in polygamy was both a duty and the mark of spiritual achievement. Romantic attachments, and the lustful behavior that they encouraged between husband and wife, were inconsistent with the reproductive ethic of a marital form that commanded women to "receive, conceive, bear, and bring forth in the name of Israel's God." Instead of indulging their sexual inclinations in destructive excess, or their petty jealousies and exclusive yearnings, women were to be dedicated to producing children for the church and raising them in the faith. Brigham Young also counseled husbands "[n]ever [to] love your wives one hair's breadth further than they adorn the Gospel."[13]

Thus, "consent" by the faithful to participation in celestial marriage did not replicate the concept of choice contemplated by non-Mormon legal and political theory. Members of the Church of Jesus Christ of Latter-day Saints made their most important choice when they testified to the truth of the New Dispensation. From this life-changing decision, others flowed. Mormons were expected to either "take sides with the mother of harlots, and with her monogamy, and celibacy, and prostitution, or take sides with the Almighty, and with His holy law of polygamy, and sexual purity." Those who had the "ability to obey and practice [the revelation] in righteousness and will not," assured Mormon leaders, "shall be damned." The struggle to accept polygamy was understood as a trial, to be sure, but one that every man and woman was capable of enduring—if their faith was strong and motives pure enough. Free consent to marriage was essential and evidence of the faith necessary to assure exaltation in the celestial worlds. But consent occurred within the faith; the capacity to affirm the doctrines central to the faith—including plural marriage—was the core freedom granted to all Saints.[14]

This religiously specific concept of choice affected other areas of Mormon life, as well. In territorial Utah, democracy was a concept with a particular meaning. The sovereignty of the people was related directly to the people's acceptance of the sovereignty of God, and of the counsel of God's representatives in the restoration. One twentieth-century scholar concluded that the government of Deseret paid "lip service" to democratic practices such as constitutional conventions and free elections. The "centralized and autocratic control" of the leaders of the church, however, actually determined both the officers of the state and the substantive disposition of political and legal questions. The participation of the people, according to Parley Pratt, constituted "a sanction, a strength and support to that which God chooses. But [the people] do not confer the authority in the first place, nor can they take it away." Mormons translated the ecclesiastical structure of the church into a government, as they built their Zion with the guidance and sustenance of faith.[15]

THE CRISIS OF A LIFE—ENTERING INTO POLYGAMY.

Fanny Stenhouse, an apostate Mormon, depicted a plural marriage ceremony in her book *Tell It All: The Tyranny of Mormonism; or, An Englishwoman in Utah,* first published in 1872. Courtesy of University of Pennsylvania Library.

The legislature that resulted from this faith-driven process enacted laws that further blurred the line between civil and ecclesiastical governments. Mormon leaders drafted legislation that consigned vital questions directly to the church itself. The 1851 Act for Incorporation of the Church of Jesus Christ of Latter-day Saints, for example, provided that all rules and laws for marriage promulgated by the church "could not be legally questioned." As Brigham Young explained the purpose behind the act, it guaranteed that "if the Latter-day Saints wish to have more wives than one to live Holy & raise up Holy seed unto the Lord [then we shall] let them have that privilege."[16]

The legislature also created probate courts staffed by powerful appointive local officials whose jurisdiction included the powers of county commissioners and courts of general criminal and civil jurisdiction but whose mandate forbade them to cite legal precedent, to apply the common law, or to enforce the collection of lawyers' fees. In these ways, the Mormon legislature assured that the structures of faith were replicated in the structures of government. The probate courts, for example, were frequently staffed by the same Mormon bishops who also ran "Bishop's courts" for the resolution of civil disputes among the brethren and who were charged with administering the laws of God on earth. Such devices, while created by democratic processes and bearing secular labels, effectively placed the church (especially Brigham Young, the "American Moses," as his biographer called him) in the position of "law giver." Scholarly studies of the probate and church courts have concluded that they generally were administered fairly and impartially. To outsiders, however, the overlap between church and state in Utah was evidence that the church really held the reins of secular power. As one federally appointed territorial governor complained, Young was still the only ruler the Mormon people obeyed, even after he was technically removed from office by Congress in the late 1850s.[17]

Mormons responded that they were deeply committed to democratic processes and that the will of the people was central to all church doctrine. Democracy, in this light, was the opportunity provided by an inspired government to the people to voice their consent to the gradual perfection of humankind according to the New Dispensation. The rule of law in such a system meant the rule of divine law, as manifested by those invested with priestly authority, who were empowered by God's covenant with the new Israel to know the will of the Lord. The choice, then, was between obedience to the revealed will of God and the first step on the road to apostasy. If many nineteenth-century Americans relied implicitly on religious belief and affiliation in their political lives, Mormons made such reliance explicit. Their embrace of religious precepts as the basis of government action galvanized Mormons' opponents, who frequently preferred that the precise relationship between church and state remain ambiguous. Mormon theorists rejected such dodges, priding themselves on their open acknowledgment of the role of latter-day faith in political authority in Utah.

The franchise, for example, reflected not so much a commitment to rigorous and pointed political debate as a chance for the people to affirm the choice of God with their acclamation. As future Mormon president John Taylor put it, explaining the meaning of democracy to Mormons in a sermon preached at the very brink of civil war in the states in 1861, "The proper mode of government is this—God first speaks, and then the people have their action. . . . We have our voice and our agency, and act with the most perfect freedom; still we believe there is a correct order—some wisdom and knowledge somewhere that is superior to ours; that wisdom and knowledge proceeds from God through the medium of the holy Priesthood." The political kingdom of God that Taylor described was a "theodemocracy," a term first used by Joseph Smith to describe the government envisioned in his presidential campaign. As Smith explained it, his presidency would ensure that "God and the people hold the power to conduct the affairs of men in righteousness." George A. Smith elaborated on the concept in 1865: "Our system should be Theo-Democracy—the voice of the people consenting to the voice of God." Because God spoke through the Mormon restoration in these latter days, the will of God could actually be known with some certainty, and conveyed to the people. In such a system, unanimity and the absence of "hostile [political] parties" were evidence of the smooth working of God's law rather than any tyranny or "ignorance" on the part of Mormon leaders or followers. There was a choice at work in Mormon theo-democracy, but it was the choice between salvation and damnation, a choice structured and conditioned by a belief system in which voluntarism had a particular meaning.[18]

The voice of God was heard, and heeded by faithful Saints in marital as well as political affairs. Thus the consent of Mormon wives to the marriage of husbands to one (or more) additional wives, which was required for a valid plural marriage by the 1843 "Revelation on Celestial Marriage," must be understood in the context of divine command and the limits of human sovereignty within nineteenth-century Mormonism. Moreover, subsequent historical research has shown that a first wife's consent "was not always sought nor willingly given." Wives who refused their consent without justification (that is, simply because they opposed the Principle), the revelation promised, would be "damned." Women as well as men struggled with the concept, but they understood clearly that it was part of latter-day faith. "The principle of Celestial Marriage was considered the capstone of the Mormon religion. Women would never have accepted polygamy had it not been for their religion," reflected one polygamous wife. As another first wife explained it, she could not otherwise have given her consent "for my dear husband whome I loved as I did my own life . . . to take more wives. This I could not have done if I had not believed it to be right in the Sight of god, and believed it to be one principal of his gospel once again restored to earth, that those holding the preasthood of heaven might be obeying this order attain to a higher glory in the eternal world." To be called a Latter-day Saint, according to Mormon leaders in the mid-nineteenth century, was to accept (and if qualified to do so, practice) plural marriage. Polygamy affected all aspects of life and law in territorial Utah. As one scholar put it recently, plural marriage was "the most honored and most sacred" form of marriage. Its defenders reached for new tactics to counter new threats against the kingdom of God.[19]

The voices and example of Mormon women became staples in pro-polygamy strategy shortly after the Civil War, as the completion of the transcontinental railroad in 1869 threatened the incursion of outside ideas and capital. In addition to Mormon dissidents in Salt Lake fielding a rival candidate for mayor, condemnations of Mormon polygamy increased in the late 1860s in Congress as the Morrill Act was revealed as ineffective. Brigham Young took several protective steps. Loyal church members were counseled to boycott non-Mormon businesses, and the church set up a centralized economic steering committee. Last but not least, Mormons gave women the vote early in 1870.[20]

Outside Utah, the belief that polygamy was akin to slavery, and the claim (made repeatedly by woman's rights activists in the states) that the franchise was a badge of freedom, meant that allowing Mormon women a political voice denied to monogamous women in the East was a powerful means of calling their opponents' bluff. "Was there ever a greater anomaly known in the history of society?" queried the popular *Phrenological Journal.* "That the women of Utah who have been considered representatives of womanhood in its degradation, should suddenly be found on the same platform with John Stuart Mill and his sisterhood, is truly a matter for astonishment." The Female Suffrage Bill passed the territorial legislature unanimously and without significant debate, an unprecedented event in the annals of woman suffrage. The franchise was extended to all female citizens over twenty-one, and also to all the wives, widows, or daughters of native-born or naturalized men.[21]

Contrary to the predictions of Eastern suffragists, who argued that "the vote of the [Mormon] women will be found a powerful aid in doing away with the horrible institution of polygamy," the woman's vote followed the standard Mormon pattern, increasing the Mormon majority to more than 95 percent in territorial elections. In all aspects of life, political, economic, and spiritual, explained their defenders, latter-day faith was the guiding star of Mormon women, many of whom viewed themselves as pioneers of the spirit as well as the soil. As one apologist put it, "[N]o sooner was suffrage granted to the Mormon women, than they exercised it as a part of their religion, or as the performance of woman's life duties, marked out for her in the economy of divine providence. In this apostolic spirit, they took up the grant of political power." From the perspective of the faithful, Mormonism imbued women's political participation with divine meaning, consistent with the natural and divine law of woman's nature, and woman's rights.[22]

Like many of their opponents, Mormon theorists emphasized the role of marriage in women's lives and progress. In Mormon theology, however, women's salvation was intimately connected to their status as wives. Only through marriage could a woman ally herself with a righteous man, participate in his progressive glory on the road to godhood, and raise children in the knowledge that they would increase their parents' exaltation. Thus the basic right of every woman, Mormons argued, the single right that eclipsed all others in both this world and the celestial kingdoms, was that of marriage. Plural marriage guaranteed that every woman would have the opportunity to be married. Thus, none would be "degraded" in the true sense of the word; that is, none would be prostitutes or condemned to celibacy. As one outraged editorial in the Mormon *Woman's Exponent* put it: "We affirm just as strongly as our opponents that instead of degrading, plural marriage elevates women; we and hundreds of others have proven it by practical experience." Almost all women in Utah married, frequently at a young age. Plural marriage, as Mormons pointed out, meant that even the poorest women could ally themselves with worthy men.[23]

By the end of the 1860s, a group of elite Mormon women were visible defenders of their (and their sisters') right to be married women—enfranchised, organized, and faithful. And while antipolygamists dismissed the women as victims of false consciousness, their presence, and their courage, gave heart to the embattled and misunderstood brothers and sisters of Zion. At a mass meeting called in January 1870, a group of "leading sisters" addressed an audience of Mormon women (and a few male reporters), breaking silence so publicly only to defend the faith against "a corrupt press, and an equally corrupt priestcraft . . . leagued against us." Rather than leading to degradation, as popular opinion would have it, argued Phoebe Woodruff, plural marriage exalted Mormon women by allowing them to live according to their nature and to fulfill their destiny: "We are sealed to our husbands for time and eternity, that we may dwell with them and our children in the world to come; which guarantees unto us the greatest blessing for which we are created."[24]

Herein lay a central aspect of arguments for plural marriage. Polygamy, Mormons insisted, was based not only on the concept of wifehood and motherhood as the central spiritual and social accomplishment of every woman's existence, but on the "right" of every woman to be granted the opportunity to participate in these "honorable and sacred callings." In monogamous Babylon, as Brigham Young put it, "I doubt whether there is one man in three who has a wife." Men did not "do what is right towards the females," and women everywhere outnumbered men, according to Young's analysis. Outside Utah, he charged, women were denied their right of marriage. As Orson Pratt put it in 1869, "Since old pagan Rome and Greece,—worshippers of idols,—passed a law confining a man to one wife, there has been a great surplus of females, who have had no possible chance of getting, married."[25]

In contrast to the iniquities of the monogamic states, where men tainted by adultery charged honorable Mormons with licentiousness even as they turned away the very children born of their own illicit unions, in Utah plural marriage had "a tendency to elevate the entire sex, and give all the privilege of being honored matrons and respected wives. There are no refuse among us,—no class to be cast out, scorned and condemned; but every woman who chooses can be an honored wife and move in society in the enjoyment of every right which woman should enjoy to make her the equal of man as far as she can be his equal." In "monogamic systems," however, women, whose natural yearning ("necessary for health and happiness") was for union with man, were forced to make a cruel choice. Many of them, faced with being deprived of "gratification of those feelings altogether, have, in despair, given way to wickedness and licentiousness; hence the whoredoms and prostitution among the nations of the earth where the 'Mother of Harlots' has her seat."[26]

The cure for such abominations, compensating for men who refused to marry and surplus women alike, was plural marriage. As Mormon leaders argued incessantly, women and marriage were protected by the law of patriarchal marriage, which "[threw] a shield around our families and sacred domestic institutions." Only when antipolygamists had devised an effective remedy for the ills that plagued them, charged Emmeline B. Wells, editor of the *Woman's Exponent,* could they claim any ground for lecturing the Saints on morals. "[H]ave you some balm to offer for the woes of [the thousands of women in the states] outraged and oppressed by men; some sure path by which they may return into the presence of their Creator[?]" queried Emmeline B. Wells. "[I]f you have, then help them, for they are sorely in need of succor. . . . Ask Congress to make, or devise some method by which women may be protected and avenged for wrongs committed against their most sacred feelings, their virtue and their honor; beseech them to provide for the neglected progeny which swarm the cities of the United States, and growing up in infamy and crime are filling the prisons with criminals." Patriarchal marriage was such a balm, argued Wells, granting honor to all women, assuring their place in this world and the next through the right to be married.[27]

Emmeline Wells defended polygamy for women and charged critics of plural marriage with disregard for women's true interests. From Orson Whitney, *History of Utah.* Courtesy Princeton University Library.

But there was a price. The divine and natural law of marriage could be satisfied only by women's sacrifice of selfishness, exclusiveness, jealousy, and even love. That the sacrifice was possible, Mormon leaders had no doubt; that it was supremely difficult, most of them also openly acknowledged. Describing the "Women of Mormondom" as the contemporary Sarahs of the Abrahamic covenant with the New Israel, writer Edward Tullidge praised their sacrifice. Their patient nature, their dedication to the exaltation in heaven, even at the expense of happiness in earthly life, would be rewarded in the afterlife: "If [the Mormon woman, like Sarah] dared to bear the patriarchal cross, was it not because she saw brightly looming in her destiny the patriarchal crown? In this life only the cross—in all the lives to come a crown of glory!"[28]

The sacrifice of the self that patriarchal marriage required for women was often offered as evidence of its divinity. Urging women to stifle the "rebellion [in their hearts] against the principle," Mormon politician George Q. Cannon explained that plural marriage was only the most taxing of the many trials that Mormon women had already endured for their purification in the faith:

> Every law of the gospel has a trial connected with it, and the higher the law the greater the trial; and as we ascend nearer and nearer to the Lord our God we shall have greater trials to contend with in purifying ourselves before Him. He has helped us this far. . . . [W]hen our sisters seek unto Him He . . . gives them strength to overcome their selfishness and jealousy. . . . You, sisters, whose husbands have taken other wives, can you not bear testimony that the principle has purified your hearts, made you less selfish, brought you nearer to God and given you power you never had before?

Such purification often had the effect of distancing husbands and wives. Their focus turned to celestial glory rather than earthly satisfaction. Especially for women, such distance could provide meaningful independence and self-reliance. They learned not to rely on the presence of a husband whose multiple families caused his absence at times of stress and the strict division of his attention and affection. Brigham Young cautioned the faithful in 1856 that only the security of a glorious resurrection rendered a spouse worthy of "the full measure of love." Security of this sort came at the end of a life of dedication to the Principle, not at the beginning.[29]

The struggle to contain and channel emotions and yearnings, to direct all of life to observation of God's moral law in preparation for the Millennium, demanded (and frequently obtained) a sense of purpose and zeal that confounded antipolygamists for decades. Divisive as it was for those wavering in the faith, polygamy connected the Saints in kinship and sacrifice as they "lived their religion." The demonstration of loyalty and commitment that plural marriage symbolized for the faithful meant that its practitioners occupied a special,

Religious and political leader George Q. Cannon argued that polygamy was difficult for men, too. From T. B. H. Stenhouse, *Rocky Mountain Saints*. Courtesy of The Huntington Library, San Marino, Calif.

honored place within the territory. The exhilaration produced by the conviction of righteousness and community sustained and strengthened the logic of resistance.[30]

Sarah Kimball declared at a mass meeting of women called to protest proposed antipolygamy legislation in 1870 that "[w]e are not here to advocate woman's rights, but man's rights." The right of plural marriage, argued Mormon leaders, was not only fully borne out by women's lives, biblical research, and latter-day revelation, it was also reflected in the natural constitution of men, whose inclination to sexual activity (as the prevalence of prostitution in the United States proved) simply could not be denied. Instead, boasted George Q. Cannon, Mormon men married enough wives to keep them from bothering unmarried women or the wives of other men. This honorable resolution of the question, he maintained, required men to take material and spiritual responsibility for their natural (and thus divinely ordained) inclinations.[31]

The vaunted sacrifice of men in polygamy has traditionally been dismissed by detractors as less than credible. Certainly Mormon theories of male sexuality and creativity provided a justification in natural law for a marital system that took patriarchy to an extreme. Women's subordination was keyed in part to their inferior fertility (for their reproductive capacity, already far more limited than that of men, ceased decades earlier than in men of corresponding age), and in part to the "greater physical and mental strength" of men. The physiology of polygamy, argued Cannon, meant that men were likely to be gratified by plurality, but outsiders underestimated the real price of rectitude:

> A lady visitor remarked to me not long ago in speaking upon this subject: "Were I man, I would feel differently probably to what I do; to your sex the institution cannot be so objectionable." This may be the case to some extent, but . . . the difficulties and perplexities connected with the care of a numerous family, to a man who has any ambition, are so great that nothing short of the revelations of God, or the command of Jesus Christ, would tempt men to enter this order; the mere increase of facilities to gratify the lower passions of our natures would be no inducement to assume such an increase of grave responsibilities.[32]

The charge that sexual indulgence was the motivating factor behind Joseph Smith's marital experimentation, of course, is almost as old as the church itself. And although church leaders after 1850 avoided claims that polygamy was anything other than a reproductive mandate awarded to worthy men, latter-day faith was also committed to the connection between sexuality and divinity. In this perspective, the procreative force of a man, whose wives in theory could be multiplied a hundredfold without exhausting his capacity, meant that plurality reflected (and strengthened) his spiritual nature. As the historian Carmon Hardy put it, polygamous men "were administering not only to the body, but, *pari passu*, were engaged in a calisthenic of the spirit."[33]

Fundamental to such theories of physiology was the conviction

The Juvenile Instructor

VOL 3.　　　　SALT LAKE CITY, OCTOBER 15, 1868.　　　　NO. 20.

HAGAR AND ISHMAEL.

ABRAHAM was one of the mightiest men that ever lived. His power did not consist in the great armies he controled, or in the greatness of the nation over which he ruled; but it was in the power which he obtained with God through his faith. He is called "the father of the faithful" and "the friend of God," and God made as great promises to him as probably could be made to any mortal being. There is not much written about his early life that has come down to us, of Ur, of the Chaldees. Haran had two daughters—Sarai and Milcah. Abraham married Sarai—her name was afterwards changed by the Lord to Sarah—and his brother Nehor married Milcah. By the command of the Lord Abraham took his wife and all who would accompany him and moved out of Chaldea into Canaan. Abraham and Sarah lived together as man and wife for a great many years; but they had no children. The Lord, however, had revealed unto

and we shall not write anything respecting it at present; but allude to that portion of his life in which the incident occurred that is illustrated in the accompanying engraving.

Abraham had a wife, the Bible calls her his sister, the daughter of his father Terah; but in his own record, which the prophet Joseph translated, he informs us that she was the daughter of his brother Haran, and, consequently, the sister of Lot. Haran died during a famine which raged in the land Abraham the law of celestial marriage. He knew that it was his privilege to have more wives than Sarah. Sarah, herself, understood this law, and when God commanded her husband she took her handmaid, whose name was Hagar, and gave her to Abraham to be his wife. She did this because it was the law, and if Abraham had not obeyed this law, the promises of God could not have been fulfilled to him wherein He told him that his seed should be as the dust of the earth or the

The Mormon magazine *The Juvenile Instructor*, edited by George Q. Cannon, explained to young readers in 1868 that Sarah understood Abraham had a right to additional wives under the law of celestial marriage and gave Hagar to Abraham as a plural wife. Courtesy of Harvard College Library.

that a woman who interfered with a man's natural inclination to generative activity violated his spiritual rights. Disdain for women who subjected their husbands to "pettycoat government" and for the men who failed to exercise their patriarchal authority by ensuring the subordination of women to men in marriage was trenchant and pointed. "[I]t is not the privilege of a woman to dictate the husband, and tell who or how many [wives] he shall take, or what he shall do with them when he gets them, but it is the duty of the woman to submit cheerfully," explained Brigham Young. "It is the man who has need to worry and watch himself, and see that he does right." If he did not do right, Young cautioned, his wives would be taken from him and given to another. Equally important, respect among the Saints hinged upon the proper control of wives when the topic of plural marriage was broached. For "[a]ny man who permits a woman to lead him and bind him down [by preventing his practice of polygamy] is but little account in the church and Kingdom of God."[34]

Only in families (rather than as individuals) could Mormons achieve the highest level of salvation, known as "exaltation." Control of families living in the Principle, the most exalted of all structures of governance, was clearly and unequivocally vested in husbands. Patriarchal governance required a husband to command obedience, to preserve harmony among wives, and to ensure the celestial progress of wives (and children) through his own exaltation after death. If the mark of the Lord was upon him, Brigham Young preached in 1870, such government would flow naturally, extending even beyond the family, to "my neighbors and the people around me." "If I am controled by the Spirit of the Most High I am a king, I am supreme so far as the control of self is concerned; and it also enables me to control my wives and children. . . . [T]hey will be perfectly submissive to my dictates." Such perfect command was not tyranny, as those outside the faith would have it. Instead, control of the family applied "the principles of our government—the principles of our religion, which, in their very nature, are bound to make those who will be guided by them healthy, wealthy and wise."[35]

The commitment to male supremacy over all women was paired with a complementary hierarchy of worthiness among men. "Among the great and numerous family of spirits," explained Orson Pratt, "there are some more intelligent than others." Such noble spirits, waiting for bodies "in the fulness of times," would be sent by God to the chosen—the fathers of the new Israel. Only such men as were granted the blessing of Abraham through the restored covenant of the latter days, and among them only such men as were righteous (for there would "be the foolish among the wise") and were chosen by the Lord's anointed (the priesthood acting under direction of the president and prophet of the church), would be exalted through plural marriage to "hold the keys of power."[36]

Thus would the race be perfected by the moral and physical invigoration of worthy men through polygamous marriage. George Q.

The Apostle Heber C. Kimball.

Heber C. Kimball claimed that polygamy kept men young and sprightly. Courtesy of The Huntington Library, San Marino, Calif.

Cannon, for example, predicted that in Zion would be "raise[d] a race of men who will be the joy of the earth, whose complexions will be the complexions of angels." Elder Moses Thatcher argued that polygamy would produce a dominant race that would eventually rule the earth according to the law of "the survival of the fittest." Heber Kimball, in an oft-quoted statement about the effects of polygamy, even claimed that plural marriage lengthened the life and increased the virility of its practitioners. "I have noticed that a man who has but one wife, and is inclined to that doctrine, soon begins to wither and dry up, while a man who goes into plurality looks fresh, young, and sprightly. . . . For a man of God to be confined to one woman is small business." The "vigorous polygamic hordes" throughout history proved the superiority of polygamous societies, even where the absence of the sanctity of the New Covenant undercut the righteousness of its practice. "Narrow and contracted," "pinch-backed" monogamists could not embody the divinity of manhood, for they "live[d] all their days under the domination of one wife" and could not exercise their powers of procreativity to their fullest.[37]

The essential logic of Mormon polygamy, then, can roughly be described as ensuring the potential equality and exaltation of all women (at an emotional cost, to be sure, but one that if bravely faced and patiently endured would bring great spiritual reward) and the potential exaltation to godhood of some men (those who were found worthy by the priesthood to enter plural marriage, who lived their religion with dignity, rectitude, and loyalty, and thus earned progression in celestial kingdoms). While such a simple formula cannot capture the subtleties of doctrine, or the experience of husbands and wives in polygamy, there can be no doubt that the logic of polygamy provided a powerful explanation for its efficacy as a force governing the lives and actions of nineteenth-century Mormons. Their salvation lay within their control—the struggle to succeed was, theoretically at least, open to every man, who could marry as many women as received him as their patriarch. The mandate was clear, its opponents were steeped in iniquity, and natural and divine law confirmed its truth.

The great obstacle lay in the "laws of man"—not with the federal Constitution, especially the First Amendment's protection of religious freedom, but with the corrupt institutions that enforced (or, from the Mormon perspective, transgressed) the constitutional protection of religious rights. Mormons brought with them to Utah vivid memories of their suffering at the hands of outsiders. In the years before the martyrdom of Joseph Smith, Mormons repeatedly petitioned Washington for aid. Their constitutional rights, they argued, were violated by state officials in Ohio, Illinois, and Missouri (whose governor, Lilburn Boggs, for example, declared in 1838 that Mormons must be "exterminated, or driven from the State if necessary for the public peace"). Inevitably, political officials in Washington, from President Martin Van Buren to individual congressmen, told the supplicants that the national government was powerless to intervene. According to one newspaper account, Smith derided Van Buren for his perfidy, for he "will not so much as lift his finger to relieve an oppressed and persecuted community of freemen, whose glory it has been that they were citizens of the United States."[38]

Mormons were told that they must look to the states for protection and justice, despite their claim that the states themselves were the problem. The story is a tangled one, filled with charges and countercharges of deceit and violence; the broad outlines are seared into the memory of Mormons. Put in starkest terms, Mormon settlements were controversial (or quickly became a source of controversy) in each of their incarnations, though not at first because of polygamy. There was rank religious persecution, as well as significant fear of "Joe Smith's" state-building. The "gathering" of the Saints crucial to the establishment and progression of the kingdom of God, Smith's political influence and economic enterprises, and, by 1840, Smith's assumption of military titles and the drilling of his "Nauvoo Legion," all were evidence to outsiders of the conspiratorial nature of Mormonism. Blending rumors of "Avenging Angels" and "spiritual wifery" into an explosive compound of fear and hatred, anti-Mormon neighbors claimed that Smith and his followers were not just different, they were dangerous. Political and military exercises embroiled the prophet in more or less continual conflicts with the legal and political systems of the states in which Mormons established their communities.[39]

The failure of the federal government to protect its Mormon citizens from harassment by state officials, or to ensure them compensation for depredations of anti-Mormon mobs, or even to entertain Smith's 1843 petition to grant independent status to Nauvoo as a federal district, outraged the prophet and his followers. It also gave them a crash course in American federalism. Such matters, explained even those politicians who sympathized with the sufferings of a religious minority, were the prerogatives of the states. The protection of the religious freedom of individual citizens was a local rather than a national affair. The Bill of Rights (whether the protection of private property against seizure in the Fifth Amendment, or the free exercise of religion in the First Amendment) simply did not limit a state's ability to persecute Mormons or invade and destroy their property. Instead, the federal Constitution guaranteed only that the *federal* government must respect the religious freedom of its citizens; the states were not affected by constitutional provisions aimed explicitly at the national sovereign. The law on this question was as clear as anything in the constitutional order.[40]

Such harsh realities of the limits of constitutional freedoms filled Joseph Smith with a disgust for all aspects of states' rights ("they are a dead carcass—a stink, and they shall ascend up as a stink offering in the nose of the Almighty"), and a conviction that for the Constitution to be properly understood and enforced, he would have to assume the U.S. presidency. Smith's candidacy in the campaign of 1844 ended when he was murdered. His successor, Brigham Young, took from the experience a healthy respect for local powers of sovereignty in the American federal system. He and his fellow Mormons had also learned a stark and painful lesson in the limits of law. Even in Illinois, where the Mormon settlement of Nauvoo was granted extraordinary powers of self-government, and Governor Thomas Ford sincerely desired to prevent the mob violence that had lynched the prophet in Carthage, government was rendered powerless by the overwhelming force of the anti-Mormon majority. The federal Congress was no better, for representatives bowed meekly to the demands of their constituents, refusing to take unpopular stands in defense of the Constitution they were charged with upholding. The very murderers who boasted of their foul deed were acquitted, in no small part because potential Mormon witnesses knew that their appearance at trial would mark them as future victims. The sympathetic Stephen Douglas advised the Mormons that the state could not ensure their safety. The people of Illinois (especially those near Nauvoo) simply would not tolerate their continued presence. To survive, the Mormons had to flee.[41]

There can be little doubt that Young understood that he was not leaving the political orbit of the United States, even as he and his emigrant wagon trains traveled beyond the states in search of a place of refuge in the late 1840s. But Young took with him an acutely developed sense of the power of majorities in American government, and a healthy skepticism about the capacity (and willingness) of the federal government to intervene in local affairs. Such a political reality, while devastating to the Saints in the states, provided a powerful justification for separation from the world as a means, paradoxically enough, of acquiring this-world power. For if the Mormons constituted the overwhelming majority in their new home in the Great Basin, then, according to the logic of federalism, their political power could not validly be questioned. Even if such questioning did occur, moreover, the essential weakness of the central state would ensure that local majorities nonetheless could accomplish their wishes in spite of legal mandates or even constitutional provisions. In the states, these had been bitter lessons. Transplanted to the Rocky Mountain fastness of the new Zion, they provided an equation for "political deliverance."[42]

What the Mormons needed, in the political tradition of American federalism, was a republican form of government, and a population at or close to 60,000. These two requirements satisfied, the argument went, there was no obstacle to formal recognition—that is, statehood. In the scramble for settlers that characterized the far Southwest in the mid-nineteenth century, Mormons crafted a far-ranging and superbly organized and self-financing missionary system, and a financial support plan for converts known as the Perpetual Emigrating Fund. To people the kingdom was to follow the mandate of the New Dispensation, and simultaneously to build political strength within (as well as against) Babylon.[43]

Jan Shipps has described the Mormon exodus to Utah as a spiritual journey "backward into a primordial sacred time." What bears emphasizing here is the Mormons' realignment to American constitutionalism. The journey took Mormons into constitutional space. From an exclusive emphasis on the protection of religious minorities in the Bill of Rights, to an embrace of the political rights of local majorities in a federal system, Mormon theorists reaffirmed their fundamental allegiance to the inspired quality of the national Constitution and its importance to the progress of their faith. In Utah, they absorbed and redeployed the very theories of local sovereignty that had been used against them so brutally in the states.[44]

Once the labor and dedication of the Saints established them as a permanent fixture of the Great Basin, Young exercised his newfound majoritarian power on many levels. The most vital of these strategies was the drive for statehood. At the time of the first petition for admission of "Deseret" as a state in 1849, the population, even in the extraordinarily large area (almost four times the current area of Utah, including most of California, Nevada, and Colorado) claimed by the Mormons, did not approach 60,000. But more important still to Congress was the reluctance to grant to a single political entity the control of such a vast portion of the trans-Mississippi West.

Most ominous, and portentous of things to come, was the congressional action actually taken. With the Compromise of 1850, Utah was admitted to the union as a territory, not a state. Further, its proposed area was drastically reduced. It was not granted the sovereign equality accompanying statehood, or the name Mormons had chosen. The debates over the organization of Utah and the other territories that were acquired in the Mexican War of the late 1840s revealed deep, dangerous divisions between North and South over the expansion of slavery. Conflicts over slavery changed the rules of the game, virtually as soon as the Mormons began to play. Questions of tyranny in "peculiar domestic relations" and their effects on the men who wielded power in such forms of private governance, exploded onto the national stage, just as Mormons petitioned for the right to govern themselves.[45]

Hoping to take advantage of the mounting crisis, and then of the Union's collapse, Mormon-controlled constitutional conventions twice petitioned for statehood for Utah in the late 1850s and at the outbreak of the Civil War. The petition failed each time. The primary stumbling block, according to contemporary observers and recent historical research, was polygamy.[46]

After the Civil War, federally appointed territorial officials made polygamy and the church's control of the political and legal systems the centerpiece of their complaints to Washington. Mormons countered that carpetbaggers had no valid authority. Instead, the hypersensitized Mormons (with memories of Missouri and Illinois still fresh, and their hard-won settlement of Utah evidently winning little praise from what should have been a grateful nation) protested what one scholar has termed "every real or imagined encroachment . . . [and] usually got their way." Fighting for every inch, as well as keeping a weather eye out for opportunities to obtain statehood, served Mormons well for two decades. As late as 1865, according to one contemporary observer, two-thirds of all territorial officials in Utah were Mormon polygamists.[47]

But by the mid-1870s, a third layer of strategic behavior was added, as Mormon leaders calculated their likelihood of success in judicial, as opposed to political, centers of power in Washington. The battle to control the legal system of Utah was especially persistent and bitterly fought. As members of the federally appointed territorial judiciary learned, the probate courts established by the local Mormon majority in the early 1850s made them virtually superfluous. Not only were their dockets severely limited by the grant of original civil and criminal jurisdiction to the probate courts, but the jury lists for territorial courts were drawn up by the local marshal, rather than a federal official. Mormon control of jurisdiction and procedure deeply offended the federal judiciary, who charged the Mormons with obstructing the course of justice, perjury, and blind obedience to Young in open defiance of federal law.[48]

The Poland Act of 1874, which for the first time since 1862 expanded the reach of federal power in Utah Territory, was passed only after much debate. Profound and organized opposition from Mormons in Utah included the mass meeting of women at the tabernacle in 1870. Mormon representatives and lobbyists in Congress (among the best known of whom were Leland Stanford and A. A. Sargent, senators from California and impresarios of the powerful "railroad lobby") struggled unsuccessfully to derail the bill and preserve Mormon legal control. But at last the act reduced the powers of the territory's probate judges and provided for jury pools to be selected by the U.S. marshal as well as his territorial counterpart. Such amendments to jurisdiction and procedure were not the stuff of sensation, to be sure, but they represented a significant loss for Mormon juridical independence. More important to territorial officials, the act eroded the general immunity that Mormon leaders, especially Brigham Young, had enjoyed since the exodus to Utah.[49]

The Poland Act was also, in substantial if indirect part, the product of extraordinary legal events in Utah itself. Turbulence in the courts of the territory highlighted the need for regular legal process and connecting such process to the successful (and dignified) prosecution of polygamists. Battles over liquor licenses and compensation for jurors, spats between local Mormon officials and territorial officers over control of the penitentiary, and so on escalated throughout the 1860s and early 1870s, with the conflict between the "laws of man" and the revelation on celestial marriage ever in the background. One particularly resourceful federal judge even impaneled a grand jury that indicted Brigham Young for "lewd and lascivious cohabitation." The judge cited a provision of a territorial statute designed, so said outraged Mormons, to punish openly immoral behavior, not the sanctified marriages of the president and prophet of the church. The indictment was a cheap conspiracy of anti-Mormons, they charged, to "wreak . . . partisan spite upon their religious and political opponents . . . as dishonest as it was despicable."[50]

Even more dramatic was the legal maneuvering from within Young's own household. In the summer of 1873, one of Young's wives apostasized, sued him for divorce, and undertook one of the most spectacularly successful lecture tours of the nineteenth century. Ann Eliza Young, billed as "The Rebel of the Harem," described her courtship, marriage, and eventual separation from Young in excruciating detail. She also claimed that the superficial harmony of Young's households masked what was in fact a systematic torture of women, riven by jealousies, violence, and deception. The publicity surrounding the suit, and Ann Eliza Young's unflinching and personal attack on the president and prophet, attracted large audiences and press attention. In the spring of 1874, her tour took her to Washington, where President Grant and his wife as well as numerous congressmen went to hear her speak.[51]

The groundswell of antipolygamy sentiment fueled by this exposé

AT THE WALKER HOUSE. MY FIRST AUDIENCE.

Ann Eliza Young began to give "talks" on her experiences in Salt Lake City, which evolved into full-blown antipolygamy lectures that she took on tour around the country. From Young, *Wife No. 19.* Courtesy of The Huntington Library, San Marino, Calif.

from the very heart of what the judge in Young's divorce suit called the "polygamic theocracy" was instrumental in the passage of the Poland Act that summer. In addition to the procedural erosion of Mormon legal power, the act also provided for appeal of polygamy convictions to the U.S. Supreme Court. Mormons at the time dismissed the legislation as a "defeat" for the antipolygamy conspiracy, arguing that it was "more ornamental than useful." But the Poland Act opened procedural and jurisdictional inroads into the local legal structure that was the outer layer of Mormon self-government. The Poland Act also clearly granted the Mormons what they claimed to have long wanted—a test case.[52]

As soon as the Poland Act took effect, federal prosecutors began harrying Mormon leaders. Territorial delegate George Q. Cannon was arrested shortly before he was due to depart for Washington in October 1874. Since any polygamy conviction could be appealed to the highest court, and since Mormons had the reasonable hope of being vindicated by the Supreme Court, Cannon and other Mormon leaders determined quickly that a test case with a less infamous defendant would be preferable on several grounds. The leadership had a clear interest in protecting the likes of Cannon from harassment and humiliation, and a younger and less well known defendant would diffuse the political implications of the trial.

The entry for 16 October 1874 in the diary of George Reynolds reads: "[I]t had been decided to bring a test case of the law of 1862 . . . before the court and . . . to present my name before the grand jury."[53] Reynolds met Cannon as he strolled with his second wife in Temple Square. There Reynolds learned for the first time that he had been selected to stand in as the exemplary Mormon polygamist in a test case that, according to Mormon sources, had been arranged with the U.S. attorney, William Carey. Reynolds was to provide the information that would form the basis of his own indictment. In return for Reynolds's cooperation, Carey reportedly agreed to drop all charges against Cannon and other recently arrested leaders, and to waive all "infliction of punishment" should Reynolds be convicted. Reynolds was duly indicted several days later. He pled innocent and was released on $2,500 bail.[54]

George Reynolds was in several ways an ideal candidate for what was to prove a long and arduous test of his mettle. A mild and obedient man, Reynolds had been a polygamist only since August, when he married Amelia Jane Schofield, his second wife. He was bookkeeper and private secretary to a succession of Mormon Church presidents and had a flair for devotional writing (stressing, among other things, the duty of obedience for every Saint). His standing within the church was respectable but not remarkable. In 1874, Reynolds was only thirty-two years old and the husband of only two wives. In an atmosphere saturated with claims that grizzled tyrants monopolized scores of women, Reynolds's youth and modest stature within the church belied the stereotype.[55]

Strategically speaking, then, George Reynolds was an appealing defendant. His selection reflected considerable awareness of the advantages to be gained from his cooperation, as well as the trust placed in his spiritual and emotional stamina by his mentor, George Cannon. Yet the strategy itself was an extraordinarily risky one, a radical departure from the prior tactics of delay and partisan maneuvering. Indeed, it is not clear that the church leadership (which had to date functioned without professionally trained legal talent in inner counsels) understood that proving polygamous marriages would be all but impossible in a faith in which records of such marriages were not public in any way. Unless the parties themselves provided the testimony or the celebrant could be prevailed upon to concede his part in the marriage, proof of plural marriages did not exist, as prosecutors (and polygamists) learned quickly enough. In the years following the

Reynolds litigation, convictions for polygamy remained exceedingly rare, as Mormons withdrew behind a wall of silence.[56]

Convinced by the time of trial that they had been betrayed by federal judges and prosecutors, each of the witnesses called by the prosecution (drawn from the same list Reynolds had given to George Cannon six months earlier in anticipation of a nonconfrontational "test" case) denied any specific knowledge about the marital status of Reynolds and the various members of his household. Orson Pratt could not recall whether records of marriages were kept by the church; the man who performed the marriage could not recall whether he had officiated, and so on.

As the prospects for conviction faded, jubilation erupted among the Mormon spectators. At that moment, a non-Mormon lawyer suggested to the marshal that he bring Reynolds's second wife to testify. When she appeared, Amelia Jane (Schofield) Reynolds, who had not been named on the original list supplied by Reynolds, was uncoached in the strategy of obfuscation and visibly pregnant. She testified forthrightly that she had been married to Reynolds by the man who only moments earlier could not recall the ceremony. An observer sent from Washington to report on the trial described this unexpected turn of events: "As the marshal stepped aside . . . and revealed the person of Mrs. Reynolds No. 2 framed in the doorway, the consternation of the Mormon crowd was startling. The ghost of Joe Smith would scarcely have produced a more profound sensation. Reynolds settled himself low in his seat with a look of hopeless terror, while the general look of dismay spread through the entire Mormon auditory."[57]

After conferring overnight, defense lawyers conceded that a plural marriage had been proved. They argued instead that polygamy for Mormons was a "divine institution, [to which they believe] they will be indebted for their highest happiness in another life to their fidelity and obedience to it in this." The judge ruled that such claims of conscience were irrelevant in the adjudication of "external acts." The jury returned a guilty verdict after half an hour's deliberation.[58]

At long last, the Morrill Act had produced a conviction. The Mormons appealed to the territorial supreme court, which reversed, on the grounds that the grand jury had been improperly impaneled. Reynolds was jubilant, exulting in his "signal triumph" over those intent on "persecuting the people of God." This victory, too, was short-lived. Federal prosecutors brought a second indictment against Reynolds as soon as the grand jury reconvened the following October. At the opening of the second trial, Amelia Jane Reynolds was nowhere to be found. The court ruled that her prior testimony could be admitted in the second trial, since Reynolds himself had told the marshal that all attempts to find his second wife would fail, and that she would never testify. This time the territorial supreme court sustained the conviction. The appeal to the U.S. Supreme Court was noticed in October 1876.[59]

Suddenly and irrevocably, local squabbles over legal process appeared on the national judicial stage. At stake were the constitutional interpretations Mormons had relied on for decades. The Supreme Court would now decide whether the protection of religious freedom in the First Amendment included protection of polygamy, and whether national intervention in domestic affairs violated the constitutional deference to popular sovereignty that was the essence of the federal system. The logic of resistance would never be the same.

PART TWO

Days of Judgment

CHAPTER 4

Law and Patriarchy at the Supreme Court

George Reynolds recorded in his diary that territorial delegate George Q. Cannon had assured the Mormon leadership that the first conviction for polygamy "will be overturned in any event."[1] As it turned out, Cannon's optimism was misplaced; yet in the 1870s the turn to jurisprudence instead of political argument offered promise. At best, Mormons felt, the judicial branch would rescue their embattled constitutional rights from the clutches of federal tyrants and the political hacks sent to govern the territory.

Like many litigants before and since, however, George Reynolds and the Saints saw the Supreme Court simplify and reconstruct their constitutional claims in ways that channeled their arguments into long-established grooves. The freshness and power of the New Dispensation shriveled on the pages of the Supreme Court Reports; Supreme Court justices used the power of judicial review not to protect the practitioners of the Principle but in the service of its enemies.

Reynolds v. United States was argued at the United States Supreme Court in November of 1878. Mormon leaders, notwithstanding confident public statements, were far from sanguine.[2] The church hired George Washington Biddle, dean of the Philadelphia bar and lifelong Democrat, to counteract the "excitement and agitat[ion of] the public mind" that the case would be sure to provoke. Attorney General Charles Devens, a native of Massachusetts and a highly partisan Republican, argued for the government personally, a clear indication of the importance the Hayes administration attached to the case.[3]

There was good reason to take seriously the first polygamy prosecution to reach the Supreme Court. First, the penalties and reforms imposed on the former Confederacy after the end of the Civil War,

The U.S. Supreme Court at the time of the decision in *Reynolds v. United States.*
Courtesy of Library of Congress.

known as Reconstruction, crumbled in the 1870s. With the departure
of federal forces and federal support, the "reclamation" of the South
by white former slaveholders began in earnest at the end of the decade. The erosion of a national commitment to reform in the South
actually increased the attention paid to Utah, and to polygamy.
Growing doubts about Republicans' commitment to humanitarian
principles highlighted the potential value of decisive action on the
"twin relic of barbarism."[4]

And the Supreme Court itself was at something of a jurisprudential (and institutional) turning point. By the late 1870s, the Court
had reined in the applicability of the Reconstruction amendments to
the daily lives of those who claimed that the federal government
should now protect their rights. Therefore, one category of potentially transformative rights—the "privileges and immunities" clause of
the Fourteenth Amendment invoked by African Americans and white
women—had recently been rejected, and the conflict receded in constitutional interpretation. The development of an alternative body of
limitations on affirmative government power lay in the future. The
blossoming of the constitutional doctrine of substantive due process,
or the theory that the protection of "due process of law" included in
the Fourteenth Amendment meant that there were substantive limits
on what state and federal legislatures could regulate or proscribe, did
not occur until the end of the nineteenth century. *Reynolds v. United
States* lies on this fault line between constitutional interpretations.

George Reynolds was indicted and tried for polygamy in the 1870s. His case became a landmark in constitutional law and undermined Mormons' claims to the right to practice plural marriage. Courtesy Historical Department, Church of Jesus Christ of Latter-day Saints.

The opinion in the case provides insight into the rejection of the new constitutional claims at issue in earlier cases. *Reynolds* also exemplifies the development of constitutional doctrines drawn from common-law concepts of contract and property that eventually were subsumed under the label of substantive due process at the turn of the twentieth century.[5]

Equally important, the opinion in *Reynolds* immediately and irrevocably raised the pitch of antipolygamy activism. The Supreme Court's power to make history (and to interpret it) was nowhere more evident than in this first polygamy case, which gave constitutional texture to the long-standing theories of antipolygamists. The opinion reassured congressmen, lobbyists, newspaper editors, and husbands and wives in the states that the marital structure they inhabited was indeed the very marrow of the Constitution, the highest expression of civilization, and the essential building block of democracy. An entire generation of activists gained new confidence that true human happiness and sacred meaning found expression in monogamy. In *Reynolds*, the Supreme Court connected constitutional law to increased federal power and Protestant humanism.

Reynolds was the first Supreme Court case to apply a provision of the First Amendment and determine its meaning in law. Previous cases had dismissed the contention that the protections of the original amendments to the Constitution provided federal protection for citizens against the power of the states. The Bill of Rights was addressed explicitly to Congress, held the Supreme Court, and it meant what it said. Any other interpretation would undermine the sovereignty of the states. And yet in *Reynolds*, the Supreme Court decided that the establishment and free exercise clauses would not protect local difference in domestic relations. The Court upheld the criminal punishment of participants in a marital system that was perceived by the majority of the nation as a fundamental violation of humanitarian precepts, a sexual analogue to slavery. The fact that the Court decided the case on First Amendment grounds indicates that at the end of the 1870s, Chief Justice Morrison Remick Waite and his brethren were beginning to think of the amendments to the Constitution as entailing a positive vision of the moral limits on the American federal system. This was a sea change in federalism, even applied against a territory, but one that was cloaked in a comforting layer of familiarity. The states provided the template for this new constitutional law of federalism, blending respect for the (past) local development of law with a (present and future) national rendering and harmonization of local tradition.[6]

The court's opinion in *Reynolds* drew heavily on the jurisprudential lessons of the states, relying on state precedent to explain and delineate the meaning of the religion clauses of the federal Constitution. State courts had long wrestled with questions of religious liberty, marriage, and political legitimacy. State constitutional jurisprudence provided the pattern for federal constitutional analysis. If the federal Supreme Court respected and even replicated the jurisprudence of state supreme courts, especially against as unpopular a system as that of the Mormons in Utah, then its constitutional analysis would not be susceptible to charges of radicalism or abandonment of first principles.

The lawyers' arguments in the case framed the central questions: would the Court validate the traditional theories of the limitations of federal power to change (or even to investigate) the decisions of majorities in areas of law traditionally reserved for local populations? Mormon leaders and their counsel relied primarily on the lessons of majority power over local government that had been painfully and violently inflicted on the faithful before the exodus to Utah. The government, on the other hand, focused directly on polygamy. Attorney General Charles Devens stressed the individual and social inequities he claimed were inherent in a form of marriage that sacrificed the sensibilities of women at the behest of priests.

Biddle's argument for the church addressed a number of technical issues, including a claim that the trial judge's charge to the jury, which referred to "innocent women" and children whose lives were blighted by polygamy, was unfairly prejudicial (see later discussion). The meat of Biddle's argument, however, was a classic restatement of the theory of popular sovereignty so dear to Democrats before and after the Civil War: "[T]here is always an excess of power, when any attempt is made by the Federal Legislature to provide for more than the assertion and preservation of the right of the General Government over a Territory, leaving necessarily the enactment of all laws relating to the social and domestic life of its inhabitants, as well as its internal police, to the people dwelling in the Territory."[7]

Biddle claimed that the Morrill Act of 1862 was unconstitutional on its face because it violated Article 4, Section 3, giving Congress "power to dispose of and make all needful rules and regulations respecting the territory or other property belonging to the United States." Article 4, Biddle argued, conferred only the power to make "needful" rules and regulations to protect the national interest, not the authority to intervene in local concerns. This was the constitutional provision on which the Missouri Compromise, which limited slavery to land below the Mason-Dixon line, was based. The Supreme Court, however, held that such interference with local decision-making was unconstitutional in 1857 in *Scott v. Sandford*, known popularly as *Dred Scott*. In that case, the majority opinion also held that Article 4 did not confer upon Congress "powers over person and property" in the territories but limited the reach of the national government there as in the states. The prohibition against national action contained in the Bill of Rights, wrote Chief Justice Roger Brooke Taney, "is not confined to [protecting the sovereignty of states], but the words are general, and extend to the whole territory over which the Constitution gives it power to legislate, including those portions of it remaining under Territorial Government, as well as that covered by States." Thus the "citizens of a Territory" were on the "same footing with citizens of the States," protected by the Bill of Rights against tyranny from the center. Any other position, Taney insisted, would be to treat the territories as "colonies . . . to be ruled and governed at the [federal government's] own pleasure." Thus any attempt by Congress to prohibit slavery, interfering in the territories' sovereignty "over person and property," would be unconstitutional. Slavery's "twin," considered from the perspective of the *Dred Scott* case, would be equally protected against congressional interference.[8]

By invoking Article 4 and relying upon the majority decision in the *Dred Scott* case, however, George Biddle touched nerves still raw after the Civil War. *Dred Scott* stands out as among the most controversial decisions in the history of the Supreme Court. The Court, and especially Chief Justice Taney, were also controversial at the time. Many contemporaries blamed the onset of the Civil War on the decision. Historians generally agree that *Dred Scott* did not single-handedly precipitate the war but that it did drastically undermine the prestige (even the power) of the Court. Yet the opinion also had many supporters and was relied upon in congressional debates and Supreme Court argument, especially by Democrats, into the 1870s and 1880s, and beyond. Slavery may have been removed from the powers of local majorities by the Thirteenth Amendment, but considerable doubt lingered about the effect of the Fourteenth Amendment on the basic tissue of the federal system. Questions of domestic relations, which traditionally had been the centerpiece of localism, were among the most troubling and contentious of the areas of law potentially unsettled after the Civil War.[9]

The Fourteenth Amendment, despite the imprecision of its language protecting of the "privileges and immunities" of citizens against state deprivations, nonetheless provided a plausible if hotly contested basis for the claim that the entire power structure of the country had been changed by the war and its constitutional aftermath. According to its more nationalistic interpreters, basic civil rights, including the rights to life, liberty, and property, were secured against state infringement by the new amendment. Such a restructuring of power over the lives and fortunes of citizens in areas that were by definition "local" and "domestic" (especially marriage) would spell the demise of all state government, replied opponents of Reconstruction and its attendant constitutional amendments. To illustrate the potentially catastrophic consequences of a broad interpretation of federal power after the war, traditionalists harped on the absurdity of removing any of the "domestic relations" from state control. Opponents of the federal Civil Rights Act of 1866, for example, argued that its inevitable result would be interference in the private relations between husband and wife.[10]

Republicans assured themselves and their colleagues across the aisle that no such control of the marital bed was contemplated, but the nature and power of state sovereignty was nonetheless clouded. There can be little doubt that most legislators were committed to an interpretation of the Fourteenth Amendment (and civil rights legislation) that did not affect the law of husband and wife, or remove its enforcement to the federal courts. Instead, as one scholar put it, "[C]ongressional Republicans recast the achievement of emancipation as a question simply of race." In this sense, the Civil War was memorialized as a war over slavery, however vehemently it was denied as the fighting raged.[11]

In the early 1870s, the Supreme Court's decisions reassured many conservatives and moderates. As the Court closed the door to radical reinterpretations of federal power through the postwar amendments in case after case, the power of federal courts in the South declined, Reconstruction atrophied, and the rhetoric of states' rights revived. In other words, the power of local majorities to challenge the authority of the central government waxed as Reconstruction waned. The reinvigoration of prewar localism affected lawyers' arguments at the Supreme Court, as well as at the more overtly political arenas of the capitol.

As George Biddle put it on behalf of the Mormon defendant, the power to create a territory did not confer upon the federal government the power to rule the inhabitants as "mere colonists, dependent upon the will" of the center. Migration to a territory, Biddle stressed, citing *Dred Scott* as his authority, did not strip citizens of the United States of their political rights to self-governance. Instead, like the residents of states, the residents of territories were "most competent to determine what was best for their interests." They were protected in such self-determination by the very "genius of the Constitution." The American Revolution, indeed, had been fought in part to establish the rights of the periphery against the central government of the British empire. Biddle's arguments aligned this powerful, insurrectionary tradition with the Mormon claim to local self-determination.[12]

Such arguments were by definition dangerous; Biddle was more cautious than Chief Justice Taney had been on the same question of territorial sovereignty two decades earlier. Much had changed in the intervening years, especially in the desire to find moral limitations on the powers of local majorities. Biddle borrowed from religious tradition to tame the radical import of his constitutional claims. Congress, he maintained, was empowered only to establish such political and judicial structures as would ensure the vitality and integrity of local self-governance. When necessary, the central government might act positively to prohibit things that were clearly contrary to the law everywhere—only those things "*mala in se*" ("law latin" for "evil in themselves" rather than as a result of some positive declaration), such as murder, false swearing (perjury), and like offenses affecting the rights of others that would undermine republican government. The Ten Commandments, Biddle stressed, provided the catalog of such offenses, and polygamy (like slavery, it is worth noting here) fell outside this "general moral code" that described and circumscribed the legislative power of Congress.[13]

Biddle conceded that while the "teachings of the New Testament" might be construed to prohibit polygamy, such an interpretation was a matter of theological rather than legal dispute. "[A] majority of the people of this particular Territory deny that the Christian law makes any such prohibition," he stressed. Thus, Biddle concluded, the statute criminalizing polygamy constituted an abuse of power by the center against the periphery, an exercise of tyranny over the inhabitants of Utah: the national government acted without express constitutional or biblical authority and against the manifest wishes of the majority of the territory's inhabitants.[14]

For the government, Charles Devens defended the Morrill Act by focusing on humanitarianism, on the perception of the essential foreignness of polygamy (and, by implication, of Mormons themselves)—on everything, that is, but the central question of federal power to outlaw polygamy. Devens evaded explicit constitutional analysis, both in his brief and at oral argument. Instead, he played relentlessly on the public perception of the human costs of polygamy. He dredged up a series of analogies that had played to good effect for decades and that would eventually appear in only slightly altered form in the *Reynolds* opinion itself.

Renowned for his sonorous voice, striking looks, and fierce patriotism, Devens had long been a popular speaker. His capacity for touching the emotions of an audience served him well in *Reynolds*, as he sidestepped the dry abstractions and jurisdictional arguments of his opponent. According to press reports of the oral argument, Devens focused on the potentially gory consequences of allowing polygamists to escape criminal punishment. Should George Reynolds go free, Devens argued, the territories would soon be home to all manner of religious atrocities. "Hindu widows [would] hurl themselves on the funeral pyres of their husbands, East Islanders . . . expose their newborn babes, Thugs . . . commit gruesome murders," all in the "name of religion." He closed with a "moving reference to the Mountain Meadows massacre," homing in on the blood that Mormons reputedly had spilled already.[15]

The murder in 1857 of some 125 members of a wagon train in Mountain Meadows by a group of Mormons and Indians was, by 1878, when Devens argued the *Reynolds* case, an old and well-worn story. Its currency, however, had been revived by the trial in Utah of ringleader Mormon bishop John D. Lee, who was not captured until 1873. Lee's trial for murder and its associated publicity rekindled tales of "Avenging Angels," "blood atonement," and other real and imagined offenses associated with the virulent and isolationist rhetoric of the Mormon Reformation in the 1850s. Many non-Mormons believed that Lee had long been shielded by Brigham Young, who they charged had ordered (or at least countenanced) the slaughter. Young turned him over to federal officials, antipolygamists maintained, when the scandal of the massacre showed such persistence that the continued lack of any official punishment was more costly than the loss of one of the faithful. Whatever the merits of such a theory, stories of murderous bands of Mormon zealots extracting revenge for transgressions made good copy and added spice to the claim that behind polygamy lurked bloodshed. Human sacrifice, Devens claimed, was the logical consequence of the sacrifice of humanitarianism at the behest of local religious majorities in the territories.[16]

These were familiar themes to antipolygamists. But their deployment in court changed the tenor of the claims. Depicting the galloping wrongs that would follow on the mistaken extension of rights is a classic form of legal argument. Lawyers for the federal and state governments had, by 1879, frequently made such arguments at the Supreme Court as they wrestled over the meaning of the Fourteenth Amendment. The lesson that lawyers and judges had taken from the results of such arguments in cases involving individual rights against state and local majorities was that for most purposes the power of the federal government remained inaccessible to individual citizens. The Fourteenth Amendment, for example, did not extend to the protection of small butchers against a city ordinance that established a local monopoly over the slaughter of animals. Nor did the amendment apply to a woman who wanted to practice law despite the state's limitation of legal practice to men, or immunize from criminal prosecution a woman suffragist who had voted knowing that local law restricted the franchise to men. Arguments against the extension of rights in such a climate were both predictable and intimately tied to the recent jurisprudence of the Court.[17]

In *Reynolds*, the thrust of such claims was more complicated. For the denial of a "right" to religious freedom in this case was tantamount to the protection of its victims in the eyes of antipolygamist reformers. If the extension of rights was typically the empowerment

The Mountain Meadows massacre of 1857 remained a topic of interest and speculation until the 1870s, when Mormon bishop John D. Lee was finally brought to trial and executed for participating in the murder of more than 125 members of a wagon train from Missouri. From T. B. H. Stenhouse, *Rocky Mountain Saints*. Courtesy of The Huntington Library, San Marino, Calif.

of those who had been subordinate, in *Reynolds* the equation was reversed. The extension of a right to Mormons to practice their faith in plural marriage was construed by liberals to be a violation of humanitarian principles. Thus one could satisfy the humanitarians by denying the power of a local majority and at the same time argue against the extension of rights, which was traditionally the constitutional conservatives' position.

Either way, the Mormons lost. And the Constitution protected the presumably enslaved women of Utah but did not insulate the patriarchs of the Mormon Church. The list of offenses that Devens insisted were the logical correlatives of polygamy (suttee, exposure of newborns, ritual murder) also countered Biddle's claim that polygamy was not prohibited by the Decalogue. If murder and human sacrifice were the ineluctable result of the protection of polygamy, then the recognition of a right to practice plural marriage was tantamount to licensing murder at the hands of the same men who claimed the right.

The connections between Christian family structure, human rights, and stable government could not have been more clearly drawn. As Devens hammered the connections between polygamy and

Asian religions, he also distinguished the Christian localism sanctioned by the Constitution from the "foreign" practices of the majority in Utah Territory. None of the states had ever (or would ever, Devens implied) authorized such an abuse of the law of marriage. The point has some irony, to be sure, since enslaved persons were formally prohibited from marrying in Southern states before the Civil War.[18]

After the war, according to the government's argument, all states were once again empowered with full control over the civil rights of their inhabitants, with the explicit exception of the rights protected by the Fourteenth Amendment. And because the Reconstruction amendments were themselves designed to erase slavery and its incidents, the happy blending of antipolygamy and antislavery theory in political and cultural venues spilled over into the government's strategy at the Supreme Court. If the "overshadowing and efficient cause" of the Civil War was slavery, and the extension of federal power through constitutional amendment after the war was directed explicitly at slavery, as the Supreme Court had said in 1873, then how could the Constitution be validly invoked only six years later to shield slavery's analogue, polygamy? The very moral meaning of the Constitution was contrary, Devens argued. Equally vital was the fact that state law on the question was uniform. Bigamy was a felony everywhere except Utah at the time of the passage of the Morrill Antipolygamy Act in 1862. This meant that even those states that had been "wrong" on slavery were "right" on polygamy. There was no call, on humanitarian grounds, to interfere with the uniform practice of the states.[19]

Yet uniformity, as lawyers in the nineteenth century well knew, hardly described the law or the practice of the states with regard to marriage. The mobility of the population after the Civil War undercut the ability of state governments to control the law of marriage and divorce. Migration also raised questions of fundamental interstate relations as peripatetic husbands (and sometimes wives) probed the boundaries of the new federalism. As recent scholarship has shown, illicit (or just extralegal) remarriage without a formal divorce in another jurisdiction was endemic to a culture in which disappearing was as easy as walking away from a failed relationship. And several jurisdictions openly (or implicitly) countenanced divorce for reasons far less grave than adultery or desertion. Polygamy thus marked the outer edge of a legal system riven by jurisdictional difference and transient populations. Preoccupation with rising divorce rates, abandonment, the relationship of marriage to political stability—all could be conveniently channeled into the condemnation of polygamy. By attacking plural marriage in Utah, one could pretend that the legal experience of husbands and wives in the rest of the country was more uniform—more monogamous—than it actually was.[20]

The hard-fought lessons of the Civil War, especially that of the dangers of fundamental moral difference by region, were nowhere so seamlessly applicable as they were to Utah Territory. The aura of polygamy colored the case. The arguments at a Supreme Court tainted with the controversy over *Dred Scott* and an uncomfortable proslavery past produced the desire to distinguish the present from such barbarism. In this political and jurisprudential atmosphere, polygamy described the limit beyond which a husband, or a state, might not go.

The Supreme Court's opinion in the case was handed down in early 1879. The decision held that Mormon polygamists had no constitutional right to engage in a form of marriage directly prohibited by Congress. In the process, the Court explored the interdependence of marriage and political structures, and the importance of religion to both. Subsequent decisions sustained and amplified the essential premise of *Reynolds*, which remains a frequently cited precedent. The staying power of antipolygamy jurisprudence is remarkable, for many nineteenth-century cases were buried under the weight of twentieth-century rights doctrines that consciously eschew the nineteenth-century Court's restrictive interpretation of civil rights.[21]

At the time, and for many decades afterward, *Reynolds* was a popular and politically important decision. It marked a watershed in antipolygamy activity and theory, galvanizing reformers, politicians, and lawyers into renewed commitment to the cause. The carefully crafted jurisdictional arguments of the Mormons evaporated in Chief Justice Waite's analysis for the Court. They were replaced with a lesson in historiography that has dominated the constitutional analysis of law and religion ever since.

Reynolds used historical analysis of the legal experience of the states in the service of federal power. The decision translated the politics and jurisprudence of disestablishment and free exercise at the state level into a mandate for dismissing the constitutional claims of George Reynolds. The research that went into the *Reynolds* opinion raises interesting questions about the institutional stature of the Supreme Court in the 1870s, and the relationship of the federal Supreme Court to state jurisprudence. Until recently, the postwar Court has not been viewed as any great improvement over what came before. And before the Civil War, of course, there was *Dred Scott*. The apparent rigidity and class bias of the Court's decisions, legal scholars maintain, revealed a deep concern with formal distinctions between public and private life that frequently obscured basic questions of justice and humanity. Certainly most Mormons at the time, and legal historians of Mormonism since, have echoed those sentiments.[22]

The jurisprudential harvest of the polygamy cases supports a more nuanced interpretation of the late-nineteenth-century's moral philosophy of law. At the Supreme Court, litigation over Mormon polygamy was the vehicle for the development of a jurisprudence that explored and delineated what one scholar has felicitously called "the sharp moral edges [of] complex legal problems." *Reynolds* stands as the first, and the foundation, of the complex legal problems brought to the Supreme Court by the Saints of Utah.[23]

The new forum in which litigants and decision makers deployed their legal stratagems was also affected by the logic of resistance. By the time the Court decided the *Reynolds* case, polygamy had been illegal for more than sixteen years. Yet in all appearances, Mormon polygamists remained defiant and impervious to congressional command or public condemnation. They maintained, as they always had, that the federal government had no power to punish a local majority's domestic relations.

Instead of addressing the Mormons' jurisdictional claim directly, the Court invoked the religion clauses of the First Amendment, only to reject their applicability to the question of Mormon plural marriage. The issue crept in sideways, not as a direct argument. George Biddle, in his brief and again at oral argument, had stressed the prejudicial effect of the charge to the jury in the second *Reynolds* trial. First, the judge refused to charge the jury that religious belief vitiated criminal intent, thus undermining the Mormon contention that latter-day celestial marriage had nothing in common with the venality of garden-variety bigamy in the states. Instead of focusing on the religious nature of plural marriage, the judge charged the jury to consider the "innocent" victims of polygamy (that is, the wives and their children) as they deliberated the fate of George Reynolds. Biddle argued that these procedural decisions had unfairly conveyed to the jurors the message that Reynolds was in fact a criminal. He cited extensive case law to bolster this argument, which was unquestionably one of criminal procedure rather than First Amendment right. Biddle's constitutional argument, on the other hand, was jurisdictional, based on the powers of Congress over the territories, and far from gritty questions of sexual behavior and religious mandates or even mens rea.[24]

As Chief Justice Waite reframed the argument, however, the claim that the jury charge was unduly prejudicial was tantamount to admitting that the plural marriage had in fact taken place, and that the religion clauses were used as an excuse. The claim, in other words, was for an exemption from an otherwise valid law. Clearly, this misconstrued Biddle's central constitutional claim, which relied on a far more powerful and more traditionally focused concept of local sovereignty and corresponding limitations of the powers of central government.

The majority opinion recast the argument as follows: "The inquiry is not as to the power of congress to prescribe criminal laws for the Territories, but as to the guilt of one who knowingly violates a law which has been properly enacted, if he entertains a religious belief that the law is wrong." This inquiry led the Supreme Court into an elaborate exercise in constitutional historiography. The *Reynolds* opinion became a study in the meaning of disestablishment and free exercise. Waite began by noting that "the word 'religion' is not defined in the Constitution. We must go elsewhere, therefore, to ascertain its meaning, and nowhere more appropriately, we think, than to the history of the times in the midst of which the provision was adopted."[25]

So began the judicial designation of state constitutional and statutory provisions as the source of meaning for the federal religion clauses. The irony is that when they were introduced, debated, and ratified, the religion clauses were designed in significant part to protect local decision-making against federal interference. Addressed explicitly to Congress, the religion clauses were a check on federal power rather than a model for local behavior. State practices, which were hardly consistent when the First Amendment was adopted in 1791, were protected by it from federal intervention.[26]

Even more ironic from the perspective of the broad sweep of religion and law in the first half of the nineteenth century is that Virginia, home of the most infamous deist (Thomas Jefferson, the "Virginia Voltaire" himself), was the state to which the Court turned for historical understanding of the meaning of religion in American constitutions. Waite first gave a thumbnail sketch of disestablishment in Virginia in 1785 as the model for the federal religion clauses enacted several years later. The preamble to the Virginia Act, Waite stressed, declared "that it is time enough for the rightful purposes of civil government for its officers to interfere when principles break out into overt acts against peace and good order."[27] Waite also cited Thomas Jefferson's "Letter to the Danbury Baptists," written in 1802, in which Jefferson explained the First Amendment: "Believing with you that religion is a matter which lies solely between man and his God; that he owes account to none other for his faith or his worship; that the legislative powers of the government *reach actions only*, and not opinions,—I contemplate with sovereign reverence that act of the whole American people which declared that their legislature should 'make no law respecting an establishment of religion or prohibiting the free exercise thereof,' thus building a wall of separation between church and State."[28]

Because this letter was written after the adoption of the Bill of Rights, and by a man so vital to their enactment, Waite maintained, Jefferson's description of the extent of the protections provided by the religion clauses was "almost an authoritative declaration of the scope and effect of the amendment thus secured." Applied to the federal context, Waite concluded, religious freedom meant that Congress was prohibited from legislating on questions of "mere opinion" but was free to address overt actions if they violated "social duties" or were "subversive of good order." This doctrine, known as the "belief-action distinction," allowed Waite to determine that Mormons were perfectly free to believe in plural marriage but could validly be punished for committing the act of polygamy.[29]

Thus, Thomas Jefferson was used as a viable source of legal doctrine for the religious life of the Republic, in a case in which the Supreme Court deployed Jefferson's deeply skeptical, and profoundly local, disestablishmentarian ethos *against* local deviance. Equally striking is that Jefferson's legacy was invoked as precedential in a case tinged with the aura of antislavery moral constitutionalism. There was precedent for such manipulation of the Jeffersonian legacy by those whose ethic was so fundamentally at odds with the states' rights vision that equated centralization with tyranny. The legacy of the Declaration of Independence, which by 1860 had become a central text in the moral constitutionalism that animated the Republican Party, illustrates how Jefferson's image had been appropriated and manipulated by the time *Reynolds* was decided in 1879.[30]

In 1865, in a eulogy to Lincoln after his assassination, the historian George Bancroft credited Jefferson and Lincoln as co-equal partners in the progress of human liberty. The Father of Democracy and the Great Emancipator, in this construction, were both members of a humanitarian "tradition" in which the moral proposition of the Declaration ("Liberty to All") was realized with the Emancipation Proclamation. This continuity was steadfastly maintained by Lincoln himself and colored with the patina of martyrdom after Lincoln's death.[31]

Less than fifteen years later, George Bancroft fed his friend and neighbor "Mott" Waite with documents and historical interpretation. The chief justice used Bancroft's research as a mandate to redeem Jefferson from the aura of proslavery that clung to his memory. By deploying Jefferson as the key to the abolition of slavery's "twin," Waite gave Jefferson's plausibility as a humanitarian republican greater substance, and jurisprudential significance.[32]

The use of Jefferson, and Virginia, as exemplars of freedom indicated the Court's willingness to reintegrate them into the constitutional mainstream. At the same time, the qualities that made Jefferson a vaguely troublesome figure in Northern thought during and after the Civil War reconciled many Southerners to the imposition of national authority on the people of Utah. Jefferson's Virginia (the epicenter of the local rule that pitted states' rights against human rights) had already decided the question. The Virginia legislature, as Waite was careful to point out, passed a statute imposing the death penalty for bigamy and polygamy three years after enacting the Statute for Religious Freedom. Perhaps the identification of antipolygamy with antislavery was not so ineluctable after all.[33]

The Court's use of history also provides clues to the changing nature of American federalism. George Biddle, relying on *Dred Scott*, had argued that "no constitutional lawyer should hesitate to give his assent to the negative proposition that citizens of the United States who migrate to a Territory cannot be ruled as colonists, . . . [rather i]n regards to all local matters it would be more advisable to commit the powers of self-government to the people of the Territory as most competent to determine what was best for their interests." Because polygamy, as a domestic relation, was quintessentially a "local matter," Biddle claimed, Congress exceeded its powers by interposing the national government in business best handled by local democratic processes. Waite's opinion breezed over this argument, dismissing what had been the dominant concept of congressional power over the territories. Instead, Waite relied on the legal history of religion in Virginia to determine the scope of local sovereignty for Utah, and for all territories.[34]

This jurisprudential sleight of hand substituted the democratic experience of one jurisdiction—Virginia—for a process that would have allowed each jurisdiction to determine for itself the meaning and scope of the law of religion within its boundaries. This substitution was profoundly nationalizing. At the same time, it was deferential to the lived experience of states in the definition of federal constitutional terms and the development of constitutional doctrine.

The Court's analysis of the belief/action distinction for federal purposes tracked state law theory, especially antebellum blasphemy jurisprudence. Emphasizing that religious "opinion, whatever it may be," was fully protected by state freedom-of-conscience provisions,

Waite explained that "acts of licentiousness" that manifested "defiance to all public order" were properly subject to criminal punishment, whether or not they were religiously motivated. The definition of "public order" as it was explained by state courts, of course, had deep roots in Christian principle as the faith of the people. The confluence of "order," democracy, and religion embraced in such state court opinions was a democratically constructed yet indelibly Protestant public morality. Open and active defiance of public morality, in this view, became the object "of primary regard by the laws."[35]

The question thus became whether polygamy violated public morality and was subversive of good order. Traditionally, Waite pointed out, the offense of polygamy had been considered one against Christianity but had been punished by civil courts in England since the reign of James I. Magistrates had assumed the authority formerly exercised by ministers, that is, of protecting through civil courts "this most important feature of social life." The substitution of secular regulation, of course, undercut the power of ecclesiastics. Arguably, it also impinged upon the religious nature of marriage. Yet even Jefferson's Virginia, the Supreme Court implied, had understood that monogamy was so integral to the very concept of marriage that its violation had been made punishable by death.[36]

The use of Jefferson here as well also subtly rehabilitated Jefferson's reputation as a free lover and miscegenist. Not only had Jefferson dallied with his slave Sally, engaging in an extralegal and interracial affair, he was hardly respectable on divorce. Jefferson supported liberal divorce laws, much to the dismay of conservative Christians. Prodivorce activists in the mid-nineteenth century used the Declaration of Independence as a justification for separation as a means of escaping relationships gone sour, and they claimed Jefferson as an ally. The validity of the Revolution as a remedy for the breach of the rights of the colonies, and the usefulness of the Declaration in cataloging the breach and justifying the remedy, argued advocates of liberal divorce, also had consequences for other dissolutions. Jefferson, already vilified as an infidel, had also maintained unorthodox opinions of the permanence of marriage. From time to time, he allowed that he was as committed to familial as to political separations when "continuance" undermined the purpose for which the union had been created. By showing that Jefferson's own statute for religious freedom had never been understood to excuse bigamy (or divorce), and thus implying that federal protection of religious freedom would not excuse Mormon polygamy, the Supreme Court integrated the protection of Christian marriage into the First Amendment.[37]

The Court also connected marriage and its legal protection to

THE CARRION CROW IN THE EAGLE'S NEST.

This cartoon, published in the 25 January 1882 issue of *Puck*, shortly after the *Reynolds* decision, illustrates the theory that Utah was isolated among American jurisdictions—a "carrion crow" that had insinuated itself into the eagle's brood. Courtesy of Yale University Library.

questions of political legitimacy more generally considered. The use of marriage as a metaphor for political life was especially poignant in the postwar period. The romance of reunion after the Civil War was punctuated not only by references to the South as a wayward yet adorable lover but also by heightened interest in the permanence of civil unions, marital as well as political. The reach and moral purchase of legal rules were complicated, of course, by federalism. Uniformity (despite the claims of conservative clerics) was never a hallmark of religious mandates for marriage in America. The embarrassing fact of Utah revealed the deep seams dividing Americans' faiths. In such an environment, riven by multiple beliefs as much as multiple laws, the constitutional meaning of marriage was freighted with significance not only for religion and law but also for their interaction with each other and for the negotiation of power within each.

Marriage was the site of potential abuse, suffering, and spiritual meaning. Yet Biddle had claimed that Reynolds was no criminal— that the trial judge had unduly prejudiced the jury against his client by raising the specter of "innocent" victims of celestial marriage. This issue of criminal procedure also raised the humanitarian question at stake in *Reynolds*. Without the presence of "victims," the moral question would not be clearly presented, or understood. In a case that otherwise involved only men, the incursion of a reference to women grounded the issue where it truly belonged, according to many anti-polygamists whose primary motives were religious and humanitarian. The focus shifted away from limitations on the central government and onto the effect of this brand of local sovereignty over Christian marriage and Mormon women.[38]

This shift was crucial not only to the decision in *Reynolds* but to the course of religion clause jurisprudence generally. Without the question of marriage, the political practices of Mormons might be of considerable interest to reformers in the East, but they would be elusive in terms of constitutional litigation. Secular control of the law of marriage, as much a product of the Protestant Reformation as the extraordinary flowering of religious variety and fervor, was also at stake in the case, and gave the case moral purchase. Here again, the question is more tangled than any simple tale of secularization.

The relationship of religion to the law of marriage was a topic of considerable jurisprudential interest in the nineteenth century. By the late 1870s, a series of eminent treatise writers had tackled the notoriously eclectic jurisprudence of the states. The connections between private structures of faith and the adjudication of disputes was most clearly present in precisely those relationships that connected the authority of husbands and fathers (that is, voters with the power to determine the course of public government) with restraints imposed on private governance by Christian principle. As Joel Prentiss Bishop stressed in his *Commentaries on Marriage and Divorce*, marriage was vital to the welfare of all society, the subject of civil regulation and individual state control. It was also, as treatise-writer Christopher Tiedeman emphasized, naturally productive of state security only when "founded in purity and rest[ing] upon sound spiritual foundations."[39]

Revelatory injunctions (the mandate for considering husbands and wives "one flesh" is the obvious example) had explicit legal force in the jurisprudence of marriage despite the separation of church and state that disestablishment implied. For neither the Bible nor the "general doctrines" of Christianity, according to jurists, should be confused with a formal alliance between church and state. In the eyes of Michigan Supreme Court justice Thomas Cooley and other state judges, the enforcement of biblical mandates was an example of the relationship between law and religion, a relationship that existed in the vital yet invariably abstract realms occupied by the most fundamental rules of right living. Among the most influential and brilliantly crafted of the postwar treatises was Cooley's *Constitutional Limitations*, first published in 1868. Cooley explained in a chapter titled "Religious Liberty" that Christianity and the common law were united in marriage and the law of the family. Thus the force of religion in secular law was undeniable, although neither Cooley nor other writers acknowledged the tension between perfect religious freedom and enforcement of "general" Christian rules for marriage.[40]

George Biddle in his argument on behalf of the Mormon defendant had, with considerable acuity, attempted to limit the range of such a relationship between religion and law to the Decalogue. But as Biddle undoubtedly knew, the supreme court of his home state of Pennsylvania had held that Christianity was part of the common law for purposes of the punishment of blasphemy and the enforcement of sexual norms. The same court also stressed that the incorporation of Christian principles was entirely distinct from an establishment of religion, which necessarily entailed denominational particularity.[41]

Secular control of the law of marriage thus existed in some theoretical tension with a widely shared perception of the religious roots of marriage itself. The boundaries between the spiritual and the secular in marriage remained more or less comfortably amorphous in much of American law. In this area, too, Mormons explored and exposed the tension. To the rest of the country, polygamy in Utah exposed the unstated yet undeniable assumption that the spiritual life of its constituent parts affected the structure and security of the central government. In other words, the debate over polygamy highlighted the vital ways in which the "private" law of marriage had undeniably "public" dimensions. *Reynolds* challenged the Court to articulate how the intersection of spiritual and secular law in marriage was fundamental to all of political life, territorial, state, and federal.[42]

In response, the Supreme Court drew together the threads that connected marriage to political life and law, holding that the Mormons' attempt to redefine the family for Utah Territory justified the intervention of the national sovereign. The jurisprudence created in *Reynolds* and the Court's subsequent polygamy cases defined the power of the federal government over domestic relations in the territories, and conveyed to other governments the constitutive (if unspoken) role of faith in all of the constituent parts of the Union. In part, the very immunity of the states to federal oversight created the opportunity for federal judges to develop a theory of the difference between states and territories—to define for the states, that is, the boundaries of their own power.

In 1852, the territorial legislature of Utah had granted to the Mormon Church power over marriage for the faithful. From one perspective, the Saints only recovered for Utah the ecclesiastical control that Protestants had sacrificed in what one scholar has called "the[ir] historic willingness . . . to desacramentalize marriage and place it under the aegis of civil law."[43] The concession was a source of irritation to many clerics, whose power over marriage was compromised by the exclusive (and increasingly exercised) control of secular law over divorce. Antidivorce theorists, especially, argued for the reimposition of religious law of marriage in the states. They were countered from the other end of the spectrum by liberal feminist Elizabeth Cady Stanton, who claimed that marriage should be entirely a matter of civil contract—private, that is, except for the protection of the vulnerable provided by rules of eligibility and conscionability.[44]

In *Reynolds*, the potentially "un-Christian" consequence of religious control over the law of marriage in a country of vigorous yet diverse faith provided a valuable caution. Invoking higher law, as we saw in Chapter 2, had invigorated such moral analysis and was frequently urged by Christian conservatives. But in the "wrong" hands, higher law carried an explosive charge that could be fatal not only to theories and justifications of secular authority as a whole but also to particular legal structures, even the law of marriage. From this perspective, polygamy in Utah was the literal incarnation of the theoretical danger. Ironically, then, one could protect Christian practice by clipping the formal power of the Mormon Church in Utah. Thus the secular power of the federal government over marriage, exercised in opposition to the expressed wishes of a local religious majority, was coated in polygamy cases with a sweet deference to Protestant mandates. Despite this deference, there is no escaping the fact that the power deployed was secular, and the power attacked was religious. Marriage and its attendant legal protections were simply too vitally important as a matter of politics to be relinquished back to ecclesiastical control. Thus the idea that monogamous marriage was central to the very concept of democratic governance in nineteenth-century America was painfully, undeniably exposed by the challenge of Mormon polygamy.[45]

The court's conviction that the private structure of governance known as marriage was the very basis of political life was clearly articulated and cogently analyzed. Waite stressed that "society may be said to be built" upon marriage. The connection between the state and marriage was one of structure as well as interest: "[A]ccording as monogamous or polygamous marriages are allowed, do we find the principles on which the government of the people, to a greater or lesser extent, rests." Here was the nub of the problem, and the point at which both Brigham Young and Morrison Waite would have agreed. For Young and the Saints were as committed to the integral relationship between political and marital structure as any jurisprude. Waite did not stop with the assertion of the political importance of marriage; he pushed on into an analysis of the consequences of polygamy from the perspective of political science, a new and powerful academic discipline in the nineteenth century. Political as well as social regression was the hallmark of polygamy, argued America's most influential political scientist. "Professor Lieber says," Waite wrote, "polygamy leads to the patriarchal principle, and which, when applied to large communities, fetters the people in stationary despotism, while that principle cannot exist long in monogamy."[46]

By the mid-nineteenth century, Francis Lieber had become widely known as a dedicated antipolygamist. His *Political Ethics* had also become the standard work cited in legal treatises and lawyers' briefs on the proper respect for, and restriction of, women in politics and law. Indeed, it was from a late edition of Chancellor Kent's *Commentaries* that Waite drew his reference to Lieber's works. Kent, author of the landmark opinion in *People v. Ruggles* discussed in Chapter 2, stated outright that "[t]he direct and serious prohibition of polygamy contained in our law is founded on the precepts of Christianity, and the laws of our social nature, and it is supported by the sense and practice of civilized nations." Lieber's analysis of the social retrogression and disorder inherent in polygamy, Kent emphasized and Waite noted with approval, was "equally striking and profound."[47]

The opinion in *Reynolds* made this point explicitly. Noting that "marriage [is] . . . from its very nature a sacred obligation," the court moved quickly to the validity of secular regulation. "[I]n most civilized nations," Chief Justice Waite stressed, marriage "is . . . a civil contract, and usually regulated by law."[48] Indeed, the embrace of marriage in secular law was capacious, and growing, by the late 1870s. Just two years earlier, the Supreme Court held that a Michigan statute providing for the solemnization of marriages did not invalidate a so-called common-law marriage, celebrated informally "by contract per verba de proesenti" (that is, the couple having declared their intention to marry one another without the benefit of civil or ecclesiastical officiation). "Marriage," the court declared in a case upholding the right of a daughter of the informal union to inherit from her intestate father, "is everywhere regarded as a civil contract. Statutes in many of the States, it is true, regulate the mode of entering into the contract, but they do not confer the right." The embrace of informal means of marrying extended the benefits of marriage to men and women who would otherwise fall outside the pale of legitimate relationships. Although the means of celebration were unorthodox, the resulting duties of protection and obedience were enforceable in marriage. Without the legal relationship, courts could not hold couples to the responsibilities of marriage. The presumption in favor of legitimacy embodied the theory that marriage was central to the political objectives of every responsible government.[49]

Polygamy challenged the logic of the civil law of marriage. States retained control over the law of marriage and divorce, of course, and the humanitarian sensibilities that animated abolitionism stalled at the bedroom door. But the legal defense of polygamy amounted to a claim that a religious mandate should sanctify one of the civil law's least admirable by-products. The informal ability of husbands to abandon an unhappy or inconvenient or just plain dull marriage in one jurisdiction and to contract a second marriage in another deeply disturbed conservatives who opposed easy divorce. Nobody thought such transience was a *good* thing, however much they felt incapable of devising a satisfactory solution. The impermanence of marital relationships, in fact, traveled uneasily alongside theoretical arguments of the illegality of marital escape. Mormon polygamy, to many outsiders, appeared to elevate such regrettable conduct to the status of a virtue. Thus the Supreme Court could hold by the 1880s that an unsavory legislative divorce and subsequent remarriage in the West without notice to a wife in the East was valid (if distasteful) as a matter of federal law. But the claim that Utah Territory had a right to so limit the obligations of husbands, that even such a sham divorce was unnecessary before remarriage, drew a scathing indictment from the same Supreme Court justice.[50]

Questions linger, nonetheless. If the presumption in favor of marriage was so strong in the late nineteenth century, why was the Supreme Court unwilling to extend the presumption of legitimacy to Mormon plural marriage? Surely part of the answer lies in the essentially religious nature of polygamy in territorial Utah. If one goal of recognizing even informally celebrated marriage was to extend the arm of the (secular) state to such relationships, polygamy was, avowedly, the extension of a theocracy into marriage. Certainly, prejudice against Mormons and their alternative faith played a role in the decision. As Waite put it for the Court in *Reynolds*, "[U]ntil the establishment of the Mormon Church, [polygamy] was almost exclusively a feature of the life of Asiatic and of African people."[51]

The invocation of race in a polygamy case had a special meaning. After the Civil War, polygamy's racial overtones migrated away from slaveholders and onto those who had been enslaved. Attacks on the morality of freed slaves in the late 1860s and 1870s, for example, hammered the presumption that "[Negroes] ungovernable propensity to miscellaneous sexual indulgence" meant that they would be easy prey for Mormon missionaries. Concern over the sexual purity of freedpersons became a prime object of Freedmen's Bureau officials, who urged monogamy on freedmen as key to their advancement. Republican politicians also made it plain that monogamy was expected of former slaves. In the late nineteenth century, antimiscegenation statutes increasingly marked the racialized boundaries of many jurisdictions' concept of marital integrity and "purity." The analogy of Mormon practices to those of Asia and Africa invoked the two continents whose peoples were most frequent targets of American prohibitions against interracial marriage. Such labeling, inevitably, carried racial and racist messages, as well as religious ones.[52]

The "fettering" of the people in the "stationary despotism" of "patriarchy," of course, also harkened back to theories of the static and barbaric qualities of slavery. It raised questions of patriarchy's inconsistency with democracy, a central concern of most antipolygamy theory. This concern helps explain how Mormon polygamy provoked such persistent and determined jurisprudential opposition, while common-law marriage, or disputes between Shaker communities and former members, or even disgruntled members of the Oneida perfec-

In the 1870s, cartoonist Thomas Nast captured the widespread fear of "foreign" clerical power over secular laws and institutions in this drawing that unites anti-Catholicism and anti-Mormonism. Courtesy of Library of Congress.

tionists, did not raise such thorny legal issues, or produce such innovative judicial analysis. In a legal regime that tolerated diversity of laws, diversity of beliefs, and even diversity of property rights for religious communities, Mormon polygamy defined the limits of tolerance.

As the Supreme Court explained it, the difference between Mormons and other religious separatists was the fundamental inconsistency of plural marriage with the very maintenance of political stability. Polygamy, like slavery, was inherently expansionist, the Court held, eroding the freedoms of neighboring jurisdictions. Political power was the essence of the problem, and the use of power to invest religious leaders with legal authority over marriage was the first step on the road to despotism and its close relative, anarchy. Waite wrote: "An exceptional colony of polygamists . . . may sometimes exist for a time without appearing to disturb the social condition of the people who surround it," but the appearance was deceptive. The "principles" of government were so different in the two systems that the tolerance of the difference would undermine the liberty that depended on monogamy.[53]

To grant an exemption to George Reynolds would be to "make the professed doctrines of religious belief superior to the law of the land. . . . Government could exist only in name under such circumstances." The fear of the state's erosion through the loss of the secular law of marriage runs like a seam through the opinion. *Reynolds* reveals the depth of anticlericalism at the heart of the Supreme Court's jurisprudence of family law. The opinion also indirectly discloses the reliance Chief Justice Waite placed on his and other husbands' exercise of governing authority without despotism. The "foreign-ness" of polygamy, together with the power over law that Waite and other justices held was at the root of the *Reynolds* case, marked the question as one of despotism versus liberty at the most fundamental levels.[54]

The sense of the interdependence of political and sexual structures, the conviction that some forms of patriarchy were essentially at odds with democracy and republicanism, and the focus on marriage as the connecting point between religious and secular law, all these elements had already been present in the speeches of Justin Morrill in the late 1850s. And yet the change of venue from the halls of Congress to the Supreme Court and the passage of two decades altered the meaning, and the tone, of antipolygamy in its jurisprudential incarnation.

The moral meaning of the Constitution had shifted in the meantime, seared into the hearts and minds of Americans by the Civil War. The price of union was high indeed; the goal of stability precious beyond all calculation. The end of Reconstruction in the 1870s meant the abandonment of the freedpersons in the South. The reconstruction of white supremacy stands as a caution to historians tempted to make too much of the "centralization" of power during and after the Civil War. In its Fourteenth Amendment jurisprudence, the Supreme Court played a central role in dismantling Reconstruction in the South, and limiting the reach of new constitutional provisions in the lives of freedpersons. And yet there was a counterpoint in Utah, a second "Reconstruction" in the West. In the political world of Justin Morrill in the late 1850s, polygamy and slavery, gender and race, had been "twin" concepts of Republican rhetoric. In the jurisprudential world of Morrison Waite in the late 1870s, the white women of Utah became substitutes for the black women and men of the former Confederacy, giving antipolygamy theory and jurisprudence a new constitutional and moral purchase. Yet as the Supreme Court revitalized the antipolygamy movement, it also revealed the seams dividing the systems that earlier Republicans had called twins. As the pressure from Washington slackened in the South, it increased in Utah. The "fetters of stationary despotism" were visible in 1879 to the judges on the Supreme Court in *Reynolds*, however invisible they were to the Northern politicians who sanctioned the Compromise of 1877, and the dismantling of Reconstruction.[55]

The immediate inspiration for the second reconstruction, it is worth noting, came from the judiciary rather than from Republicans in Congress. *Reynolds*, which had seemed to Mormon leaders to have the potential to rescue the embattled Zion, instead provided an invaluable service to its foes, revivifying and redirecting the energies of antipolygamists in Congress and elsewhere. With the blessing of the Supreme Court, Congress turned to dismantling the patriarchy of Utah in the avowed service of democracy, liberty, and law.

CHAPTER 5

The Erosion of Sympathy

In Utah, *Reynolds* changed everything but the determination to resist. As one prominent polygamist put it, "I will not desert my wives and my children and disobey the commandments of God for the sake of accommodating the public clamor of a nation steeped in sin and ripened for the damnation of hell." The betrayal of constitutional principle, argued Mormons, bankrupted the decision, the court that issued it, and the nation that supported it. *Reynolds*, said the *Latter-day Saints Millennial Star*, was "the product of base cowardice, [and] pandering to anti-Mormon fanaticism." Defiance was rendered more desperate by the erosion of the constitutional logic of resistance. But the New Dispensation was at stake, and the foul pronouncements of judges in the East could not corrode the exultation of sainthood.[1]

Resistance also worked. From 1879 to 1890, the government brought only seventy-eight indictments for polygamy. Proving a second (or third or fourth) marriage in a jurisdiction that had no official registration provisions, in a church that purportedly kept no records of marriages, and in the midst of a recalcitrant population was a burden prosecutors could not meet. As a test case, *Reynolds* was both indispensable and insufficient.[2]

The determination to avoid compliance, combined with the shrewd activities of territorial representative George Q. Cannon in Congress, had long served the interests of the church. The end of Cannon's tenure in Washington (he served from 1872 to 1882) marked the boundary of resistance as an effective political strategy. Cannon's tireless advocacy of peaceful coexistence rested on theories of localism and respect for privacy, as well as energetic opposition to antipolygamy proposals. His aim was to make Utah all but invisible politically,

A cartoon in the 23 February 1881 issue of *The Daily Graphic* called for the sword, "national authority," to slay polygamy, the "twin relic," completing "the work begun by the Republican Party twenty years ago." Courtesy of Yale University Library.

until an opportune moment arrived to insinuate yet another petition for statehood, which might finally slip through. One opening, the bitter election dispute of 1876, backfired when Democrat Samuel Tilden, to whom Cannon had promised "the gratitude of the [Mormon] people," lost the battle for the presidency to Rutherford B. Hayes.[3]

Cannon's most costly strategy, as it turned out, was to turn to law in the hope of tying up Republicans in the tangles of Supreme Court doctrine. Instead, the Court made the situation materially worse, not only exposing but painfully highlighting Mormon polygamists. Cannon wrote immediately and passionately to demonstrate why *Reynolds* was wrong, claiming that the definition of religion announced by the Court wrested control over the content of religion from majority will and placed it in the hands of potentially ungodly and irreligious civil judges. Outside the faith, Cannon's attack on the Court fell on deaf ears.[4]

Reynolds had galvanized the Eastern antipolygamists, and non-Mormons from Utah were eager to pitch in, too. The battle over the source of constitutional rights and the scope of protection for religious difference was no longer the central issue. New constitutional law had changed the rules of their conflict; now antipolygamists of all stripes could plausibly argue that polygamy and polygamists had no constitutional claim to protection. The Supreme Court's decision translated Mormon Utah from an alternative society (however dangerous) into unconstitutional deviance (with all the resonance of treason such a label carried). Resistance was cast as criminal and undemocratic rather than different or independent. Invisibility in such a climate was no longer sustainable. Not only was Utah more vulnerable after *Reynolds*. Cannon himself became a target.[5]

Antipolygamy legislation poured out of Congress in the 1880s, finally crushing Mormon resistance. Throughout most of the decade, the Mormons' capacity to resist appeared inexhaustible, and infuriating to Republican leaders. As the decade wore on, Republicans' patience wore thin. Exasperation eroded sympathy for Mormon women in particular, who declared their willing participation in a marital system that outsiders claimed was the essence of oppression for women, even as the full force of federal law turned upon their husbands. The erosion of sympathy for the "victims" of the twin relic of barbarism and the implementation of antipolygamy laws in the courts characterized Congress's turn to coercion in the second half of the 1880s. Women, and their role in marriage of all kinds, became the central focus of one powerful strand of antipolygamy law and theory in the 1880s.

The creation and active enforcement of antipolygamy laws on a reluctant population had been gradual, hesitant, and unsteady in the 1870s. The desire to avoid punitive measures, to work toward reconciliation rather than confrontation, compromised many moderate Republicans' support for antipolygamy bills before 1880. As the powerful Senator John Sherman, Republican of Ohio, put it in 1873, Mormons were as likely "misguided" as immoral and if subjected to the leavening force of "civilization" would abandon polygamy. Perhaps the railroad would bring light to the benighted people of Utah, or time and patience might allow polygamy just to fade away. The question of whether exposure to American law and political institutions would "rehabilitate" Mormon men, or whether American law and institutions must actively provide a rehabilitative mechanism, was effectively answered by the Mormon response to the *Reynolds* decision. Resistance goaded antipolygamists after 1879.[6]

Republicans, especially those of reformist stripe, responded to changed legal circumstances with new political strategies. In 1880, President Hayes traveled to Utah accompanied by his wife, Lucy, who was herself the chairwoman of a missionary organization with strong antipolygamist leanings. After returning to Washington, Hayes called forcefully and directly for legislation to impose monogamy on Utah. He denied that time and civilization were eroding polygamy; he charged that polygamy had inevitable and deleterious political consequences: "The political power of the Mormon sect is increasing. It now controls one of our wealthiest and most populous Territories, and is extending steadily into other Territories. Wherever it goes it establishes polygamy and sectarian political power."[7]

Republicans rededicated their party to antipolygamy, and none more effectively than George Edmunds, senator from Vermont, chairman of the Senate Judiciary Committee for two decades, and an able and articulate constitutional lawyer. "Public opinion, acts of Congress, and decisions of the Supreme Court" condemned polygamy and the Mormons who practiced it, Edmunds charged in an article supporting his proposed antipolygamy bill. Unanimity in moral and legal doctrine had been insufficient, he argued, because the Mormons were impervious to any will but that of their leaders. Not only did they continue to assert the rightfulness of polygamy, but they "set up for themselves and maintain[ed] an exclusive political domination in the Territory of Utah, and . . . so frame[d] and administer[ed] the laws as to encourage rather than repress polygamy." One of every three Mormon men, Edmunds charged, had more than one wife. The system had not declined over time—it had mushroomed. The result was a "crime against the political institutions of our country."[8]

Gone were theories of the beneficent effects of railroads or of progress over time or through the advance of civilization. Antipolygamists in Congress were never a monolithic or a conflict-free bunch, but after *Reynolds* they understood that they had acquired constitutional power. They wielded it with increasing vigor, recycling provisions of failed proposals from previous years and introducing new ones. Antipolygamy legislation in the 1880s also played on many current political and economic themes, highlighting especially the relationship between race and gender in national politics. The antipolygamy Edmunds Act of 1882, for example, replicated in crucial ways the penalties imposed on the former Confederacy after Appomattox. Like Reconstruction reforms, antipolygamists insisted, keeping the targets of prosecution out of power would allow the legal system to function smoothly. Edmunds claimed that increased and effective enforcement of antipolygamy laws involved a simple correction in two fundamental points of law: the constitution of juries (that is, keeping those who believed in polygamy off grand and petit juries in polygamy cases) and proof (because the secrecy of polygamous marriages gave Mormon witnesses the ability to deny all knowledge of a given ceremony). Once legal process mirrored substance, Edmunds argued, the rest would be easy: "If we really mean to exterminate polygamy in Utah, it can easily be done by lawful and just means, and without doing any injury even (but rather a good) to the morally innocent persons involved in its practice, and their children."[9]

Put this way, there was little choice. The most partisan Democrats had long been chary of giving statehood to Utah in all but their weakest moments. Cannon recognized this and railed against the entire Democracy as "tender footed," cowardly, and disorganized on the Mormon Question. With public opinion and political tides running against them, many Democrats (including some Southerners) embraced antipolygamy politics in the early 1880s, arguing that federal oversight of the territories included the power to define and enforce the law of sexual relations. This shift in position had a strategic benefit. The implicit contrast between federal power over domestic relations in the territories and federal powerlessness in similar matters in states was itself a potential shield against the central government's interference in the hardening lines of Jim Crow in Southern states. Focusing on the "twin relic" of slavery in Utah, in other words, deflected attention from the aftermath of slavery. Southerners implicitly screened the legal and political disabilities imposed on former slaves as the reinvigorated law and politics of antipolygamy took flight.[10]

"VIOLATORS OF THE LAWS OF THE LAND."
COLUMBIA. "Even (G. Q.) Cannon shall not open these Doors to you."

In the 28 February 1882 issue of *Harper's Weekly*, cartoonist Thomas Nast pictured George Q. Cannon as "attacking" Congress, which was defended by an outraged Columbia. Courtesy of Yale University Library.

Edmunds was attuned to the timing of the bill and the importance of his leadership in crafting the turn to coercion. His proposed legislation included the new offense of "unlawful cohabitation" (living simultaneously with more than one woman as wives, a misdemeanor punishable by six months in prison and a $300 fine) and the exclusion of jurors who believed in polygamy. The bill would also disfranchise all polygamists—strip them of the vote and the right to hold "place of public trust, honor, or emolument." As an admitted polygamist, territorial delegate George Q. Cannon would be disqualified, would no longer be able to take his seat in Congress and work against antipolygamy legislation. Edmunds knew that revocation of suffrage for polygamists would destroy neither the Mormon majority in territorial elections nor the private power of polygamists. It was public display, especially the presence of a spokesman for polygamy in the capital at federal expense, that he and the Republicans targeted.[11]

None of these provisions was unprecedented; they had appeared in earlier failed antipolygamy bills, adapted from the domestic-relations laws of the states and congressional Reconstruction. But they were received in a far different political climate. By 1882, the inclusion of unlawful cohabitation and the exclusion of jurors were unexceptionable, even to Southerners. Suffrage was another matter. Linking suffrage to domestic relations, to loyalty to law dictated from the center, smelled strongly of Reconstruction. Joseph Brown, Confederate governor of Georgia and now senator, said that he had "a little taste of the rule that we now propose to apply to Utah. I stood by the polls, disfranchised and not permitted to vote, while my former slaves, emancipated, walked up and deposited their ballots." Mormon "impropriety with a female" was an act of marriage, not politics, Wilkinson Call of Florida charged. "A man who has been guilty of polygamy . . . may still have a large proprietary interest; he may have and ought to have a very numerous family to protect by his ballot. . . . It is scarcely to be supposed that a man . . . of this character has disqualified himself . . . from casting an intelligent vote."[12]

The connection to politics, of course, was the key concept on which much of antipolygamy theory was based: Republican antipolygamists claimed that political corruption was the wellspring of polygamy's danger to the rest of the nation. The *Reynolds* opinion explicitly drew such a connection, and Republicans insisted on the link between marital and political legitimacy. Without it, Edmunds responded to his Southern senatorial colleagues, the federal government could not "mak[e] the practice of . . . Utah and of its inhabitants conformable to what is essential to the republican safety of every one of the States . . . and of them all under the Union." With only Southern conservatives opposing it, the Edmunds Bill passed the Senate in early 1882 and was quickly seconded by the House. The Edmunds Act tied the revocation of the political franchise to the absence of a supporting marital structure. The act yoked private virtue to public privilege, the ability to deliberate the fate of others (that is, to be a juror) to personal morality, freedom itself to marital structure.

For the first time, federal statutory law expressed openly and directly the conviction that democratic government, national and local, depended on the law of marriage, and on the kinds of power that men had over women, and thus finally on women themselves.[13]

The Edmunds Act also included significant enforcement powers. Twenty years earlier, the last major congressional redefinition of law for Utah, the Morrill Act, had been unenforceable until the *Reynolds* case. Even then, the conviction of George Reynolds rested on a fluke—his second wife had not been coached when the marshal first brought her to testify and had naively admitted her marriage. After her initial, disastrously frank testimony in her husband's first trial, she could "not be found" for his second. Surely other witnesses would be equally difficult to locate. Edmunds designed his revision of criminal law and procedure to make the federal system an effective mechanism of punishment at multiple levels, ensuring that legal process would not be slowed by strategies of resistance. The act provided for an alternate means of punishing even the appearance of plural marriage (that is, "unlawful cohabitation"). A common feature of state domestic-relations law, unlawful cohabitation was the flip side of the presumption of legitimacy for marriage. Those relationships that literally could not be rehabilitated in law (such as bigamous unions) were routinely treated as criminal offenses, matching the legal protections for marriage with legal penalties for its "abuse." Deploying the concept of unlawful cohabitation against Utah, Congress adapted a familiar state-law concept to new circumstances. The resonance of the new law, as well as its coercive powers, was profoundly insulting to Mormons. They contrasted their celestial unions with the typical target of such laws. Unlawful cohabitation described the most irregular, thoughtless sexual liaisons, a far cry from the religious and moral fortitude demanded by the Saints from patriarchs practicing the Principle.[14]

With the passage of the Edmunds Act, the turn to coercion after *Reynolds* carried messages to antipolygamists throughout the country, to Southerners, to states, to other religious groups. It also conveyed clearly the moral responsibility of men—husbands—for the connected integrity of political and personal life. The Edmunds Act was aimed at men: unlawful cohabitation was made by definition gender-specific—the crime of living with two women simultaneously as wives. Jury service was limited to men—the disqualification thus affected men called to sit in judgment upon each other. The franchise, of course, was more complex. Women, while they had the right to vote in Utah, were not allowed to hold office. And of course Cannon was widely believed to be the prime target of disfranchisement as a political strategy. Later in the decade, the revocation of the privilege of political consent for women became a key component of anti-polygamy strategy. But for now the focus on women in Utah was on what George Edmunds called their "moral innocence."

Federal enforcement mechanisms were directed against the most visible patriarchs in Utah. But determined resistance eventually required federal officials in Utah and antipolygamists in the rest of the country to reassess their strategy. Mormons in general were not convinced by the Edmunds Act (as they had not been persuaded by the Morrill Act, or the *Reynolds* opinion) that they should foreswear the practice of the Principle at the behest of Babylon. Those who wavered in the face of punishment learned quickly that stoicism was expected of patriarchs. Mormons' ability to endure—even welcome—condemnation and to evade prosecution challenged the theory that criminal penalties were sufficient for the task.

As Mormon historian Orson Whitney, himself an indicted polygamist, wrote in the early twentieth century, "The Federal courts, and not the mountain fastnesses, became the battleground of the great contest, which was fought out with laws, arguments and judicial rulings in lieu of swords and bayonets." By the mid-1880s the territorial courts were awash in indictments, arraignments, trials, and appeals. The gradually accelerating pace of legal process defined the course of events in Utah, affecting all aspects of life. The "Raid," as it was commonly called by Mormons (non-Mormons in Utah called it the "Crusade"), consumed the territory in the 1880s, raising the cost of resistance and changing the structure and tone of antipolygamy in the territory and around the country.

Mormon witnesses and defendants feared martial law even more than the Raid, despite its attendant sorrows and indignities. Mormon legal strategies were developed with one eye on the threat of army occupation and the other on the promise of statehood. There were benefits to such a strategy, even though the price was also high. The professionalization of Mormon legal arguments and strategies through the long and painful defense of the Principle produced some notable victories, both in Utah and at the Supreme Court.

The records of federal prosecutions in the 1880s, and the stories contained in them, are treasures of social history. There are approximately 2,500 criminal cases in the court records from 1871 to 1896, when statehood was finally achieved. More than 95 percent are for sexual crimes, ranging from fornication to bigamy. This level of enforcement far exceeds anything historians have found elsewhere in the country. It is, literally, unique in American legal history, far exceeding, for example, that of seventeenth-century Massachusetts. Almost every sex offense, and many nonsexual prosecutions for crimes like "illegal voting" and "perjury," involved plural marriage in one way or another.[15]

The sheer size of the Raid was astonishing, and unprecedented. Mormons and their historians remember the pain of a world in which their leaders, and many more ordinary folk, were hunted as common criminals, separated from families and from freedom itself for "living their religion." Frequently, they have focused on the sacrifice demanded, and often willingly given, by the Saints and on the betrayal of tolerance by the rest of the country; on everything, that is, except the way the Raid was actually implemented. The rest of the world, by and large, has forgotten the struggle.

The disruption of lives recorded in the territorial courts is often conveyed only obliquely; but in many cases there is detailed testimony, appeals for mercy—evidence of the devastation wrought by the legal reconstruction of a society. The records also reveal the ebb and flow of legal argument, plea bargaining, and strategizing in general. Behind the riveting individual cases and the (less unique, but no less poignant) general numbers, one can discern the outlines of moves and responses. The strategic choices made by both sides, each attempting to outwit the other, provide the answers to two basic questions posed by the reconstruction of Utah. First, why were there so many cases? Second, what was the role of women in the prosecution of sex crimes in the territory?

The larger scene, the pattern of charge and countercharge, mirrored the bloodless tourney of lawyers. Most of the time the people involved did not employ guns, knives, or hatchets; their weapons were subterfuge and legal process. Still, some players descended into violence, as in 1885 when Sarah Nelson beat two deputies with a broomstick as they attempted to serve process on her husband's other wives. There were structural incentives on both sides to avoid open violence, however. Mormons knew well that they could not win a shooting war. Territorial court personnel also had little interest in turning their jobs over to the army: their employment and their importance in the territory depended on the perception that the court system was the most effective means of dealing with defiance of federal law in Utah.

A typical record contained a complaint, an arrest warrant, a bail record, and an indictment, including the names and residences of wives and the government's witnesses. One judge required his clerk to note the result of a prosecution, including any sentence, on the back of the indictment. If one looks carefully, therefore, there is a great deal of information to be gleaned even from an apparently sparse record. Some records are gold mines of information, with verbatim testimony of witnesses, proposed jury charges, and so on. There is some information about the result (e.g., a guilty plea, a jury verdict, or a dismissal) in about 50 percent of the unlawful cohabitation cases; the precise sentence is included in about half those cases. One can get a pretty good idea of the big picture of the Raid from this sampling.[16]

Of the many cases decided by Charles Schuster Zane, chief justice of the territory and judge of the Third Judicial District (which included Salt Lake), none was more important than that of Rudger Clawson. Clawson was convicted of polygamy and unlawful cohabitation in 1884 after marshals tracked him to a boardinghouse and found him with one of his wives, Lydia Spencer. The *Clawson* case was the first prosecution using a jury in which those who practiced or believed in polygamy had been struck for cause under the Edmunds Act. It was also the first polygamy trial to take place in years.[17]

At sentencing, Zane asked Clawson whether he knew of any reason why judgment should not be pronounced, standard criminal procedure. Clawson's reply—that the laws of his country had come into conflict with the laws of his God and that he would always choose the latter—was soon to become the classic Mormon position. Zane's response was also formulaic. The first humans, Zane said, were promiscuous, until they had gradually progressed to polygamy, and finally to monogamy, which marked the transition from "barbarism and superstition to civilization." He sentenced Clawson to four years in prison and fines of $800, one of the most severe sentences imposed on a polygamist in the Raid. The sentence was made harsher, Zane said, because of Clawson's open defiance of the law.[18]

The *Clawson* case marked the beginning of the Raid. Prosecutors set to work within months of Clawson's conviction. According to the records, there were more than 1,400 indictments for unlawful cohabitation from the time the Edmunds Act was enacted in 1882 through the close of the territorial period in 1896. More than half the total number of 2,500 criminal records for a twenty-six-year period, therefore, were cases of unlawful cohabitation. The prosecutions were heavily concentrated in the years 1886 to 1889—only one indictment each was handed down in 1882, 1883, and 1884. The numbers began to climb in 1885, with 136 indictments, 46 convictions after jury trial, 35 guilty pleas, 3 acquittals after trial, and 11 dismissals. Federal officials brought almost 900 indictments for unlawful cohabitation alone (that is, not counting indictments for polygamy, adultery, fornica-

Judge Charles Zane of the Utah Territorial Court heard the cases of hundreds of indicted Mormon polygamists in the 1880s. Courtesy of Utah State Historical Society.

tion, and miscellaneous offenses such as perjury and illegal voting) between 1886 and 1888.

These astoundingly high numbers represent a reaction to church policy rather than a preconceived commitment to incarcerate each and every polygamist. Shortly after the *Clawson* case, church officials determined that evasion was their best option. They went "Underground," as the process of flight was called by Mormons in another reference to pre–Civil War concepts of freedom and slavery, in early 1885. The Underground was a blow to prosecutorial strategy. Just as the prospect of jailing the entire first presidency of the church appeared possible, the leadership disappeared. The records are full of arrest warrants on which is written in a deputy's painful scrawl that the defendant could not be located after a diligent search. Church leaders (including George Reynolds, who married a third wife while in hiding in 1885) led a fly-by-night existence, sleeping in hay ricks, hiding under floorboards, conducting church business far from Salt Lake. According to one polygamist's diary, those in the Underground (and those who helped them, which translates into the great majority of territorial residents) developed a code to communicate with each another about the presence of deputies, or likely indictments. The code name for Judge Zane, for example, was Nero. The game of hide-and-seek was conducted on a massive scale; federal prosecutors complained that the Mormons controlled the railroad and telegraph systems so completely that their every move was known as soon as they made it. Before they even appeared in a town, they complained, the residents would be aware of their coming and would unite in their refusal to cooperate. The best-laid plans frequently failed to net the fugitives the federal officials sought.[19]

George Q. Cannon, to give the most dramatic example, escaped from federal officials briefly after jumping (he claimed he had fallen) from a train bringing him from Nevada back to Utah. He was recaptured and brought to Salt Lake under military guard, only to forfeit the astronomical $45,000 bail bond set by Judge Zane and disappear once again. Most higher echelon church officials remained underground for several years.[20]

The exception was Apostle Lorenzo Snow, captured in November 1885. He had been hiding in a specially constructed room underneath his living room floor. Snow was convicted on three indictments for unlawful cohabitation—each count for a calendar year. This policy of dividing cohabitation into discrete periods was popularly known as "segregation" and quickly became a favorite tactic of federal prosecutors. Segregation allowed for multiple-count indictments, and thus for the lengthy punishment of notorious offenders, since each offense carried a maximum $300 fine and six months' imprisonment. This practice greatly increased the potential punishment for unlawful cohabitation, consistent with the instructions of U.S. attorney general Augustus Garland, who advised his underlings in Utah in 1885 that "[t]he practice of polygamy may be more successfully met by the conviction of large offenders than by the conviction of every offender in the community."[21]

As a legal strategy, segregation countered the Underground; even if the government could not effectively prosecute the entire church leadership, segregation allowed prosecutors to seek severe penalties for those who were caught. Some U.S. attorneys used the multicount indictment, and others procured separate indictments for each six-, nine-, or twelve-month period. One unlucky "cohab" received a nineteen-month sentence; five (including Snow) were given eighteen months, one was given fifteen months, and two were given twelve months.

These sentences, and the prosecutorial practice upon which they were based, were invalidated in 1887 by a major victory for the defense bar, and a substantial setback for prosecutors. Appealing his conviction, Lorenzo Snow won at the U.S. Supreme Court in an opinion holding that unlawful cohabitation was a continuous offense rather than one that could validly be considered divisible by periods. Segregation was henceforth prohibited, and prisoners serving more than six months on unlawful cohabitation convictions were immediately released. As Orson Whitney put it, the decision "fell like a funeral pall upon the crusaders." Frustrated by the Underground, and without the benefit of segregation, the reconstruction of Utah flowed into less august channels. The tedium of numerous and frequently unsuccessful investigations daunted many officials.[22]

Most prosecutions were of less notorious polygamists. That population was both more vulnerable, because it was less able to call upon the machinery of the church and the Underground and more likely to be distressed by serving time in prison and fines. The policy behind wholesale prosecution is evident: if the government could not have spectacular trials of church leaders, could not sentence infamous polygamists to long jail terms, it would grind down the practice by catching every fish in the pond, however small and obscure. The combined effects of the Underground and the Supreme Court's disapproval of segregation meant that federal officials had to cast their nets into scattered and remote settlements where outsiders (especially federal marshals) were unwelcome. The small-time patriarch, often a farmer with two or three wives, was now exposed to federal justice. The suffering that such prosecutions imposed on Mormon families was undeniable; many officials dismissed such misery with a callousness that betrays the depth of the conflict between two systems of law, faith, and marriage.[23]

Such a process was also slow and expensive. And in many cases it was unsuccessful. Even those polygamists who could not afford to leave their families for lengthy periods found that the effective early warning system created by a sympathetic populace meant that they could often evade arrest, even if only temporarily. If the "cohab" held out long enough, there was a good chance after 1890 that the indictment would be dismissed. Lot Darney's case, for example, was dismissed in 1892, along with nineteen others, on the motion of the prosecution. Darney, who had been indicted for unlawful cohabitation in 1886, was formally discharged "for the reason that in each [of the twenty cases dismissed that day] it is impossible to secure evidence sufficient to justify a conviction, and because, in the judgment of said District Attorney, the ends of justice do not require the trial thereof."[24]

The Underground, as an extralegal strategy, therefore, was effective, though it exposed the less mobile to prosecution and incarceration. It is possible, of course, that the increase in prosecutions was anticipated by the leadership. Many Mormons argued that theirs were crimes of conscience, for which punishment was inappropriate in the first place and prison sentences a patent violation of justice. Church officials may have hoped that the public would be outraged by prisons peopled by humble and otherwise law-abiding men. It is also possible that Mormons counted on winning a war of attrition, forcing the government into prolonged and costly prosecutions while the church leadership watched and waited in hiding, holding out until the public and the government wearied of this legal guerrilla war.

A second defense strategy, which spanned the spectrum from combativeness, to "forgetfulness," to actual falsehood, was also widely practiced, especially by Mormon women. As one contemporary put it: "The effect of [testifying in polygamy cases] upon the minds of modest wives and maidens may readily be imagined. That they should be averse to appearing in this class of cases, and seek to protect themselves with hatchets or any other weapons against those who came to drag them before courts and juries to be interrogated upon subjects of this kind, is not surprising." Here in a nutshell is the contemporary Mormon spin on the federal courts: the abuse of women was a product rather than a cause of law enforcement and a justification for evasive, even violent, tactics by women when confronted with federal officials.[25]

Mormon women's most common approach to the service of a summons was not to use hatchets. Instead, they crafted an adaptation of the Underground's policy of flight. Those who could not hide, lied. Mormon witnesses, especially the wives and local leaders who were suspected of having performed or witnessed plural marriage ceremonies, would not provide meaningful testimony. In a few early cases, before they learned that forgetting provided more protection than silence, wives were jailed for contempt of court after they refused to answer questions. John Zane described such a contempt situation in his father's courtroom: "The witness was an innocent-faced, red-cheeked, buxom looking young woman, who had been told what she must do. . . . [T]he judge . . . told her how idle it was for her to suppose that she could defy her country's laws. The witness was now in tears. Then . . . he referred in scathing language to a man who would lead a young woman into such a forlorn situation . . . that she could not state whether she was married or not, . . . where she must suffer imprisonment . . . to shield him from his crime." The description shows how an antipolygamist interpreted the situation, placing the blame for the misery of the woman on Mormon men, in stark contrast to the Mormons' interpretation of the same course of events. However one characterizes it, outright refusal to testify was a costly strategy both for the government (which had no space to house female prisoners) and, of course, for Mormon women.[26]

Within months of this episode in Judge Zane's courtroom, Mormon witnesses, especially wives, resurrected a practice first tried in the *Reynolds* trials in the mid-1870s. Instead of refusing to answer questions, witnesses simply "forgot" the material elements of crimes associated with plural marriage. The records are full of testimony that meets this description, in all kinds of cases. Members of an accused polygamist's family would deny all knowledge of their husband's or father's other wives, could not remember the last time they had seen him, and did not know where the other families lived, even if they all resided in a tiny village. Bishops forgot whether they had performed marriage ceremonies, could not remember whether they had ever heard that records were kept of marriages. Frustrated federal prosecutors railed against this annoyingly effective tactic: "[Mormons] study the *art* of forgetting what they have seen and heard, and so it often happens that a Mormon . . . goes upon the witness stand, and testifies that he cannot remember having performed a marriage ceremony that took place within a week past. . . . They all have wonderful powers of forgetting—I have never found one who had a retentive memory when a polygamy case was on trial." In legal terms, such forgetfulness is perjury. Like the Underground, it was an extralegal strategy, but it, too, was successful in many cases. Polygamy prosecutions were especially unworkable with forgetful witnesses undermining the government's ability to prove a marriage had taken place. There was an additional payoff for forgetful witnesses: even if obfuscation did not result in the dismissal of charges against the defendant, at least his families (or his friends) were not implicated in his conviction.[27]

Often, prosecutors claimed that actual falsehoods, rather than just creative forgetfulness, was involved. In a few such cases, women were prosecuted for perjury. Marintha Loveridge, for example, was charged with perjury in 1887 after she testified at her father's trial for unlawful cohabitation that she could not remember ever meeting his other wife, and had never heard it reported in the family that he had another wife. Several cases involved attempts by wives to exonerate their husbands by claiming that the illegal act at issue (either a marriage ceremony or unlawful cohabitation) had occurred more than three years before the initiation of the prosecution, and thus was barred by the statute of limitations. Often the question was the age of the youngest child. A child born two years and three months before the date of an indictment would allow the plural wife to claim plausibly that she had had no contact with her husband for three years. There are many cases in which the age of the youngest child was predictably three years old, although no one, even the mother, could ever remember precisely. One woman who made such a claim was convicted of perjury after a jury trial, although there is no record of a sentence in her case.[28]

A second case illustrates the danger of such evasive or untruthful answers for women, and the fragility of the uneasy truce that existed for decades between Mormons and territorial officials. Agnes McMurrin, one of Royal B. Young's wives, claimed in 1885 that she had married him in 1881, rather than 1882. The three-year statute of limitations would have precluded Young's punishment for polygamy if McMurrin's testimony was correct. One Mormon observer claimed that McMurrin was later charged with perjury in part because the prosecutor was convinced she had lied to the grand jury, but primarily because she had resisted arrest "with hatchet in hand" until her husband had arrived and counseled her to submit. Young was convicted of both polygamy and unlawful cohabitation after a jury trial in 1885. He was convicted again of three counts of unlawful cohabitation in 1886.[29]

The perjury case against McMurrin highlights the vulnerability of Mormon women. At one level, the requirement that they appear in court to testify about the intimate details of their married lives threatened their very self-identity as respectable women of the nineteenth century. Most important, however, the actions of these women, who were courageous from the perspective of their coreligionists but contemptible to outsiders, challenged their status as passive victims.

By the mid-1880s, Mormon women were revealed as active participants in the perpetuation of polygamy and its attendant "vices" (untruthfulness, for example, was widely perceived to be characteristic of all Mormons). They could hardly be treated as innocent victims. Especially among antipolygamist women, however, there was considerable resistance to the notion that Mormon women were *really* so deeply committed to polygamy and the church. For example, some non-Mormon women in Utah still argued that plural wives would abandon their marriages if only they could, and even built an elaborate "Industrial Home" to house escaped wives and train them as domestic servants. Yet others embraced the turn to coercion. They argued that Mormon women could not be trusted to know the evils of their situation. At best, they were victims of delusion, in need of forcible rehabilitation. To federal officials, and to many antipolygamists by the mid-1880s, Mormon women required punishment as well as pity. Their very evasiveness, both physical (running away) and verbal (perjury, "forgetting"), translated Mormon women from victims into moral agents, tainting them with criminality.[30]

Territorial officials importuned Congress for tools to punish Mormon wives, claiming that the women were the lynchpin of the system; that women lied and cheated and ran away as often as the men; that they were complicitous, in other words, in their own sexual enslavement. Many antipolygamist activists outside Utah also shifted in the 1880s from calling for the liberation of Mormon women to unhappily admitting that Mormon women were just possibly part of the problem. The intransigence of women in Utah was confirmed by their apparent desire to shield their own oppressors. Leading Mormon women held rallies opposing the Raid and even traveled to Washington on public relations tours in desperate defense of the faith.

"These are strange times," charged popular lecturer Kate Field in 1886, "when a female Mormon lobby asks Congress to give to Utah the liberty of self-degradation!" As the recalcitrance of Mormon women battered theories of their involuntary sexual servitude, the erosion of sympathy highlighted other manifestations of women's consent in Utah, and the connections of such "consent" to marital integrity. Many antipolygamists capitalized on the women's resistance to hammer home the links between public and private power. To antipolygamists such as Field, Utah was the negative illustration of the vital role of the law of marriage in establishing and then protecting legitimate structures of authority. She called for the "dynamite of law" to blow up Mormon polygamy and the power of the church that sustained and justified its practice.[31]

Early in 1886, the Senate began debate on a second Edmunds bill. The new proposal would provide for the registration of all marriages; establish the crimes of adultery, fornication, and incest; create a right of dower—or the statutory right for a widow to claim a portion of her husband's estate—for first wives; revoke woman suffrage; and escheat

In her popular lecture "The Mormon Monster," antipolygamist Kate Field called upon Congress to use "the dynamite of law" to destroy Mormon polygamy. Courtesy of Princeton University Library.

extensive church property to the government (this final provision is treated at length in Chapter 6). Polygamy, argued antipolygamist congressmen and lobbyists, could be finally undermined only by the imposition of positive law. They insisted that the sole effective remedy was the transplantation of the marriage laws of the states to Utah Territory. Edmunds's new bill would impose on the Saints the protective legal hedge around marriage that defined and insulated the private governance of households in all the states and territories but Utah. For the first time, this new law would also replicate the punitive aspects of marriage law for women involved in unlawful relationships. The protection of first wives through establishing the crime of adultery and imposing the protections of dower (and, arguably, through incest provisions, which addressed the practice of marrying sisters, a niece, or even a mother and daughter) was matched by provisions for punishing plural wives as "fornicators." Fornication, traditionally associated with promiscuity and even prostitution, was the standard device in the states for punishment of "loose" women—thus implicitly a protection for respectable women's legitimate relations. Based on the theory that polygamy affected the political legitimacy of the women's as well as men's franchise, the new law would also silence the explicit political voice of all the women in the territory by revoking their right to vote.[32]

The bill originally proposed by Edmunds also illustrates the importance of traditional rules of state law, hived off and imported into federal legislation. As Senator Edmunds first wrote the bill, it would have compelled a first wife to testify against her husband in a case involving polygamy. Under state law in the early nineteenth century, marital unity as well as the prerogative of husbands explained why a wife could not testify either against or in support of her husband—to allow such testimony would be to recognize the distinction between husband and wife—in law presumed to be "one flesh." There were occasions, of course, when courts and legislatures shattered the fiction of unity, especially when the rule was belied by the facts. When there was no longer any family whose "peace" would be preserved by the fiction, or when abuse reached extraordinary levels, judges routinely invaded the privacy of the relationship. A man who savagely beat his wife or, "with brutish feelings, introduced lewd women with her into his household" had trespassed against the sanctity and inviolability of marriage that would otherwise protect him from her testimony. Woman's rights advocates were perennial critics of the rule, too, arguing that a separate legal identity was precisely what marriage law should ensure (rather than presume away) for women.[33]

In Edmunds's formulation, the introduction of plural wives mirrored the traditional justification for disaggregation of the fictional unity of husband and wife. Despite his lawyerly arguments about the justification for the abolition of the rule in polygamy cases, Edmunds was met with a barrage of protest from marital conservatives and with only lukewarm support from his more liberal colleagues in the Senate. Marital unity, however pockmarked by legislative reform and judicial construction by the late nineteenth century, retained significant religious and cultural purchase. Indeed, to many of its critics, polygamy was a "problem" *because* it divided a husband into many parts, violating the mandate for one flesh that "God and nature had established." Edmunds, whose bill arguably would undermine the sacred unity of the one relationship in Utah that antipolygamists believed merited legal protection (that is, the marriage of the "legal," or first, wife), ran into a buzz saw. His colleagues disputed his interpretation of state law and rested on the sanctity of marital privacy. An amendment proposed by Senator Joseph Brown of Georgia would have allowed a wife's testimony with her husband's express consent and only on matters not deemed "confidential at common law." This provision would have prohibited outright testimony about private relations between a husband and his first wife, the woman presumed to be most injured by his polygamy. The proposal failed in the Senate but was reintroduced in the House and became part of the conference committee's final report to both houses.[34]

As enacted, the final text of the Edmunds-Tucker Act provided that the wife of a man accused of polygamy or unlawful cohabitation "shall not be compelled to testify . . . without the consent of the husband" and further prohibited testimony on "confidential" matters altogether. Edmunds did not publicly defend his earlier proposal. In so restricting the testimony of first wives in Utah, many antipolygamists less learned in the law than Edmunds believed that they protected and respected marriage in the same ways that the states did. By replicating in Utah the laws that they believed made marriage the "foundation-stone of every Christian society" in their home states, antipolygamists reassured themselves that their own homes were "in the lead of progress in the Christian era." Antipolygamists also solidified the notion that the laws of the states were essential to the federal as well as local government, "the fair and pure sisterhood of these American states."[35]

The regularization of marriage law for Utah thus played on and highlighted many concerns outside the territory, especially worries and theories about the permanence (and permeability) of marriage. Particularly poignant and cogently argued was the connection between woman suffrage and the survival of monogamy. The forcible imposition of monogamy on Utah explicitly tied the legal mandate for union in marriage ("one flesh"), patrolled by criminal and civil laws such as those regarding adultery, dower, and spousal testimony, to the assumption that a separate political voice for women would undermine marriage. The woman's franchise in Utah raised a host of doubts and fears, none of which were entirely separable from the issue of polygamy, but all of which implicitly raised questions about the consequences of the woman's vote anywhere. The franchise, which by 1886 had existed in Utah for fifteen years, drew attention to the relationship of the vote to marriage for all women. The debate over the woman's vote in Utah took place against a backdrop of debate elsewhere in the country. Polygamy, Kate Field, George Edmunds, and many other antipolygamists claimed, was the mockery of marriage. It also made a mockery of woman suffrage in Utah, they argued, where voting privileges for women had not led to a change in marriage practice. Instead, claimed Edmunds and even some advocates of woman suffrage for the states, the women's vote in Utah had only increased the power of the church and its hold on political power in the territory.

Antipolygamists could safely condemn the woman's vote in Utah (one antipolygamist quipped that "woman suffrage in Utah means only woman suffering") and by implication, woman suffrage everywhere because by the mid-1880s almost everyone was agreed that it had failed to emancipate Mormon women. Many conservative and moderate Americans treated Utah as a test case for woman suffrage. Outside Utah, suffragists claimed in the 1870s that any attempt to revoke the "franchise [for] the women of Utah, [would be] a movement in *aid* of polygamy." Women in Utah were to prove to the rest of the nation that their votes would be more thoughtfully cast than those of their husbands. They would legislate their own freedom and moral redemption. The Utah experiment was thus freighted from the start with an impossible cultural and political burden.[36]

Instead of demonstrating the benefits of woman suffrage, however, the vote for women in Utah played into the hands of those who opposed suffrage as an attack on marriage. Tales of degraded and browbeaten women driven to the polls by the wagon load catered to stereotypes, undermining respect for women as voters. Women in Utah had "no adequate political expression," conceded proponents of woman suffrage, they were the mere "catspaw of the priesthood." Their political participation, in other words, was vitiated by a marital system that antipolygamists believed contradicted their most basic civil liberties.[37]

Liberal Republicans who had supported woman suffrage outside

FEMALE SUFFRAGE.
Wouldn't it put just a little too much power into the hands of Brigham Young, and his tribe?

Opponents of woman suffrage for Utah accused Mormon polygamists of attempting to increase their own power by dictating how their wives voted. From *Frank Leslie's Illustrated Newspaper*, 5 October 1869. Courtesy of General Research Collection, New York Public Library, Astor, Lenox and Tilden Foundations.

Utah in the late 1860s were discomfited by Mormon appropriation of the idea. The *New York Times*, which had supported the enfranchisement of women in Utah as part of federal legislation, argued after the Female Suffrage Bill passed the Utah legislature in 1870 that "the downfall of polygamy is too important to be imperiled by experiments in woman suffrage." Bills and resolutions calling for disfranchisement, styled as "purification" of elections in Utah, were introduced in Congress at almost every session.[38]

Mormon rhetoric exacerbated the criticism. A widely publicized

At the urging of Angie Newman and other antipolygamy women in Utah, the massive Industrial Christian Home was built in the late 1880s with federal funds. They argued that the home would serve as a refuge for "escaped" plural wives, who could then be trained as domestic servants. The home, which never attracted more than a few dozen residents, was closed in the early 1890s, and the building was eventually torn down. Courtesy of Utah State Historical Society.

interview given to a San Francisco newspaper by a Mormon bishop played on Eastern fears: "The women of Utah vote, and they never desert the colors of the church; they vote for the tried friends of the church. . . . In some great political crisis the two present political parties will bid for our support. Utah will be admitted as a polygamous State, and the other Territories we have peacefully subjugated will be admitted also. We will then hold the balance of power, and will dictate to the country." Easterners heard the threat and condemned woman suffrage in Utah.[39]

The problem became acute in 1880 when non-Mormon women in Utah began publishing the *Anti-Polygamy Standard*, a newspaper dedicated to "every happy wife and mother" and asking for "sympathy, prayers and efforts to free her sisters from this degrading bondage." The paper took an early editorial position against woman suffrage for the territory, proclaiming that "moral and mental liberty should take precedence [over] political enfranchisement." In Utah, the editors claimed, the franchise tightened women's bonds, "increas[ing] the spread of polygamy and the consequent degradation of woman, to make them, if possible, greater slaves than before." In 1884, Woman's Christian Temperance Union activist Angelina French Newman joined the growing clamor against suffrage for Mormon women. Newman submitted a petition that had been circulated among women attending Methodist Home Missionary Society meetings. The petition, which called for the revocation of woman suffrage, received an astronomical 250,000 signatures. Even the renowned suffragist Susan B. Anthony was reduced to arguing that "suffrage is as much of a success for the Mormon women as for the men." By the time Anthony spoke, the popular image of Mormon women had come full circle. They were no longer thought of as likely sources of a new monogamous liberty as they had been in the prosuffrage vision of the 1870s. Instead, they were conceived as objects of reform.[40]

Moderate Republicans led the campaign to "redeem" the political system of Utah by purging it of the votes of Mormon women. A few prosuffrage Republicans and woman's rights activists argued against sacrificing principle to expediency. And a few Southern Democrats, all of whom opposed woman suffrage as a matter of federal policy, argued that suffrage was a local matter and should be left to states and territories to deal with as they saw fit. But overwhelming sentiment was in favor of revocation. By 1886, George Edmunds had successfully translated the franchise into a bondage from which Mormon women, if only their true voices could be heard, would beg to be freed. His bill, Edmunds said, would "relieve the Mormon women of Utah from the slavehood of being obliged to exercise a political function which is to keep her in a state of degradation." The franchise became a cruel joke, in this view. The women's vote in Utah played into traditional theories that the best and truest "protection" of married women was by their husbands, not political power. Women who consented to a legitimate marriage, said many conservative theorists, had made their choice and should thereafter defer to the political voice of their husbands, who would "represent" the interest of the household at the polls. Woman suffrage for Utah seemed to validate the theory that women *could* have no independent political voice, or alternatively that religious difference meant that Mormon women were as guilty as Mormon men. In either case, many antipolygamists claimed, woman suffrage was based on an erroneous understanding of the vote in Utah. The nineteenth century's most important test of the woman's franchise became a victory for defenders of a vision of marriage in which women's power to consent was both greatly valued and tightly confined.[41]

The role of consent in the nineteenth century was complex and ambiguous—implicated in the Civil War, in Unionism, in the very concept of national authority. Marriage and wage labor were the essential consensual rights that Americans subsumed under the "freedom of contract" label. They were also the voluntary legal relations denied to slaves. By the mid-1880s, Republican antipolygamists had long argued that the marital half of the slavery equation was replicated for women in Utah. Like slaves, they charged, Mormon women were denied the central legal privilege of women. Mormon husbands' "tyranny" undermined women's ability to contract valid marriages. Polygamy could never be truly voluntary, according to antipolygamists, despite the delusions of the women involved in plural marriage.[42]

Consent, manifested in a series of contractual agreements (the "social contract," the marital contract, the employment contract), was so closely identified with freedom and civic responsibility that lack of consent described lack of freedom. In the nineteenth century, theories of consent and contract traveled across venues and genres, coloring the analysis not only of polygamy and slavery but also of poverty, prostitution, and free labor. The "will theory" of contract, for example, the notion that there must be some "meeting of the minds" to form an enforceable agreement, was peculiarly a creature of the nineteenth century. The will theory implied that contracts were based on positive choice—that a contract was the child of consent.[43]

The picture was significantly more complicated than such cozy theories presume. Opposition to Mormon polygamy highlighted the ways that consent was not *really* there in many aspects of marriage, or labor, or politics. Consent, although the trigger for valid relationships of authority, was not necessary to sustain such a relationship. The emphasis on consent (voluntary *entry* into the relationship) should not be confused with voluntarism *within* the relationship. Marriage, a domestic relation created by consent, was neither negotiated as to terms, nor could it be terminated at will, argued conservative theorists of marriage; the essence and the central meaning of marriage was its permanence, its irrevocability once consensually celebrated.[44]

The tensions between marriage and politics, and the connection of consent theory to both, were played out in antipolygamy thought. Frequently, antipolygamists were as critical of the notion that one could revoke consent to an on-going marriage as they were of the fraudulent procurement of consent at the outset. In this they shared a fundamental opposition to divorce with defenders of traditional marriage, many of whom joined the ranks of antipolygamists. A sermon delivered by Brigham Young in 1856 (long before his marriage and eventual divorce from Ann Eliza [Webb] Young) figured for decades in antipolygamist arguments: " 'My wives have got to do one of two things—either round up their shoulders and endure the afflictions of this world and live their religion, or . . . leave. . . . I will go into heaven alone, rather than have scratching and fighting around me. I will set all at liberty. What! first wife too? Yes, I will liberate you all.' " That Brigham Young even contemplated "liberating"—that is, divorcing—his wives for failing to endure their "afflictions" silently was as shocking as the existence of polygamy. Shocking, but not surprising. Many antipolygamists maintained even in the late 1880s that no woman *could* really consent to a system as fundamentally contrary to her interests as polygamy, thus Mormon women's participation must be forced. Lax exit (divorce) from marriage, when paired with the presumption of forced entry, appeared as a coherent whole, two sides of a corrupt coin. Antipolygamists charged that easy divorce among Mormons devalued consent where it was vital, allowing it to rule where most inappropriate. Southern Democrats countered such statements with claims that more people in New England practiced "consecutive polygamy" through divorce and remarriage than Mormons practiced simultaneous polygamy. New Englanders would do better to cleanse their own immoral jurisdictions, charged Joseph Brown of Georgia in debates over the new Edmunds bill in the mid-1880s, than to meddle in the affairs of Utah, as they had in the South.[45]

The connection between prohibition of polygamy and advocacy of stringent divorce laws was widely accepted in the North as well as the South. One clergyman, arguing that divorce and polygamy came from the same "allegorical lake," asked rhetorically, " 'What made Mormon polygamy *possible*, in this country?' The . . . truest answer is, 'the *unchastity* that makes divorces easy, and popular.' " Antidivorce activists added to their popular appeal by calling divorce "the polygamic principle" or "polygamy on the installment plan." Whatever treated marriage as permeable, vulnerable to whim and caprice, they argued, was cut from the same cloth.[46]

What, one might ask, had happened to the principle of consent? Hadn't the Mormons at least gotten half the equation right, allowing miserable marriages to be dissolved at will? In most contracts, one could buy out of the agreement. The marital contract described by antidivorce theorists, however, was impossible to breach without committing a crime (that is, without adultery or, in some proposals, extraordinarily violent domestic abuse). This is where "liberty" and "consent," argued conservative antipolygamists, should be distinguished from license. Freedom of contract contained the power to participate in domestic relations, not to restructure them at will. The marriage contract was drafted by the state and triggered by the consent of the parties but not constructed by their idiosyncrasies. Like other political structures in a democracy, according to conservatives and many moderate defenders of marriage, the creation of a marital union was not only an exercise of individual liberty by husband and wife. It was also an exercise of sovereignty, which rested in the whole people. Exit was a matter for which the will of the spouses was necessary but not sufficient.[47]

Judge Noah Davis of New York, in an 1884 essay addressing the subject of divorce, began with freedom of contract: "[The state] should require nothing but the one essential element; and that is, the consent to the matrimonial contract of parties capable in law of making it." In the next breath, Davis explained that consent to end a valid marriage was not enough; "they have no power or right to annul [the contract] without the consent of the State." Furthermore, the state had a vital interest in the "life-unity of one man and one woman," contrary to the spurious individualism of easy divorce. This selfishness, charged Davis, "is the culminating thought of the harem. It has been the curse of woman, making her the slave and man the master, . . . bought and sold at the price of lust." Divorce and polygamy, so the theory went, were twisted strands, already strangling society through the destruction of marriage. If only the country had the clarity of vision to perceive the danger. The "price of lust," as Davis put it, was the treatment of sexual relations as if they were properly subject to negotiation, exchange, sale. Polygamy bore a strong resemblance, in this view, to prostitution. Antipolygamists, who had for decades called polygamy "white slavery," were among the earliest to connect concepts of the purchase of slaves to illicit "traffic in women." Both polygamy and prostitution, they argued, allowed men to purchase women (and, of course, women to treat their sexuality as subject to negotiation and temporary alliances).[48]

Arguments about the evils of divorce did not go unanswered, although it was far more popular to defend lifelong monogamy than to risk the taint of being seen to support polygamy. Elizabeth Cady Stanton inveighed against "marriage as a compulsory bond enforced by law and rendered perpetual by that means," charging that all forms of coercion replicated slavery. Most suffragists avoided the question of divorce raised by Stanton for both strategic and philosophical reasons. By the 1880s, the political price of the "anti-marriage" label, always substantial, became virtually unbearable. As one antipolygamist put it, the "sacred atmosphere of Christian homes" was a trope that only grew in stature as antipolygamy gathered momentum in the 1880s. Even activists Susan Anthony and Belva Lockwood became, as one Mormon adviser lamented, "very defensive about their loyalty to monogamy" and cautious about supporting Mormons.[49]

The marriages that Utah promoted, according to antipolygamists, combined with the territory's apparently boundless self-declared authority to dissolve unions created elsewhere, exacerbated tensions over religious difference and local sovereignty. As one critic of liberal divorce put it, "Mormons," like "feminists, Fourierites, Spiritualists, Perfectionists, socialists, anarchists and free lovers," advocated matching their spiritual infidelity with marital infidelity. Such a lineup not only reveals the widespread misunderstanding of the tenets of Mormonism and other dissenting groups, it also reveals fears about allowing legal difference by jurisdiction. By introducing disruptive religious and political ideas into the federal system, charged conservatives, proponents of liberal divorce would erode the permanence (and perhaps even the existence, in the most extreme formulations) of marriage in the rest of the nation.[50]

Antipolygamists and their antisuffragist allies had good reason to play the divorce card. Alarm at spiraling divorce rates prompted several states to repeal omnibus divorce clauses in the 1870s, but divorce rates grew swiftly and steadily from 1860 to 1880. Liberty, argued antidivorce theorists, could not long tolerate such decay. Theodore Woolsey, president of Yale, pointed to the effects of rising divorce and marital infidelity on one flourishing civilization, ancient Rome. In a series of popular magazine articles and then a book devoted to the topic, Woolsey claimed that the Roman Empire perished from within, eroded by divorce. His investigation of history, Woolsey insisted, provided a powerful example of the price paid by a system that downplayed the political importance of family life.[51]

The West was especially troublesome to those concerned about the breakdown of marriage. Indiana was the earliest Western "divorce mill," but other Western states and territories offered lax residency requirements and omnibus divorce clauses in the 1870s and 1880s. Antipolygamists insisted repeatedly that Utah was the worst-case example. The territorial legislature in 1852 enacted a divorce statute that only required the petitioner to demonstrate that he or she was "a resident or wishes to become one." Utah's divorce law also included an omnibus clause that allowed a divorce "when it shall appear to the satisfaction and conviction of the Court, that the parties cannot live in peace and union together, and that their welfare requires a separation," making Utah the most permissive of any American jurisdiction. Probably designed to allow converts whose spouses did not become Mormons to obtain a quick civil divorce and remarry within the faith, the statute was construed outside Utah as evidence of Mormon disregard for marital integrity. As one commentator put it, the statute gained "instant notoriety" for the territory "among Americans concerned about the decline of marriage and the family." The "slimy folds" of polygamy not only allowed one man to marry "sisters, mothers, and daughters," one outraged congressmen railed, but "in order that no element of . . . loathsomeness may be wanting, it includes facility of divorce. . . . As well might religion be invoked to protect cannibalism or infanticide."[52]

Travelers to Utah commented on the ease of divorce in the territory, shoring up the theory that divorce, like polygamy and woman suffrage, was a peculiarity of Mormonism. Indeed, scholars have concluded that divorce was more common among nineteenth-century Mormons in Utah than in other jurisdictions. The rate of divorce in Utah was extraordinarily high, especially when divorces in polygamous marriages (granted exclusively by ecclesiastical courts because of the illegality of plural marriage after 1862) are included in the total. Utah was a "consent divorce" jurisdiction, charged antipolygamists in the 1880s, using a label that implied all the disunionism they argued was associated with polygamous marriage.[53]

The problem had grown worse in the 1870s after the completion of the transcontinental railroad. The territory's residency standard allowed Eastern lawyers to flood local courts with divorce petitions. The practice was so common, according to U.S. labor commissioner Carroll Wright, that lawyers used forms on which preprinted intention to become a resident and incompatibility allegations required only names, dates, and localities to be filled in. The unbearably tangled issues raised by Ann Eliza Young's divorce suit against Brigham Young also shocked outsiders. There was the delicate question of whether an illicit union—that is, a polygamous marriage that to outsiders was presumptively nonconsensual in the first place, at least on the wife's part—should entitle an estranged "wife" to alimony. This prospect raised the specter of multiple and precipitous marriages and divorces, with consequences spreading far beyond the boundaries of any single territory. Tales of abuse of process flowed into the press and courts outside Utah.[54]

By the 1880s, as concern about divorce rates preoccupied the rest of the country, the ease of divorce in Utah was a handy counter to arguments made by Mormons and their defenders that "consecutive polygamy" was practiced by Easterners who divorced and then remarried, whereas in Mormon society, divorces were "unknown." Kate

What is the use of Mormonism, when a man can change his wife whenever he likes?—*Graetz.*

Popular equation of divorce and polygamy depicted men as seeking "variety" through a corrupt and compliant legal system. "What is the use of Mormonism," queried a bemused cartoonist, "when a man can change his wife whenever he likes?" From *Puck*, 13 February 1884. Courtesy of Yale University Library

Field, for example, told of an "excellent, kind[-]hearted woman," whose husband "got a divorce without [her] knowledge." Wives in Utah, Field argued, were powerless to prevent their husbands' polygamy, or even to be sure they were still married. Not only were the courts corrupt, she insisted, but Mormon leaders profited by granting church divorces. Brigham Young, Field claimed, "drove a thriving business by untieing his own people."[55]

A "United States marriage law" was to be the cure. This notion, popularized in a *New York Tribune* editorial, called for uniform marriage and divorce laws to protect American society from corruption from within. Divorce was sapping the nation's moral strength, the *Tribune* charged; the source of the corrosion was in the West, where free-love advocate Robert Dale Owen had first turned Indiana into a divorce haven for freethinkers, and then Utah, where polygamy and divorce went hand in hand. These areas, antipolygamists charged, lured men from other jurisdictions who might otherwise remain married and thus politically responsible. Utah especially revealed the weaknesses of the federal system and created a mandate for national action.[56]

Arguments about the necessity of protecting marriages against unilateral dissolution also highlighted the currents flowing between marriage and race in the second half of the nineteenth century. During the Civil War, Unionists argued and fought for the proposition that a constitution, like a marriage, was more than a compact formed with the possibility of dissolution in view. As President Buchanan put it bluntly in 1860, the national union was not "a mere voluntary association . . . to be dissolved at pleasure by any one of the contracting parties."[57]

Abraham Lincoln memorialized the quandary in 1858 in a revealing metaphor, as applicable to marriage as to government: "A house divided against itself cannot stand." The "house" that became such a powerful metaphor for political union was (in theory) built by the voluntary association of citizens whose consent transformed the nature of their relationship. There was no going back, said Unionists, even if the initial consent had evaporated—the "bonds of affection," as they referred to the political ties among the states, could not unilaterally be sundered. The war was in this sense a rejection of the claim that revocation of consent could accomplish the same objective as absence of consent at the outset.[58]

The irrevocability of such marital and political unions stood in stark contrast to the emphasis that Unionists placed on the necessity of consent to their creation. An act of will—of love, of trust, at the very least of hope—was isolated in the nineteenth century as traditional hierarchies collapsed or were reconfigured as consensually based. The duty to make a good bargain (rather than the ability to get out of a bad one) led defenders of political and marital permanence to dismiss with callousness the erosion of emotional commitment. Catharine Beecher put the problem succinctly when she charged that unhappy wives and employees should have chosen husbands and masters more carefully, for their voluntary actions subordinated them to unworthy men. Similarly, implied Beecher, foolish wives were protected by men whose choice had placed them in positions of authority. The "right" to choose created an "obligation" to live with the consequences of the choice, so the argument went. The rights and obligations of constituent parts of the country were central to Unionist thinking in the Civil War era, of course, and justified the discipline of Southerners and their states after Appomattox. The similarity between the "house" that Lincoln described and the marital union was picked up at the end of the war, as well. The "national household" became a favorite trope in congressional debates over Reconstruction, wherein the national union was constantly portrayed in terms of marriage.[59]

Uncle Sam is pictured in this 1883 *Daily Graphic* cartoon urging Congress to dip into the bucket called "Extreme Measures" to clean the "blot" of Mormonism off the country, represented here as a womanly "fair statue." Courtesy of Yale University Library.

The language of unity resonates with the traditional common-law doctrine of "one flesh." The presumption that a separate political identity (for women, or for regions) would undermine the unity, the necessary submersion of the self in the relationship, became the rallying cry of conservative theorists of marriage. One Democratic senator, alive to the multiple implications of Lincoln's metaphor, argued that the franchise for women would recreate the same division of authority that precipitated the war, a "family with two heads—a house divided against itself" rather than one of "perfect union." As one activist pithily explained her opposition to divorce, "I am a Unionist, not a secessionist."[60]

Antipolygamists, especially in the 1880s, understood the power of such arguments. Pro-unionism, pronationalism, only "extreme measures," they claimed, could combat Mormon resistance. They capitalized on the sense that politics and marriage were mixed together in unprecedented ways and that whatever the proper solution, the Mormons had gotten the formula terribly wrong. The politics of Utah, and the marital system on which politics must rest, they insisted, were the expression of what could happen if Americans compromised the politics of union.[61]

The Edmunds Bill passed the Senate in 1886, as a similar bill sponsored by John Randolph Tucker of Virginia worked its way to the floor of the House. A conference committee reported out a harmonized version in early 1887. The Edmunds-Tucker Act, as the *Deseret News* reported to the desperate faithful in Utah, passed both houses without serious opposition. Its message to Mormons was clear—and devastating. Fornication, adultery, and the revocation of woman suffrage brought women as well as men into the criminal and political focus of federal law. Enforcement by the federal government demanded ever greater sacrifice from Mormons and caused ever more dislocation and dismay. Life in Utah by the late 1880s was riven by law and legal process. The territory was consumed with the punishment, defense, or flight of polygamists and their wives. Kate Field had called for "the dynamite of law" to blow up polygamy; with the enactment of the Edmunds-Tucker law, Congress delivered much, although never all, of what Field had asked for. There was no "United States Marriage Law," but there was now a full-blown legal structure imposed on all territories (although without question motivated by polygamy and Mormon resistance in Utah). Equally important, the substance of the new law was drawn from the laws of the states, with all the "privileges" that nineteenth-century monogamy extended to women. The "protection" of marriage went hand in hand with the silencing of an explicit political voice for women and their exposure to criminal penalties.[62]

Given the tools to prosecute women, federal law enforcement officials for the first time began the wholesale indictment of pregnant women in plural marriages for fornication. Almost 200 women were indicted between 1887 and 1890, a stunning transformation in their perceived status as victims of Mormon men. Many antipolygamists in Congress and elsewhere finally accepted the truth of what Mormons had been saying all along—that Mormon women would not voluntarily abandon their religion, even if given the vote, or if their husbands were prosecuted for sexual offenses. Indicted as fornicators, with no vote, these women had gone, in less than a decade, from being called victims to being labeled criminals.

Whether out of compunction or because there was no prison space to house women (much less pregnant ones or nursing mothers), prosecutors rarely pursued fornication charges beyond indictment and arraignment. In contrast to men, women rarely pled guilty, and often pled not guilty if they were arraigned at all. Of the 188 indictments against women for fornication brought between 1887 and 1890, for example, the records contain only one case in which a woman was found guilty after a jury trial; four were acquitted, and four women pled guilty, one of whom was given a suspended sentence. There is no record of any woman incarcerated for fornication. The arrest and indictment of plural wives appears to have been a means of securing their testimony against their husbands.

The charge of fornication, the standard provision used for the punishment of prostitutes under state law, labeled women in plural marriages as fallen rather than just kidnapped or duped. The acceptance of the essentially criminal nature of these wives—their transformation into the legal equivalent of prostitutes—may have reconciled Eastern antipolygamists to a legal regime that in fact punished Mormon women. The stigma attached to the fornicator label apparently was deeply felt. None of the contemporary histories mention such indictments, nor have modern scholars unearthed this prosecutorial strategy. Women jailed for contempt for refusing to testify appeared in the Mormon press and histories as heroines; the wives indicted for fornication received no such play. The victims were criminalized and then forgotten.

CHAPTER 6

The Marital Economy

Another more visible facet of antipolygamy existed in the 1880s. Chief Justice Taney had declared in 1857 that Congress was prohibited from legislating on questions of "persons and property." *Reynolds* had answered the "persons" part of Taney's holding, sustaining interference in local domestic relations. But the complementary power, over property, remained untested and ever more tempting to congressional antipolygamists. By the mid-1880s, it was easy to see the structural supports for polygamy in Utah, legal and financial. The church's role in the struggle stood out in sharp relief as the attempted punishment of polygamists failed to achieve the capitulation of Mormon men. The ability of polygamists to disappear, and thus to escape the wheels of justice, depended on the organization that governed the faithful, so lamented their opponents, more effectively than did the national sovereign. As antipolygamists absorbed the news from Utah of church-organized hero's parades for convicted polygamists and heard from Mormon pulpits the veneration of resistance, they turned their attention to the church itself. In 1886, Senator George Edmunds railed against the power of the church and its leaders over law and life in Utah. He blamed the apparent failure of the Raid on the legal power of the church and its leaders: "[Mormons] have been the masters of the situation, and have gloried in it, . . . for the propagation not merely of polygamy . . . [but] of a political government, . . . because when you take their statutes and codes together and run them through one after another you will find that everything runs up to the first president of the church . . . for the management of the whole affairs of society in the Territory, and as long as they can persuade Congress or tender hearted members of it, . . . to touch them with

The Judge, 9 January 1885, showing the punitive atmosphere of Congress in the mid-1880s. Courtesy of Yale University Library.

velvet and leave them alone, they will rejoice." The authority of church leaders, especially their ability and willingness to command followers to disobey the law and sacrifice personal interest for the benefit of the broader Mormon community, confirmed to Edmunds and many other antipolygamists that the very church was criminal. Federal officials were unsuccessful at jailing the highest Mormon leaders, so their focus shifted to the seat of patriarchal power—the Church of Jesus Christ of Latter-day Saints.[1]

The Edmunds-Tucker Act, as its preamble proclaimed, was designed to punish the institution that sponsored and shielded polygamy, as well as the men and women who practiced it. In addition to regularizing marriage law for Utah, and most devastating to the church, the act abolished the church corporation and directed the attorney general to begin escheatment proceedings against church property. Ownership of real property was limited to a total of no more than $50,000. Escheated property was to be used to fund the public schools of Utah, to train its children for greater independence and judgment than that shown by their parents. The act also abolished the Perpetual Emigrating Fund, the revolving pool that financed the "gathering" of the faithful through migration of converts from England, Scandinavia, and Europe to the Great Basin kingdom.[2]

This extraordinary piece of legislation has been criticized by twentieth-century historians of Mormonism, who argue (with some plausibility) that the wide sweep of the act and its openly redistributive mandate demonstrate that antipolygamists in Congress were more interested in economic control than they were in the protection of women. Yet there is more to the story. Congressional antipolygamists were integral to the development of a national political economy in the 1880s, and especially of the belief that marital structure, separation of church and state, and competitive behavior were related.

The political world in which the Edmunds-Tucker Act took shape was galvanized by change and growth in corporate law and in the power and reach of corporations. Changes in the broader economy affected antipolygamists' thinking, as it did the rest of the country. In the 1880s, the potential frustration of republican principles and government by despotic men holding the reins of mammoth corporations gained new visibility. Regulation of corporate behavior in its antipolygamy guise touched populist, antimonopoly, and nativist chords that connected traditional common-law remedies to changed economic circumstances. Once again, antipolygamists drew on state law to create a national vision, imposing on Utah many of the same rules and structures that they believed guaranteed the flourishing of civilization, and Christianity, in their home states.

The Edmunds-Tucker Act was the culmination of a series of intellectual and political developments after the Civil War that focused attention on the "marital economy" of territorial Utah. The Supreme Court decision that upheld the act finally crushed the long tradition

Frontispiece from Walter Hill Crockett, *George Franklin Edmunds*. Senator George Edmunds crafted antipolygamy legislation by drawing on state laws and traditions, and applying them to Utah through new federal statutes. Courtesy of American Philosophical Society.

of Mormon resistance. With *Reynolds* marking the beginning and *Late Corporation of the Church of Jesus Christ of Latter-day Saints v. United States* marking the end, the Supreme Court in just over a decade created and sustained an entirely new branch of federal constitutional law. And yet this new constitutional world was already cracking in 1890, even as it reached its zenith. The arguments in the *Late Corporation* case, the opinions themselves, and the constitutional and corporate law that resulted from the litigation reveal cleavages in corporate theory and constitutional law that divided the Court and legal thinkers as they wrestled with change in the final decade of the nineteenth century.

The Mormon tradition of resistance that survived, however battered, into the late 1880s provoked American judges and legislators to imagine a national law of religion, marriage, and economic structure. They created a new law based on the shared wisdom of the states, and at the same time they recast a tradition of localism against local difference. Equally important, the final stage took Congress, and the Supreme Court, further into the realm of coercion than they had ventured before. Put bluntly, the Edmunds-Tucker Act recognized the connections between faith, marriage, and property in Mormon culture; then it set out to destroy them. Victory, in this sense, was the creation of a legal community possible only with the destruction of an alternative one.

Economic imagery and language had figured in antipolygamy efforts since the 1850s, but only in the 1880s was positive legislation to restructure the economy of Utah finally enacted. Antipolygamists in Congress turned popular concerns about corporate power in the broader secular economy against the Mormon Church. Long-standing fears of the church's financial and legal power metastasized as church leaders continued to control the church's substantial assets, even while they were "underground."[3]

Added to the open and defiant practice of polygamy, according to the church's opponents, was the capture of the economic, legal, and political systems of the territory. As the House report on the Edmunds-Tucker bill put it,

> [The policy of the Mormon Church] is shown from the enormous power of the corporation to increase its means and influence in the infant State. All the reasons which have induced the mortmain acts of the mother country, and all the evils which must follow unlimited power of the church to take and hold lands and other property, which evils are beginning to show themselves in our own country, should lead the legislative authority to look with jealousy on this tendency and to check it in its beginnings. Ecclesiastics clothed with property, which is so potential an influence in every state, would invade the province of the state as disastrously to religion and corruptly for the state as when the state invades the province of the church. And these reasons increase in force when, as in this case, the church has shown such an inherent tendency to control the state and master its fate.

As many antipolygamists saw it, Protestants in England had rebelled against just such priestcraft, which had now been smuggled into a land of religious freedom by the Latter-day Saints. The growth of the church's wealth, as well as its political power, they charged, was the predictable result of priestly authority in politics and law. The answer, claimed the House Committee on the Territories, was to apply the traditional remedy against "ecclesiastics clothed with property." Express enforcement of the limitations on the power of religious organizations to acquire and hold property, which were part of the Morrill Act, passed more than two decades earlier, seemed to many antipolygamists to be an essential final step in the regularization of law for Utah. The proof of the devastating consequences of such power in the hands of priests, they argued, was in the dual forms of authority exercised by the leaders of the church. The marital practice of Mormon men and the domination of Utah's economy by the multifaceted business, financial, and industrial interests of the church appeared deeply and inseparably connected. This overlap, a sign of harmony, virtue, and cooperation to Mormons, became a sure sign of corruption to their opponents.[4]

The relationship between the marital and the political economies appeared ever more frequently in antipolygamy thought, prompted by continued Mormon resistance. As Mormons endured the Raid in the 1880s, antipolygamists gradually rationalized their failure as the result of the heretofore partially obscured relationship between monogamy and economic equality. According to many congressional antipolygamists, polygamy created a host of economic consequences, all of them irretrievably at odds with liberty, democracy, competition —in short, with capitalism. The habits of home life, the argument went, determined the political economy of the territory. As one antipolygamist lobbyist put it, "The man with four wives must have the means of supporting them; he must monopolize power, property, and privilege; while the man not permitted to marry one wife is deprived of other rights and reduced to an inferior position."[5]

Henry Blackwell, dedicated woman's rights activist and husband of American Woman Suffrage Association president Lucy Stone, argued in *The Woman's Journal* in 1879 that the property consequences of polygamy were immediate and devastating. In polygamy, Blackwell charged, the "toil and economy" of one wife could be aggrandized by the husband to his own benefit, or even to the benefit of other wives. The "matrimonial firm," when expanded beyond the exclusive and cooperative partnership of monogamy, he argued, introduced perverse incentives, undermining the wife's position and jeopardizing her interest in "the joint accumulations of married life."[6]

Such attacks not only criticized the patriarchy that antipolygamists insisted was central to Mormon plural marriage. They also presumed that the toil and economy of wives in monogamous marriages was not expropriated by domineering husbands. Plainly, this did not describe the experience of many wives, as antipolygamists knew well. Like other aspects of the common law of marriage, the property rights of married women were subject to searching and constant debate and criticism in the second half of the nineteenth century. In many states, married women's property acts and earnings statutes formalized the sense that coverture was hardly a real protection against an abusive husband. The union of estates, the complement to the union of persons in the metaphor of "one flesh," had long been subject to disunion in courts of equity, which were by definition not bound by common-law rules. And yet the idea that property was somehow "naturally" distributed in monogamy grew up around the core of antipolygamy sentiment. The Mormon Church looked too *rich* and polygamous Mormon husbands, too *powerful* and too closely connected with the wealth of the church, for wives (or monogamous or unmarried men, for that matter) to be getting their due. Other households and other churches, almost any household or church outside Utah, these antipolygamists implied, seemed benign by contrast. They blamed the legal power of the church.[7]

Two aspects of the corporate charter of the Church of Jesus Christ of Latter-day Saints were particularly galling to observers outside Utah. The first was that the Mormons had set up a legal entity, the corporation, empowered to own unlimited amounts of personal and real property. Second was the perceived structural connection linking mandatory tithing by all faithful Mormons, the wealth of the church corporation, and the practice of polygamy. The church's capacity to acquire property, especially when combined with its apparent power to exact contributions from the faithful, argued opponents, marked this religious corporation as a front for the aggrandizement of Mormon leaders.[8]

Antipolygamists claimed that the church corporation was a sham. The church's ostensibly harmless purpose as a religious organization cloaked the reality, they maintained, which was the oppression of all women and the gullible masses of men. Here was a species of fraud of a sort that seemed akin to other kinds of abuse that preoccupied much of late-nineteenth-century politics.[9] By the 1870s, the political power of corporations at the state (and even the federal) level was unprecedented and intimately connected to growing fears of monopoly.

These two photographs of Utah, the first (above) showing Brigham Young's residences and the second (below) claiming to be "representative of life in the rural districts," illustrated the wide economic disparity many antipolygamists assumed characterized Mormon life. From *The Great West Illustrated.* Courtesy of The Huntington Library, San Marino, Calif.

"Robber barons," the stereotypical unscrupulous men who acquired dazzling wealth through shady and even piratical dealings, seemed to exist outside the legal system, exploiting the liberties that should be carefully preserved. Fabulous new fortunes and predatory business dealings shocked (and inspired) the nation in the decades after the Civil War. The railroads and their flamboyant developers played a central role in the obsession with corruption in business and in anti-monopoly politics and theory. After the Civil War, the rate of railroad construction spiraled upward, spurred by Eastern investment and a focus on the West as key to economic as well as physical expansion. And, mistakenly as it turned out, the railroad had long been expected to bring "civilization" to Utah, eroding polygamy and the power of the Mormon Church.[10]

The boom in construction, however, was matched by the rate of bankruptcy among railroads and by charges of unfair dealing and predatory pricing policies. Throughout the 1870s and 1880s, road after road went into receivership, transforming the corporate landscape and debt structure of capitalism. Railroad systems and their powerful leaders also transformed markets, creating and then endangering whole networks of exchange and dependency. Resistance to such change and the erosion of independence for farmers and small producers that accompanied massive development, especially in Midwestern and Western states, rekindled old antimonopolist concerns; fear, that is, of officially sanctioned privileges exercised at the expense of ordinary people.[11]

In the late nineteenth century, dread of monopolies and monopolists was used against both corruption and foreigners. Populist theories, especially, joined fear of economic domination with distrust of railroads. As one antimonopolist put it, the "power of capital and monopoly" had "seized upon" tens of thousands of square miles of prime agricultural, mining, and forest land, turning would-be homesteaders into "hired pawns." And indeed land grants to railroads were massive; claims that the roads controlled whole legislatures in some states hardly exaggerated the intimate relationship between government subsidies and the transportation revolution.[12]

The connections between distrust of corporate privilege and manipulation of markets in the broader economy and antipolygamy theory were powerful and multilayered by the 1880s. The wealth and influence of a "corrupt" Mormon lobby was a constant refrain in antipolygamy rhetoric in Congress and on the lecture circuit. And not without reason; subsequent research into the relationship of the Mormons to railroad interests (including payments to California senator Leland Stanford to act as a pro-Mormon lobbyist) reveals that significant amounts of money actually did change hands. Mormon representatives, desperate for relief and protection, attempted to buy better press, and better political results, by allying themselves with big business Democrats.[13]

As robber barons organized themselves behind seemingly innocuous corporate facades, their foes lobbied for new methods of dealing with business practices that in this century we have since prohibited with antitrust laws or have labeled as "white collar crime." George Edmunds, for example, was a perennial opponent of the railroad lobby, a proponent of limiting the size and political influence of corporations generally, and committed to the separation of wealth and faith. As one antipolygamist senator put it, "The sentiment of the Senate will be that every corporation should have some limit to the amount of property that it may acquire, and particularly a religious corporation." From this perspective, the threat to freedom flowed from the wealth and power of any corporation that sponsored and shielded a religious equivalent of the railroad speculator. And the very speculators whose roads that brought thousands of new converts to Utah (instead of the civilization previous generations had hoped for) created unholy political alliances with their counterparts in "Mormondom."[14]

The disease, antipolygamists charged, was spreading rapidly; whatever may be the assessment of the gravity of the threat after more than a century, "spread" was the operative word. Between 1886 and 1889, the church organized more than 100 communities for settlement *outside* Utah. Colonies of Mormons sprouted up in Idaho, Arizona, New Mexico, Colorado, and Wyoming. There was a simple explanation for expansion: Mormon missionaries had been so successful, and Mormon women were having so many babies, that in only forty years the population had outgrown Utah and was overflowing in all directions. The dispersal of the faithful, of course, also undermined federal attempts to enforce antipolygamy laws. Remote valleys in new locations provided isolation and refuge for indicted or suspected polygamists and, frequently, their families.[15]

Fear of foreigners also connected antipolygamy to broader antimonopoly theory by the 1880s. The same conviction that accused railroad entrepreneurs of plotting to people the West "with the paupers of Europe on the one side, and those of Asia on the other," and of consigning "the [native] children of the soil into the most abject slavery," fueled distrust of domination by corporate hierarchies. Anti-Chinese and antipolygamy nativism coalesced in claims that Chinese immigrants were slaves "rigidly under the control of the contractor who brought [them] as ever an African slave was under his master in

UNCLE SAM'S NIGHTMARE.

As *The Wasp* (24 March 1882) saw it, Mormons and Chinese tormented a sleeping nation. Courtesy of Yale University Library.

South Carolina or Louisiana." Similar charges connected polygamy to the immigration of impoverished converts and especially to the proselytizing in the slums of England and Scandinavia. Without the work of Mormon missionaries in Europe, charged antipolygamists, polygamy would atrophy for lack of new and ignorant women who could be duped into becoming plural wives. As *The Nation* put it in an editorial in late 1883, the Chinese Exclusion Act of 1882 established the principle that immigrants could validly be excluded "as a remedy for social or political evils." Extending the principle to Utah, wrote the popular editor E. L. Godkin, would dictate that the "low, igno-rant peasant" women who had converted to Mormonism should be barred from entrance into the territory altogether. This "somewhat Oriental" treatment, Godkin maintained, was the most likely solu-tion to an archaic and entirely foreign institution.[16]

   In one sense, the connection between immigration and polygamy was justified. By the mid-1880s, the missionary force sent abroad from Utah ballooned, as refugee polygamists left to escape prosecution under the Edmunds Act. At the same time, they recruited new Saints, swelling the population of Utah and surrounding states. Subsequent research has supported the claimed connection between immigration

"The Wolves and the Lambs." The arrival of Scandinavian converts with Mormon missionaries at Castle Garden en route to Salt Lake City. From *Frank Leslie's Illustrated Newspaper*, 15 December 1883. Courtesy of General Research Collection, New York Public Library, Astor, Lenox and Tilden Foundations.

and new plural marriages. Single women who emigrated to Utah generally married quickly, and upsurges in plural marriages generally followed increases in immigration. Especially during the 1880s, when Mormon leaders urged unwavering commitment to the Principle, indicted polygamists traveled abroad as missionaries to evade arrest as well as to recruit new wives. The success of the missionary program fueled charges that the church itself was the source of the "problem." No other religious group had such an organized (and successful) means of expanding its membership; the efficiency of Mormon recruitment added to the chagrin of antipolygamists.[17]

Diplomatic efforts proved fruitless. In 1879, Secretary of State William Evarts sent a circular to American diplomatic and consular officials in England and Europe directing them to urge their host governments to prevent the emigration of "law-defying Mormons" to Utah. European governments replied that it was impossible to justify detention of Mormon converts simply in anticipation of some future offense against the United States. Newspapers in the East reported the frequent arrival of Mormon converts destined for trains westward to Utah, even as convicted polygamists rode to Eastern prisons on the same roads.[18]

By the mid-1880s, antipolygamists used such publicity to draw attention to the legal and financial structures of immigration to the kingdom, as well as to the mother church itself. As anti-Chinese sentiment grew in the late nineteenth century, calls for the nationalization of immigration law dovetailed neatly with antipolygamists' claims that Mormon polygamy fed on a constant diet of "fresh victims." The Perpetual Emigrating Fund, incorporated in 1850 with the power to manage and finance the gathering of the faithful, provided loans to converts, whose repayment then financed the immigration of future converts, and so on. In this way, charged antipolygamists, Mormons wrested control over immigration from the national or state government, or even the forces of natural law. The work of missionaries and the Perpetual Emigrating Fund created a "Church and State machinery," claimed the federally appointed governor of Utah Territory, that financed the voyages of recruits destined for oppression and exploitation. Mormons were accused of cloaking the real fate of impoverished immigrants with a fraudulent layer of religion. Such recruits, antipolygamists charged, should be excluded by the federal Contract Labor Act of 1885, which prohibited the importation of foreigners into the country under contracts of employment with private employers.[19]

The managerial style of Mormon leaders bolstered the perception outside Utah that the church corporation was bent on domination of everything its opponents insisted should remain secular. Antipolygamists routinely claimed that the entire territorial economy was controlled by invisible threads emanating from church offices, especially the office of president and prophet of the church. Church rank and personal wealth frequently were closely related. One study has determined, for example, that high-ranking church officials were likely to hold ten times as much wealth as other Mormons. The most notorious, of course, was Brigham Young, who his opponents claimed was the religious counterpart to the robber barons whose ally he had become. Spoofs of Young and his followers played on the instant recognition that his name, and his church's marital practices, produced in audiences at home and abroad. Comedian Artemus Ward, for example, referred to Mormons' "bigamy, Brighamy and ninnygavinny" in his lectures. Even Young's death in 1877 did not dispel the rhetorical value of his piratical and tyrannical public image. As litigation over his estate revealed, Young created hundreds of enterprises—from cotton and silk farms, to theater companies, to railroads—managed by the church, often in his own name.[20]

One of the first projects of the territorial legislature in 1850 had been to grant President Young and the church leadership control of social and property structures and match them to the dictates of faith. Young used his church's power over property and marriage to marry twenty-seven women and ran his several households according to bureaucratic discipline. He also oversaw the settlement and development of Utah, frequently down to the smallest details. Young supervised where his followers went, which crops they grew, which professions they entered, and so on. This top-down style of leadership was coordinated, according to Young's critics, with an iron determination to control the economy of the territory. In theory, tithing was mandatory for all the faithful; the church used its funds to finance factories, retail stores, banks, newspapers, utilities, logging, and transportation, just to name a few of the church's extensive entrepreneurial ventures. To outsiders, such a mingling of enterprise and faith smacked of abuse. The mandatory tithe, antipolygamists claimed, replicated in Utah the oppression of the poor and uneducated that marked the centuries of Catholic power in England and Europe. They also argued that Utah went further still, for Mormon leaders, they charged, united sexual self-indulgence with economic control.

The same men who had plural wives served as the leadership for church enterprises. Young was at one time governor of Utah Territory, on the boards of utilities, banks, and factories in the territory, and head of the church. The overt interlacing of religious, political, and economic power, never as complete within the territory as imagined by those without its bounds, nonetheless conveyed with some accuracy the vision that many antipolygamists claimed was the essence of a rule of men, rather than a rule of laws. The Mormons, George Edmunds charged, had created a "one-man power" in the church hierarchy, with all authority "run[ning] up to the first president of the church (and all he has to do with the church is to have [the title of first president])." Mormons responded that the rule was one of faith rather than of men. But outside the territory, such arguments went largely unheeded, or were derided as "blasphemous ravings."[21]

Added to the control of settlement and industry were the landholdings of church leaders, to whom the territorial legislature granted valuable tracts of land, including water courses, grazing tracts, timber stands, and so on. Thus the escheatment of church property contemplated by the Edmunds-Tucker Act was not so much an infringement of religion, its supporters hastened to explain, as the liberation of land and resources from acquisitory men who stole the property of the United States and then hid behind a veneer of religion. As Democratic representative John Randolph Tucker of Virginia put it in the final debates in the House on the bill, "[Mormon leaders] took possession of the forests; they took possession of everything that they deemed valuable. . . . That hierarchy has been kept up ever since its organization, inside the United States and controlling one of its Territories. . . . [T]o-day we are rooting out an unjust possession of the soil which belonged to the people of the United States, and should have been left open and free to them." In that sense, the informal establishment of the Mormon Church was different than anything the formal establishments in Massachusetts or Virginia had ever achieved. It combined profound religious belief with the Yankee fever to experiment with new technology and with organizational forms. In many aspects, the behavior of the church hierarchy replicated (even anticipated) the managerial revolution that transferred American business in the late nineteenth century from the control of personal capitalists—that is, individual entrepreneurs—to hierarchies of managers. In other words, Salt Lake was a company town whose corporate religion really was religion.[22]

As the Edmunds-Tucker Act was introduced and gathered strength in Congress in the early and mid-1880s, the church designated trustees to be equitable owners of its business property and real estate. These "trustees-in-trust," as they were called, like many of the enterprises they controlled and the system of tithing through which development was financed, were viewed by faithful Mormons as divinely sanctioned agents for group investment and group savings. To outsiders, they were another indicator of the anticompetitive nature of the entire church, and the essential inability of all but the church's leaders to act in their own interest. The popular minister and novelist Henry Ward Beecher, for example, charged Utah with "treason" against all that was free and pure in the United States, calling the Mormon Church a political monopoly of greedy priests: "It is a union of church and state, which we fear, and to prevent which we lift up our voice: a union which never existed without corrupting the church and enslaving the people, by making the ministry independent of them and dependent on the state, and to a great extent a sinecure aristocracy of indolence and secular ambition, auxiliary to the throne and inimical to liberty."[23]

Antipolygamists said in many different ways that the exercise of political, legal, and entrepreneurial power by a religious corporation was antithetical to everything the country stood for. They also claimed that they played fair, and on a level playing field, unlike the Mormons. The Saints, many antipolygamists charged, had violated the implicit text of disestablishment by dabbling (and doing well) in areas that other faiths knew were properly secular. The Mormons had thereby accorded themselves an unfair advantage, especially as compared to the Protestant denominations whose missionaries labored mightily for few converts in Utah. "The passion for equality in religion as well as secular matters is everywhere in America far too strong to be braved, and nothing excites more general disapprobation than any attempt by an ecclesiastical organization to interfere in politics," wrote one English observer in the late 1880s as he explained to his readers why Mormonism was so galling to Americans. To many antipolygamists, Young's leadership combined polygamy and the worst elements of a religious establishment with the tangled and tortuous paper trail of contemporary corporate abuses of liberty. They turned their gaze to the broad structures of politics and the economy in Utah, which, they argued, were by definition unequal and kept the people of Utah in servitude.[24]

The maintenance of the church, antipolygamists insisted, was based not on informed and willing obedience by the faithful but on enforced ignorance. Aggravating the religious monopoly of the territorial economy, claimed non-Mormons was the church's opposition to free education in Utah. Many American Protestants, glancing over the role of anti-Catholicism in practices such as Bible reading (King James version, of course) in the public schools of many states, claimed that public education was "secular" and should be extended to every child as an essential means of preparation for citizenship and self-governance. Public education in the nineteenth century was not experienced by many Catholic children and their parents as liberating, however, but oppressive. Even as the majority of Utah Territory, moreover, Mormons frequently brought with them memories of the power of Protestant morality deployed against their faith. In this sense, to protest against the dominant culture by instituting plural marriage was also, implicitly, to challenge prevailing Protestant theories of child-rearing and education.[25]

Although Mormon leaders consistently explained that they were not opposed to private education, merely to taxation in support of public schools, reformers claimed that children in Utah were unlettered and dependent and thus unfit for American citizenship. They also charged that the leadership wanted it that way. Indeed, the majority of Mormon children did not attend school until the 1890s. Throughout the polygamy period, many Mormon leaders were self-

This picture of the Cannon Family School was taken sometime in the 1880s and shows the teacher (front row, third from right) with sixteen pupils, of whom only five were girls. Courtesy Utah State Historical Society.

taught. In vain did the Saints protest that their love of learning had made them an extraordinarily literate society, and point to the founding of institutions of higher learning almost from the moment the territory was settled. Even those most articulate and learned, including George Q. Cannon, frequently combined a vigorous program of reading and inquiry with the conviction that education was a private matter. Cannon built a schoolhouse on his family compound outside Salt Lake to educate his forty-three children, but many Mormons could not afford such private solutions. Local schools, although they did exist in many communities by the 1880s, generally were privately financed, and understaffed. Equally important, antipolygamists were concerned that Mormons inculcated their children with an anti-democratic, unchristian faith, instead of the "secular," republican curriculum that non-Mormons supported for the territory. Lack of formal (and publicly financed) schooling became a key ingredient in the assumption that genuinely competitive behavior and equality were inconsistent with Mormonism. As one Mormon proponent of public schools quipped shortly before he was excommunicated, how could Brigham Young understand the value of education when he could "hardly spell half-a-dozen consecutive words correctly" or "write a correct sentence in his mother tongue"?[26]

All these symptoms of apparent domination—control of the legislature and enterprise and even opposition to public education—by men who were themselves polygamists were by the 1880s understood as the inevitable result of a faith that "perverted" the underlying marital economy. The failure to practice monogamy, in other words, spread monopoly like a contagion throughout the territory. Antipolygamists honed their arguments as the Raid failed to produce capitulation. The basic premise was that monogamy, or the legitimate monopoly of one spouse by the other, was the basis in natural law for productive competitive behavior in the rest of the economy. By multiplying the ability of a few men to monopolize many women, competitive behavior in the rest of the economy was drastically reduced. Antipolygamists claimed, in other words, that Mormons got the equation backward: they mandated intense competition where it was inappropriate, that is, among men for wives, and then among wives for the attention of their husband, while at the same time restricting competition where it was most vital—in business, industry, and finance.[27]

To ensure that a more independent (and self-sufficient) generation did not dislodge them from their positions of comfort and command, according to many antipolygamists, Mormon leaders denied most of the children of the territory the capacity to succeed, damning them through ignorance to a life of subservience. The very minds of the Mormon people were monopolized by their leaders, argued those outside the faith. Elizabeth Cady Stanton, for example, on a trip to the territory in 1871, summarized her impressions of Brigham Young and Utah, concluding that the failure to allow individual initiative in the economy and to respect "true marriage as the union between two, [which] will not allow . . . sharing the affections," had stifled rather than promoted development. "[W]hen you think that [Young]," she said, "has had a quarter of a century to build up one very poor city, composed chiefly of small, cheap houses, without free schools or sidewalks; when you see the impoverished condition of the masses, compelled to pay a tenth of all their earnings to the church, and the slavery in which their minds are held to dogmas, traditions and revelations; when you contrast Utah with California, one must feel that that master mind has blocked rather than pushed forward civilization in the territory under his control."[28]

The antipolygamist theory that competition outside the home depended on monopoly of affection in the home represented a popular moderate position in a hotly debated field. The relationship of marriage to monopoly was the subject of scrutiny by theorists of both Left and Right in the 1880s. Frequently, commentators focused on marital structure as the barometer of the economic order. Some theorists even opposed monogamy as a key factor in the concentration of wealth. For instance, Frederick Engels, disciple and financier of Karl Marx and influential socialist theorist in his own right, wrote in his famous *Origin of the Family, Private Property, and the State, in Light of the Researches of Lewis Henry Morgan* in 1884 that monogamy was a symptom of inequity rather than a recipe for the cure. The monopoly of a woman by a man, Engels claimed, was the result of what he called "considerable concentration of wealth" in a few men and their determination to transmit their control of capital to the next generation. Such a marriage was based not only on the "absolute supremacy" of the husband, he wrote, but also on his absolute hypocrisy. Monogamy, Engels argued much in the same vein as Mormon apologists, was "supplemented by adultery and prostitution." The sexual freedom of promiscuity, Engels continued, was denied only to women. Monogamy and prostitution were "inseparable contradictions, poles of the same state of society" in which the "single family" stifled the "unconstrained sexual intercourse" of women, but not men. He claimed that only abolition of the monopoly of wealth and power created and justified by capitalism would break the cycle of sexual and economic subservience for women and duplicity and patriarchy for men.[29]

Social Darwinist William Graham Sumner, by contrast, argued that monopoly and the concentration of capital, rather than being the cause of monogamy, were its logical consequence. In an essay titled "The Family Monopoly," first published in 1887, Sumner approved "monogamic marriage as monopoly" and claimed that marriage was at "the root of" monopoly in the "capital and industrial system." He defended the "great monopoly" of monogamous marriage against the Mormons ("sects which have perceived this and made it an object of their agitation"), calling monopoly a positive good. Engels, in Sumner's view, had correctly diagnosed "the fact that property and the family are inextricably interwoven with each other from their very roots in the remotest origin of civilization." But he had reached the wrong conclusion. Permanent families and permanent property were mutually dependent, in Sumner's eyes, and mutually beneficial. Both were fundamental to "the decline of polygamy" and to the corresponding "advance of luxury." The virtues of monopoly, in his view, were determined by their basis in the family: "The reason why I defend the millions of the millionaire is not that I love the millionaire, but that I love my own wife and children, and that I know no way in which to get the defense of society for my hundreds, except to give my help, as a member of society, to protect his millions."[30]

Sumner and Engels represented extreme positions; antipolygamists, by and large, hewed a more popular middle path. The example of Utah, they argued, revealed that polygamy rather than monogamy produced monopolistic behavior in society. The reintroduction of competitive behavior would tend to undermine polygamy and the concentration of wealth in the hands of polygamists. Thus, they could embrace monogamy, contra Engels, and condemn monopoly in the economy, contra Sumner. It was only logical, argued George Edmunds, that a polygamous corporate giant would erode the independence, the integrity, of the rest of the territory's political economy. Polygamy conveniently explained the apparent desire to keep the population in uneducated "serfdom," the manipulation of the political process, and, of course, the vast land and business holdings of the church and its leaders.[31]

As the power wielded by the new corporate giants in the rest of the country grew both in real terms and in public perception in the 1880s, the corporate power of the Mormon Church also became more visible. The failure of earlier statutes to eradicate polygamy was more comprehensible: legislation that criminalized polygamy or disfranchised polygamists left the all-important economic leg standing. Mormon leaders, through their control of the economy, still controlled the legislature, claimed antipolygamists. Mormon polygamists, they said, coerced the mass of followers to act against their own interests in sustaining the inordinate power of a few men. Thus, by the mid-1880s, many antipolygamists were unmoved by claims that the criminal indictment of Mormon leaders, and the threat of imprisonment as well as the inability of polygamists to vote, was all that was necessary.

Only by dismantling the monopoly of Utah's economy, it was argued, could the polygamous power structure be finally and truly destroyed and the territory freed from religious domination. George Edmunds explained the problem. The corporate powers granted by the territorial legislature to the Mormon Church, he argued, were based on the "propagation of polygamy." The church corporation, Edmunds charged, "is devoted to . . . the purpose of imposing upon [ignorant and degraded people] the doctrines and the practice of polygamy." The Report of the House Judiciary Committee in 1886 hammered home the connection between economic and marital structures. Polygamy, the report claimed, "assumed the garb of religion . . . and sought through the rapid propagation of the species under the economy of celestial [marriage and] its church [corporation] . . . to make Utah the permanent seat of Mormon supremacy and power." To ensure the perpetuation of polygamy, argued one senator, the corporation granted to "priests and apostles and bishops and other men in authority . . . a degree of duress [over individuals], not merely spiritual duress, but personal and physical duress and control over their property, which shall compel them to bow in submission to any decree that the church may put forward."[32]

This domination had been accomplished, according to antipolygamists, not through true faith but through the manipulation of law. In their view, the legal power of the corporate form shielded Mormon leaders and increased their sway over the people and the economy. As Democratic senator John Tyler Morgan of Alabama put it, the "act of legal incorporation . . . is the one act from which [the Mormon Church] has derived all its power to do mischief in that Territory." To cleanse the corporation of its temporal excesses, George Edmunds stressed, was to put it on the same legal footing as other religious organizations (themselves a highly competitive group by the late nineteenth century). The forfeiture of the church's extensive enterprises and landholdings would force the Saints to recognize that they were just one among many other religious groups, he claimed. The implication, of course, was that real competition would encourage Mormons in Utah to shift their allegiance to other faiths. Almost anything, implied Edmunds, would be better than Mormonism. Missionaries from many Protestant denominations, already active in the territory, were eager to step in.[33]

Belief in the virtues of a marketplace of religion, was all but unquestioned among Protestants after the Civil War. They congratulated themselves that the "voluntary principle" of separation of church and state had produced a vigorous market for moral progress. As one state supreme court put it shortly before the Edmunds-Tucker Act was introduced, "Let religious doctrines have a fair field, and a free, intellectual, moral and spiritual conflict. The weakest—that is, the intellectually, morally, and spiritually weakest—will go to the wall, and the best will triumph in the end. This is the golden truth which it has taken the world eighteen centuries to learn, and which has at last solved the terrible enigma of 'church and state.' "[34]

Here was a handy solution to two quandaries, as well as a justification for the eradication of polygamy and for the confiscation of extensive Mormon Church property. On the one hand, the theory that the religious marketplace would winnow out the unworthy, rather than the weak (but very possibly deserving), resolved the moral dilemma raised by the Social Darwinism of theorists such as William Graham Sumner. In this view, natural selection of religion through competition would always reward the most morally advanced rather than the strongest, or the slickest, or the loudest. On the other hand, the notion that religious organizations, like their commercial cousins, should participate in the free-for-all of the market, albeit on a spiritual rather than material level, fit in nicely with a capitalist political and moral economy.[35]

Theories of the relationship between the distribution of property, education, and citizenship affected Congress's treatment of Native Americans as well as Mormons in the 1880s. The Dawes Act of 1887, which mandated the "allotment" of American Indian reservation land away from tribes and to individual members, was conceived as a means of assimilating native peoples. Individual ownership of land, maintained sponsor Senator Henry L. Dawes, Republican of Massachusetts, was key to the real flourishing of native groups. Antipolygamists recognized the overlap between the corporate communalism of the Mormon Church and the tribal structures that controlled the land base for many Indians. The Dawes Act was "a mighty pulverizing engine to break up the tribal mass," as Theodore Roosevelt put it at the turn of the twentieth century. The act was designed to confer upon Indians the benefits of competition and mobility, replicating the common law of property in the states within Indian Territory. In the House, Representative John Randolph Tucker drew the parallel between citizenship and property in Utah. For Mormons, as for Indians, he insisted, "[w]e dissolve tribal relations of the Indians in order to make the Indian a good citizen; so we shatter the fabric of this church organization in order to make each member a free citizen of the Territory of Utah."[36]

Equally important, George Edmunds explained in debates on the bill, the church's former wealth would be rededicated to an economically progressive, quintessentially American purpose. To rehabilitate the unduly dependent and ignorant population of Utah, as the Edmunds-Tucker Bill proposed, the forfeited property of the church was to fund public education in the territory. Edmunds and other supporters of the bill argued that free schools would ensure that the residents of Utah would understand the virtues of planning, and enterprise, and discipline as elements of character that come from within rather than are imposed from without. Polygamy would never again gain a foothold in the territory if the people were inculcated with the lessons of competition in the market and monopoly at home. Once the formal legal powers that the church corporation held over the "most ignorant and superstitious class of the people" were

THE THREE TROUBLESOME CHILDREN.

Wasp cartoonist Frederick Keller imagined the "Mormon Question," the "China Question," and the "Indian Question" as troublesome children plaguing the mother country. Courtesy of Yale University Library.

stripped away, Edmunds predicted, the residents of Utah would be transformed into an "industrious, thrifty, and economical people," freed from the exigencies of the tithe and trained in school for self-government and self-sufficiency.[37]

Once again, Congress drew the strategy for breaking up the Mormon monopoly of production and reproduction in Utah from state law, this time from the law of corporations, including traditional rules of mortmain inherited from England, as well as the state's power to revoke corporate charters once issued. The fear of monopolization of property by religious corporations was an ancient one indeed. As the House Committee on the Territories stressed, the Protestant Reformation in England included the forfeiture of much of Catholic property, as well as restrictions on the power of churches to acquire new property. Protestants in the United States were also wary of the economic power of clerics. State statutes throughout the nineteenth century commonly restricted the ability of religious organizations to hold real and personal property. As one senator put it, his home state (Illinois) restricted religious groups to the ownership of $50,000 in property—why should not the same rules be imposed on the Latter-day Saints in Utah? The Utah territorial legislature's explicit grant of unlimited property rights to the Mormon Church was, from this perspective, extraordinary. The wealth of the church, as well as its opposition to public education, struck many antipolygamists as a reincarnation of Roman Catholic (especially papal) despotism on American soil. They argued that traditional remedies for Catholic despotism were already in place throughout the country and should be as valid in Utah as elsewhere. State mortmain statutes, of course, were inherited from a vigorous English tradition of anti-Catholicism, which migrated across the Atlantic. Antipolygamists further adapted the tradition to suit the new "theocracy" in the West, imposing the $50,000 limitation on the Saints in Utah. As Edmunds's cosponsor in the House explained his support for the bill, "I have, in reality, attempted to engraft the polity of Old Virginia upon the polity of Utah. . . . We do not allow the church to have any property except the property upon which the church building stands and that upon which the parsonage for its pastor is erected."[38]

The Edmunds-Tucker Act, reaffirming and reinforcing earlier antipolygamy legislation, also dictated that the corporate charter—that is, the authorization in law for the church to exercise corporate privileges—was formally revoked. Revocation of a corporate charter as a device for undermining monopoly power was also a familiar, if recent, characteristic of state law. By the mid-1880s, several states had brought suit under common law and statutory antimonopoly principles. Those suits sought revocation of corporate charters by the sovereign entities that granted them legal existence in the first place on the theory that corporations that had joined monopolistic trusts had violated fundamental legal doctrines restricting all of corporate action. The Edmunds-Tucker Act, from this perspective, was the federal version of such state suits, but with the added interest of religion at one end of the spectrum of issues and marriage at the other.[39]

Taken together, the provisions of the Edmunds-Tucker Act were a powerful endorsement of an imagined world of marriage, faith, and individual initiative in the economy. The small producer, the nuclear household, and disestablished religion were revealed as the key components of a political economy in which women (and, by implication, wealth) were equally distributed. The household, in such a vision, was the basis for economic competition as well as the wellspring of democratic legitimacy, the site of engagement with the external, competitive structures of democracy and commerce. The act homed in on the core of Sainthood in late nineteenth-century Utah—the corporate, communal nature of Mormon identity so deeply tied to polygamy and the group-focused ethic that set Mormons apart as a sanctified people.[40]

Edmunds met stiff opposition to his proposed linkage between faith, marriage, and the market. Some critics argued that the church corporation could not be guilty; the law already punished the men who led it. Others claimed that revocation of the charter was warranted but that the proceeds should go back to the donors. Edmunds, defending his plan for public education, pointed out that returning property to donors would actually increase the wealth of polygamists. Unless the church corporation were dissolved, further explained Tucker in the House, polygamy could never be effectively stamped out. The "power of the hierarchy is complete and absolute," Tucker claimed. "[A]s long as that organized power of the church continues, so long will every member of that church be under its control." Thus, *only* by revoking the corporate charter of the church, and limiting its capacity to acquire new property, claimed supporters of the bill, could Mormons in Utah become "free citizens" acting without the "superstitious reverence [of the] concentrated and corporate wealth" of the church. After more than a year of debate and parliamentary maneuvering, only thirteen senators voted against the Edmunds-Tucker Act, and the legislation passed the House by a comparable margin in 1887. In the end, the statute's connections between corporate behavior, concentration of wealth, and personal freedom seemed self-evident to many antipolygamists. Their formula, which relied on state legal tradition to promote a national political economy based on corporate restraint and respect for individual households, eventually supported further federal intervention.[41]

In 1890, only three years later, Edmunds made similar arguments about the interdependence of competition, property, and individual character in the debates over the Sherman Act, the statute that still governs the legal treatment of monopolistic entities and behavior in the United States. Edmunds was a profound believer in the virtues of competition and the essentially corrupt nature of monopoly, whether exercised by railroads, by trusts, or by religious corporations. Edmunds was in fact the author of most of the provisions of the Sherman Act, including the forfeiture clause, which requires that all profits made by monopolistic behavior be disgorged by the guilty corporation. Edmunds's wholesale reconstruction of Utah's economy was a powerful precedent for the effectiveness of his vision and its benign relationship to the law (and power) of the states.[42]

The antitrust bill, Edmunds argued, like his earlier antipolygamy bill, was designed to do no more than apply nationally what the states had already crafted locally and through the wisdom of the common law—a vigorous defense of competition in the interests of freedom. National antitrust and antipolygamy legislation were adaptations, claimed Edmunds, rather than alterations of state law at the federal level. Such laws, reassuring in their familiarity, Republican antipolygamists argued, constituted the distillation rather than the abrogation of tradition. Replying to those who claimed that such drastic measures were beyond anything they had previously done to Utah, George Edmunds dismissed their doubts and waverings as uninformed. His purpose, he argued again and again, was only to require Mormons in Utah to observe the legal rules that all the states required of their own citizens. By removing the "special privileges" accorded to the church and its leaders, Edmunds insisted, he simply reduced them to the same level as other corporations and men of faith.[43]

As he had been instructed, Attorney General Augustus Garland ordered a bill filed in the territorial supreme court, asking for the appointment of a receiver to hold and manage all the property of the dissolved corporation. The court appointed Frank Dyer, a former territorial official with strong antipolygamist credentials, as receiver. Church authorities voluntarily "surrendered" real property, including the Temple Block (which was later held not to be subject to forfeiture), the General Tithing Office, and the ornate Gardo House, all of which were rented back to the church. Escheated personal property, including stock, cash, and cattle, totaled some $400,000, but without question far less than the true value and extent of the church's property. Mormons later claimed that Dyer's self-interest, combined with his antipathy to the Saints, brought maximum benefit to his own pocketbook.[44] The church's leaders were in jail or on the lam, its political power eroded fast as non-Mormons swelled the ranks of legal voters, and its financial resources were abolished in one fell swoop. Even church property was now subject to invasion by antipolygamists. Although it is by no means clear that federal officials found and seized more than a fraction of church property, Mormons knew well that their ability to resist was devastated by the new act. Dire necessity prompted the church quickly to perfect its appeal to the Supreme Court.[45]

At the Supreme Court, the role of traditional legal theories and the power of the central government to adopt and adapt the legal structures of the states formed the nucleus of a bitter debate among the justices. The use of legal structures to reform local societies in the interest of Protestant morals and monogamous marriage, of course, lay at the heart of the connection between polygamy and property in the Edmunds-Tucker Act. Such reformation was an exercise of power at the national level that raised fundamental questions of the independent powers of corporations, the disposition of their property, and the authority of legislatures to decide such questions. At the Court, the exercise of federal control over legal entities (corporations) whose powers and responsibilities confronted jurists as well as legislators in the late nineteenth century required the justices to grapple with legal tradition in changed circumstances. Finally, the church's constitutional challenge to the Edmunds-Tucker Act in *Late Corporation of the Church of Jesus Christ of Latter-day Saints v. United States* forced the federal judiciary to contend with Congress's use of the traditional judicial power known as equity. Managing and redistributing legal and financial power of dissolved corporations in the interests of the broader society was traditionally a judicial prerogative.

James Overton Broadhead, a well-known Missouri Democrat hired by the church to argue the case for the church, made essentially three claims: first, that the Edmunds-Tucker law was an unconstitutional repudiation of an executed contract and second, that even if Congress did have the power to dissolve a corporation by disapproving the legislation that created the charter, the time lag between the date of incorporation (1850) and the date of disapproval (1887) created a presumptive approval that could not thereafter be revoked by the government. Finally, Broadhead argued that by directing the attorney general to institute proceedings against the former corporation, by ordering the territorial court to decide the case, and by specifying the manner in which the assets of the corporation were to be administered and disbursed, Congress had exceeded the bounds of its proper authority and had engaged in "judicial legislation."[46]

For the United States, Attorney General Garland devoted considerable attention to the question of the validity of the Edmunds-Tucker law. At the same time, he took repeated jabs at the obduracy of the Mormon Church, at the distastefulness of its morals, and—most important—at the financial and legal power it wielded in the territory. Garland made short work of the power to dissolve territorial corporations. By the late 1880s, Garland was on stable ground in arguing that the express power to annul territorial legislation in the organic act that created the territory gave Congress the right to act at any time.[47]

Garland focused instead on the nature of the charter itself. Not only had Congress expressly reserved the same kind of power that allowed states to modify or abolish corporations, but this corporation, he argued, was void ab initio: the very charter violated the Constitution. Because it granted a religious organization the right to make laws that affect society, most conspicuous among them control over marriage and the right to tax citizens through the tithe, Garland claimed, the territorial legislation that had first created the Mormon Church corporation violated the establishment clause. Not since the Inquisition, argued Garland in an appeal to the popular equation of Mormonism and Roman Catholicism, had a church obtained such open-ended power to define (and execute) the laws.[48]

By any reading of the charter itself, this was an exaggeration of the powers granted to the Mormon Church. Still, the influence of the church did determine the political and legal life of the territory, and the territorial statute incorporating the church provided that church decisions on marriage and other aspects of membership "could not be legally questioned." What Garland was attempting, therefore, was to ratchet up a largely de facto establishment into an explicitly de jure one, and then argue that de jure establishments in the territories violated the federal establishment clause. This question, of course, had been a central issue in the debate over polygamy. The power of territorial governments to control their internal workings in the ways that states did (including the power to establish a religion) had been lost in *Reynolds* and the Morrill Act. Nobody was safe, Garland argued, when a group of men could form a company, call themselves a religion, and exercise such legal control over the personal and financial lives of their unfortunate adherents.

Garland, too, tapped into powerful veins of anti-Mormon feeling by highlighting the connections between corporate structure, the property of the corporation, and the maintenance of polygamy. Polygamy, he argued, was integral to Mormon corporate power; destroy that inordinate power, and polygamy would fall as well. The cure for polygamy, claimed the attorney general, required the nation to treat the related symptoms (political monopoly of the government of the territory and economic monopoly of the resources of the territory) as well as the core (the introduction of competition into the marital household).[49]

Counsel hastened to reply in a supplemental brief that (even if valid in other respects) the punishment inflicted was disproportionate to the crime. At the forfeiture proceedings, the territorial supreme court found as a matter of fact that approximately 20 percent of the adult Mormon population was directly involved in polygamy. To confiscate most of the property of an organization as penalty for the crimes of a minority of its members, the church argued, was unwarranted:

> Will it do to enter upon a system of general confiscation and forfeiture of all Church funds, and of all charitable funds, wherever it can be found that *one out of five* of the Church members, or *one out of five* of the beneficiaries of the charitable fund, is unworthy and immoral? If that were the law, . . . it would soon bankrupt many Churches and close up many charitable institutions and asylums by confiscation of their property and funds. . . . [L]ove of justice, equity and fair dealing, and a firm belief in the rights of property and the protection of all persons in their rights to acquire and use and enjoy their property, compels the . . . strongest condemnation of the high-handed acts of confiscation and spoliation attempted by the act of March 3, 1887.[50]

The Supreme Court's decision in *Late Corporation* was announced in late May 1890, more than a year after the case was argued. According to several sources, the delay was designed to give the church time to abandon polygamy before the axe fell. There were cracks along the polygamous seam among the Mormon leadership by the late 1880s. Democratic clubs, dominated by young Mormon lawyers who had little patience for continued insistence that antipolygamy legislation was unconstitutional, demonstrated that traditional allegiance to the Mormon People's Party was wavering. George Q. Cannon (who was also campaigning hard—and unsuccessfully—to be named president of the church after John Taylor died in mid-1887) took the lead in

This photograph, taken in 1888, shows George Cannon surrounded by other "cohabs" and "polygs," all serving sentences in the Utah Penitentiary. Cannon's surrender to federal officials was part of an effort to demonstrate that Mormons would no longer defy federal statutes criminalizing polygamy. Courtesy of Utah State Historical Society.

advocating the disavowal of the Principle, although he was himself a "much-married man," as antipolygamist wits put it. In late 1888, Cannon even surrendered to federal officials, demonstrating that the highest church officials considered themselves subject to the law. He was brought to trial quickly and received an extraordinarily light sentence, reportedly at the behest of Attorney General George Jenks.[51]

The church also publicized that no new polygamous marriages were authorized in 1888 and 1889. Territorial representative John T. Caine even gave a speech in Congress titled "Polygamy in Utah—A Dead Issue." But several factors undermined the value of such public relations efforts. First, there was evidence that plural marriages did in fact take place, whether or not specific approval had been granted. Then, on his release from prison, church leader Rudger Clawson delivered a fiery sermon defending polygamy, promising that "we will not make the promise to do away with [celestial marriage] any more than we will promise to do away with the principle of faith." The sermon was picked up by Eastern papers, tarnishing the claim that plural marriage was on the wane. The church also did not promise a commitment to prohibit polygamy forever. The provision declaring polygamy a "misdemeanor" in a draft constitution in 1887, which presaged yet another unsuccessful bid for statehood, was widely understood outside Utah as a ploy to divert attention. Such a ploy would remove unlawful cohabitation from the criminal code and deliver polygamy into the hands of state prosecutors, who were themselves members of the church. Some antipolygamists had argued that the Edmunds-Tucker Act went too far, that instead lawmakers should allow criminal process to take its course. But by the late 1880s, delay and compromise would not satisfy the majority of the justices of the Supreme Court, or the country; they wanted to win the war for monogamy outright, and quickly.[52]

An additional factor may also help explain the delay in handing down an opinion in the case. The justices disagreed on the merits. A 6–3 majority, in a long and scholarly opinion by Justice Joseph Bradley, upheld both the dissolution of the church corporation and the forfeiture of its assets. But Chief Justice Melville Westin Fuller was joined in dissent by Stephen Field and Lucius Quintius Cincinnatus Lamar (himself a relic of the Old South and an opponent of anti-polygamy legislation during his tenure in the Senate). The debate between the justices revolved around traditional common-law theories of the corporation as a public trust and the relationship of such theories to the law of equity.[53]

Bradley's majority opinion knit together many internal, court-centered concerns of precedent and interpretation with the external political and humanitarian antipolygamy ethic. By 1890, exasperation colored the Court's vision, lending Bradley's opinion an impatience that denied some of the very real suffering of Mormons. Given the obduracy of the church corporation, Bradley queried rhetorically: is "the promotion of such a nefarious system and practice, so repugnant to our laws and to the principles of our civilization, . . . to be allowed to continue by the sanction of the government itself"? Bradley turned the question into one that depicted the Mormons asking the government, through maintenance of the corporate form, for official support for criminal activity. The intended answer was so plainly "no" that it raised the issue of why this rogue corporation had been allowed to exist for so long: "It is unnecessary here to refer to the past history of the sect, . . . to the attempt to establish an independent community, to their efforts to drive from the territory all who were not connected with them. . . . The tale is one of patience on the part of the American government and people, and of contempt of authority and resistance to law on the part of the Mormons. Whatever persecutions they may have suffered in the early part of their existence, . . . they have no excuse for their persistent defiance of law of the government of the United States."[54]

Bradley was also sensitive to the international embarrassment occasioned by the existence of a polygamous sect in Utah and by the role of immigration in the maintenance of the church's power. The spread of Mormonism through foreign missionary work undermined the progress of American civilization, Bradley maintained. The church itself was culpable: "[I]ts emissaries are engaged in many countries in propagating this nefarious doctrine [of polygamy], and urging its converts to join the community in Utah. The existence of such a propaganda is a blot on our civilization. The organization of a community for the spread and practice of polygamy is, in a measure, a return to barbarism. It is contrary to the spirit of Christianity and of the civilization which Christianity had produced in the Western world."[55]

"Barbarous" customs, Bradley emphasized, could not enjoy legal protection simply because their practitioners claimed that faith impelled them: "The practice of Suttee by Hindu widows may have sprung from a supposed religious conviction. The offering of human sacrifice by our own ancestors in Britain was no doubt sanctified by an equally conscientious impulse. But do we, on that account, hesitate to brand these practices, now, as crimes against society?" The language of civilization and barbarism, of course, resonated with decades of Protestant humanitarianism in general and antipolygamy in particular. It also allowed the Court to explain why this corporation had failed and must now be dissolved, and how the diversion of its assets to public education could survive judicial scrutiny. As Bradley explained it, the Church of Jesus Christ of Latter-day Saints exemplified the threat posed by the corporate form in the hands of the undeserving. The Mormon Church, he said, had no respect for law or civilization. In a legal system preoccupied with organized corruption, the existence in Utah of a "contumascious organization," a community dedicated to the overthrow of civilization through the corruption of marriage, Bradley insisted, exemplified abuse of the corporate form.[56]

The connection between Christian civilization and corporate integrity was vividly illustrated by a "charity" (that is, a religious organization) that belied the very definition of philanthropy. In Bradley's analysis, the "pretence" of religion by the Mormon Church was "sophistical," an attempt to cloak a practice that was "obnoxious to condemnation and punishment by civil authority." By turning what should have been donations into mandatory contributions through the tithe, and by the dedication of the proceeds to an unlawful and nefarious use (the propagation of polygamy), the church corporation literally exceeded the "religious and charitable uses" of any such organization. By definition, then, this was a "failed" charity, a corporation whose existence depended on a violation of the "civilization which Christianity had produced." Dissolution, Bradley reasoned, was the most appropriate means of vindicating the "sovereign dominion" of the people of the United States, themselves a Christian people.[57]

After dissolution of the church corporation, the disposition of its considerable assets became the central question and the nub of the dispute among the justices at the Supreme Court. At common law, the real property (that is, land and buildings) of a dissolved corporation reverted to the grantors, and the personal property (money, legal interests, and so on), to the state. By the 1880s, however, the proliferation of private corporations and the frequency of their dissolution led many states to modify the common-law rule. The assets of dissolved corporations, instead of reverting automatically to the government, were treated as a trust for creditors and stockholders. The Edmunds-Tucker Act, however, declared that the real and personal property of the church corporation was to be forfeited to the national government, then to be dedicated to public education in the territory.[58]

The majority opinion dealt at length with the propriety of such disposition of the church's property. As Justice Bradley explained it, the "ancient rule" still applied to charitable corporations. Because charities were by definition engaged in endeavors of interest to the state, it was only appropriate that the personal property of failed charities should revert to the state. And, applying the common-law rule for real property to the situation at issue, Bradley held that it was evident that the federal government, as the sovereign who organized the territory and gave it political life, was itself the grantor of the land in question. Thus, both the real and personal property reverted to the government under the applicable law of corporate dissolution. In addition, the United States could not validly be called upon to dedicate the property, real or personal, to the purposes for which the individual members of the church had originally made their gifts, as Mormon lawyers argued it should. The Mormon Church's property, whether acquired through business dealings, or "taxes imposed upon the people" (tithes), or voluntary gifts, had been acquired in direct contravention of legal mandates. The church corporation, through its abuse of the laws against polygamy, Bradley held, was dedicated to nefarious ends. The "character" and "objects" of the corporation, he concluded, because they were so intimately tied to the "spread and practice of polygamy," contradicted even the basic claim that such a corporation could validly be labeled "charitable."[59]

Charity, as the Court explained it, was a concept rooted in Christianity, governed by the laws of Europe and especially of England. In England, the failure of a charitable gift, especially when the desired use was declared void by statute, empowered the king in his sovereign capacity to honor the charitable intent of the donor and redirect the gift to an analogous use. Included among such failed gifts were those made for "superstitious uses," contrary, that is, to the Protestant faith of his majesty and the people he ruled. Applying the statute against superstitious uses in the late seventeenth century, for example, the Lord Chancellor upheld the redirection of a bequest for establishing a synagogue (which failed because it would propagate "the Jewish religion") to a foundling hospital. Known as the doctrine of cy pres, the rule allowed the British sovereign substantial latitude to alter the recipient of a gift even when contrary to the express wishes and faith of the donor. The king and the courts that supported the doctrine claimed they honored the desire to give, rather than frustrating it by returning the gift to the grantor.[60]

In the new nation, the states succeeded "to all the rights of the crown" for purposes of charitable uses, as Justice Story held for a unanimous Supreme Court in 1815. He applied the doctrine of cy pres to lands in Vermont that had been set aside for the support of the Church of England before the Revolution, upholding the state legislature's redirection of the gift to the establishment of public schools—a charitable use in keeping with a disestablished state. The precedent—dedication to public education of property formerly reserved for a controversial religious use now unlawful and thus void—translated the English rule into American law. The democratic nature of public education made it acceptable for the traditional equitable redirection of imperfect charitable gifts in a republic.[61]

At the end of the nineteenth century, the Edmunds-Tucker Act replicated the solution reached by the Vermont legislature at the beginning of the century. As the majority opinion held, the public had an interest in the property of the former Mormon Church, because "property given to a charity becomes in a measure public property" and the failure of the gift should not reduce the overall amount of charitable funds dedicated to beneficent uses. The interest of government in the disposition of gifts, Bradley stressed, sustained Congress's desire to ensure that funds or lands donated to the Mormon Church were not returned to private owners.[62]

Further, Bradley insisted, beneficence had its origins in the "spirit of Christianity." Christian civilization, Bradley held, was both the

The General Tithing Store in Salt Lake City as it appeared in the mid-1850s. The tithing store was among the properties forfeited under the Edmunds-Tucker Act. Courtesy of Utah State Historical Society.

source of charitable impulses and the barometer against which gifts must be measured. The "principles of reason and public policy which prevail in all civilized and enlightened communities" required that charitable gifts be placed under the "guardianship of the laws," if the object of the gift had "failed, or because [the gifts] have become unlawful and repugnant to the public policy of the State." The repugnance to public policy, in this case, was the explicit dedication of charitable funds to an "un-Christian" practice (polygamy). Polygamy, and its support by the church, demonstrated that the funds in question had been misdirected and that redirection was a valid exercise of sovereign authority. In Bradley's view, the forfeiture of church property was an essential means of vindicating Christian civilization and thus affirming the international law of charities. The Vermont example, he emphasized, demonstrated that the public schools were appropriate recipients of the property of a failed charity. Mormons' traditional opposition to public education, needless to say, made the insult comparable to the diversion of synagogue funds to establish a foundling hospital in England two centuries earlier.[63]

To hammer home the connection between Christian faith and charity even in a secular republic, Bradley quoted a passage from Nathan Dane's famous *General Abridgment and Digest of American Law*, published in the 1820s, which described the place of charity within the new nation: "[T]he erection of schools and the relief of the poor are always rights, and the law will deny the application of private property only as to uses the nation deems superstitious." By the end of the nineteenth century, "superstitious" (a term that in England had been steeped in anti-Catholic and even anti-Semitic meaning) seemed to many antipolygamists to describe the Mormon faithful. Thus, the Supreme Court implied, to sustain the redirection of the property of the former Mormon Church corporation to public schools was to strike a blow against superstition, and for faith.[64]

Chief Justice Fuller, however, joined by Associate Justices Lamar and Field, argued in a brief but angry dissent that Congress exceeded its authority in the "arbitrary disposition [of the church's property] by judicial legislation." Although one source described the dissent as motivated by old-fashioned states' rights doctrines, the dissenters were in fact more solicitous of separation of federal powers than local sovereignty. The corporation, they conceded, accumulated property for illegal purposes but argued that the "doctrine of *cy-pres* is one of construction [that is, of judicial interpretation], and not of [legislative] administration." Legislative incursions into equity, a decidedly judicial power, whether by state or federal representatives, cut into the powers of the judiciary. The openly redistributive mandate of the Edmunds-Tucker Act could as readily be turned against a lay corporation as against a spiritual one.[65]

The equity powers of the federal judiciary were significant and frequently deployed by 1890. From "friendly receiverships" for railroads that cut out small investors, to labor injunctions that prohibited unionization and strikes, equitable remedies for corporate distress were a judicial innovation of the late nineteenth century. "Government by injunction," as critics put it, allowed courts new remedies and sweeping powers to protect traditional rights in property and contract, or to restructure debt so effectively that the redistributive efforts of legislatures could hardly survive the surgical force of judicial craft.[66]

The relationship of the equitable powers of judges to traditional legal rules of property and contract brought the dissenters at the Supreme Court into direct conflict with the remedial structure of the Edmunds-Tucker Act. Congress, conceded Chief Justice Fuller implicitly, had the power to create or abolish a corporation, and thus the dissolution of the church corporation was valid. But the distribution of corporate assets after dissolution was peculiarly the domain of courts. In an atmosphere in which bankruptcy filings dominated the life of many industries, the power to distribute corporate assets meant considerable judicial influence. Equity empowered the judiciary to wield new public power, even as it veiled the exercise with the rhetoric of traditional doctrine.

Fuller and his fellow dissenters in *Late Corporation* bristled at what they saw as the congressional appropriation of this influence in the name of state law tradition—even when deployed against Mormons and wrapped in the rhetoric of civilization and Christianity. Yet it is important to emphasize here that the dissenters did not advocate protection of the church corporation, or even that the public schools were necessarily an invalid beneficiary of the forfeiture. Instead, they bristled at the idea that Congress could instruct the Supreme Court on the proceeds of the dissolution.

Without question by 1890, therefore, antipolygamists had established the plenary authority of the federal government in the territories. Even more important, antipolygamists demonstrated the political and legal power of absorbing state law into federal reform legislation. The practice, as George Edmunds proved in the statutes that bore his name in the 1880s, allowed Congress to adopt and adapt state law. The use of state structures in federal law reform insulated such innovation with layers of familiarity and tradition. By 1890, when the Supreme Court decided *Late Corporation*, the dissenters at least understood that the legislative use of state common-law traditions entailed a potentially significant reduction in judicial power to control the newfound power of the national political economy.

The struggle over which branch of government would wield particular aspects of increased federal power had begun. The battle between the federal judiciary and federal (and state) legislatures continued, escalating until the New Deal precipitated what has sometimes been called the third American revolution, a story that is beyond the scope of this book but whose roots are in part revealed by the battles over polygamy.

Still, by 1890, the issue so central to the campaign against Mormon plural marriage had been decided; outside Utah, the authority to punish polygamy was virtually unquestioned. So deeply had antipolygamists' moral constitutionalism been absorbed into executive, legislative, and judicial thought and action that the deployment rather than the existence of authority over marriage was the locus of friction.

With the decision in the *Late Corporation* case, the constitutional battle over polygamy, finally, was over. The logic of resistance lay in tatters.

The pain of resistance overwhelmed the Saints, their church, and their commitment to legal difference. After four long decades of conflict, the victory was as eagerly anticipated by most antipolygamists as it was dreaded by many Mormons. Mormon leaders understood that survival and resistance had finally come full circle. The journey away from the political systems of the states and into a constitutional space where Saints were the majority could not protect the Principle from a changing constitutional world. In September 1890, Wilford Woodruff, the last of the Mormon presidents to have made the great journey westward with Brigham Young, capitulated. After much prayer, Woodruff received a communication from God that counseled abandoning the legal claim to practice the Principle to ensure the survival of the church. Issued as a "Manifesto," Woodruff's statement assured all concerned that he would no longer advise the faithful to engage in unlawful practices. The Manifesto was controversial among many Mormons. Non-Mormons in Utah challenged Woodruff to bring the revelation to a popular vote. With widespread silence construed as approval, Woodruff claimed the habitual "unanimous" consent of the faithful to this radical departure from doctrine.[67]

As antipolygamists grew more confident of victory in the early 1890s, the stranglehold on the church relaxed. Prosecution of vocally defiant Mormons continued for several years in the territorial courts, but hundreds of pending cases were dismissed on the motion of the prosecutors, sometimes "in the interests of justice" but usually for the more noncommittal "for reasons on file." Similarly, all personal property of the church that had been confiscated in 1887 was returned in 1894; real property, in 1896. Presidential pardons of convicted or indicted polygamists, conditioned only on the promise to obey the law in the future, were issued in 1893 and 1894.[68]

EPILOGUE

The (Un)Faithful Constitution

Few antipolygamists questioned the means to the end or the merits of the moral constitutionalism they had imposed on Utah. Pockets of antipolygamy rhetoric survived, especially among women's auxiliaries of the home mission movement and the missionaries they funded, and from time to time in Congress. But the enemy had formally conceded the field: once the Saints abandoned the claim to a higher law of marriage endorsed by a local majority, they ceased to pose a direct threat to the law of the center. Some Mormons might still practice polygamy (although never so unabashedly as before 1890), but they did not openly claim they had a legal right to do so.[1]

The abandonment of Mormons' claim of a constitutional right to legal difference gradually relaxed enmity between antipolygamists and Mormons. In the end, constitutional law was what antipolygamists fought for, and their opponents had surrendered. They were content, by and large, with a symbolic victory. Just as many Northerners had argued and fought for emancipation but their commitment to freedpersons had eroded by the mid-1870s, constitutional victory in Utah exhausted many antipolygamists' commitment. Once Mormons abandoned their legal claim, mere contrary social fact, while uncomfortable, or embarrassing, or the butt of jokes, generally was not compelling at the constitutional level. The church continued its extensive economic activity and regained its corporate stature. By and large, plural marriages were not dissolved, yet statehood was granted in 1896. Mormonism has survived and flourished in its new accommodationist incarnation.[2]

Yet the country itself was different, however little the faith of Mormons had been shaken. In their encounter with Mormon resistance, American politicians, lawyers, and judges fought for and eventually realized constitutional power and Christian meaning in their political culture. They had crafted and then imposed a new constitutional vision. The Christian structure and meaning of marriage, antipolygamists reasoned, was essential to the flourishing of a democracy. And Christian marriage was best protected by a government composed of men whose religious beliefs and marriages were private and monogamous. Theirs was a journey of multiple paradoxes, the most poignant of which entailed the dismantling of public religious power to protect private Christian faith, a profoundly Protestant understanding of religious voluntarism and its relationship to political legitimacy. The insistence that the Constitution enshrined such a Protestant vision in the religion clauses of the First Amendment invigorated antipolygamists' conviction of the righteousness of the founding document and the country it described.

Mormons learned many lessons about the changeable nature of constitutional law and theory, as well as the fear of religious difference across the country. They endured the faithlessness of the nation and its lack of real commitment to a constitution that created space for latter-day inspiration. The loss of the battle for polygamy was bitter and still resonates in Mormons' historical scholarship. The authority of the Constitution, instead of vindicating difference and local power, reflected the interests of the enemies of Zion. The outrage and the pain of betrayal, combined with the lingering sense of defeat, led traditional historical treatments of the subject to focus on Mormons as victims of a powerful and oppressive legal order.[3]

Mormons made law, however, as well as had law imposed upon them. The power of their faith and their commitment to a new legal order constructed the challenge to the rest of the country, not only at the initial stages before the enactment of the first antipolygamy legislation in the early 1860s, but well beyond. Mormons' resistance to legal rules imposed from the outside, and their deployment of law and legal argument as tools of resistance, required the rest of the country to grapple with the meaning and limits of religious liberty as never before. The Saints *forced* their opponents to take them seriously and to explain how localism should be limited in unprecedented ways. Mormons' creativity and tenacity require us to recognize them as legal actors and constitutional theorists, as well as eventual losers in the battle for constitutional legitimacy and local difference. Mormons witnessed the creation of a new, constitutional authority in opposition to their faith; the contest over polygamy was key to its creation.

THE DAILY GRAPHIC

AN ILLUSTRATED EVENING NEWSPAPER

39 & 41 PARK PLACE

VOL. XXXIX. All the News. Five Editions Daily. NEW YORK, WEDNESDAY, DECEMBER 16, 1885—TWELVE PAGES. 20 Per Year in Advance. Single Copies, Three Cents. NO. 3973

DRIVING THE LAST NAIL INTO THE MORMON COFFIN.

THE SUPREME COURT DECIDES THAT THE MORMONS MUST GO—THE DECISION IN THE CASE OF ANGUS M. CANNON.

The mallet titled "Decision of the U.S. Supreme Court" is poised to drive the final nail into the coffin of Mormonism, as lightning strikes the Mormon Tabernacle behind. From *The Daily Graphic*, 16 December 1885. Courtesy of Yale University Library.

The new constitutional authority dispersed traditional religious power to individual husbands and wives, endowing them with political as well as spiritual capacity through their union. This solution, which entailed both the privatization and politicization of marriage, was appealing in its assertion of moral authority. It also ratified the theory that private structures were the source of public power, heartening Americans with the conviction that state interference was warranted only in egregious cases. The example of polygamy provided the comforting reassurance to the rest of the country that whatever complaints woman's rights activists or antidivorce theorists had about the law of marriage, at least nothing they could point to held a candle to Utah. And Protestants could make common cause even with Catholics against Mormons. Facing stark religious difference, many antipolygamists discovered that their commitment to monogamy gave them reason to treat with those who were otherwise unlikely allies. They also determined that legal and religious truth were united in Christian monogamy.

To protect monogamy, antipolygamists learned to their lasting satisfaction, was to observe the common law in its most appealing aspects—the union of husband and wife, their mutual obligation, their respective duties and responsibilities. Accordingly, the essential qualities of marriage, though shot through with religious meaning, were not alterable at the whim of clerics or heretics. As antipolygamists saw it, these qualities described the contours of liberty, which validated a particularly Protestant morality, if not in all details, at least in situations where it was really warranted—that is, against Mormon polygamy.

At the outset, constitutional law would not have admitted such national interference with local affairs. The federal government, although it was conceded to have more power in the initial organization of the territories than at any point in the states, was broadly thought to be limited to basic questions of the structure of public government. Once the "necessary and proper" structures of governance were in place, issues of "domestic governance" were matters for local debate and local disposition. However, arguing that no civilized group could disagree about such a fundamental question of domestic relations, antipolygamists claimed that Mormons *must* be barbaric, and thus undemocratic, inhumane, un-American. The uniform conclusion of all the states that polygamy was a crime provided antipolygamists with the mandate for constructing and then enforcing a new kind of federal control. They hoisted state law out of its local home and thus nationalized constitutional law in ways that were still respectful of state tradition, and familiar in terms of legal concepts and principles. The ambiguous legal status of territories allowed for the importation of state law into federal legislation and Supreme Court jurisprudence. The message it sent to other states and territories was that all Americans had much in common: the cumulative power of their own local customs confirmed their national character, justifying the forcible reconstruction of an aberrant local difference. The legal world that was created by the contest over polygamy took local law seriously, even as it eviscerated the tradition of localism.

The Constitution would not tolerate religious license, antipolygamists were pleased to learn; they labored long and hard to ensure that Protestant Christianity and religious liberty seamlessly reinforced one another. The popular conviction that the lessons of antipolygamy were woven into the fabric of constitutional law and political culture is particularly apparent in a case decided by the Supreme Court shortly before *Late Corporation* crushed the last vestiges of resistance. Writing for a unanimous Court in *Davis v. Beason*, Justice Stephen Field sustained "test oaths" for Mormons in Idaho Territory. The territorial legislature in the late 1880s, reacting to the influx of Mormons, restricted the power of the new settlers by limiting the franchise to those who could swear they did not adhere to any group that advocated plural marriage. The tone of Field's opinion for the Court illustrates how deeply antipolygamist ethics had been absorbed at the highest levels of government. The opinion also reveals the intolerance and exasperation at the heart of antipolygamists' turn to coercion in the 1880s. The legacy of the antipolygamy campaign includes not only the power of moral argument and its relationship to disestablishment and legal structures generally but also the layers of coercion and inhumanity that lurked within a movement ostensibly dedicated to the preservation of individual liberty and humanism through law.

Justice Field expressed the outrage of the justices when confronted with recalcitrant Mormon polygamists. "Few crimes are more pernicious to the best interests of society [than polygamy] and receive more general or more deserved punishment," he wrote for the Court. About such a question, Field stressed, "there can be no serious discussion." Of course, "serious discussion" was precisely what sustained four decades of focused debate, litigation, and constitutional theorizing and proved that serious difference over the meaning of faith in American life and law was anything but out of the question. The Mormon Question would not have provoked such virulent and long-lived responses had there been unanimity on the issue. Yet Justice Field, like many other antipolygamists, was so deeply invested in the

Justice Field was a trenchant critic of polygamy and held that no civilized person could reasonably defend its practice. Courtesy of Library of Congress.

assumption of a valid political interest in the monogamous structure of the household that he imagined that no "difference of opinion" on the question was possible.[4]

Davis was an appeal from a conviction for conspiracy, not polygamy. Samuel Davis was convicted of conspiring to swear falsely that he was not a member of an organization that encouraged its adherents to practice polygamy "as a doctrinal rite of such organization." Anti-polygamists frequently accused Mormons of stifling political competition and political debate to protect a local religious majority from real challenge at the polls. In the end, the local religious majority in Idaho Territory, which had seen the expansion of the Mormon population there in the 1880s, deployed a similar tactic. To qualify as a voter in territorial Idaho in 1890, each male of twenty-one years or more had to pass a "test," to swear that his religious affiliation was not to Mormonism.[5]

Justice Field held that "religion" for purposes of the franchise, as for the free exercise clause, was bounded by the concept of "general Christianity," which precluded protection for "acts, recognized by the general consent of the Christian world in modern times as proper matters for prohibitory legislation." Field dismissed the idea that the Constitution would shield alternative moral structures under the "pretense" of religion, insisting that this confused the concept of religion with that of "the *cultus* or form of worship of a particular sect." The result would undermine the "good order and morals of society." Instead, religious liberty was designed to protect individual citizens against attempts to "control the[ir] mental operations, and enforce an outward conformity to a prescribed standard" rather than to excuse attempts to redefine legal or political structures in light of religious belief. Notwithstanding such perfect toleration, "[h]owever free the exercise of religion may be, it must be subordinate to the criminal law of the country, passed with reference to actions regarded by general consent as properly the subjects of punitive legislation." Because the franchise was the epitome of political expression, the Court held, a propolygamy vote, a form of expression contrary (and dangerous) to legitimate political goals, would pervert liberty into license by twisting freedom to produce despotism. The consequences would be dire indeed. To protect the holy estate of matrimony, and thereby to preserve freedom, Field stressed, it was necessary "to prevent persons from being enabled by their votes to defeat the criminal laws of the country."[6]

Davis's crime was the intention to undermine the validity of the test oath. According to his prosecutors, in other words, Davis would lie because his belief system was fundamentally at odds with orthodox Christian notions of punishment for false swearing. The problem of lying, of course, had long troubled judges and prosecutors in polygamy prosecutions, as well as in older state blasphemy cases. As the Pennsylvania Supreme Court put it in 1824, failure to punish blasphemers would be to destroy the legal system, paving the way for "perjury by taking a false oath upon the book, fornication, and adultery." From this perspective, polygamy and the subornation of perjury were the predictable results of Mormons' claim to a new moral and legal dispensation. Much was at stake, antipolygamists believed, for the perversion of the Word might well entail the destruction of law itself. The Constitution, Justice Field reasoned, must allow for the self-protection contained in the test oath.[7]

Yet there was also a fundamentally antidemocratic logic to the *Davis* opinion, which was, rhetorically at least, not present in earlier state or federal religion clause jurisprudence. As the Delaware Supreme Court emphasized in an important antebellum blasphemy case, the people, should they decide to adopt another religion, could democratically alter the legal protection of Christianity. Majority rule, in other words, justified the criminal punishment of blasphemers. The decision in *Davis* precluded just such an alteration on the theory that the moral difference of Mormonism was itself evidence of the perversion of democracy.[8]

Antipolygamists' moral constitutionalism hardened into law in the Supreme Court's opinions in the polygamy cases. As the Civil War taught Northerners that religious commitment not only revealed to believers the sin that was slavery but also sustained the Union by its expiation, so the Supreme Court taught attentive Americans that, at its core, the Constitution was an essential expression of "general" Christian humanitarianism. The abolition of slavery's "twin relic," moreover, was accomplished within the parameters of a Constitution already written and ratified (for that matter, with portions of the Constitution that were part of the original document or amendments that were themselves incorporated by 1791) long before Mormon polygamists claimed access to a higher law. The lesson imposed upon Mormons, and telegraphed to the entire nation, was that the Constitution had been, morally, a Protestant document all along.

And yet, antipolygamists maintained, there was an essential distance between the government created by the Constitution and the institutional manifestations of religion. The constitutional morality was based on principles of a general Christianity that presupposed separate institutional structures for church and state, as well as legal protection for private governance imbued with profound religious meaning. Truly the separation of church and state "by no means involve[d] a separation of the nation from Christianity and Christian morality," as one contemporary put it. Nor did democracy in the second half of the nineteenth century entail the ability to restructure authority in light of faith, especially in areas of "private" (that is, sexual and domestic) governance.[9]

Antipolygamists sought, and were sure they could find, spiritual

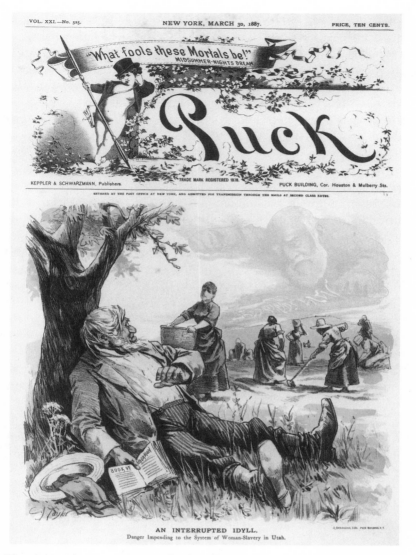

VOL. XXI.—No. 525.   NEW YORK, MARCH 30, 1887.   PRICE, TEN CENTS.

"What fools these Mortals be!"
MIDSUMMER-NIGHTS DREAM

Puck

KEPPLER & SCHWARZMANN, Publishers.   TRADE MARK REGISTERED 1878.   PUCK BUILDING, Cor. Houston & Mulberry Sts.

ENTERED AT THE POST OFFICE AT NEW YORK, AND ADMITTED FOR TRANSMISSION THROUGH THE MAILS AT SECOND CLASS RATES.

AN INTERRUPTED IDYLL.
Danger Impending to the System of Woman-Slavery in Utah.

The theory that women were "enslaved" in Utah and the implication that women elsewhere in the United States were "free" are illustrated in a cartoon that appeared in the popular magazine *Puck* in the mid-1880s. Courtesy of Yale University Library.

security and individual happiness for men and women within this constitutional vision. The power of this vision blinded most anti-polygamists to inequality and suffering in monogamous marriages, however. The investment in monogamy, and the denigration of po-lygamy, freighted the "right" kind of union with a spiritual and constitutional power that implicitly denied that patriarchal structures and betrayal could exist outside Utah, too. Once more, the analogy of antipolygamy to antislavery provides insight; if one focuses on the gross facts of institutionalized, legally supported involuntary servitude, the subtler features of unfair bargaining conditions for "free laborers" may be rendered invisible. The "home of liberty" imagined and defended in the novels of Metta Victor in the 1850s had become ubiquitous and all but unchallenged by the end of the polygamy period.

Antipolygamists' investment in marriage as the spiritual center of governance had increased over the course of the nineteenth century. In 1882, for example, the influential activist Frances Willard wrote the introduction to a collection of antipolygamy stories and articles that was published under the title *The Women of Mormonism*. The aim of the book, as its editor Jennie Anderson Froiseth explained, was to call attention to the abuse of women, and lack of respect for law and individual freedoms, in Mormon Utah. Willard, whose presidency of the Woman's Christian Temperance Union (WCTU) launched the organization into wide-ranging political and religious activity, lent her considerable influence to the antipolygamy campaign not only because Western (and many Eastern) members of the WCTU were also active in antipolygamy circles but also because polygamy challenged in fundamental ways what Willard labeled the "beloved Home Religion."[10]

The phrase captured both the significance of religion in home life in much of late-nineteenth-century political theory and the answering embrace of the importance of marriage in Protestantism. Willard and her fellow antipolygamists, using law and legal rhetoric in the service of monogamy, urged the country to prevent Mormons from restructuring the law of marriage in light of their peculiar religious faith. Indeed, Willard argued, the flourishing of the country depended on respect for women in marriage, because women's "relation to the Home, Society, and the State, shall determine [mens'] degree of elevation or ignorance." Only in monogamous marriage, Willard insisted, were women truly valued and respected. The isolation of Utah was not a reason for discounting the breadth and urgency of the threat, either. As Willard saw it, "each woman degraded means the potential degradation of all women." Christian "manhood's indignation and woman's righteous wrath" were the only sure protectors of the natural law of marriage, the "Gospel of Him who came not only to redeem the world but to restore . . . the beloved Home Religion in every Home."[11]

By the time Willard wrote of the "beloved Home Religion" in the early 1880s, antipolygamy theorists had been wrestling with the crisis of authority known as the Mormon Question for three decades. Their solution to the "problem" was the reconstruction of marriage as the centerpiece of private governance, an arena of profound religious meaning and safety for women, and the source of political legitimacy for men. Thus, the "beloved Home Religion" contained a legal mandate, as well as a spiritual prescription—the marriage of duty and sentiment. From its beginnings in sentimental fiction, through the moral constitutionalism of early Republican policy, into the turn to coercion, and finally in its triumph as Mormon resistance crumbled, the "Home Religion" mapped the contours of authority in monogamous marriage for Americans. Antipolygamists might disagree about the wisdom of requiring the testimony of a legal wife, or the justice of confiscating church property, but their sense of the importance of marriage and faith united the movement.

The lessons of this battle over faith in marriage, including respect for its private aspects as an element of essential governance, are everywhere in American life and law. Learning to understand the language of the past, to appreciate the gestures of committed pro- and antipolygamists, teaches us that the constitutional conflict over polygamy remade American legal consciousness.

The Constitution, however, has not been a reliable friend. The "Christian nation" that antipolygamists hoped was etched in constitutional bedrock has proven elusive. They, too, have found that law can be a treacherous tool. Motivated by a deep sense of the intrinsic Christianity of their country and a conviction of the vulnerability of liberty, antipolygamists fought for, and eventually enforced, a Constitution in which explicit political power was prohibited to religious organizations, and yet secular law fit comfortably within central Protestant tenets. Like their Mormon opponents, antipolygamists relied on constitutional lessons they had learned in the states. They, too, "used" the past as a tool in the construction of a constitutional world for the future. In the states, Protestants had learned that their own power grew after disestablishment. They were convinced that their brand of Christianity would blossom in Utah, if only the tyrannical Mormon Church could be got out of the way.

As it turned out, however, most Mormons remained faithful to their church, even in its defeat. Despite the predictions of antipolygamists, the Mormon Church survived the capitulation to federal authority, adapting itself to new circumstances after 1890. Protestant missionaries, especially, were chagrined. They found that Mormonism flourished in its new, ostensibly nonpolygamous guise as it had in its old. Competition for converts, they learned, was not greatly improved by disestablishment of the Mormon Church, or even by public education. Predictably, these missionaries lost much of their enthusiasm for free markets in souls, where Mormons competed with all other religions on a level playing field.[12]

Shortly after the turn of the twentieth century, clergy from the same Protestant denominations that earlier had pressed Congress to impose the rules of the market on religion in Utah, met in an interdenominational group. Competition had not brought in waves of new converts to evangelical denominations, nor had it weakened Mormon membership. So, the group compromised its commitment to the market rather than live with its failure to make significant inroads into Mormon communities. They created the Home Missions Council, their own version of a trust. They divided up the new state of Utah among themselves, each receiving exclusive missionary rights to a given area.[13]

According to the council's "Statement of Principles," each of the evangelical churches agreed not to proselytize or establish a church in a community where another member church was already operating, without prior consent of the council. If a congregant of one church moved to a community where another of the churches in the council had exclusive jurisdiction, then the affiliation of the member would be automatically transferred to the existing denomination in the new town. As one delightfully naive commentator observed, "It is through this type of cooperation that the evangelical churches have succeeded in establishing flourishing churches in many small towns in the twentieth century, which they failed to do when three or four denominations were competing for members in the same town." The "level playing field" that antipolygamists found they needed was in fact a variation on the "monopoly" they charged was characteristic of Mormonism.[14]

The logic of coercion that sustained antipolygamists, one might say, was based on the belief that to build constitutional law on any other than a Christian foundation was to betray the true source of constitutional rights and liberties. The "meaning" of liberty, in this sense, was deeply Protestant, humanitarian, and voluntaristic. That does not mean that antipolygamists were committed to the codification of biblical rules and injunctions as a general matter. Rather, they believed that "general" Christianity was the basis of secular law: all of human legal reasoning and constitutional thought was the product of God's law. In other times and other settings, "neutral" legal principles had served Protestants well. Thus, the legal tools they used were secular, in the sense that they were debated and enforced by those who themselves had no formal religious power, and in a government in which formal religious power was constitutionally prohibited. The justifications for the punishment of polygamists and the dismantling of the Mormon Church corporation were as frequently social and moral as religious, not because God's word was irrelevant, but because it underlay all of society and morality.

In retrospect, these were dangerous strategies, even though the success of such a construction of the role of faith in the Constitution was undeniable by 1890. In the twentieth century, however, secular rationality and disestablishment undermined many of the constitutional principles antipolygamists believed in and fought for. The distinction in constitutional law between "belief" and "action," once so useful in the prosecution of polygamists, was turned against believing Protestants in the twentieth century. The Word was buffeted: school prayer and Bible reading have formally been excised from public education; questions of the origins of human life challenge the "literal" truth of Genesis and have profoundly affected public education. Abortion, parochial school funding, and many more questions divide twenty-first century Christians. Marriage, now, is impermanent everywhere as a matter of law. "Consent" divorce is the rule. Sunday closing laws are a distant memory. "Unlawful cohabitation" laws are unenforced. Blasphemy is no longer prosecuted. Same-sex commitment ceremonies are performed by Christian clergy, and Vermont has recently legalized same-sex "civil unions." Liberal Christians in the twenty-first century have long accepted that the biblical text cannot be understood literally, and they often concede a basic difference between faith and rationality.[15]

Frequently, conservative Christians find their faith exists in tension with the secular rationality that looked like a safe harbor in the nineteenth century. Many find themselves agreeing with Mormons more often than they disagree, especially on questions of "family values." The change in the position of Mormons and Mormonism relative to the rest of the country, especially to evangelical Protestants and Catholics, is the product of changes within Mormonism as well as the sense among Christian conservatives that the country has abandoned core principles. By the middle of the twentieth century, Mormons had revolutionized their own approach to the law of marriage. Emerging as defenders of the traditional family, they proved especially effective in challenging the proposed Equal Rights Amendment in the 1970s. In some senses, contemporary Mormons' defense of marriage and family is consistent with the centrality that Mormon doctrine has always accorded to relationships that, after all, will endure for all time, governing life in the "celestial worlds" after death as in life.[16]

The abiding sense of pain and persecution that many Mormons bring to the study of their past does not translate into a mandate to relive its trials, or make them sympathetic to others' arguments for reshaping the structure of marriage. In response to the gay marriage movement, for example, the church strongly supported the federal Defense of Marriage Act in the mid-1990s. The act explicitly recognized heterosexual monogamy as the only form of marriage endorsed by the national government, empowering states to refuse to recognize marriages composed of anything other than one man and one woman. Legal and moral differences by region, especially in areas of sexual practice and marital structure, disturb twenty-first century Mormons as they did antipolygamists a century and more earlier.[17]

In some aspects, therefore, Mormons have adopted and made their own the constitutional and moral philosophy of law created in opposition to their own forebears. Conservative columnist George Will, memorializing this reunion and the newfound common ground between Mormons and other conservative Christians, recently called Mormonism the "most American" of religions. A century ago, those outside the faith invested heavily in the notion that Mormonism was un-American. Ironically, this reunion between Mormons and other Christian conservatives has itself contributed to the obscurity of the antipolygamy movement of the nineteenth century.[18]

Like the Protestant missionaries who found that evangelizing in Utah was not materially improved by increased competition, many Mormon leaders also compromised, especially after 1890. When the church formally and publicly renounced the practice of polygamy, Mormon leaders (and, frequently, their families) used what the historian Carmon Hardy has called "pretzled language" to distance rumors and questions about continued plural relations and the celebration of new polygamous marriages. Such tactics hid the practice from many within the faith as well as the outside world. Clearly, many Mormons were uncomfortable with the layered quality of communication about the Principle and struggled to hold on to shreds of candor. Yet the practice of denial frequently involved them in evasive tactics that came perilously close to creating the secret, double life around illicit unions that they charged were typical of non-Mormon men.

Deployed to quiet the concerns of those in the faith but not in on

A caricature pictured a harried Mormon president Joseph F. Smith coming to Washington with a long line of trailing wives and many babies to testify at the congressional hearings on the election of Mormon apostle Reed Smoot to the Senate. From *Life* magazine, 31 March 1904. Courtesy of Princeton University Library.

the secret, as well as outsiders, propolygamists created a hierarchy of truths that shielded the fact of ongoing plural marriages. Such language included outright denial of polygamy, often in the conviction that the questioners themselves assumed a promiscuity that was entirely foreign to celestial union. Frequently, lack of candor involved linguistic sophistry, such as the ruse that allowed a man to deny he was married polygamously because, according to Mormon custom, women were sealed to men, rather than vice versa, or another in which a man denied having a wife "among the living," because his first wife was at that moment standing in a graveyard.[19]

Although the central battle, the constitutional conflict over religious and legal difference, concluded with the *Late Corporation* decision and the Manifesto, the de facto continuation of plural marriage provoked sporadic aftershocks of the antipolygamy campaign into the early twentieth century. The specter of polygamy even kept indicted but subsequently pardoned polygamist B. H. Roberts out of Congress in 1898 and provoked an intense and long-lived Senate hearing into the election of Mormon apostle Reed Smoot as the junior senator from Utah in 1904. The practice of dissemblance came apart during the hearings, which revealed fatal inconsistencies in the testimony of Mormon president Joseph Fielding Smith and other leaders about whether or not polygamous marriages were still secretly condoned and even supported by the church. Smoot was finally seated in 1907, but not before many Mormons were treated to the acute embarrassment of seeing their president exposed and his church humiliated as the keeper of a dirty secret. After the Smoot affair, Mormon leaders gradually, but with increasing conviction, internalized an antipolygamous ethic that, while it did not deny the truth of the "Revelation on Celestial Marriage," held that its practice would be forbidden across the board.[20]

Within a decade, patriarchs who refused to come into harmony with the brethren found themselves ostracized. Splinter groups dedicated to the perpetuation of the Principle, formed as self-styled "fundamentalist" Mormons, continue to plague the central church into this century. The subject of criminal and civil investigation and prosecution in several states (including Utah, often with the active support of central church leaders) since the early 1920s, polygamists over the last century have been tried for bigamy, incest, child abuse, welfare fraud, statutory rape, and neglect. As one legal historian of Mormonism put it recently, polygamists in contemporary Utah occupy much the same legal and political space with regard to Mormons as Mormons did to the rest of the country in the late nineteenth century.[21]

From a different perspective, modern legal scholars question the very premises of the conflict. They challenge the antipolygamist notion that polygamous marriage will erode the moral and political integrity of the participants. They don't accept the central tenets of pro-polygamy argument, either, especially those that rely on a reunion of faith and law and the requirement of a religious dispensation for the validity of plural marriage. Contemporary scholars often discount theories of the importance of marriage to all forms of governance. Instead, they maintain that marriage is best understood as a question of personal choice rather than a divinely mandated order underlying all valid political action. Civil libertarianism, or the theory that the government has no business inquiring into private and personal lives of citizens, has eroded scholarly consensus for compulsory monogamy. A shallower understanding of marriage as a private "lifestyle choice" has papered over the nineteenth century's richer and far more politically driven understanding (and embrace) of power relations within marriage.[22]

Small cracks have appeared even in the jurisprudence of antipolygamy. A lone dissent by Supreme Court justice Frank Murphy in 1946 argued that a Mormon polygamist should not come within the meaning of the Mann Act of 1910, a federal statute known popularly as the "White Slave Act" that prohibited taking women across state lines for illicit sexual purposes; that is, for prostitution. Murphy maintained that polygamy was simply another form of marriage rather than a real analog to slavery, however much the beliefs and mores of modern society might condemn it. Even though one might well believe (as he did) that monogamy was morally superior to polygamy, Murphy argued, plural marriage was a far cry from sexual enslavement. In 1964, Mormon legal scholar Orma Linford added to the reinterpretation of the polygamy cases, publishing the first full description of all the cases. He attacked the Court as an institution where "neither balance nor measurement" of the merits of Mormonism or polygamy was attempted. A vision of marriage as the key to political structure had all but disappeared from the analysis—now the jurisprudence was described as anti-Mormon, rather than antipolygamy.[23]

In 1972, the trickle of criticism became a flood. In *Wisconsin v. Yoder*, the Supreme Court held that children might be withdrawn from school before they reached the age prescribed in the state education statute because their parents, members of the Old Order Amish Church, demonstrated that a full four years of high school for Amish children would undermine the order's ability to survive. Justice William O. Douglas, author of the majority opinion in the Mann Act case and a believer in the analogy of polygamy to slavery, disagreed. He argued that *Yoder* implicitly overruled *Reynolds*, implying that it was only a question of time before polygamy would reappear in America.[24]

Picking up on Douglas's prediction, modern libertarian scholars have argued that current lifestyles render the prohibition of polygamy ridiculous. Mormon scholars have also weighed in. In their study of the legal history of the Mormon Church, for example, Edwin Firmage and Richard Mangrum claimed in the 1980s that the prosecution of Mormon polygamists had degraded the oppressor—the federal government—and chilled the freedoms and slowed the social advance of all Americans.[25]

Although polygamy is now rarely discussed in public by Mormon leaders, a countertrend (in support of the Supreme Court's basic holding in the polygamy cases) among some Mormon legal scholars is also discernible. "The Manifesto Was a Victory" is the title of one recent article that celebrates the integration of Mormons into the broader American culture. A second, tackling libertarianism head-on, argues that "legalizing polygamy would signal a deterioration of traditional values." The author claims that the Supreme Court's decisions were based on beliefs that most Mormons now subscribe to, even as social acceptance of "unrighteous lifestyles" has infected the rest of the country. Mormon leaders are now commonly known as vocal opponents of polygamy, feminism, and gay rights.[26]

As these various reinterpretations of the basic premises of the debate illustrate, we no longer live in the world made by the conflict over polygamy. There can be no doubt, however, that the conflict shaped national politics, religious debate, and especially constitutional law in the nineteenth century. The contours of the law of church and state in America, as well as the limits of local sovereignty, were forever changed by the battle over polygamy. Faith, marriage, and constitutional law, all complex and charged with moral meaning, are wrapped in layers of history, argument, and theory. Untangling the strands that brought Mormons and antipolygamists into conflict in the nineteenth century brings to light a world of struggle for legitimacy and power, furious battles over the meaning of the Constitution and the relationship of liberty to faith.

NOTES

ABBREVIATIONS

AHR	*American Historical Review*
AQ	*American Quarterly*
CG	*Congressional Globe*
CR	*Congressional Record*
DC	*Doctrine and Covenants*
JAH	*Journal of American History*
JD	*Journal of Discourses*
JMH	*Journal of Mormon History*
"Mormon Monster"	"The Mormon Monster" Lecture, delivered by Kate Field, in the Congregational Church, corner of 10th and G Streets, Washington, D.C., Wednesday evening, Dec. 15, 1886, reported by John Irvine, MS 3111, Historical Department, Church of Jesus Christ of Latter-day Saints, Salt Lake City
UHQ	*Utah Historical Quarterly*
YJLH	*Yale Journal of Law and the Humanities*

INTRODUCTION

1. Then as now, members of the Church of Jesus Christ of Latter-day Saints (LDS) were popularly called Mormons. In the nineteenth century, the label "Mormon," drawn from the scripture the *Book of Mormon*, was frequently deployed as an insult and experienced as such by its targets. In the twentieth century, however, the name Mormon for most intents and purposes lost its derogatory connotation and is widely used by contemporary Mormon historians to describe church members in the nineteenth century. See, for example, Leonard J. Arrington and David Bitton, *The Mormon Experience: A History of the Church of Jesus Christ of Latter-day Saints* (New York, 1978). The professional historical association, moreover, is called the Mormon History Association, and its periodical, the *Journal of Mormon History*. This book follows the common practice and uses the term "Mormon" to describe LDS church members.

The traditional Mormon term for all non-Mormons is "Gentile." This term however, and is not widely accepted. It is not considered appropriate to describe, for example, Jews. This book, therefore, uses the term "non-Mormon" wherever possible.

The term "polygamy" is in fact an umbrella term that comprises both polygyny, or the marriage of one man to two or more women (which was practiced by Mormons in the nineteenth century), and polyandry, or the marriage of one woman to two or more men (which was not practiced by Mormons). Polyandry has been rare in human history, whereas polygyny traditionally has been the most common form of marriage (George Peter Murdock, "World Ethnographic Sample," *American Anthropologist* 59 [August 1957]: 686). So dominant is the polygynous variety of polygamy that the word polygamy is popularly understood as the marriage of a single man to multiple women. This book follows the common practice, using polygamy to describe the polygyny practiced by nineteenth-century Mormons.

2. For an example of the "barbarism" label applied to polygamy, see the Republican Party platform of 1856, which called both polygamy and slavery the "twin relics of barbarism" (Kirk H. Porter, comp., *National Party Platforms* [New York, 1924], 48). See also the extended discussion of civilization and barbarism in Chapter 2.

3. For the purposes of this book, the "Mormon Question" captures the debate over the elusive yet vital relationship between religious conviction and governmental structure in American history. For much of that history, the relationship has been abstract, however important. In the nineteenth-century conflict over marriage and law, it became concrete and visible as participants defined and defended starkly divergent theories of the role of faith in the Constitution. For examples of antipolygamists' claims about the relationship of the Constitution and monogamy, see *Davis v. Beason*, 133 U.S. 333, 341 (1890), and *Murphy v. Ramsey*, 114 U.S. 15, 45 (1885).

4. Parley P. Pratt, *Marriage and Morals in Utah* (Liverpool, 1856), 2, 4; Lucy W. Kimball, in *Reorganized Church of Jesus Christ of Latter Day Saints, Complainant, vs. Church of Christ at Independence, Missouri; . . . Complainant's Abstract* (Lamoni, Iowa, 1893), 375 (quoted in B. Carmon Hardy, *Solemn Covenant: The Mormon Polygamy Passage* [Urbana, Ill., 1992], 104).

5. Kenneth R. Bowling, "A Tub to the Whale: The Founding Fathers and the Adoption of the Federal Bill of Rights," *Journal of the Early Republic* 8, no. 3 (1988).

6. *Permoli v. First Municipality of New Orleans*, 44 U.S. (3 How.) 589, 593 (1845); *Barron v. Mayor and City of Baltimore*, 7 Pet. 243 (1833).

7. Rhys Isaac, *The Transformation of Virginia, 1740–1790* (New York, 1982), 273–95; Rhys Isaac, " 'The Rage of Malice of the Old Serpent Devil': The Dissenters and the Making and Remaking of the Virginia Statute for Religious Freedom," in *The Virginia Statute for Religious Freedom: Its Evolution and Consequences in American History*, ed. Merrill D. Peterson and Robert C. Vaughan (Cambridge, Eng., 1988); R. Laurence Moore, *Selling God: American Religion in the Marketplace of Culture* (New York, 1994), 66–89.

8. For an overview of state establishments and disestablishment, as well as religious qualifications for office and prohibitions on clerical officeholding, see Anson Stokes Phelps, *Church and State in the United States*, 3 vols. (New York, 1950), 1:358–444. A prohibition on clerical officeholding in Tennessee was held unconstitutional in 1978 (*McDaniel v. Paty*, 435 U.S. 618 [1978]). The Mas-

sachusetts case is *Baker v. Fales*, 16 Mass. 492 (1820). The New York Court of Appeals decided in 1854 that the trustees of a religious society were charged not with preserving doctrinal purity as understood by the society's founders but with carrying out the wishes of the present members of the society (*Robertson v. Bullions*, 11 N.Y. 243 [1854]). See also Mark DeWolfe Howe, *The Garden and the Wilderness* (Chicago, 1965), 41–42. On the decade-long erosion of establishment in Massachusetts after the *Baker v. Fales* case, see William G. McLoughlin, *New England Dissent, 1630–1833: The Baptists and the Separation of Church and State*, 2 vols. (Cambridge, Mass., 1971), 2:1189–1276. On nativism, see David Brion Davis, "Some Themes of Countersubversion: An Analysis of Anti-Masonic, Anti-Catholic, and Anti-Mormon Literature," *Mississippi Valley Historical Review* 47 (September 1960).

9. *People v. Ruggles*, 8 Johns., 294–97 (1811); Article 38, New York Constitution, 1777. On the distinction between liberty and licentiousness, see Sarah Barringer Gordon, " 'The Liberty of Self-Degradation': Polygamy, Woman Suffrage, and Consent in Nineteenth-Century America," *JAH* 83 (December 1996): 815, 817–23. See also William J. Novak, *The People's Welfare: Law and Regulation in Nineteenth-Century America* (Chapel Hill, N.C., 1996), esp. 10. For an analysis of the concept of "the sovereign people" in antebellum political rhetoric, see Daniel T. Rodgers, *Contested Truths: Keywords in American Politics Since Independence* (New York, 1987), 80–111.

10. On anti-Mormon violence in Missouri, see Stephen C. LeSeuer, *The 1838 Mormon War in Missouri* (Columbia, Mo., 1987); Alexander L. Baugh, "Missouri Governor Lilburn W. Boggs and the Mormons," *John Whitmer Historical Association Journal* 18 (1998): 111–32; and Marie H. Nelson, "Anti-Mormon Violence and the Rhetoric of Law and Order in Early Mormon History," *Legal Studies Forum* 21 (1997): 353–88.

11. John C. Fitzpatrick, ed., *The Writings of George Washington*, 39 vols. (Washington, D.C., 1931–44), 35:229. Donald G. Mathews, "The Second Great Awakening as an Organizing Process, 1780–1820: An Hypothesis," *American Quarterly* 21, no. 1 (1969): 23–43; Perry Miller, *The Life of the Mind in America: From the Revolution to the Civil War* (New York, 1965), 3–95; Robert H. Abzug, *Cosmos Crumbling: American Reform and the Religious Imagination* (New York, 1994); Louis J. Kern, "Sectarian Perfectionism and Universal Reform: The Radical Social and Political Theory of William Lloyd Garrison," in *Religion and Secular Reform in America: Ideas, Beliefs and Social Change* (New York, 1999), 91–120.

12. David Brion Davis, "The New England Origins of Mormonism," *New England Quarterly* 26 (June 1953): 154–85; Jan Shipps, *Mormonism: The Story of a New Religious Tradition* (Urbana, Ill., 1985); Charles C. Sellers, *The Market Revolution: Jacksonian America, 1814–1846* (New York, 1991), ch. 7; Gordon S. Wood, "Evangelical America and Early Mormonism," *New York History* 61 (October 1980): 356–86; Nathan O. Hatch, *The Democratization of American Christianity* (New Haven, Conn., 1989), 113–22, 167–70; R. Laurence Moore, *Religious Outsiders and the Making of Americans* (New York, 1986), 25–47; Whitney R. Cross, *The Burned-Over District: The Social and Intellectual History of Enthusiastic Religion in Western New York, 1800–1850* (Ithaca, N.Y., 1950).

13. On the language of corruption and the war of words, see Church of Jesus Christ of Latter-day Saints, *History of the Church of Jesus Christ of Latter-day Saints*, 2d ed., 7 vols. (Salt Lake, 1963), 1:4, 6.

14. Shipps, *Mormonism*, 25–39.

15. For the theory that American history is in significant part the story of the rise of religious liberty, see Sanford Cobb, *The Rise of Religious Liberty* (New York, 1905), and *Everson v. Board of Education*, 330 U.S. 1 (1947). See also Robert N. Bellah, "Civil Religion in America," *Daedalus* 96 (Winter 1967): 13: "[T]he relation between religion and politics in America has been singularly smooth. . . . [T]he civil religion was able to build up without any bitter struggle with the church powerful symbols of national solidarity and to mobilize deep levels of personal motivation for the attainment of national goals." Quoting from Tocqueville, Bellah continues, "[Americans] brought with them into the New World a form of Christianity which I cannot better describe than by styling it a democratic and republican religion" (Tocqueville, *Democracy in America* [1985; reprint, New York, 1830], 311). Mark DeWolfe Howe's *Garden and the Wilderness* is a classic but frequently overlooked counter to such scholarship. The argument that the dismantling of Reconstruction in the South was an abandonment of national moral oversight is qualified by the creation of a second Reconstruction in Utah. For examples of such arguments, see Eric Foner, *Reconstruction: America's Unfinished Revolution, 1863–1877* (New York, 1988), 609–12.

16. See, e.g., *Reynolds v. United States*, 98 U.S. 145 (1879), and the extensive discussions of Supreme Court jurisprudence in Chapters 4 and 6.

CHAPTER ONE

1. For useful descriptions of how Mormonism was both unique and uniquely American, see Whitney R. Cross, *The Burned-Over District: The Social and Intellectual History of Enthusiastic Religion in Western New York, 1800–1850* (Ithaca, N.Y., 1950), and Jan Shipps, *Mormonism: The Story of a New Religious Tradition* (Urbana, Ill., 1985). On Smith, see Richard Bushman, *Joseph Smith and the Beginnings of Mormonism* (Urbana, Ill., 1984).

2. Shipps, *Mormonism*, 52. For the quoted language, see Church of Jesus Christ of Latter-day Saints, *History of the Church of Jesus Christ of Latter-day Saints*, 2d ed., 7 vols. (Salt Lake, 1963), 1:4, 6. On the cultural power of the *Book of Mormon*, see Timothy L. Smith, "The *Book of Mormon* in a Biblical Culture," *JMH* 7 (1980): 3–22, and Paul Gutjahr, "The Golden Bible in the Bible's Golden Age: The *Book of Mormon* and Antebellum Print Culture," *American Transcendental Quarterly: Nineteenth-Century American Literature and Culture* 12 (December 1998): 275–93. On the importance of ongoing revelation, see Harold Bloom, *The American Religion* (New York, 1992), 77–128.

3. Mormonism and Smith's leadership were by no means static between the founding of the church in 1830 and Smith's death in 1844. For an analysis of the relationship of multiple internal and external challenges to Smith's leadership and their profound effect on the structure of Mormon doctrine and governance in the Kirtland and Nauvoo periods, see Marvin S. Hill, *Quest for Refuge: The*

Mormon Flight from American Pluralism (Salt Lake, 1989), and Fawn M. Brodie, *No Man Knows My History: The Life of Joseph Smith, the Mormon Prophet* (New York, 1945).

4. For basic elaborations of church experience and doctrine in the nineteenth century, see Shipps, *Mormonism,* and Leonard J. Arrington and David Bitton, *The Mormon Experience: A History of the Church of Jesus Christ of Latter-day Saints* (New York, 1978), 3–240.

5. For a review of the evidence of polygamy prior to 1843 (and after 1890), see D. Michael Quinn, "LDS Church Authority and the New Plural Marriages, 1890–1904," *Dialogue* 18 (Spring 1985): 9–105, and Richard Van Wagoner, *Mormon Polygamy: A History,* 2d ed. (Salt Lake, 1989), 3–12, 17–25, 29–36. On Emma Smith's cleverly worded denials of polygamy after her husband's death, see Linda King Newell and Valeen Tippets Avery, *Mormon Enigma: Emma Hale Smith,* 2d ed. (Urbana, Ill., 1994), 292, 298, 301, 302.

6. *DC,* 132:63, 13–14, 5.

7. B. Carmon Hardy, *Solemn Covenant: The Mormon Polygamous Passage* (Urbana, Ill., 1992), 1–38; John L. Brooke, *The Refiner's Fire: The Making of Mormon Cosmology, 1644–1844* (Cambridge, Eng., 1994).

8. For a discussion of early polygamy and the secrecy that surrounded the practice, see Van Wagoner, *Mormon Polygamy,* ch. 3. According to the *The Book of Mormon, Another Testament of Jesus Christ* (1830: Salt Lake, 1989), "Behold, David and Solomon had many wives and concubines, which thing was abominable before me saith the Lord" (Jacob 2:24), and "Wherefore, my brethren, hear me, and hearken to the word of the Lord: For there shall not any man among you save it be one wife; and concubines he shall have none" (Jacob 2:27). Theologically, the revelation given to Smith in 1843 superseded earlier commands. On the breadth of attacks on Mormons before the public announcement of polygamy in 1852, see Chad Flake, *A Mormon Bibliography, 1830–1930: Books, Pamphlets, Periodicals, and Broadsides Relating to the First Century of Mormonism* (Salt Lake, 1978), and *A Mormon Bibliography: Ten Year Supplement* (Salt Lake, 1989), which lists only one of the hundred or so anti-Mormon books and pamphlets published prior to 1852 as primarily an antipolygamy tract. Published privately by the author in 1847 in Lynn, Massachusetts, the pamphlet appears not to have been widely circulated.

9. Hardy, *Solemn Covenant,* 102. On Smith's plural marriages, see Todd Compton, *In Sacred Loneliness: The Plural Wives of Joseph Smith* (Salt Lake, 1997).

10. On the deterioration of relations between Mormon settlements and surrounding communities in the 1830s and 1840s, see R. Laurence Moore, *Religious Outsiders and the Making of Americans* (New York, 1986), 25–47; Cross, *Burned-Over District*; and Marie H. Nelson, "Anti-Mormon Violence and the Rhetoric of Law and Order in Early Mormon History," *Legal Studies Forum* 21 (1997): 353. On the relationship between faith and economic industry, see Charles C. Sellers, *The Market Revolution: Jacksonian America, 1814–1846* (New York, 1991), 237–68. For a detailed account of Smith's murder, see Brodie, *No Man Knows My History.*

11. On Young's leadership, see Leonard Arrington, *Brigham Young, American Moses* (Chicago, 1986).

12. The church remains one of the fastest growing religions in the world. Due to a large and highly structured missionary program that trains young Mormon men (and in recent decades, Mormon women as well) and sends them all over the world on two-year missions, church membership in South America and the South Pacific (including Polynesia and the Philippines) has grown steadily, and the demographic makeup of the church (once primarily Yankee, English, and Scandinavian) has changed dramatically (Arrington and Bitton, *Mormon Experience*, 285–86).

13. D. Michael Quinn, *The Mormon Hierarchy: Origins of Power* (Salt Lake, 1994), 53–56, 115, 214–15; Howard Roberts Lamar, *The Far Southwest, 1846–1912: A Territorial History* (New Haven, Conn., 1966), 315–26.

14. On this first petition for statehood and the role of William Smith, Joseph Smith's brother, in defeating the admission of Deseret, see David L. Bigler, *Forgotten Kingdom: The Mormon Theocracy in the American West, 1847–1896* (Spokane, Wash., 1998), 46–48. The territorial statute incorporating the church is reprinted in Dale Morgan, "The State of Deseret," *UHQ* 8 (1940): 223–25.

15. See, for example, John Gunnison, who wrote of his stay in Salt Lake in 1850: "That many [Mormon leaders] have a large number of wives in Deseret is perfectly manifest to anyone residing among them" (*The Mormons, or, Latter-day Saints in the Valley of the Great Salt Lake* [Philadelphia, 1852], 66). The proceedings of the entire conference were published in the September 1852 edition of the *Latter-day Saints Millennial Star*. See also David J. Whittaker, "The Bone in the Throat: Orson Pratt and the Public Announcement of Plural Marriage," *Western Historical Quarterly* 18 (July 1987): 293–314.

16. Young's sermon is reprinted in *JD*, 4:50 (21 September 1856). In 1870, just to give one example of later uses of such sermons, a leading antipolygamist senator from New York dredged up the 1850s sermons in support of legislation that would have limited the jurisdiction of Mormon-controlled courts and juries. See *CG*, 41 Cong., 2 sess., 2144 (22 March 1870) (quoting sermon of Brigham Young on 21 September 1856), and ibid., 3575 (23 March 1870) (quoting discourse of Heber Kimball on 9 November 1856). The fact that most Mormon men married only one wife—despite the command to participate in plural marriage—is evidence, some scholars maintain, that even among the faithful, polygamy may have been quietly disapproved. Public dissent went hand-in-hand with excommunication. See Stanley S. Ivins, "Notes on Mormon Polygamy," *Western Humanities Review* 10 (Summer 1956), and Arrington and Bitton, *Mormon Experience*, 203.

17. On church control of the natural resources and industries of Utah, see Lamar, *Far Southwest*, 327–77, and Leonard Arrington, *Great Basin Kingdom: An Economic History of the Latter-day Saints, 1830–1900* (Cambridge, Mass., 1956). On the leadership of those who practiced plural marriage, see *JD*, 1:53 (Orson Pratt, "Celestial Marriage"). On the overlap between political and religious power, see Klaus Hansen, *Quest for Empire: The Political Kingdom of God and the Council of Fifty in Mormon History* (East Lansing, Mich., 1967).

18. John Cairncross, *After Polygamy Was Made a Sin: The Social History of Christian Polygamy* (London, 1974); Leo Miller, *John Milton among the Polygamophiles* (New York, 1984).

19. Paul Johnson and Sean Wilentz, *The Kingdom of Matthias* (New York,

1994); Lawrence Foster, *Religion and Sexuality: Three American Communal Experiences of the Nineteenth Century* (New York, 1981); Louis Kern, *An Ordered Love: Sex Roles and Sexuality in Victorian Utopias: The Shakers, the Mormons, and the Oneida Community* (Chapel Hill, N.C., 1981).

20. Gordon S. Wood, *The Radicalism of the American Revolution: How a Revolution Transformed a Monarchical Society into a Democratic One Unlike Any That Had Ever Existed* (New York, 1992); Hatch, *The Democratization of American Christianity.*

21. Edmund S. Morgan, *American Slavery, American Freedom: The Ordeal of Colonial Virginia* (New York, 1975), 363–87; Amy Dru Stanley, *From Bondage to Contract: Wage Labor, Marriage, and the Market in the Age of Slave Emancipation* (Cambridge, Eng., 1998), 1–35; Ronald G. Walters, *The Antislavery Appeal: American Abolitionism after 1830* (New York, 1978); Eric Foner, *Free Soil, Free Labor, Free Men: The Ideology of the Republican Party before the Civil War* (London, 1970), 301–17; Lewis Perry, *Radical Abolitionism: Anarchy and the Government of God in Antislavery Thought* (Ithaca, N.Y., 1973).

22. Ralph Waldo Emerson called the faith "an afterclap of Puritanism." As Emerson saw it, the authoritarianism and communal ethic of Mormonism replicated explicit connections between belief and social standing that many nineteenth-century Americans associated with Puritan colonists of the seventeenth century. The quote is from a reminiscence published by James Bradley Thayer a dozen years after Emerson visited Salt Lake with a party of friends in 1871. In response to an observation by one of the party that Mormonism appealed to common people through biblical names and imagery, Emerson is reported to have said, "Yes, it is an after-clap of Puritanism. But one would think that after this Father Abraham could go no further" (*A Western Journey with Mr. Emerson* [Boston, 1884], reprinted in William Mulder and A. Russell Mortensen, eds., *Among the Mormons: Historic Accounts by Contemporary Observers* [New York, 1958], 384).

23. Metta Victoria Fuller Victor, *Mormon Wives, A Narrative of Facts Stranger than Fiction* (New York, 1856), viii.

24. Arthur Conan Doyle, *A Study in Scarlet* (London, 1887), opened with a blood-curdling murder in London, fulfilling the murderer's long quest for revenge against Mormons who had captured his young fiancée for the seraglio of an elder. By the time Conan Doyle wrote in the 1880s, anti-Mormon fiction was a well-known literary device in both the United States and England. Michael W. Homer, "Sir Arthur Conan Doyle: Spiritualism and 'New Religions,'" *Dialogue* 23 (Spring 1990): 97–121, 101, and Jack Tracy, *Conan Doyle and the Latter-day Saints* (Bloomington, Ind., 1978), 10–14. For the quoted language condemning novel-reading for Mormons, see *JD*, 15:222 (Brigham Young, 9 October 1872), and *Juvenile Instructor* 5 (8 January 1870): 4, and 16 (15 April 1881): 15.

25. Victor, *Mormon Wives*, vii–viii.

26. Ibid., 226, 316. Despite its claim to a factual basis, *Mormon Wives* clearly is fiction—one of the earliest antipolygamy novels. There have been several studies of antipolygamy fiction in recent decades, including Terryl L. Givens, *The Viper on the Hearth: Mormons, Myths, and the Construction of Heresy* (New York, 1997), 97–152; Leonard J. Arrington and Jon Haupt, "Intolerable Zion: The Image of Mormonism in Nineteenth-Century American Literature," *Western Humanities*

Review 22 (Summer 1968): 243–60; Charles A. Cannon, "The Awesome Power of Sex: The Polemical Campaign against Mormon Polygamy," *Pacific Historical Review* 43 (February 1974): 61–82; Karen Lynn, "Sensational Virtue: Nineteenth-Century Mormon Fiction and American Popular Taste," *Dialogue* 14 (Fall 1981): 101–12; and Gail Farr Casterline, " 'In the Toils' or 'Onward for Zion': Images of Mormon Women, 1852–1890" (master's thesis, Utah State University, 1974).

27. Scholars who have studied antipolygamy fiction have concluded that these novels were products of the need for a "handy, ready-made Other," "vehicles of erotica," products of a widespread "fear of sexuality," or deeply suppressed rape fantasies on the part of authors and readers. See Givens, *Viper on the Hearth*, 23; Arrington and Haupt, "Intolerable Zion," 244, n. 5; and Charles A. Cannon, "Awesome Power of Sex," 67. Other standard works of Mormon historiography attribute the success of antipolygamy fiction to non-Mormons' "palpitating desire to be shocked by the hideous aspects of Mormondom" or simply to "fantasy." See Lynn, "Sensational Virtue," 108; Norman Furniss, *The Mormon Conflict, 1850–1859* (New Haven, Conn., 1966), 82–83; Kern, *Ordered Love*, 54–55; and Kimball Young, *Isn't One Wife Enough?* (New York, 1954), 25. The content of antipolygamy fiction, these scholars agree, reveals more about the views of the authors than actual Mormon practice or experience. Mistakes of fact are rife in the portrait of polygamy that emerges from these novels. For the quoted language, see Cornelia Paddock, *The Fate of Madame La Tour* (Detroit, 1882), copy in Firestone Library, Princeton University.

28. For lists of antipolygamy novels (newspaper and magazine serials are not included but are plentiful), see Arrington and Haupt, "Intolerable Zion," 257–60, and Karen Lynn, "Sensational Virtues," 110–12. For examples of later fiction, see, e.g., Mrs. Cornelia Paddock, *In the Toils; or, Martyrs of the Latter Days* (Chicago, 1879); Mrs. Jennie Anderson Froiseth, ed., *The Women of Mormonism; or, The Story of Polygamy as Told by the Victims Themselves* (Detroit, 1882); and [Mrs. Rosetta Luce Gilchrist], *Apples of Sodom: A Story of Mormon Life* (Cleveland, 1885), which replicate the literature of the 1850s in many essentials. For the quoted language, see Alfreda Eva Bell, *Boadicea; The Mormon Wife. Life Scenes in Utah* (Baltimore, Md., 1855), 82.

The legal relevance of sentimental storytelling in nineteenth-century America has been established by studies of lawyers' courtroom strategies and their validation of strategic storytelling in jury verdicts. See Hendrik Hartog, "Lawyering, Husbands' Rights and the 'Unwritten Law' in Nineteenth-Century America," *JAH* 84 (June 1997): 67–96; Daniel A. Cohen, *Pillars of Salt, Monuments of Grace: New England Crime Literature and the Origins of American Popular Culture, 1764–1860* (New York, 1993), 195–246; and Robert A. Ferguson, "Story and Transcription in the Trial of John Brown," *YJLH* (Winter 1994): 37–73. Lawyers deployed sentimental formulas to answer legal questions, such as whether a given man was capable, in light of his open and honest character, of adultery. See Laura Hanft Korobkin, *Criminal Conversations: Sentimentality and Nineteenth-Century Legal Stories of Adultery* (New York, 1998). The goal of antipolygamy fiction, although related to such litigation strategy, was more ambitious: the reconstruction of law to reflect emotional and spiritual truths.

On the use of pain as a means of creating sympathetic identification, see Robyn R. Warhol, *Gendered Interventions: Narrative Discourse in the Victorian Novel* (New Brunswick, 1989); Elizabeth B. Clark, " 'The Sacred Rights of the Weak': Pain, Sympathy, and the Culture of Individual Rights in Antebellum America," *JAH* 82 (September 1995): 463, 470–75, 479–87; Philip Fisher, *Hard Facts: Setting and Form in the American Novel* (New York, 1985), ch. 3; Jane Tompkins, *Sensational Designs: The Cultural Work of American Fiction, 1790–1860* (New York, 1985); and Shirley Samuels, ed., *The Culture of Sentiment: Race, Gender, and Sentimentality in Nineteenth-Century America* (New York, 1992). Tales of virtuous women, legally bound to men who indulged their basest desires, figured prominently in the work of antebellum reform fiction. Mormon polygamy was just one of their targets: Victor, for example, wrote temperance and antislavery novels as well as antipolygamy fiction. Another antipolygamy author also wrote anti-Catholic stories, and Harriet Beecher Stowe was well known as an antipolygamist, as well as an abolitionist.

29. Clark, " 'Sacred Rights of the Weak,' " 475–81. See also Sandra S. Sizer, *Gospel Hymns and Social Religion: The Rhetoric of Nineteenth-Century Revivalism* (Philadelphia, 1978); David S. Lovejoy, *Religious Enthusiasm in the New World: Heresy to Revolution* (Cambridge, Mass., 1985); John Mullan, *Sentiment and Sociability: The Language of Feeling in the Eighteenth Century* (New York, 1988); Daniel Walker Howe, *The Unitarian Conscience: Harvard Moral Philosophy, 1805–1861* (Cambridge, Mass., 1970); and Ann Braude, *Radical Spirits: Spiritualism and Women's Rights in Nineteenth-Century America* (Boston, 1989). Elizabeth B. Clark's "Anticlericalism and Antistatism" (unpublished manuscript on file with the author), 2–13, documents the multiple intellectual and spiritual sources of this shift from external measures to subjective conscience as the only reliable guide to authenticity.

For the growth of sentiment in popular literature, see Ann Douglas, *The Feminization of American Culture* (New York, 1977); Tompkins, *Sensational Designs*; Fisher, *Hard Facts*; and David S. Reynolds, *Faith in Fiction: The Emergence of Religious Literature in America* (Cambridge, Mass., 1981). For legal storytelling, see Cohen, *Pillars of Salt*, ch. 4; Laura Hanft Korobkin, "The Maintenance of Mutual Confidence: Sentimental Strategies at the Adultery Trial of Henry Ward Beecher," *YJLH* (1995): 1; Ferguson "Story and Transcription in the Trial of John Brown," 37; and Hartog, "Lawyering, Husbands' Rights and 'the Unwritten Law.' " For the popular appeal in political rhetoric, see Harry L. Watson, *Liberty and Power: The Politics of Jacksonian America* (New York, 1990); James M. McPherson, *The Abolitionist Legacy: From Reconstruction to the NAACP* (Princeton, N.J., 1975); and Richard J. Carwardine, *Evangelicals and Politics in Antebellum America* (New Haven, Conn., 1993). For the quoted language, see Charles Grandison Finney, *Lectures on Revivals of Religion* (New York, 1835), 34, 82, quoted in Clark, " 'Sacred Rights of the Weak,' " 479.

30. Maria Ward, *Female Life among the Mormons* (New York, 1855), 325. For an anti-Catholic allusion, see Orvilla Belisle, *Mormonism Unveiled; or, A History of Mormonism from Its Rise to the Present Time* (Philadelphia, 1855), 132 ("I am no apologist for lynch or mob law, but there have occasions occurred, and may again, when the people have arisen in their might and bade the tyrant's vice and

oppression begone. So they did at Lexington and New Orleans, and so they did at Philadelphia in 1844, and so they were doing [in anti-Mormon mob violence] now.").

31. Ward, *Female Life among the Mormons*, 332. This religious corollary to the sentimental vision of marriage, according to which women as wives had primary jurisdiction over whatever affected the marital relationship and the family homestead, while clearly anticlerical, also contains interesting seeds of antistatism in a philosophy that was otherwise profoundly committed to state intervention on behalf of women. Only certain kinds of state actors, those who came to their posts without any explicit religious affiliation, were qualified to legislate the protection of women.

32. Belisle, *Mormonism Unveiled*, 230–33; Bell, *Boadicea*, 24.

33. Victor, *Mormon Wives*, 139, 313–14.

34. Belisle, *Mormonism Unveiled*, 66, 105, 115. For an insightful critique of the motivations behind such criticism, see David Brion Davis, "Some Themes of Countersubversion: An Analysis of Anti-Masonic, Anti-Catholic, and Anti-Mormon Literature," *Mississippi Valley Historical Review* 47 (1960): 224.

35. Robert H. Abzug, *Cosmos Crumbling: American Reform and the Religious Imagination* (New York, 1994), 163–82. For overviews of utopian groups, see Foster, *Religion and Sexuality* and *Women, Family, and Utopia: Communal Experiments of the Shakers, the Oneida Community, and the Mormons* (Syracuse, N.Y., 1991); Kern, *Ordered Love*; and Carol Weisbrod, *The Boundaries of Utopia* (New York, 1980). The quoted language is from J. H. Beadle, *Life in Utah; or, The Mysteries and Crimes of Mormonism. Being an Exposé of the Secret Rites and Ceremonies of the Latter-Day Saints, with a Full and Authentic History of Polygamy and the Mormon Sect from Its Origin to the Present Time* (Philadelphia, 1870), 332–33.

36. For analyses of fascination with forbidden forms of sexuality in their nineteenth-century incarnations, see Karen Halttunen, *Murder Most Foul: The Killer and the American Gothic Imagination* (Cambridge, Mass., 1998), 60–90, and Cohen, *Pillars of Salt*, 167–246. For the quoted language, see Belisle, *Mormonism Unveiled*, 201, and Victor, *Mormon Wives*, 313.

37. Timothy Dwight, *The Triumph of Infidelity* (n.p., 1815); "The Dangers of our Country," *Christian Watchman*, 4 December 1829, 195. For an example of anti-Paine rhetoric, see W. B. Reed, "Life and Character of Thomas Paine," *The North American Review* (July 1843): 1–58. The "evangelical juggernaut" phrase is used in Daniel Walker Howe, "The Evangelical Movement and Political Culture in the North during the Second Party System," *JAH* 78 (March 1991): 1226. See also Leo Pfeffer, *Church, State, and Freedom* (Boston, 1953), 119–20. As late as 1830, Senator Richard Johnson of Kentucky, chairman of the Senate Committee on the Post Office and Post Roads, accused opponents of Sunday mail delivery of "religious despotism" and treason (Richard M. Johnson, "Report . . . on the Subject of Mails on the Sabbath," 19 January 1829, 20 Cong., 2 sess. *Senate Documents*, no. 46, 4). On the Sunday mail controversy, see Bertram Wyatt-Brown, "Prelude to Abolitionism: Sabbatarian Politics and the Rise of the Second Party System," *JAH* 58 (September 1971): 316–41; James R. Rohrer, "Sunday Mails and the Church-State Theme in Jacksonian America," *Journal of the Early Republic*, 7, no. 1 (Spring 1987): 53–74; and Richard R. John, "Taking Sab-

batarianism Seriously: The Postal System, the Sabbath, and the Transformation of American Political Culture," *Journal of the Early Republic* 10, no. 4 (Winter 1990): 517–67.

38. "Female Infidelity," *Advocate of Moral Reform*, 1 August 1836, quoted in Lori D. Ginzberg, " 'The Hearts of Your Readers Will Shudder': Fanny Wright, Infidelity, and American Freethought," *AQ* 46, no. 2 (June 1994): 185. For examples of claims of freethinkers' inherent depravity, immorality, and criminality, as well as their bloodthirsty proclivities, see the sources quoted in Albert Post, *Popular Freethought in America* (New York, 1943), 199–204. On Wright, see Celia Morris Eckhardt, *Fanny Wright: Rebel in America* (Cambridge, Mass., 1984).

39. James Turner, *Without God, Without Creed: The Origins of Unbelief in America* (Baltimore, Md., 1985), 67.

40. In recent scholarship, historians have argued that Mormonism incorporated what the historian D. Michael Quinn (*Early Mormonism and the Magic World View* [Salt Lake, 1987]) called the "magic world view." See also John L. Brooke, *The Refiner's Fire: The Making of Mormon Cosmology, 1644–1844* (Cambridge, Eng., 1994).

41. Samuel Gridley Howe, "Atheism in New England," *New England Magazine* 8 (1835): 53, 54, 56. As Howe put it,

He who is prepared to let the infidels advance one step, must concede to them the whole ground; if a man has right to try to shake the belief of his neighbor's wife in the sanctity of the marriage vow, he has a right to seduce her from him; if he has a right to rail against virtue, he has a right openly to encourage vice, and by music and dancing and feasting, to add to the force of his reasonings; if he may call in question the rights of property, he may lay his hands on what he can get; if he has a right to persuade the poor and ignorant, that laws are made only *to oppress them*, he has a right to excite them to riot, and to lead them on to break open prisons, and let out the persecuted men who are not thieves, but only *dividers of property*.

42. Victor, *Mormon Wives*, 315; Catharine Beecher and Harriet Beecher Stowe, *The American Woman's Home; or, Principles of Domestic Science* (New York, 1860). On the spiritual importance of marriage, see Mary P. Ryan, *Cradle of the Middle Class: The Family in Oneida County, New York, 1790–1865* (Cambridge, Mass., 1981), and Barbara L. Epstein, *The Politics of Domesticity: Women, Evangelism, and Temperance in Nineteenth-Century America* (Middletown, Conn., 1981). According to many midcentury treatise writers, male and female alike, woman's natural state, contrary to earlier conceptions of rampant female sexuality, was one of moderation, constancy, and self-restraint in matters sexual. See Nancy F. Cott, "Passionlessness: An Interpretation of Victorian Sexual Ideology, 1790–1850," in Nancy F. Cott and Elizabeth Pleck, eds., *A Heritage of Her Own* (New York, 1979), 165–60; Carl N. Degler, *At Odds: Women and Family in America from the Revolution to the Present* (New York, 1980), 253–63; Sellers, *Market Revolution*, 242–45; and Carroll Smith-Rosenberg, "Beauty, the Beast and the Militant Woman: A Case Study in Sex Roles and Social Stress in Jacksonian America," *AQ* 23 (October 1971): 563–83.

43. Ward, *Female Life among the Mormons*, 294.

44. Ibid., iii–iv, 321: As Ward put it in the introduction to her novel, "Knowing, as I do, the evils and horrors and abominations of the Mormon system, the degradation it imposes on females, and the consequent vices which extend through all the ramifications of the society, a sense of duty to the world has induced me to prepare the following narrative, for the public eye."

45. Ibid., 172.

46. The deaths of young women and children, and the tears of release and regret that accompanied an untimely death, were a special language in domesticity. The virtuous died young in a cruel world because heaven was where they belonged. Jane Tompkins makes this point eloquently in her analysis of *Uncle Tom's Cabin*: "Stories like the death of little Eva are compelling for the same reason that the story of Christ's death is compelling; they enact a philosophy, as much political as religious, in which the pure and powerless die to save the powerful and corrupt, and thereby show themselves more powerful than those they save" (*Sensational Designs*, 127–28). Sentimental writers advocated the recreation of that heaven on earth through marriage—in the "sacred circle of home," as Metta Victor put it. Destruction of marital happiness (through polygamy or other means, such as slavery or alcoholism) meant that angels could not long survive. In antipolygamy fiction, the home was the metaphor for women's souls; it was the "charmed precinct" where "peace and love and innocent joy" were realized (Victor, *Mormon Wives*, 172, 199).

47. Victor, *Mormon Wives*, 140, 224, 319. "Discord, confusion and misery reigned supreme" in polygamous families, Maria Ward claimed. Wives refused to work in harmony with one another; one put the cutlery away as soon as another set the table. She described the household of Brigham Young, whose wives, she imagined, were consumed with jealousy of one another: "[E]ach one wishes to take precedence of the others. The eldest fancies that her age entitles her to the place of honor. The youngest, because she is a beauty, and a favorite; and the middle-aged, on account of her wealth. They will not eat together, because each one wishes to sit at the head of the table; each one also aspires to superintend and direct the affairs of the household, while the others perform the labor" (*Female Life among the Mormons*, 410, 387, 300–301).

48. This argument indirectly encouraged women *not* to follow their husbands into a faith (and perhaps into anything else) that did not appeal to their own sense of what was right. The justification for challenging the authority of husbands was usually based on a reference to an external power figure, be it a mother or a clergyman (note, however, that the appeal was made to a "female" personage, rather than a father or brother). In Ward's novel, for example, as one woman lay dying of a broken heart, she lamented that she had "forgot[ten] the dying admonitions of my mother." On occasion, women openly defied authority when commanded to enter plural marriage. "I dare to disobey any man, who seeks to make me a slave, and whose tyranny would embitter my whole life," declared a spirited young woman to her father (*Female Life among the Mormons*, 172, 358).

49. According to Ward, Smith then murdered the product of their union—his own child—and commanded Ellen to become the plural wife of another man, "who, to excessive boorishness of manner united a most repulsive countenance and forbidding disposition." Ellen's suicide came as no surprise to Mrs. Ward,

who accused Smith of her murder by asking: "Whose fanaticism blighted the hopes of that pure spirit, degraded her aspirations for love and truth, and turned the sweetness of her life to gall and wormwood?" (*Female Life among the Mormons*, 65, 79, 80).

50. Ibid., 313–14.

51. Ibid., 90, 219, 312, 428.

52. Victor, *Mormon Wives*, 103. The same was true for Arthur Guilford in Orvilla Belisle's *Mormonism Unveiled*; after losing an ill-conceived and poorly run race for governor, Arthur fled to Mormonism as a means of recovering his lost wealth and self-esteem. Greed for money soon evolved into greed for women, since Mormon converts lost control over their sense of what was right. Once he left the East, Arthur careened downward morally, finally killing his wife by his cruel treatment of her.

53. Belisle, *Mormonism Unveiled*, 145, 149–50; Ward, *Female Life among the Mormons*, 101.

54. Belisle, *Mormonism Unveiled*, 65–66, 70, 230–31. The defense of class structure as the best protection for all levels of society, of course, is deeply conservative at its core. Economic (and geographic) mobility might not have looked so threatening to the masses Belisle claimed made up the bulk of converts to Mormonism.

55. Ibid., 233; Victor, *Mormon Wives*, 323. Victor attributes the quote to a report in the *New York Times*, "of a late date." This theme is repeated several times in Cornelia Ferris's "Life among the Mormons," *Putnam's Monthly* 6 (October 1855): 378–79, as well as in book-length treatments.

56. Bell, *Boadicea*, 49, 70. Boadicea herself was the victim of physical abuse, poisoning, and even an attempted assassination at a fancy dress ball. Boadicea was a survivor, however; disguised as a man, she escaped to the East. Bell also wrote an antislavery (and anti-Confederacy) novel in 1864 titled *The Rebel Cousins; or Life in Secession: The Autobiography of the Beautiful Bertha Stephens, the Accomplished Niece of the Hon. Alexander Hamilton Stephens, Vice-President of the Southern Confederacy*, Written by herself, and prepared for Publication by Her Friend, Alfreda Eva Bell (Philadelphia, 1864).

57. Bell, *Boadicea*, 54, 34. See also Ward, *Female Life among the Mormons*, 438.

58. Ward, *Female Life among the Mormons*, 294–95.

59. Victor, *Mormon Wives*, 198.

60. Dedication to *Anti-Polygamy Standard* (1880).

61. Theirs was, as Elizabeth B. Clark, a scholar of antislavery, has pointed out in a related context, "a lay, rather than a legal[,] tradition, fluid precisely because it did not depend on the revealed word of a statute or constitutional amendment" ("'Sacred Rights of the Weak,'" 487).

62. The delicate balance between womanly spiritual superiority and the gracious act of subordination in wifehood is illustrated in Metta Victor's *Mormon Wives*. The heroine counseled her (soon to be faithless) friend that someday she would meet a man "whom you cannot help obeying" (29).

63. Ward, *Female Life among the Mormons*, 292. Metta Victor, for example, believed that when positive legislation to protect wives was in place, behavior would actually change. In her temperance novel, she pleaded for enactment of the "Maine" law in all states, arguing that human nature alone could not accom-

plish the reform of society: "As long as men must be governed, let them have as many laws as are necessary and just. If this was the millenium reign of love, when the lion and the lamb are to lie down together, we should not need those restrictions. Now they are wholesome, necessary and wise" (Metta Victoria Fuller [Victor], *The Senator's Son: or the Maine Law; a Last Refuge: a Story Dedicated to the Law-Makers* [Cleveland, 1853], 44).

64. Belisle, *Mormonism Unveiled,* 95. On the relationship between nativism and fear of violence by secret societies, see Davis, "Some Themes of Counter-subversion." The "Danites," or "Sons of Dan," were, according to many anti-polygamists, a group of Mormon vigilantes who hunted down and brutally murdered both non-Mormons and Mormons who dared to stray from the path of strict obedience to the leadership. See Kate Field, "Mormon Blood Atonement," *North American Review* 143 (September 1886): 262. See also Bigler, *Forgotton Kingdom,* 123–26. The role of the Danites, and whether their activities were supported by church officials, remains a topic of debate among Mormon historians. See, e.g., Hansen, *Quest for Empire,* 57–58; Arrington and Bitton, *Mormon Experience,* 54, 353 n. 45; and Leland H. Gentry, "The Danite Band of 1838," *Brigham Young University Studies* 14 (Summer 1974): 421–50.

65. Belisle, *Mormonism Unveiled,* 91–92.

66. Victor, *Mormon Wives,* vii–viii.

67. Ibid., viii. For an interesting parallel to this argument, see Laura F. Edwards, " 'The Marriage Covenant Is at the Foundation of All Our Rights': The Politics of Slave Marriages in North Carolina after Emancipation," *Law and History Review* 14 (Spring 1996): 81–82.

68. Hendrik Hartog, "The Constitution of Aspiration and the Rights that Belong to Us All," in *The Constitution in American Life,* ed. David Thelen (New York, 1987), 362. See also Clark, "Anticlericalism and Antistatism," 9–13, 41–47.

69. Hartog notes that his study of the career of divorce reformer Mrs. Packard "suggests the need for a rethinking of domestic feminism and its relationship to its supposed opponent, political feminism," a point that also bears emphasis in the antipolygamy context. See "Mrs. Packard on Dependency," *YJLH* 1 (December 1988): 94 n. 50, 101. A growing literature on masculinity addresses some of the issues of husbands' rights and duties raised here. See, e.g., Mark C. Carnes and Clyde Griffen, eds., *Meanings for Manhood: Contructions of Masculinity in Victorian America* (Chicago, 1990), and Hendrik Hartog, "Lawyering, Husbands' Rights and the 'Unwritten Law' in Nineteenth-Century America," *JAH* 84 (June 1997): 67–96. See also Sellers, *Market Revolution,* and Ryan, *Cradle of the Middle Class,* ch. 4, on the self-made man.

70. For an exploration of such a discourse, see Gail Bederman, " 'Civilization,' the Decline of Middle-Class Manliness, and Ida B. Wells's Anti-Lynching Campaign (1892–1894)," *Radical History Review* 52 (1992): 5–22. As historians of slavery have argued in studies of slave codes in the Old South, the manipulation of the ideological tools of the master class may have given some slaves temporary refuge from individual masters, but supplication to an ethic of restraint for slaveholders drove slaves deeper into an acceptance of paternalism, if not of slavery. See Eugene D. Genovese, "The Hegemonic Function of Law," in *Roll, Jordan, Roll: The World the Slaves Made* (New York, 1976), 25–49. Such an approach would label antipolygamist women's appeal to legislators' ethic of

husbandly restraint as a flawed form of subversion at best, a kind of false consciousness, especially if the law of monogamy was the source of wives' oppression, as the law of slavery was the source of the slaves' oppression. And yet this was precisely the concession that antipolygamists were not prepared to make. From their perspective, true slavery lay in the uncontrolled redefinition of marriage, in moral difference, and in too much patriarchy. Monogamous marriage, on the other hand, may well have needed legal reinforcement to achieve stability and to protect the sanctity of the marital unit, but antipolygamists argued that monogamy was essential to the well-being—the very spiritual nature—of women.

71. Nancy Isenberg, *Sex and Citizenship in Antebellum America* (Chapel Hill, N.C., 1998), 155–90; Linda K. Kerber, *No Constitutional Right to Be Ladies: Women and the Obligations of Citizenship* (New York, 1999), 38–39; Abzug, *Cosmos Crumbling*, 204–29; Jean Fagin Yellin, *Women and Sisters: The Antislavery Feminists in American Culture* (New Haven, Conn., 1989); MaryLynn Salmon, *Women and the Law of Property in Early America* (Chapel Hill, N.C., 1986).

72. *The Washington Tragedy [The Sickles-Key Murder Trial]* (Washington, D.C., 1859), 27, quoted in Hartog, "Lawyering, Husband's Rights, and 'the Unwritten Law,' " 90. On the limited effect of statutory reforms to the common-law rules of coverture, see Reva B. Siegel, "The Modernization of Marital Status Law: Adjudicating Wives' Rights to Earnings, 1860–1930," *Georgetown Law Journal* 82 (1994): 2127, and "Home as Work: The First Woman's Rights Claims Concerning Wives' Household Labor, 1850–1880," *Yale Law Journal* 103 (March 1994): 1073; and Richard Chused, "Married Women's Property Acts," *Georgetown Law Journal* 71 (1983): 1359.

73. Angelina Emily Grimké, *Letters to Catharine Beecher* (Boston, 1836), quoted in Alice S. Rossi, ed., *The Feminist Papers: From Adams to de Beauvoir* (New York, 1973), 320. See also Blanche Glassman Hersch, *The Slavery of Sex: Feminist-Abolitionists in America* (Urbana, Ill., 1978).

74. This dual function is not unique to antipolygamy fiction: it runs throughout the American tradition of rights talk (Hartog, "Constitution of Aspiration," 356 n. 7).

CHAPTER TWO

1. On the role of party platforms, see Jean Harvey Baker, *Affairs of Party: The Political Culture of Northern Democrats in the Mid-Nineteenth Century* (New York, 1998), 265.

2. Kirk H. Porter, comp., *National Party Platforms* (New York, 1924), 48. As a mixture of former Whigs, Free-Soilers, nativists, and sprinklings of Democrats settled into the third-party system as Republicans in the late 1850s, their distinctive brand of political rhetoric took shape. One scholar has described this retooling of politics as a fundamental precondition to accommodating the conviction that self-improvement was a universal norm. See David J. Greenstone, *The Lincoln Persuasion: Remaking American Liberalism* (Princeton, N.J., 1993), 33.

Put slightly differently, the Republican Party was in part the political manifestation of a cognitive style—the institutional response to the development of humanitarian sensibilities (Thomas G. Haskell, "Capitalism and the Origins of the Humanitarian Sensibility," part 1, *AHR* 90, no. 2 (1985): 339–61; Eric Foner, *Free Soil, Free Labor, Free Men: The Ideology of the Republican Party before the Civil War* (London, 1970). There is no current record of the process that produced the "twin relics" language, but the written proceedings report that there was "tremendous" applause at the convention following a reading of "The resolution condemning Polygamy and Slavery." See *Proceedings of the First Three Republican National Conventions* (Minneapolis, Minn., n.d.), 44.

3. Charles Sumner's "Barbarism of Slavery" speech (*The Barbarism of Slavery: Speech of Hon. Charles Sumner, on the Admission of Kansas as a Free State, in the United States Senate, June 4, 1860* [Washington, D.C., 1860]) is perhaps the best-known example of this genre, which appeared in countless other forms. See Roy Harvey Pearce, *Savagism and Civilization: A Study of the Indian and the American Mind* (Baltimore, Md., 1953), 76–104, and Robert J. Berkhofer Jr., *Salvation and the Savage: An Analysis of Protestant Missions and American Indian Response, 1787–1862* (Lexington, Ky., 1965).

4. *CG*, 36 Cong., 1 sess., 1860, app., 194.

5. *Speech of Hon. Justin S. Morrill, of Vermont, on Utah Territory and Its Law— Polygamy and Its License; Delivered in the House of Representatives, February 23, 1857* (Washington, D.C., 1857), 10, 13–14. For a discussion of the reformers' commitment to seamless morality in public and private life, see Shirley Samuels, *The Culture of Sentiment: Race, Gender, and Sentimentality in Nineteenth-Century America* (New York, 1992), 4. This integration of public and private life also provided Mormon leaders with a mandate for condemning novels and novel-reading in 1860. See T. B. H. Stenhouse, *The Rocky Mountain Saints* (New York, 1873), 300–301; John L. Brooke, *Refiner's Fire: The Making of Mormon Cosmology, 1644–1844* (Cambridge, Eng., 1994), 287.

6. *CG*, 36 Cong., 1 sess., 197 (4 April 1860).

7. *Latter-day Saints Millennial Star*, 14 February 1857.

8. On the internal causes and tenor of the Reformation, see Paul H. Peterson, "The Mormon Reformation of 1856–1857: The Rhetoric and the Reality," *JMH* 15 (1989): 59–87. The concept that some sins are so grievous that they only can be cleansed by the blood of the sinners was the subject of much speculation and condemnation in the nineteenth century. See, e.g., Kate Field, "Mormon Blood Atonement," *North American Review* 143 (September 1886). See also Klaus Hansen, *Quest for Empire: The Political Kingdom of God and the Council of Fifty in Mormon History* (East Lansing, Mich., 1967), 69–71, and D. Michael Quinn, *The Mormon Hierarchy: Origins of Power* (Salt Lake, 1994), 112–13. Federally appointed territorial judge Perry Brocchus claimed that the crowd was "ready to spring upon me like hyenas and destroy me." His letter is reprinted in *CG*, 32 Cong., 1 sess., app., 25, and excerpted in William Mulder and A. Russell Mortensen, eds., *Among the Mormons: Historic Accounts by Contemporary Observers* (New York, 1958), 250–53.

9. On Bleeding Kansas, see James M. McPherson, *Battle Cry of Freedom: The Civil War Era* (New York, 1988), 145–53, 162–69.

10. Stephen A. Douglas, *Kansas, Utah, and the Dred Scott Decision. Remarks of Hon. Stephen A. Douglas, Delivered in the State House at Springfield, Ill., on 12th of June, 1857* ([Springfield, Ill.?], 1857), 7–8; Robert W. Johanssen, *Stephen A. Douglas* (New York, 1973), 104–10, 149–50. Douglas had been a vigorous defender of the Mormons during the 1840s and had been instrumental in securing independence from state government for Nauvoo. Douglas, and the Democrats, who had thereby won the allegiance of the Mormons, at the same time lost the support of anti-Mormons, who by 1843 constituted a substantial portion of the regional population. According to one source, Douglas and others were suspected of being covert members of the Mormon Church during the 1844 presidential campaign. See J. T. Flaherty, *Glimpses of the Life of Rev. A. E. Phelps and His Co-Laborers* (Cincinnati, 1878), 61–63, quoted in Richard J. Carwardine, *Evangelicals and Politics in Antebellum America* (New Haven, Conn., 1993), 86, 352 n. 38. On the Mormon settlement at Nauvoo, and the extraordinary controversy that marked relations between Mormons and surrounding communities in the early 1840s, see Marie H. Nelson, "Anti-Mormon Violence and the Rhetoric of Law and Order in Early Mormon History," *Legal Studies Forum* 21 (1997): 353; John E. Hallwas, "Mormon Nauvoo from a Non-Mormon Perspective," *JMH* 16 (1990): 57; and B. H. Roberts, *A Comprehensive History of the Church of Jesus Christ of Latter-day Saints: Century I*, 6 vols. (Provo, Utah, 1965), 2:111–24, 193–209, 234–51.

11. The most complete history of the course of the Mormon War is Norman Furniss, *The Mormon Conflict, 1850–1859* (New Haven, Conn., 1966). See also Richard D. Poll and William P. MacKinnon, "Causes of the Utah War Reconsidered," *JMH* 20 (Fall 1994): 16–44, and David L. Bigler, *Forgotten Kingdom: The Mormon Theocracy in the American West, 1847–1896* (Spokane, Wash., 1998), 141–58, 181–88.

12. Howard Roberts Lamar, *The Far Southwest, 1846–1912: A Territorial History* (New Haven, Conn., 1966), 349. The conduit for uneasy reconciliation was Democrat Thomas L. Kane, an excitable, even neurotic, but undeniably well-intentioned Philadelphia lawyer and businessman. He was respectable enough to win a grudging mandate from Buchanan to sue for peace, and, much more unusual (even unique), a man trusted by the Mormons as their "Little Friend," their "Sentinel in the East." See Albert L. Zobell Jr., *Sentinel in the East: A Biography of Thomas L. Kane* (Salt Lake, 1965); Leonard J. Arrington, " 'In Honorable Remembrance': Thomas L. Kane's Service to the Mormons," Task Papers in LDS History, No. 22, Salt Lake, 1978; and Sherman L. Fleck, "Thomas L. Kane: Friends of the Saints," *Mormon Heritage* 1 (May–June 1994): 36–40, 42.

13. *Appendix to the CG*, 36 Cong., 1 sess., 196–97 (4 April 1860) (Rep. Lawrence M. Keitt).

14. See, for example, the remarks of Rep. Clement Vallandigham, Democrat of Ohio, *CG*, 36 Cong., 1 sess., 1519 (3 April 1860), and William Simms, Democrat of Kentucky, ibid., app., 202 (5 April 1860); and David W. Gooch, *Polygamy in Utah: Speech of Daniel W. Gooch, of Massachusetts, House of Representatives, April 4, 1860* (Washington, D.C., 1860).

15. *Illinois State Journal*, 16 April 1860, quoted in Vern L. Bullough, "Polygamy: An Issue in the Election of 1860?" *UHQ* 29 (Spring 1961): 120–26, 125.

16. Morrill, *Polygamy and Its License*, 10.

17. "Polygamy in the Territories, Speech of Mr. Nelson," *CR*, 36 Cong., 1 sess., 194 (5 April 1860) (quoting Cradlebaugh); Morrill, *Polygamy and Its License*, 10.

18. Gooch, *Polygamy in Utah*, 6.

19. Thomas M. Cooley, *A Treatise on the Constitutional Limitations Which Rest Upon the Legislative Power of the States of the American Union* (Boston, 1868), 472. On the influence of Cooley, see Clyde E. Jacobs, *Law Writers and the Courts: The Influence of Thomas M. Cooley, Christopher G. Tiedeman, and John F. Dillon upon American Constitutional Law* (Berkeley, Calif., 1954), and Alan Jones, "Thomas M. Cooley and the Michigan Supreme Court," *American Journal of Legal History* 10 (1966): 97.

20. St. George Tucker, ed., *Blackstone's Commentaries*, 5 vols. (Philadelphia, 1803), 1:442.

21. Karen Lystra, *Searching The Heart: Women, Men, and Romantic Love in Nineteenth-Century America* (New York, 1989), 227–58; Michael Grossberg, *Governing the Hearth: Law and the Family in Nineteenth-Century America* (Chapel Hill, N.C., 1985), 17–30.

22. Lystra, *Searching the Heart*, 257–58. On challenges to the law of marriage, see Elizabeth B. Clark, "Self-Ownership and the Political Theory of Elizabeth Cady Stanton," *Connecticut Law Review* 21 (Summer 1989): 905–41. On the increased visibility of wife abuse as a public problem, see Elizabeth Pleck, *Domestic Tyranny: The Making of Social Policy against Family Violence from Colonial Times to the Present* (New York, 1987), 34–66, and Robert L. Griswold, "Law, Sex, Cruelty and Divorce in Victorian America, 1840–1900," *AQ* 38 (Winter 1986): 721–45.

23. Hendrik Hartog, *Man and Wife in America, a History* (Cambridge, Mass., 2000), 103–15.

24. *Appendix to the CG*, 36 Cong., 1 sess., 19 (25 April 1860) (Thomas Nelson).

25. Kent, *Commentaries*, 2:81. For a discussion of the home as an actual space for the development of such spiritual meaning, see Colleen McDannell, *The Christian Home in Victorian America, 1840–1940* (Bloomington, Ind., 1986).

26. Morrill, *Polygamy and Its License*, 10–12.

27. Ibid.

28. Rhys Isaac made a similar point about the hobbling of religious critiques of society through disestablishment in *The Transformation of Virginia, 1740–1790* (New York, 1982), 285–95, and "The Rage of Malice of the Old Serpent Devil': The Dissenters and the Making and Remaking of the Virginia Statute for Religious Freedom," in *The Virginia Statute for Religious Freedom: Its Evolution and Consequences in American History*, ed. Merrill D. Peterson and Robert C. Vaughan (Cambridge, Eng., 1988), 139, 163. On the disabling of dissent in ostensibly tolerant political orders, see Herbert Marcuse, "Repressive Tolerance," in *A Critique of Pure Tolerance*, ed. Robert T. Paul Wolff, Barrington Moore Jr., and Herbert Marcuse (Boston, 1969), 81.

29. Gooch, *Polygamy in Utah*, 8. Such legislative limitations on the powers of churches to acquire and hold real property were common. Delaware, Illinois, Iowa, Kentucky, Maryland, Michigan, New Jersey, New York, and Ohio, according to one source, all had published case law construing mortmain statutes

in the late nineteenth century. See Carl Zollman, *American Civil Church Law* (New York, 1917), 89–93.

30. Alexis de Tocqueville, *Democracy in America*, trans. Henry Reeve, 2 vols. (1840; New York, 1990), 1:300–313. Tocqueville, although apparently not himself a believer, subscribed to the basic knowability and universality of "general Christianity": "[T]he sects in the United States belong to the great unity of Christendom, and Christian morality is everywhere the same."

31. *Baker v. Fales*, 16 Mass. 492 (1820). The imposition of majoritarian rule extended outside Massachusetts and beyond established faiths. South Carolina's 1778 constitution, for example, declared not only that "the Christian Protestant religion" was the established religion of the state but also that ministers should be chosen by "a majority of the society to which he shall minister." See Francis N. Thorpe, *The Federal and State Constitutions*, 9 vols. (Washington, D.C., 1909), 6:3255–57. See also *Robertson v. Bullions*, 11 N.Y. 243 (1854); Mark DeWolfe Howe, *The Garden and the Wilderness* (Chicago, 1965), 41–42; and William G. McLoughlin, *New England Dissent, 1630–1833: The Baptists and the Separation of Church and State*, 2 vols. (Cambridge, Mass., 1971), 2:1189–1276.

32. *People v. Ruggles*, 8 Johns. 290, 291, 293 (1811) (emphasis in original), citing *Rex v. Wollston*, Str. 834. Fitzg. 64. See also R. W. Lee, "The Law of Blasphemy," *Michigan Law Review* 16 (1918): 149. According to Perry Miller, Ruggles spoke at the door of a tavern, where he had been drinking heavily. His punishment was a "stiff fine," which he paid, and he "vanished thereupon from history" (*Life of the Mind in America: From the Revolution to the Civil War* [New York, 1965], 66).

33. *People v. Ruggles*, 294–95, 297.

34. Ibid., 296, 297–98; New York Constitution, art. 38, 1777. See also Michael Feldberg, *The Turbulent Era: Riot and Disorder in Jacksonian America* (New York, 1980), and Theodore M. Hammett, "Two Mobs of Jacksonian Boston: Ideology and Interest," *JAH* 62 (December 1976): 845.

35. *Updegraph v. Commonwealth*, 11 Serge. & Rawl. 393, 406 (Pa., 1824); *People v. Ruggles*, 295.

36. *Updegraph v. Commonwealth*, 399; Perry Miller, *Life of the Mind*, 66. At New York's Constitutional Convention in 1821 (to which Kent was also a delegate), Erastus Root, reporting that at least two indictments for blasphemy had been sustained by the courts of New York, proposed an amendment to the following effect: "The judiciary shall not declare any particular religion, to be the law of the land; nor exclude any witness on account of his religious faith" (*Convention of the State of New York* [New York, 1821], 462). After debate, in which Kent defended his opinion in *People v. Ruggles*, the amendment failed by a vote of seventy-four to forty-one (*Convention of the State of New York*, 577). For more on these issues, see Sarah Barringer Gordon, "Blasphemy and the Law of Religious Liberty in Nineteenth-Century America," *AQ* 52, no. 4 (December 2000).

37. Perry Miller, *Life of the Mind*, 239. The "Americanization" label is drawn from the work of William E. Nelson. See *The Americanization of the Common Law: The Impact of Legal Change on Massachusetts Society, 1760–1830* (Cambridge, Mass. 1975), esp. ch. 3, for an overview of prosecutions of offenses against morality and religion in the Revolutionary era.

38. Michael W. Homer, "The Judiciary and the Common Law in Utah Territory, 1850–1861," *Dialogue* 21 (Spring 1988): 97–108.

39. Andrew A. Lipscomb, ed., *The Writings of Thomas Jefferson*, vol. 26 (Washington, D.C., 1904), 48 (letter to Major John Cartwright, dated 5 June 1824). Jefferson also claimed that judges in England and America had misinterpreted the common law, translating a decision in "law french" that rested on "antien scripture" as "holy" scripture rather than on the "ancient written laws of the church." See "Whether Christianity Is a Part of the Common Law," *Jefferson's Virginia Reports*, vol. 1 (Charlottesville, 1829), 173, 138, 142.

40. *State v. Chandler*, 2 Harr. 553, 567, 557–58 (Del., 1837); Story to Edward Everett, 15 September 1824, in William W. Story, ed., *Life and Letters of Joseph Story, Associate Justice of the Supreme Court of the United States, and Dane Professor of Law at Harvard University*, 3 vols. (Boston, 1851), 1:430.

41. Joseph Story, *Commentaries on the Constitution*, 3 vols. (Boston, 1833), 3:723–24, 728, sec. 1865–71; James McClellan, *Joseph Story and the American Constitution: A Study in Political and Legal Thought* (Norman, Okla., 1971), 118–59.

42. *Commonwealth v. Kneeland*, 20 Mass. 206 (1838); Leonard Levy, ed., *Blasphemy in Massachusetts: Freedom of Conscience and the Abner Kneeland Case* (New York, 1973); Henry Steele Commager, "The Blasphemy of Abner Kneeland," *New England Quarterly* 8 (March 1935): 29.

43. Lyman Beecher, *Sermons Delivered on Various Occasions* (Boston, 1828), 138, 143–44, quoted in James Turner, *Without God, without Creed: The Origins of Unbelief in America* (Baltimore, Md., 1985), 84. In 1829, Joseph Story explained that reason and revelation were mutually reinforcing in natural law, a "check [on] the arrogance of power, and the oppression of prerogative, . . . the teacher as well as the advocate of rational liberty" ("Value and Importance of Legal Studies," in William W. Story, ed., *Miscellaneous Writings of Joseph Story* [Boston, 1852], 534–35). *Updegraph v. Commonwealth*, 406.

44. *Updegraph v. Commonwealth*, 406.

45. Thomas J. Curry, *First Freedoms: Church and State in America to the Passage of the First Amendment* (New York, 1986); Arlin M. Adams and Charles J. Emmerich, *A Nation Dedicated to Religious Liberty: The Constitutional Heritage of the Religion Clauses* (Philadelphia, 1990); William L. Miller, *The First Liberty: Religion and the American Republic* (New York, 1986).

46. *Cantwell v. Connecticut*, 310 U.S. 296 (1940); *Everson v. Board of Education*, 330 U.S. 1 (1947). For the argument that admittance to statehood depended on conformity to republican principles, see [Francis Lieber,] "The Mormons: Shall Utah Be Admitted to the Union?" *Putnam's Monthly* 5 (March 1855).

47. Lyman Beecher wailed in 1812, "[W]e shall become slaves, and slaves to the worst of masters" (*Autobiography*, ed. Barbara M. Cross, 2 vols. [Cambridge, Mass., 1961], 1:192).

48. Jesse T. Peck, *The History of the Great Republic* (New York, 1868), 205–6, 499, 562.

49. On Garrison, see Aileen Kraditor, *Means and Ends in American Abolitionism: Garrison and His Critics on Strategy and Tactics, 1834–1850* (Berkeley, Calif., 1981); *CG*, 31 Cong., 1 sess., app., 260 (11 March 1850). On northern politics in the 1850s, see McPherson, *Battle Cry of Freedom*; Carwardine, *Evangelicals and Politics*; George M. Thomas, *Revivalism and Cultural Change: Christianity, Na-*

tion Building, and the Market in the Nineteenth-Century United States (Chicago, 1989). On the reactions to Seward's speech, see Allan Nevins, *Ordeal of the Union*, 2 vols. (New York, 1947), 1:301–2.

50. Morrill, *Polygamy and Its License*, 4, 10. On Chase's approach to Constitution, see Foner, *Free Soil, Free Labor, Free Men*, ch. 3.

51. The initial quotes are from Theodore Parker, "The Destination of America," in *The Slave Power* (Boston, n.d.), and William Ellery Channing, "Slavery," in *Works* (Boston, 1841), both quoted in Merrill D. Peterson, *The Jefferson Image in the American Mind* New York, 1960), 173–74. For Nelson's speech, see *Appendix to the CG*, 36 Cong., 1 sess., 195 (4 April 1860).

52. Morrill, *Polygamy and Its License*, 10.

53. *Appendix to the CG*, 36 Cong., 1 sess., 192, 193 (5 April 1860); Thomas A. R. Nelson, *Polygamy in the Territories of the United States, to Accompany Bill H.R. No 7, March 14, 1860*, (Washington, D.C., 1860), 2.

54. [Lieber,] "Shall Utah Be Admitted to the Union?" 18–19, 24; Francis Lieber, *Political Ethics*, 2 vols. (Philadelphia, 1838), 2:9; James Russell Thayer, *The Life, Character, and Writings of Francis Lieber, A Discourse Delivered before the Historical Society of Pennsylvania, January 13, 1873*, (Philadelphia, 1873), 21–28. This indirect Christianization of constitutional interpretation may explain why a proposed amendment to the preamble of the Constitution, recognizing explicitly the authority of God's law, which enjoyed relatively strong support during the immediate Civil War era, seemed unnecessary to many believing Christians by the 1870s. The amendment was never seriously a part of either party's agenda. See Morton Borden, "The Christian Amendment," *Civil War History* 25 (March 1979): 156.

55. The only objection to the proposed legislation came from Californians who feared that it might so alienate the Mormons that they would attempt to interfere with Union communications in the West. James McDougall and Milton Latham, Democrats of California, were the only two opponents of the legislation. See *CG*, 38 Cong., 1 sess., 1862, app., 2507. Indeed, Mormon loyalty was the subject of much speculation, especially early in the war, as Brigham Young and other leaders predicted that the war was the conflagration prophesied in Mormon scripture as the end of all human government and the onset of latter-day domination of the world. See Alan E. Haynes, "The Federal Government and Its Policies Regarding the Frontier Era of Utah Territory, 1850–1877" (Ph.D. diss., Catholic University, 1968). See also David L. Bigler, *Forgotten Kingdom: The Mormon Theocracy in the American West, 1847–1896* (Spokane, Wash., 1998), 224–25.

56. Haskell, "Capitalism and the Origins of the Humanitarian Sensibility"; David Walker Howe, "American Victorianism as a Culture," *AQ* 27, no. 5 (December 1975): 507–32; William Belmont Parker, *The Life and Public Services of Justin Smith Morrill* (New York, 1924), 349–57.

57. Report from the Committee on the Judiciary, 28 February 1867, responding to the "Memorial of the Legislative Assembly of the Territory of Utah, Praying for the Repeal of [the 1862 Act]," 3. The petition, and the proposed state constitution that accompanied it, are detailed in Orson F. Whitney, *History of Utah*, 4 vols. (Salt Lake, 1892–1904), 2:172–75.

1. B. Carmon Hardy, *Solemn Covenant: The Mormon Polygamous Passage* (Urbana, Ill., 1992), 101.

2. Klaus Hansen, *Quest for Empire: The Political Kingdom of God and the Council of Fifty in Mormon History* (East Lansing, Mich., 1967), 111–20. On Cannon's role in Congress, see Mark W. Cannon, "The Mormon Issue in Congress, 1872–1882, Drawing on the Experience of Territorial Delegate George Q. Cannon" (Ph.D. dissertation, Harvard University, 1960); E. Leo Lyman, *Political Deliverance: The Mormon Quest for Utah Statehood* (Urbana, Ill., 1986), 19–23; and Davis Bitton, *George Q. Cannon, A Biography* (Salt Lake, 1999), 169–262. I clearly differ with the historian Klaus Hansen, who argues that the Fourteenth Amendment essentially undermined state sovereignty, thus reducing the value of statehood for Mormons (*Quest for Empire*, 135). In congressional debates on the amendment, however, it was abundantly clear that its proponents were by no means seeking to undermine state control over domestic relations other than slavery, especially marriage. See William E. Nelson, *The Fourteenth Amendment: From Political Principle to Judicial Doctrine* (Cambridge, Mass., 1988), 110–47. Instead, many debates over the relationship of freedom and marriage were fought out at the state level. See Amy Dru Stanley, *From Bondage to Contract: Wage Labor, Marriage, and the Market in the Age of Slave Emancipation* (Cambridge, Eng., 1998), 175–212.

3. This chapter focuses especially on theories of rights, both constitutional and natural, as well as federalism and concepts of church and state. Much excellent secondary work on polygamy as it was lived in territorial Utah (and beyond) is available to students of Mormon history. See, e.g., Hardy, *Solemn Covenant*; Richard Van Wagoner, *Mormon Polygamy: A History*, 2d ed. (Salt Lake, 1989); Jessie L. Embry, *Mormon Polygamous Families: Life in the Principle* (Salt Lake, 1987); and two bibliographic articles, Davis Bitton, "Mormon Polygamy: A Review Article," *JMH* 4 (1977): 106, and Patricia Lyn Scott, "Mormon Polygamy: A Bibliography, 1977–1992," *JMH* 19 (Spring 1993): 133–55. For surveys of propolygamy argument in more general terms, see David Whittaker, "Early Mormon Polygamy Defenses," *JMH* 11 (1984): 43–63, and Davis Bitton, "Polygamy Defended: One Side of a Nineteenth-Century Polemic," in *The Ritualization of Mormon History* (Urbana, Ill., 1994), 34–53.

4. See, e.g., "Petition of the Utah Assembly," *CG*, 35 Cong., 1 sess., 1858, 1151–52.

5. "Celestial Marriage," *The Seer* 1 (October 1853).

6. There is some disagreement among scholars about whether or not polygamy was the centerpiece either of anti-Mormon attacks or of Mormon resistance. Hansen (*Quest for Empire*, xvii–xviii) maintains that the political kingdom, the theocracy in the Great Salt Lake Valley, was in fact the primary concern of anti-Mormon agitation. Lyman (*Political Deliverance*, 2–5), on the other hand, argues persuasively that, as a national matter at least, polygamy was the crux of the matter. My reading has convinced me that, for the most part, Lyman has the better of the argument, despite the counterexamples Hansen cites as evidence. I am also convinced, however, that most antipolygamists believed that without the political power of the church to keep them in "subjec-

tion," Mormons would throw off the mantle of priestly authority and spurn polygamy. Thus I think that both Lyman and Hansen are essentially correct: that polygamy was the true center of national anti-Mormonism in the latter half of the nineteenth century but also that antipolygamists were committed to the idea that polygamy and church authority were mutually dependent. The quoted language is from An Old Timer, "Expressions from the People," *Deseret News*, 14 April 1885 (quoted in Hardy, *Solemn Covenant*, xix).

7. An example of the dangers posed by such former members is that of William Law, whose *Nauvoo Expositor* printed rumors of polygamy and other skullduggery and was suppressed after a kangaroo court trial presided over by Joseph Smith in the spring of 1844. This event provided the pretext for the arrest of Smith and his imprisonment in the Carthage jail that became the site of his murder. See Dallin H. Oaks, "The Suppression of the Nauvoo Expositor," *Utah Law Review* 9 (Winter 1965): 861, and Van Wagoner, *Mormon Polygamy*, ch. 6. Bennett's letters, originally published in the *Sangamo Journal*, were profoundly embarrassing to Smith, who had taken Bennett into his confidence after a relatively short acquaintance, treating him as his second-in-command. See also John C. Bennett, *The History of the Saints; or, An Exposé of Joe Smith and Mormonism* (Boston, 1842). Roger D. Launius, *Joseph Smith III: Pragmatic Prophet* (Urbana, Ill., 1988), ch. 11. Roger D. Launius and Linda Thatcher, eds., *Differing Visions: Dissenters in Mormon History* (Urbana, Ill., 1994); Ronald W. Walker, "The Stenhouses and the Making of a Mormon Image," *JMH* 1 (1974): 51; Robert N. Baskin, *Reminiscences of Early Utah* (n.p., 1914), 80–82.

8. *JD*, 3:71 (Orson Pratt, 8 July 1855). As Klaus Hansen put it, "[T]he Saints' . . . version of the American dream could be enforced only through the destruction of the United States in its present form" (*Quest for Empire*, 44).

9. Orson Pratt explained that Mormons respected American constitutional government "because it has good principles in it, and not that we think it will endure forever" (*JD*, 3:71 [8 July 1855]). For the assumption that the war would destroy the entire country and for the expression of Young and other leaders that the Mormons would fill the political void, see Hansen, *Quest for Empire*, 165–69. On the introduction of monogamy as a peculiarly Roman (and inherently decadent) practice, see *Discourses on Celestial Marriage, delivered in the New Tabernacle, Salt Lake City, October 7, 8 and 9, 1869, delivered by Orson Pratt, George A. Smith and George Q. Cannon* (Salt Lake, 1869), 22 (George Q. Cannon); Parley P. Pratt, *Marriage and Morals in Utah* (Liverpool, 1856), 4–5; and Hardy, *Solemn Covenant*, 100. See also *JD*, 3:71.

10. Pratt, *Marriage and Morals in Utah*, 2, 4.

11. For the quoted language, see Pratt, *Marriage and Morals in Utah*, 4, 8. See also *Discourses on Celestial Marriage* (Orson Pratt), 1.

12. *JD*, 1:63 ("A Discourse delivered by Elder Orson Pratt, in the Tabernacle, Great Salt Lake City, 29 August 1852"). For an argument that this initial defense of polygamy formed a model for all those that followed, see Whittaker, "Early Mormon Polygamy Defenses," 43. See also Van Wagoner, *Mormon Polygamy*, 97–98; Hardy, *Solemn Covenant*, 102, 124 n. 143, and sources cited therein.

13. Mormon president John Taylor, 14 October 1882, quoted in Scott Kearney, ed., *Wilford Woodruff's Journals, 1833–1898*, 9 vols. (Midvale, Utah, 1983–84), 8:126. *JD*, 3:360 (Brigham Young, 15 June 1856). The exaltation of polygamy

might also benefit the family of the wife. Heber Kimball, for example, importuned his fifteen-year-old daughter Helen to marry Joseph Smith in 1843, because of his "great desire to be connected with the Prophet" (Stanley B. Kimball, *Heber C. Kimball, Mormon Patriarch and Pioneer* (Urbana, Ill., 1981), 97). See also Van Wagoner, *Mormon Polygamy*, 93–97, and Stanley S. Ivins, "Notes on Mormon Polygamy," *Western Humanities Review* 10 (Summer 1956): 229. Erotic pleasure was only rarely a component of some propolygamy arguments, and never after the exodus to Utah. See Hardy, *Solemn Covenant*, 9, 91.

14. On the role of consent in the creation of a valid marriage, see Michael Grossberg, *Governing the Hearth: Law and the Family in Nineteenth-Century America* (Chapel Hill, N.C., 1985), 103, 121–26; Joel Prentiss Bishop, *Commentaries on the Law of Marriage and Divorce and Evidence in Matrimonial Suits*, 2 vols. (Boston, 1873), 1:3–13; James Schouler, *Laws of the Domestic Relations* (1870: Boston, 1905), 12–17. On consent to polygamy among Latter-day Saints in the nineteenth century, see "Monogamy, Polygamy, and Christianity," *Latter-day Saints Millennial Star*, 6 August 1853, 515 (quoted in Hardy, *Solemn Covenant*, 101); *JD*, 20:31 (Joseph F. Smith, 7 July 1878); Gustive O. Larson, *The "Americanization" of Utah for Statehood* (San Marino, Calif., 1971), 44; *Discourses on Celestial Marriage*, 21 (George Q. Cannon).

15. Hansen, *Quest for Empire*, 128. For the quoted language, see *Latter-day Saints Millennial Star*, vol. 5, 150 (quoted without further attribution in Hansen, *Quest for Empire*, 40).

16. Kearney, ed., *Wilford Woodruff's Journal*, 4:11. The act is reproduced in Dale Morgan, "The State of Deseret," *UHQ* 8 (1940): 223–25. See also Jacob Smith Boreman, *Curiosities of Early Utah Legislation* (Ogden, Utah, 1895?) (typescript at Huntington Library, San Marino, Calif.), 47–49.

17. "An Act in Relation to the Judiciary," 4 February 1852, Utah Territory, *Acts, Resolutions, and Memorials Passed by . . . the Legislative Assembly* (Salt Lake, 1852); Leonard Arrington, *Brigham Young, American Moses* (Chicago, 1986); Governor J. Wilson Shaffer to Senator Shelby M. Cullom, 27 April 1870, in Department of State, Territorial Papers, National Archives, quoted in Larson, *"Americanization" of Utah for Statehood*, 73. On the rejection of the common law (according to which bigamy was a crime), see *Laws of Utah* (Salt Lake, 1853–54), 16. On the jurisdiction of the probate courts, see James B. Allen, "The Unusual Jurisdiction of the County Probate Courts in the Territory of Utah," *UHQ* 36 (1968): 133, and Earl S. Pomeroy, *The Territories and the United States, 1861–1890* (Philadelphia, 1947), 59–60. For analyses of probate courts, see Elizabeth C. Gee, "Justice for All or for the 'Elect'? The Utah County Probate Court, 1855–1872," *UHQ* 48 (Spring 1980): 129, and Edwin B. Firmage and Richard Collin Mangrum, *Zion in the Courts: A Legal History of the Church of Jesus Christ of Latter-day Saints, 1830–1900* (Urbana, Ill., 1988), 140–43, 219–22.

18. *JD*, 9:10 (6 April 1861); Hansen, *Quest for Empire*, 40–41; Joseph Smith to the *Daily Globe*, 14 April 1844, quoted in D. Michael Quinn, *The Mormon Hierarchy: Origins of Power* (Salt Lake, 1994), 124–25.

19. The quoted language is from Sarah Rich, in Leonard J. Arrington, *Charles C. Rich—Mormon General and Western Frontiersman* (Provo, Utah, 1974), 288, and Annie Tanner, in *A Mormon Mother: The Autobiography of Annie Clark Tanner*, ed. Obert Tanner, ed. (1941; Salt Lake, 1973), 2. For fuller discussions see

Van Wagoner, *Mormon Polygamy*, 90–91; Embry, *Mormon Polygamous Families*, 58–60; and Kahlile Mehr, "Women's Response to Plural Marriage," *Dialogue* 18 (Fall 1985): 93–95. The 1843 revelation itself, which required consent for plural marriage, commanded Emma Hale Smith to give her consent, or be damned. See *JD*, 17:224–25 (Orson Pratt, 7 October 1874). For the effects of polygamy on the lives of women in Utah, see Kathryn M. Daynes, *More Wives than One: Transformation of the Mormon Marriage System, 1840–1910* (Urbana, Ill., forthcoming), 102.

20. On popular contemporary perceptions of the role of the railroad in western settlement and Mormon strength through immigration, see Josiah Strong, *Our Country* (Philadelphia, 1885). On the political challenge of the New Movement, see Ronald W. Walker, *Wayward Saints: The Godbeites and Brigham Young* (Urbana, Ill., 1998); T. B. H. Stenhouse, *The Rocky Mountain Saints* (New York, 1873), 622–46; and G. Homer Durham, "The Development of Political Parties in Utah: The First Phase," *Utah Humanities Review* 1 (January 1947): 122. On the response of Mormon leaders to challenges in the late 1860s, see Leonard Arrington, *Great Basin Kingdom: An Economic History of the Latter-day Saints, 1830–1900* (Cambridge, Mass., 1956), 235–56, and Orson F. Whitney, *History of Utah*, 4 vols. (Salt Lake, 1892–1904), 2:276–94.

21. S. R. Wells, "William H. Hooper, The Utah Delegate and Woman Suffrage Advocate," *Phrenological Journal* 51 (November 1870): 328, 329. On the timing and introduction of the Female Suffrage Bill, see *Salt Lake Tribune*, 15 December 1877, 2, and Alan P. Grimes, *The Puritan Ethic and Woman Suffrage* (New York, 1967), 33–40.

22. On Mormon voting patterns, see Stanley S. Ivins, "The Moses Thatcher Case," typescript [1964?], 3, Utah State Historical Society, Salt Lake. The quoted language is from Edward W. Tullidge, *The Women of Mormondom* (New York, 1877), 500.

23. *Woman's Exponent* 7 (1 May 1879): 234. See also Carol Cornwall Madsen, "Emmeline B. Wells: A Voice for Mormon Women," *John Whitmer Historical Association Journal* 2 (1982): 11; Van Wagoner, *Mormon Polygamy*, 94–95; Joan Smyth Iversen, *The Anti-Polygamy Controversy in United States Women's Movements, 1880–1925* (New York, 1997), 61–63. One recent study concludes that Mormon women were instrumental in the church leadership's assessment of the utility of woman suffrage in the defense of polygamy. See Lola Van Wagenen, "In Their Own Behalf: The Politicization of Mormon Women and the 1870 Franchise," *Dialogue* 24 (Winter 1991): 31. On the ecclesiastical and political power of women connected by ties of faith and kinship, see Jill Mulvay Derr, " 'Strength in Our Union': The Making of Mormon Sisterhood," in *Sisters in Spirit: Mormon Women in Historical and Cultural Perspective*, ed. Maureen Ursenbach Beecher and Lavina Fielding Anderson (Urbana, Ill., 1987), 153.

24. Harriet Cook Young, quoted in Tullidge, *Women of Mormondom*, 395; Woodruff quoted in ibid., 400. On the role of the elite women, see Maureen Ursenbach Beecher, "The 'Leading Sisters': A Female Hierarchy in Nineteenth-Century Mormon Society," *JMH* 9 (1982): 25.

25. *JD*, 12:261 (Brigham Young, 9 August 1868). On Mormon theories of the excess of women in the states, see *Discourses on Celestial Marriage*, 8 (Orson Pratt). The quoted language is from *Discourses on Celestial Marriage*, 7.

26. *Discourses on Celestial Marriage,* 20–21 (George Q. Cannon). The charge of hypocrisy against detractors of polygamy was a constant refrain of propolygamists. See Hardy, *Solemn Covenant,* 89, 110 nn. 38–40, and sources cited therein. *Discourses on Celestial Marriage,* 8 (Orson Pratt).

27. Pratt, *Marriage and Morals in Utah,* 8; *Woman's Exponent 7* (15 November 1878): 92.

28. Tullidge, *Women of Mormondom,* 534.

29. *Discourses on Celestial Marriage,* 21 (George Q. Cannon). On the freedom of plural wives, see Martha Hughes Cannon's quote in *San Francisco Examiner,* 8 November 1896: "If her husband has four wives, [a Mormon woman] has three weeks of freedom every month." See also Gail Farr Casterline, " 'In the Toils' or 'Onward for Zion': Images of Mormon Women, 1852–1890" (master's thesis, Utah State University, 1974), 79–81; Fanny Stenhouse, *A Lady's Life among the Mormons* (New York, 1872), 91; and Joan Iversen, "Feminist Implications of Mormon Polygyny," *Feminist Studies* 10 (Fall 1984): 505. Young quote is from *JD,* 3:360–61 (Brigham Young, 15 June 1856). See also Hardy, *Solemn Covenant,* 90–92, for a discussion of romantic love and eroticism in plural marriage.

30. On the centrifugal, unifying force of plural marriage in Mormonism, see Leonard J. Arrington and David Bitton, *The Mormon Experience: A History of the Church of Jesus Christ of Latter-day Saints* (New York, 1978), 200–205, and Jan Shipps, *Mormonism: The Story of a New Religious Tradition* (Urbana, Ill., 1985), 61–63. On the exhilaration of a life of "shared commitment to the restored Gospel of Jesus Christ" for Mormon women in the nineteenth century, see Kenneth W. Godfrey, Audrey M. Godfrey, and Jill Mulvay Derr, *Women's Voices: An Untold History of the Latter-day Saints* (Salt Lake, 1982).

31. Quoted in Tullidge, *Women of Mormondom,* 381; *JD,* 14:58 (George Q. Cannon, 15 August 1869).

32. The initial quote is from Charles W. Penrose, "Family Government," *Latter-day Saints Millennial Star,* 16 May 1868, 307. George Q. Cannon argued that the physical characteristics of men dictated that they must have sexual variety, or be engrossed in sin: "We are all, both men and women, physiologists enough to know that the procreative powers of man endure much longer than those of woman. Granting, as some assert, that an equal number of the sexes exist, what would this lead to? Man must practice that which is vile and low or submit to a system of repression; because if he be married to a woman who is physically incapable, he must either do himself violence or what is far worse, he must have recourse to the dreadful and damning practice of having illegal connection with women, or become altogether like the beasts" (*Discourses on Celestial Marriage,* 21–22). The connection between male physiology and patriarchy in Mormonism was tempered by an injunction to rule wives kindly and without excessive physical discipline. See B. Carmon Hardy, "Lords of Creation: Polygamy, the Abrahamic Household, and Mormon Patriarchy," *JMH* 20 (Spring 1994): 119.

33. Hardy, *Solemn Covenant,* 102. See also Louis Kern, *An Ordered Love: Sex Roles and Sexuality in Victorian Utopias: The Shakers, the Mormons, and the Oneida Community* (Chapel Hill, N.C., 1981), 144–52; Lawrence Foster, *Religion and Sexuality: Three American Communal Experiences of the Nineteenth Century* (New York, 1981), 125–46; and John L. Brooke, *The Refiner's Fire: The*

Making of Mormon Cosmology, 1644–1844 (Cambridge, Eng., 1994), 214–17, 262–65.

34. Kimball, *Heber C. Kimball,* 234–36. See also *JD,* 5:272–73, 276–77 (Heber C. Kimball, 27 September 1857); *JD,* 17:159–60 (Brigham Young, 9 August 1874). On the subordination of women, see also Kern, *Ordered Love,* 151–57. The final quotation is from Wilford Woodruff, in 1875 in Matthias F. Cowley, *Wilford Woodruff* (Salt Lake, 1909), 490.

35. *JD,* 13:272–74 (Brigham Young, 24 July 1870).

36. Ibid., 1:63–64 (Orson Pratt, 29 August 1852).

37. Ibid., 12:224 (George Q. Cannon, 7 April 1868); see also *JD,* 1:63 (Orson Pratt, 29 August 1852) ("noble" spirits would be sent to the Saints, whose "just and righteous parentage" will produce the "last dispensation"); *JD,* 5:26 (Heber C. Kimball, 6 April 1857) (quoted in Kimball, *Heber C. Kimball,* 238); "Discourse by Elder Moses Thatcher," *Deseret News,* 26 May 1883 (quoted in Hardy, *Solemn Covenant,* 95); *JD,* 1:60 (Orson Pratt, 29 August 1852); *JD,* 3:291 (George A. Smith, 6 April 1856). See also Van Wagoner, *Mormon Polygamy,* 92.

38. Governor L. W. Boggs to General John B. Clark, 27 October 1838, reprinted in William Mulder and A. Russell Mortensen, eds., *Among the Mormons: Historic Accounts by Contemporary Observers* (New York, 1958), 102–3; *Whig* (Quincy, Ill.), 17 October 1840, reprinted in Mulder and Mortensen, eds., *Among the Mormons,* 115.

39. See *Deseret News,* 14 September 1856 (cited in Howard Roberts Lamar, *The Far Southwest, 1846–1912: A Territorial History* [New Haven, Conn., 1966], 313). The legal troubles of the prophet occasioned his arrest on no fewer than forty-six separate occasions, according to Brigham Young. For a detailed treatment of anti-Mormon violence through the end of the Nauvoo period, see Marvin S. Hill, *Quest for Refuge: The Mormon Flight from American Pluralism* (Salt Lake, 1989). On Mormon militarism, see Paul Bailey, *The Armies of God* (New York, 1968).

40. See the discussions in the introduction and Chapter 1 on limitations of religion clauses.

41. On Smith's decision to run for president, and his crowning as "King and Ruler over Israel," see Quinn, *Mormon Hierarchy,* 117–26. Smith's language is reprinted in Joseph F. Smith, *History of the Church of Jesus Christ of Latter-day Saints,* 2d ed., 7 vols. (Salt Lake, 1963), 6:95. On the disintegration of state control over anti-Mormon mobs and the decision to abandon Nauvoo, see Hill, *Quest for Refuge,* 153–82.

42. Upon the passage in 1895 of the enabling act that would admit Utah as a state a year later, the first president of the church sent the following telegram: "We rejoice with and congratulate you on the successful termination of your labor which has resulted in Utah's infranchisement, and political deliverance of her people" ("The First Presidency to Tobias Trumbo and Clio Clawson [1895]," cited without further attribution in Lyman, *Political Deliverance,* dust jacket).

43. The pattern for admission to the United States was set by the Northwest Ordinance of 1787. See Earl S. Pomeroy, *The Territories and the United States, 1861–1890* (Philadelphia, 1947), 3–5. For a description of the organization and workings of the Perpetual Emigrating Fund, see Arrington, *Great Basin Kingdom,* 97–108, 381–83.

44. Shipps, *Mormonism*, 120.

45. James M. McPherson, *Battle Cry of Freedom: The Civil War Era* (New York, 1988), 51–77, 117–30, 182–84. See Earl S. Pomeroy, *The Pacific Slope: A History of California, Oregon, Washington, Idaho, Utah, and Nevada* (New York, 1965), 74–82, on the widespread sense of Western remove from sectional conflict and adherence to older "conservative" concepts of federal politics in the 1850s and 1860s.

46. For a summary of these attempts to win statehood, see Lyman, *Political Deliverance*, 7–10. See also Whitney, *History of Utah*, 2:36–43, 58–59, 691–707, 720–21.

47. Lamar, *Far Southwest*, 355; Samuel Bowles, *Across the Continent: A Summer's Journey to the Rocky Mountains, the Mormons, and the Pacific States* (Springfield, Mass., 1865), 109.

48. As Jacob Boreman, judge of the Second District in Beaver City put it, "[T]he juries, both grand and petit, were largely Mormons and in those days a Mormon jury could be & was dictated to by the heads of the church whenever it was possible to reach the jury." Quoted in Leonard J. Arrington, "Crusade Against Theocracy: The Reminiscences of Jacob Smith Boreman, 1872–1877," *Huntington Library Quarterly* 24 (November 1960): 28 n. 40 (original in Henry E. Huntington Library).

49. On the "Mormon lobby," see Baskin, *Reminiscences of Early Utah*, 27, and Lyman, *Political Deliverance*, ch. 3.

50. Whitney, *History of Utah*, 2:592. On this case, see Thomas G. Alexander, "Federal Authority versus Polygamic Theocracy: James B. McKean and the Mormons, 1870–1875," *Dialogue* 1 (Autumn 1966): 85. The indictment eventually was dismissed because the process by which grand jurors were impaneled in the case was reversed on appeal to the Supreme Court in an unrelated case. See *Clinton v. Engelbrecht*, 80 U.S. 434 (1872). One outcome of this and other highly publicized strike suits against Mormon leaders was the removal of the crimes of adultery and cohabitation from territorial law, which had not been intended to apply to the practice of celestial marriage (George A. Smith, *The Rise, Progress, and Travels of the Church of Jesus Christ of Latter-day Saints* [Salt Lake, 1872], 68–71; Hardy, *Solemn Covenant*, 56).

51. Ann Eliza Young, *Wife No. 19; Or, The Story of a Life in Bondage, Being a Complete Exposé of Mormonism, and Revealing the Sorrows, Sacrifices and Sufferings of Women in Polygamy, by Brigham Young's Apostate Wife* (Chicago, 1876); Irving Wallace, *The Twenty-Seventh Wife* (New York, 1961); Fawn M. Brodie, "Ann Eliza Young," in *Notable American Women*, 3:696–97.

52. *U.S. Stats. at Large* 18 (1874): 669–71. On the role of Young's lectures in the passage of the Poland Act, see Helen Beal Woodward, *The Bold Women* (New York, 1953), ch. 16; Robert McHenry, ed., *Liberty's Women* (Springfield, Mass., 1980), 458; and Jack B. Cullen, "Ann Eliza Young: A Nineteenth-Century Champion of Women's Rights" (paper presented at the Annual Meeting of the Western Speech Communication Association, Albuquerque, N.M., February 1983). After Judge James McKean ordered Brigham Young to pay $500 monthly pending the outcome of the suit, the U.S. attorney general apparently intervened in the case, querying how a plural wife could be awarded alimony for a marriage that had never legally existed ("Brigham Young Must Pay Alimony to

Ann Eliza. Opinion of Chief Justice McKean" [n.p., 1875] [pamphlet in Huntington Library]). Arrington, "Crusade against Theocracy," 39–40 n. 59. For claims that the Poland Act was mere window dressing, see Whitney, *History of Utah*, 2:740, and *Deseret News Weekly*, 1874 (quoted in Lamar, *Far Southwest*, 370, without further attribution).

53. Journal entry, vol. 5, 16 October 1874, George Reynolds, Journal, vols. 1, 3–6, Latter-day Saints Historical Archives (quoted in Bruce A. Van Orden, *Prisoner for Conscience' Sake: The Life of George Reynolds* [Salt Lake, 1992], 62).

54. Whether or not such an agreement existed, relations soured shortly after the indictment of Reynolds. Mormon sources claimed that they had satisfied their part of the bargain (that is, Reynolds dutifully provided a list of witnesses for the case) but that federal prosecutors violated the pact virtually as soon as the indictment was handed down. According to Reynolds's biographer, "numerous provocative acts" demonstrated that Carey had "violat[ed] their agreement" (Van Orden, *Prisoner for Conscience' Sake*, 63). See also Whitney, *History of Utah*, 3:46–47.

55. Reynolds recorded in his diary that he had "considerable difficulty in presiding, being better able to do as I am told than to tell others what to do" (Van Orden, *Prisoner for Conscience' Sake*, 13 [quoting Reynolds Journal, vol. 1, 25 July 1861]).

56. Of the seventy-eight polygamy indictments handed down by grand juries in Utah between 1874 and 1891, an estimated thirty-one resulted in conviction. When compared with the approximately 700 recorded convictions for "unlawful cohabitation," it is evident that proving polygamy was extremely difficult. See also *Miles v. United States*, 103 U.S. 304 (1880) (reversing conviction for polygamy on ground that testimony of plural wife as to marriage would not sustain conviction where first marriage not also proved), and Firmage and Mangrum, *Zion in the Courts*, 149–53.

57. Baskin, *Reminiscences of Early Utah*, 61–72. The quoted description by General Benjamin R. Cowan, assistant secretary of the interior, appears in ibid., 66.

58. *Salt Lake Tribune*, 2 April 1875, p. 3, col. 2. According to Baskin (*Reminiscences of Early Utah*, 64–66), the guilty verdict was the direct result of his suggestion to the prosecutor and judge that the court adjourn immediately after the testimony of Schofield. Mormon jurors, Baskin claimed, had been told before the trial to vote for acquittal in anticipation that the second marriage would not be proved. Without time to receive new instructions, Baskin assumed, the jury would have deadlocked. Baskin and other federal observers of the Reynolds trial concluded that Mormons had no respect for law.

59. The opinion reversing the first conviction is reported in *United States v. Reynolds*, 1 Utah 226 (1875). See also Reynolds Journal, vol. 5, 5 June 1875 (quoted in Van Orden, *Prisoner for Conscience' Sake*, 74). The affirmation of the second conviction is reported at *United States v. Reynolds*, 1 Utah 319 (1876). Traditionally, the second indictment of Reynolds has been cited as evidence of the lack of compassion federal officials felt for the sensibilities of Mormon polygamists. It is also worth noting, however, that Reynolds may have been the only reasonable prospect for conviction, given that his plural wife had already sworn under oath that she married Reynolds in August 1874 and that this testimony

had been corroborated in open court by the concession of Reynolds's lawyers that the marriage had been celebrated by a high officer of the Mormon Church.

CHAPTER FOUR

1. "Extract from a letter of brother Geo. Q. Cannon to Pres. J. Taylor dated Washington 19 Mch," vol. 5, March 1878, George Reynolds Journal, vols. 1, 3–6, Latter-day Saints Historical Archives.

2. As the correspondence of George Q. Cannon reveals, he determined that "we should have strong councel [*sic*]" (letter from George Q. Cannon to President John Taylor, 11 March 1878, quoted in Reynolds Journal, vol. 5, March 1878). Cannon asked someone he referred to as "our Friend" for a recommendation of "first class and at the same time moderate [*sic*] priced lawyer" ("Extract from a letter of brother Geo Q. Cannon to Pres J. Taylor"). Almost certainly this friend was Philadelphian Thomas L. Kane, longtime ally of the Mormons, negotiator of the truce in the Mormon War. See Albert L. Zobell Jr., *Sentinel in the East: A Biography of Thomas L. Kane* (Salt Lake, 1965); Leonard J. Arrington, "'In Honorable Remembrance': Thomas L. Kane's Service to the Mormons," Task Papers in LDS History, no. 22 (Salt Lake, 1978).

3. "Extract from a letter of brother Geo. Q. Cannon to Pres. J. Taylor." On Devens, see John Codman Ropes, "Introductory Memoir" to a collection of Devens's public addresses, *Orations and Addresses on Various Occasions Civil and Military* (Boston, 1891); obituary, *American Law Review* 25 (1891): 255; and obituary, Massachusetts Reports, vol. 152 (1891), 608.

4. On Reconstruction, see Eric Foner, *Reconstruction: America's Unfinished Revolution, 1863–1877* (New York, 1988), 564–601; Laura F. Edwards, *Gendered Strife and Confusion: The Political Culture of Reconstruction* (Urbana, Ill., 1997).

5. *Bradwell v. Illinois*, 83 U.S. (16 Wall.) 36 (1873), and *The Slaughter-House Cases*, 83 U.S. (16 Wall.) 130 (1873), decided on the same day, decimated the theory that the "privileges and immunities" clause of the Fourteenth Amendment would provide new constitutional rights for all citizens. See also Paula Brandwein, *Reconstructing Reconstruction: The Supreme Court and the Production of Historical Truth* (Durham, N.C., 1999), 61–95.

6. In *Barron v. Mayor and City of Baltimore*, 7 Pet. 243 (1833), Chief Justice Marshall held that the Bill of Rights did not apply to disputes between individuals and states, thus effectively foreclosing litigation on questions involving the first nine amendments to the Constitution until after the Civil War. See also *Permoli v. First Municipality of New Orleans*, 44 U.S. (3 How.) 589 (1845) (applying holding of *Barron* to religion clauses of the First Amendment).

7. Brief of the Plaintiff in Error, Reynolds v. United States, 98 U.S. 145 (1879), 55.

8. *Scott v. Sandford*, 60 U.S. (19 How.) 393, 446, 450–51 (1857).

9. For contemporary attacks on Taney and the Court, see Charles Warren, *The Supreme Court in American History*, 3 vols. (Boston, 1923), 3:1–42. See also Maxwell Bloomfield, "The Supreme Court in American Popular Culture," *Journal of American Culture* 4 (1982): 3. For support of the opinion after the war, see, for example, the statements of George Graham Vest, Confederate official during

the Civil War, Democratic senator from Missouri after the war, and counsel for the Mormon Church in *Murphy v. Ramsey*, 114 U.S. 15, 45 (1885), who maintained that *Dred Scott* was written in "letters of gold; letters which declare the essence of the Constitution and the rights of every American citizen" (*CR*, 47 Cong., 1 sess., 1158 [15 February 1882]). On Southern Democrats' defense of the Mormons, see David Buice, "'A Stench in the Nostrils of Honest Men': Southern Democrats and the Edmunds Act of 1882," *Dialogue* 19 (1982): 106.

10. William E. Nelson, *The Fourteenth Amendment: From Political Principle to Judicial Doctrine* (Cambridge, Mass., 1988), 110–47; Warren, *Supreme Court in United States History*, 3:261–69.

11. Amy Dru Stanley, *From Bondage to Contract: Wage Labor, Marriage, and the Market in the Age of Slave Emancipation* (Cambridge, Eng., 1998), 58.

12. Brief of the Plaintiff in Error, *Reynolds v. United States*, 53–54.

13. Ibid., 54.

14. Ibid.

15. The oral argument in the *Reynolds* case was reported in the *New York Times*, 15 November 1878, p. 4, col. 7.

16. Juanita Brooks, *The Mountain Meadows Massacre*, rev. ed., (Norman, Okla., 1962); John D. Lee, *Mormonism Unveiled; or, The Life and Confessions of the Late Mormon Bishop, John D. Lee* (St. Louis, 1877); David L. Bigler, *Forgotten Kingdom: The Mormon Theocracy in the American West, 1847–1896* (Spokane, Wash., 1998), 159–80, 308–9. On the antipolygamist theory that Young sacrificed Lee, see Robert N. Baskin, *Reminiscences of Early Utah* (n.p., 1914), 136–37. For the ongoing currency of tales of avenging Danites in non-Mormon popular culture, see Arthur Conan Doyle, *A Study in Scarlet* (London, 1887).

17. *The Slaughter-House Cases*; *Minor v. Happersett*, 88 U.S. (21 Wall.) 162 (1875); *Bradwell v. Illinois*, 130.

18. On pro-marriage rhetoric after the Civil War, see Laura F. Edwards, "'The Marriage Covenant Is at the Foundation of All Our Rights': The Politics of Slave Marriages in North Carolina after Emancipation," *Law and History Review* 14 (Spring 1996): 81–124. See also Stanley, *From Bondage to Contract*, 1–35.

19. The quoted language is from *The Slaughter-House Cases*, 68.

20. On marital irregularity in the nineteenth century, see Beverly Schwartzberg, "Grass Widows, Barbarians and Bigamists: Documenting and Describing Marital Irregularity in Nineteenth-Century America" (unpublished manuscript on file with author); Hendrik Hartog, *Man and Wife in America, a History* (Cambridge, Mass., 2000), 242–86; Michael Grossberg, *Governing the Hearth: Law and the Family in Nineteenth-Century America* (Chapel Hill, N.C., 1985), 129–32. Compare Jill Elaine Hasday, "Federalism and the Family Reconstructed," *University of California at Los Angeles Law Review* 45 (June 1998): 1297–1400.

21. *Reynolds v. United States*, 98 U.S. 145 (1879). The list of such disapproved (or outright overruled) cases is extensive, including but not limited to *The Slaughter-House Cases, Bradwell, Minor v. Happersett, Plessy v. Ferguson*, 163 U.S. 537 (1896), and *Lochner v. New York*, 198 U.S. 45 (1905).

22. For examples of pro-Mormon response, see Henry Reed, *Bigamy and Polygamy: Review of Reynolds v. U.S.* (New York, 1879), 20, which argued that the opinion was an example of "popular passion and sentimental fanaticism." Edwin B. Firmage and Richard Collin Mangrum (*Zion in the Courts: A Legal*

History of the Church of Jesus Christ of Latter-day Saints, 1830–1900 [Urbana, Ill., 1988], 153–56) maintain that the decision was misguided and shortsighted. On the Court in the late nineteenth century, see, e.g., William E. Nelson, *Roots of American Bureaucracy, 1803–1900* (Cambridge, Mass., 1982); Michael Les Benedict, "Laissez-faire and Liberty: A Re-evaluation of the Meaning and Origins of Laissez-faire Capitalism," *Law and History Review* 3 (1985): 293–332; Robert W. Gordon, "Legal Thought and Legal Practice in the Age of American Enterprise," in *Professions and Professional Ideologies in America,* ed. Gerald L. Geison (Chapel Hill, N.C., 1983); Charles W. McCurdy, "Justice Field and the Jurisprudence of Government-Business Relations," *JAH* 61 (December 1975): 970–1005; Morton J. Horwitz, *The Transformation of American Law, 1879–1960: The Crisis of Orthodoxy* (New York, 1992); Benjamin R. Twiss, *Lawyers and the Constitution: How Laissez Faire Came to the Supreme Court* (Princeton, N.J., 1942); J. Willard Hurst, *Law and the Conditions of Freedom* (Madison, Wisc., 1950); and Arnold M. Paul, *Conservative Crisis and the Rule of Law: Attitudes of Bar and Bench, 1887–1895* (Gloucester, Mass., 1960).

23. Norma Basch, *Framing American Divorce: From the Revolutionary Generation to the Victorians* (Berkeley, Calif., 1999), 50. Few historians have studied the *Reynolds* opinion in depth. The exceptions are Carol Weisbrod and Pamela Sheingorn, "Reynolds v. United States: Nineteenth-Century Forms of Marriage and the Status of Women," *Connecticut Law Review* 10 (1978); Orma Linford, "The Mormons and the Law: The Polygamy Cases," parts 1 and 2, *Utah Law Review* 9 (1964); (1965); Firmage and Mangrum, *Zion in the Courts*; and Nancy L. Rosenblum, "Democratic Sex: *Reynolds v. U.S.,* Sexual Relations, and Community," in *Sex, Preference, and Family: Essays on Law and Nature* (New York, 1997), 63–85.

24. *Reynolds v. United States,* 98 U.S., 147–49.

25. Ibid., 161–62.

26. Kenneth R. Bowling, "A Tub to the Whale: The Founding Fathers and the Adoption of the Federal Bill of Rights," *Journal of the Early Republic* 8, no. 3 (1988); Arlin M. Adams and Charles J. Emmerich, *A Nation Dedicated to Religious Liberty: The Constitutional Heritage of the Religion Clauses* (Philadelphia, 1990).

27. *Reynolds v. United States,* 162 (quoting 12 Hening's Stat. 84).

28. Ibid., 164 (quoting without further attribution *Works of Thomas Jefferson,* 8:113). For the political context in which the letter was written, see James H. Huston, "Thomas Jefferson's Letter to the Danbury Baptists: A Controversy Rejoined," *William & Mary Quarterly,* 3d ser., 66 (October 1999): 775–90, and the responses in the same issue. On the actual course of the law of church and state in Virginia after disestablishment, see Thomas E. Buckley, "After Disestablishment: Thomas Jefferson's Wall of Separation in Antebellum Virginia," *Journal of Southern History* 61 (August 1995): 445.

29. *Reynolds v. United States,* 164.

30. Also important to the theories that Jefferson was opposed to slavery was the Northwest Ordinance, which included a ban on slavery and which many antislavery theorists claimed had been written by Jefferson. On the tenuousness of such a claim, see Merrill D. Peterson, *The Jefferson Image in the American Mind* (New York, 1960), 189–98.

31. See George Bancroft, "The Place of Abraham Lincoln in History," *Atlantic Monthly* 25 (June 1865). On the connections of such an identification of Lincoln with Jefferson and both men with the spiritual dimension of American patriotism, see Conor Cruise O'Brien, *The Long Affair: Thomas Jefferson and the French Revolution, 1785–1800* (Chicago, 1996), 305.

32. On the likely collaboration between Waite and Bancroft in researching the history of disestablishment in Virginia, see Peter Magrath, "Chief Justice Waite and the Twin Relic: *Reynolds v. United States,*" *Vanderbilt Law Review* 18 (1965): 513–14. On Bancroft, see John Franklin Jameson, *The History of Historical Writing in America* (Boston, 1891), 103; Richard Hofstadter, *The Progressive Historians: Turner, Beard, Parrington* (New York, 1968), 14; and Russell B. Nye, *George Bancroft: Brahmin Rebel* (New York, 1945). Waite was evidently a close friend of Bancroft's and a frequent guest at his home. See M. A. DeWolfe Howe, *Life and Letters of George Bancroft,* 2 vols. (New York, 1908), 2:279, 298–99. At the time the *Reynolds* opinion was written, Bancroft was preparing for publication a study of the framing of the Constitution and the Bill of Rights.

33. The statute is discussed in *Reynolds v. United States,* 165.

34. Brief of the Plaintiff in Error, *Reynolds v. United States,* 53.

35. *People v. Ruggles,* 8 Johns. 290, 295–96 (N.Y. 1811). See also *Commonwealth v. Kneeland,* 20 Mass. 206, 221 (1838), and *State v. Chandler,* 2 Harr. 553, 567 (Del. 1837); Joel Prentiss Bishop, *Commentaries on the Criminal Law,* 2 vols. (Boston, 1856), 1:545.

36. *Reynolds v. United States,* 164–65.

37. Frank L. Dewey, "Thomas Jefferson's Notes on Divorce," *William & Mary Quarterly* 39 (1982): 212–23. This point about divorce and revolution is also made in Basch, *Framing American Divorce,* 21–30.

38. *Reynolds v. United States,* 162.

39. Bishop, *Commentaries on Marriage and Divorce,* 1:25, 35; Christopher G. Tiedeman, *A Treatise on State and Federal Control of Persons and Property in the United States,* 2 vols. (St. Louis, 1886), 2:883–84.

40. Thomas M. Cooley, *A Treatise on the Constitutional Limitations Which Rest Upon the Legislative Power of the States of the American Union* (Boston, 1868), 472.

41. *Updegraph v. Commonwealth,* 11 Serge. & Rawl. 394, 400 (Pa., 1824); Sarah Barringer Gordon, "Blasphemy and the Law of Religious Liberty in Nineteenth-Century America," *AQ* 52 (December 2000): 694–95.

42. Nancy F. Cott, *Public Vows: A History of Marriage and the Nation* (Cambridge, Mass., 2000), ch. 5.

43. Basch, *Framing American Divorce,* 89; John Witte Jr., *From Sacrament to Contract: Marriage, Religion, and Law in the Western Tradition* (Louisville, Ky., 1997).

44. See the debate between Cardinal Gibbons, Bishop Henry E. Potter, and Col. Robert G. Ingersoll in "Is Divorce Wrong?" *North American Review* 149 (November 1889): 513–38. On Stanton, see Elizabeth B. Clark, "Self-Ownership and the Political Theory of Elizabeth Cady Stanton," *Connecticut Law Review* 21 (Summer 1989): 905–41.

45. As the historian Nancy Cott put it in another context, debates over marriage dissolution in the nineteenth century "complete[d] a circuitry that

connects private and public life, and links personal choices to state policies" ("Marriage and Women's Citizenship in the United States, 1830–1934," *American Historical Review* 103 [December 1998]: 1473).

46. *Reynolds v. United States*, 166.

47. Lieber's work was cited with approval in James Kent's influential *Commentaries on American Law*, 12th ed., 2 vols., ed. Oliver Wendell Holmes Jr. (Boston, 1873), 2:81–82. See also James Schouler's *Treatise on the Law of Domestic Relations: Embracing Husband and Wife, Parent and Child, Guardian and Ward, Infancy, and Master and Servant* (Boston, 1870), 188, for the proposition that polygamy is inconsistent with Christianity, civilization, and the Germanic races. Lieber was also relied on extensively by the State of Illinois in its brief opposing Myra Bradwell's Fourteenth Amendment claim that women should be allowed to practice law. See Brief of the Plaintiff in Error, *Bradwell v. Illinois*, 2, and Weisbrod and Sheingorn, "Reynolds v. United States," 838 n. 50.

48. *Reynolds v. United States*, 165.

49. Nancy F. Cott, "Giving Character to Our Whole Civil Polity: Marriage and the Public Order in the Late Nineteenth Century," in *U.S. History as Women's History: New Feminist Essays*, ed. Linda K. Kerber, Alice Kessler-Harris, and Kathryn Kish Sklar (Chapel Hill, N.C., 1995), 107–21; *Meister v. Moore*, 96 U.S. 76, 78 (1877).

50. Justice Stephen J. Field in *Maynard v. Hill*, 125 U.S. 190 (1887), and *Davis v. Beason*, 133 U.S. 333, 341 (1890).

51. *Reynolds v. United States*, 164.

52. For the charge of sexual promiscuity, see "Negro Suffrage and Polygamy," *New York World*, 12 October 1865, quoted in Cott, *Public Vows*, 88. See also Laura F. Edwards, " 'The Marriage Covenant Is at the Foundation of All Our Rights': The Politics of Slave Marriages in North Carolina after Emancipation," *Law and History Review* 14 (Spring 1996): 90. For discussion of the Freedmen's Bureau and southern states' reactions to form slaves' sexuality and marriages, see Cott, *Public Vows*, 84–96, and Eric Foner, *Reconstruction: America's Unfinished Revolution, 1863–1877* (New York, 1988). On miscegenation statues and their enforcement, see Peggy Pascoe, "Miscegenation Law, Court Cases, and Ideologies of 'Race' in Twentieth-Century America," *JAH* 83 (June 1996): 44–64. Utah also passed a prohibition against marriage of whites to Asians in the 1860s.

53. *Reynolds v. United States*, 165–66.

54. Ibid., 167. On the relative tolerance of courts to utopian separatists in the nineteenth century, see Carol Weisbrod, *The Boundaries of Utopia* (New York, 1980).

55. On the erosion of Reconstruction in the South, see Foner, *Reconstruction*, 412–587; George M. Fredrickson, *The Inner Civil War: Northern Intellectuals and the Crisis of the Union* (New York, 1965); Stephen Kantrowitz, *Ben Tillman and the Reconstruction of White Supremacy* (Chapel Hill, N.C., 2000).

CHAPTER FIVE

1. Wilford Woodruff, June 1879, quoted without further citation in Kimball Young, *Isn't One Wife Enough?* (New York, 1954), 354; *Latter-day Saints Mil-*

lennial Star, 3 February 1879, 73. See also editorial in *Deseret News*, 7 January 1879, 7.

2. The official case files of Utah's territorial district courts from 1870 to 1896 (when the territory achieved statehood) comprise some fourteen cubic feet of material ranging from preprinted criminal complaint forms from H. H. Bancroft's printing company in San Francisco with the offense "unlawful cohabitation" stamped on the cover, to stained and often illegible scraps of paper with scribbled jury verdicts in faded ink. Criminal prosecutions outnumber civil cases by more than twenty to one. The records are housed in the National Archives, Rocky Mountain West Division, in Denver, Colorado. The records have been microfilmed (thirty-six reels) and indexed (they are arranged, very roughly, in alphabetical order and, also very roughly, by district and by year). The index is a list of the names of the defendants but does not contain further information that could be of use to historians. The index does not, for example, tell the researcher what the case was about or what result, if any, is contained in the records. Nor are the records complete. To take just one example, the indictment of Brigham Young and other leading Mormons on charges of "lascivious cohabitation" in 1871 is not included in the criminal files, nor is Ann Eliza's divorce suit in 1873 included in the civil records (both suits are discussed in Chapter 3). But these are by far the most complete records available to students of antipolygamy, invaluable resources for assessing both the run-of-the-mill and many of the more spectacular polygamy prosecutions. In addition to several cases mentioned in the text and endnotes of this chapter, D. Michael Quinn, an independent scholar working on Mormon history and the author of several books and articles, has noted some thirty cases reported in the *Deseret News* that do not appear in the records (Letter from D. Michael Quinn, 3 August 1993, in author's possession).

3. On Cannon's effectiveness and financial support of railroad interests in Congress, see E. Leo Lyman, *Political Deliverance: The Mormon Quest for Utah Statehood* (Urbana, Ill., 1986), 69–95; Howard Roberts Lamar, *The Far Southwest, 1846–1912: A Territorial History* (New Haven, Conn., 1966), 383; and Frank J. Cannon and Harvey J. O'Higgins, *Under the Prophet in Utah: The National Menace of a Political Priest Craft* (Boston, 1911), 85–91. For detailed accounts of Cannon's life and activities in Washington, see Davis Bitton, *George Q. Cannon, A Biography* (Salt Lake, 1999), 169–205, 215–32, 234–44, 248–64, and Mark W. Cannon, "The Mormon Issue in Congress, 1872–1882, Drawing on the Experience of Territorial Delegate George Q. Cannon" (Ph.D. diss., Harvard University, 1960).

4. George Q. Cannon, *A Review of the Decision of the Supreme Court of the United States, in the Case of George Reynolds vs. United States* (Salt Lake, 1879), 39, 10–14.

5. The image of Mormons as treasonous was especially powerful in the 1880s, but its roots go back to the Mormon War of 1857–58 and to doubts about the loyalty of Mormons to the Union during the Civil War. See Sarah Barringer Gordon, " 'The Liberty of Self-Degradation': Polygamy, Woman Suffrage, and Consent in Nineteenth-Century America," *JAH* 83 (December 1996): 832.

6. *CG*, 42 Cong., 3 sess., 1790 (26 February 1873). On theories that the railroad and associated immigration would erode Mormons' commitment to

polygamy, for example, used as an argument against the enactment of new legislation in the late 1860s and early 1870s, see the debates over the Cullom Bill in 1870, a complex proposal of forty-one sections, including a hodge-podge of political and procedural measures, each one designed to eat away at the ability of polygamists and their church to find shelter in local government. The bill passed the House but failed in the Senate. See *CG*, 41 Cong., 2 sess., 2143–45 (22 March 1870). Many of the provisions of the Cullom Bill were eventually codified in the Poland Act of 1874, the Edmunds Act of 1882, and the Edmunds-Tucker Act of 1887, and proposed in the Cullom-Struble Bill of 1890.

7. James D. Richardson, comp., *Messages and Papers of the Presidents, 1789–1897*, 10 vols. (Washington, D.C., 1897), 10:4458. See also Chester Arthur, "President's Annual Message," *CR*, 47 Cong., 1 sess., 23–30 (6 December 1881).

8. George F. Edmunds, "Political Aspects of Mormonism," *Harper's Magazine* 64 (January 1882): 285–87. See also Howard Lamar, "Political Patterns in New Mexico and Utah," *UHQ* 28 (Summer 1960): 384–85.

9. Edmunds, "Political Aspects of Mormonism," 287.

10. Quote from Mark W. Cannon, "Mormon Issue in Congress," 167. On growing Southern support for antipolygamy lesiglation, see Senator Augustus Garland of Arkansas, a former Confederate official, who argued on behalf of the Edmunds Act: "Desperate cases need desperate remedies, and I am of the opinion that every provision in this bill is well sanctioned by the organic law and precedents under the organic law as any bill that has ever received the sanction of Congress" (*CR*, 47 Cong., 1 sess., 1158 [15 February 1882]).

11. As George Cannon explained it, Edmunds was "like a block of ice—polished, cold and hard . . . determined to do all in his power to strike down plural marriage and with it our supremacy in Utah" (George Q. Cannon Journal, 13 February 1882, quoted in Bitton, *George Q. Cannon*, 252).

12. *CR*, 47 Cong., 1 sess., 1198, 1205, 1208 (16 February 1882).

13. Ibid., 1213, 1214.

14. In a case decided two years after *Reynolds*, the Supreme Court demonstrated how ineffective the Morrill Act really was. John Miles, who married three women on the same day, was prosecuted for polygamy upon the complaint of the (now disgruntled) second wife. He admitted his marriage to her, which disqualified her testimony as to his bigamy, until another witness established the existence of another marriage—an unlikely occurrence. As the Court put it, "It is made clear by the record that polygamous marriages are so celebrated in Utah as to make the proof of polygamy very difficult. They are conducted in secret, and the persons by whom they are solemnized are under such obligations of secrecy that it is almost impossible to extract the facts from them when placed upon the witness stand. If both wives are excluded from testifying to the first marriage, as we think they should be under the existing rules of evidence, testimony sufficient to convict in a prosecution for polygamy in the Territory of Utah is hardly attainable" (*Miles v. United States*, 103 U.S. 304, 315 [1880]).

15. See, e.g., David Flaherty, "Law and the Enforcement of Morals in Early America," in *American Law and the Constitutional Order: Historical Perspectives*, ed. Lawrence M. Friedman and Harry Scheiber (Cambridge, Mass., 1988), 53–66. Although Flaherty does not give percentages for the records he studied, he cites a study of Virginia as following the typical pattern for prosecution of sexual

crimes. Out of 490 cases, approximately 125 involved sexual offenses. See Arthur P. Scott, *Criminal Law in Colonial Virginia* (Chicago, 1930), 281.

16. The total number of indictments for polygamy between 1870 and 1891, including those for unlawful cohabitation, polygamy and bigamy, adultery, fornication, and incest, and with the odd prosecution for illegal voting, bribery, perjury, and resisting officers, is in the neighborhood of 2,300. Estimating the total number of convictions is more difficult. The record contains convictions in approximately 935 cases, acquittals in 135, and dismissals in 112, for a total of results in 1,182 cases, roughly 50 percent. For unlawful cohabitation I find some 1,400 indictments, with a record of convictions in 711. Multicount indictments, or separate indictments included in the same case file, are common; I have treated all such indictments as a single prosecution.

Some information can also be gleaned from other sources. Stewart L. Grow, in "A Study of the Utah Commission" (Ph.D. diss., University of Utah, 1954), 268, basing his numbers on the reports of the Utah Commission, says that there were 33 convictions for polygamy and 1,004 for unlawful cohabitation. See also Richard D. Poll's "The Twin Relic: A Study of Mormon Polygamy and the Campaign of the U.S. Government for Its Abolition, 1852–1890" (master's thesis, Texas Christian University, 1938), 206–24, in which he claims that there were "1,004 convictions for unlawful cohabitation under the Edmunds Act between 1884 and 1893, and another 31 for polygamy." Rosa Mae McClellan Evans, basing her findings on the lists of prisoners at the Utah prison, concludes that 780 men did time for unlawful cohabitation between 1884 and 1895, 146 for adultery, 13 for polygamy, and one for incest ("Judicial Prosecution of Prisoners for LDS Plural Marriage: Prison Sentences, 1884–1895" [master's thesis, Brigham Young University, 1986]). Gustive O. Larson (*The "Americanization" of Utah for Statehood* [San Marino, Calif., 1971], 183), without citation to sources, says that "over twelve hundred Mormon polygamists" were housed in the penitentiary in the last half of the 1880s.

17. By his own estimation, Judge Charles Zane alone was responsible for the imprisonment of as many as a third of those convicted by 1890 for violation of antipolygamy laws. See Charles S. Zane, "The Death of Polygamy in Utah," *Forum* 12 (1891–92): 368. The *Clawson* record is contained in Records of the Territorial Courts of Utah, 1870–96, National Archives, Rocky Mountain West Division, Washington, D.C., case file 425. See also the discussion of the trial in Orson F. Whitney, *History of Utah*, 4 vols. (Salt Lake, 1892–1904), 3:293–314. Appealed to the U.S. Supreme Court after the territorial supreme court affirmed, Clawson's conviction and the grand and petit jury procedures that it secured were upheld unanimously. See *Clawson v. United States*, 114 U.S. 477 (1885). On the trial and Clawson's experiences in prison, see his *Prisoner for Polygamy: The Memoirs and Letters of Rudger Clawson at the Utah Territorial Penitentiary, 1884–1887*, ed. Stan Larson (Urbana, Ill., 1993). See also Thomas G. Alexander, "Charles S. Zane . . . Apostle of the New Era," *UHQ* 34 (Summer 1966): 314.

18. On the Clawson trial and the penalties imposed by the church on men who promised to obey the law in future in return for light sentences or fines, see James B. Allen, " 'Good Guys' vs. 'Good Guys': Rudger Clawson, John Sharp and Civil Disobedience in Nineteenth-Century Utah," *UHQ* 48 (Summer 1980): 148. Zane's speech is paraphrased in Whitney, *History of Utah*, 3:318.

Clawson's petition for a writ of habeas corpus was denied in *Clawson v. United States*, 114 U.S. 55 (1885).

19. Diary of Moses Franklin Farnsworth, reprinted in Larson, *"Americanization" of Utah for Statehood*, 120. P. T. Van Zile, assistant district attorney for Utah, fulminated against the conspiracy to prevent the capture of polygamists. His speech to the Michigan State Association of Congregational Churches, 21 May 1880, is reprinted in Mrs. Jennie Anderson Froiseth, ed., *The Women of Mormonism; or, The Story of Polygamy as Told by the Victims Themselves* (Detroit, 1882), 312–36.

20. Cannon surrendered in 1888, evidently in return for a promise of leniency. He was sent to the "pent," the federal prison just outside Salt Lake. Church president John Taylor died on the Underground, despite the best efforts of Marshal Ireland. The indictment of Taylor is another item missing from the official records.

21. Records of the Territorial Courts of Utah, case files 2237–39. For the quoted language, see Attorney General Garland to [U.S. marshal] Elwin A. Ireland, 11 November 1885, Instruction Books, Records of the Dept. of Justice, Record Group 60, National Archives, Washington, D.C.; Stephen Cresswell, *Mormons, Moonshiners, Cowboys, and Klansmen: Federal Law Enforcement in the South and West, 1870–1893* (Tuscaloosa, Ala., 1991), 113.

22. The Supreme Court's decision was the second of Snow's appeals to Washington. The first, in which the Court decided that defendants in unlawful cohabitation cases had no right of appeal to the Supreme Court, was succeeded by a habeas corpus proceeding, in which Snow challenged his eighteen-month sentence (*In re Snow*, 120 U.S. 274 (1887)). See also Ken Driggs, "Lorenzo Snow's Appellate Court Victory," *UHQ* 58 (1990): 81–93, and *History of Utah*, 3:543–44. *In re Hans Nielson*, 131 U.S. 176 (1889), expanded the holding of *Snow* to adultery cases, reversing a conviction for adultery that rested on precisely the same facts as an earlier conviction for unlawful cohabitation. For the perspective of federal officials on the course of the Raid and its effects on Mormons, see the collection of essays included in Froiseth, ed., *Women of Mormonism*.

23. One anonymous correspondent urged Mormon president John Taylor to abandon polygamy, given that the court of last resort had sustained Reynolds's conviction. He also argued that many Mormons viewed the Underground as an abandonment of the Mormon people: "The people say that you and Cannon . . . have run away and left the masses to go to the penitentiary or humiliate themselves before the courts. . . . You will force men to go to the pen when you will not go yourselves" (letter dated 11 January 1886, Samuel W. Taylor Collection, Historical Department, Church of Jesus Christ of Latter-day Saints, Salt Lake, cited in Richard Van Wagoner, *Mormon Polygamy: A History*, 2d ed. [Salt Lake, 1989], 127). On the experiences of Mormon men in prison, see William Mulder, "Prisoners for Conscience' Sake," in *Lore of Faith and Folly*, ed. Thomas E. Cheney (Salt Lake, 1971), 135–44; Melvin L. Bashore, "Life Behind Bars: Mormon Cohabs of the 1880s," *UHQ* 47 (1979): 22–41; and M. Hamlin Cannon, ed., "The Prison Diary of a Mormon Apostle," *Pacific Historical Quarterly* 16 (November 1947): 393–409.

24. Records of the Territorial Courts of Utah, case file 640.

25. Whitney, *History of Utah*, 3:348.

26. John M. Zane, "A Rare Judicial Service; Charles Shuster Zane," *Transactions of the Illinois State Historical Society*, publication no. 33 (1926), 93–94.

27. P. T. Van Zile, "The Twin Relic of Barbarism," in Froiseth, ed., *Women of Mormonism*, 320–21.

28. Records of the Territorial Courts of Utah, case file 1465. Loveridge pled not guilty. There is no record of what happened after the arraignment. Her husband, Ledru, was charged with unlawful cohabitation in 1886 and again in 1887. He pled not guilty at his first arraignment, but the record in the second case against him shows him changing his plea to guilty. There is no record of any sentence. See ibid., case files 1460 and 1461. Susan Parry was convicted of perjury in 1886 for swearing that her child was over three years old. Given that the statute of limitations for unlawful cohabitation was three years, Joseph Parry (who eventually pled guilty) could have argued that he had not cohabited with his plural wife within the operative time. Although it is evident from the record that Susan was tried by a jury in front of Judge Henderson, there is no record of any sentence. See ibid., case files 1864 and 1865.

Fanny Whiting, plural wife of Lucius Whiting, was also indicted in 1889 for perjury for swearing that she had not seen her husband for the two months prior to the time he was sent to prison. Fanny had been indicted one year earlier for fornication (and a complaint for unlawful cohabitation against Lucius was changed to adultery in the indictment), a sure sign that she had conceived. It appears from the record that Fanny was represented and that the case went to trial (there are several proposed jury instructions included), but there is no indication of what the outcome of the trial was. See ibid., case files 2544, 2564, 2565, and 2567.

29. Ibid., case file 1490. McMurrin's brother Joseph was also involved. At the time the subpoena was served on Agnes, Joseph had exchanged "warm words" with Deputy Marshal Henry Collin. Some time later, Joseph was wounded by two shotgun blasts in the stomach. He claimed, with what many believed to be his dying breath, that Collin was the one who had shot him. Salt Lake City soon seethed with tension, with Mormons charging that Collin had attempted to murder McMurrin for his resistance at the time of his sister's arrest, and many non-Mormons countering that Collin was a victim rather than an aggressor and that a riot was imminent. The situation was diffused after McMurrin fled to Europe; Collin eventually was discharged after a grand jury investigation (Whitney, *History of Utah*, 3:345–48).

30. In the 1880s, conflict over the most effective means of "reforming" Utah pitted those who advocated the punishment of all Mormons who practiced polygamy against those who believed that Mormon women were victims. The Industrial Christian Home, sponsored by women who insisted that plural wives were in fact prisoners, was controlled by federal territorial officials. Proponents of the home claimed that its male administrators, whose commitments were to punishment rather than to sympathy, ensured that only a handful of women were accepted into the home. On the home, see Jeannette H. Ferry, *The Industrial Christian Home Association* (Salt Lake, 1903), and Peggy Pascoe, *Relations of Rescue: The Search for Female Moral Authority in the American West, 1874–1939* (New York, 1990), 22–30, 184.

31. "Kate and the Mormons: Miss Field's Arraignment of the Apostolic

Women of Utah," *The Chicago Tribune*, 6 June 1886, 2. For another report of a Field lecture, see "Mormon Monster." On Field's career, see Lilian Whiting, *Kate Field, a Record* . . . (New York, 1909); "Kate Field," *Notable American Women*, 3 vols. (Cambridge, Mass., 1971), 1:612–14; Helen Beal Woodward, *The Bold Women* (New York, 1953), 201–14; and E. L. Godkin, "Woman in the Lyceum," *The Nation*, 13 May 1869, 371–72. Although newspaper accounts and notes taken at Field's lectures provide a relatively good idea of the content of her talks, the texts of the lectures themselves have not survived. Field also apparently varied her talks considerably, responding to one or another recent event, even changing her recommendations for legislation for Utah. There appears to have been more than one lecture in the initial series, at least. See Edward Increase Mather's, "Kate Field's New Departure," *Bay State Monthly* 3 (November 1885): 433, in which he described a "course of three lectures" in Boston to "spellbound" audiences. On lecturing in the nineteenth century, see Donald M. Scott, "The Profession that Vanished: Public Lecturing in Mid-Nineteenth-Century America," in *Professions and Professional Ideologies in America*, ed. Gerald L. Geison (Chapel Hill, N.C., 1983), 12–28; Woodward, *Bold Women*, 217–36; and Major James Burton Pond, *Eccentricities of Genius: Memories of Famous Men and Women of the Platform and Stage* (New York, 1900), 143.

32. The act also expressly disapproved of territorial laws allowing illegitimate children to inherit from an intestate father but exempted all children born within twelve months of the passage of the act and all children legitimized by the 1882 Edmunds Act. See Section 11, *CR*, 49 Cong., 2 sess., 1896 (18 February 1887). On the complexities of the law of inheritance in territorial Utah, see Barry Cushman, "Intestate Succession in a Polygamous Society," *Connecticut Law Review* 23 (Winter 1991): 281–332, and Kathryn M. Daynes, *More Wives than One: Transformation of the Mormon Marriage System, 1840–1910* (Urbana, Ill., forthcoming), 83–86, 176–82.

33. Hendrik Hartog, *Man and Wife in America, a History* (Cambridge, Mass., 2000), 108–10; St. George Tucker, ed. *Blackstone's Commentaries*, 5 vols. (Philadelphia, 1803), 1:442–43; James Wilson, *Works*, ed. Robert G. McCloskey (Cambridge, Mass., 1967), 602.

34. See the remarks of Senator Brown, *CR*, 49 Cong., 1 sess., 519 (7 January 1886), and Senator Van Wyck of New Hampshire, *CR*, 49 Cong., 1 sess., 552–53 (8 January 1886).

35. *CR*, 49 Cong., 2 sess., 1896 (18 February 1887) (final text of statute as enacted); *CR*, 49 Cong., 2 sess., 593 (12 January 1887) (remarks of Representative John Randolph Tucker, Democrat of Virginia). *Bassett v. United States*, 137 U.S. 496 (1890), reversed a conviction for polygamy based on spousal testimony.

36. Elizabeth Cady Stanton, Susan B. Anthony, and Matilda Joslyn Gage, eds., *History of Woman Suffrage*, 6 vols. (Rochester, N.Y., 1881–1922), 2:780 (resolution adopted at the annual meeting of the National Woman Suffrage Association, May 1870). The memorial of the New York Suffrage Association is reprinted in U.S. Congress, House, "Memorial of the New York Woman Suffrage Society . . . ," in *Miscellaneous Documents*, 42 Cong., 3 sess., H. Doc. 95 (17 February 1873). For additional discussions of woman suffrage in Utah, see Angelina French Newman, "Woman Suffrage in Utah," *Miscellaneous Docu-*

ments, 49 Cong., 1 sess., S. Doc. 122 (8 June 1886), 9, and "Mormon Monster," 13.

37. Fanny Stenhouse, an apostate Mormon, described the practice of Mormon men when faced with a contested election: "I have often seen one solitary man driving into the city a whole wagon load of women of all ages and sizes. They were going to the polls and their vote would be one. Many have voted two or three times. . . . It is easy to see how the influence of the priesthood has been exerted and the women themselves have been made the instruments for riveting still more firmly their own fetters" (quoted in the Newman, "Woman Suffrage in Utah," 4). See also Ross Evans Paulson, *Woman's Suffrage and Prohibition: A Comparative Study of Equality and Social Control* (Glenview, Ill., 1973), 90 (citing newspaper stories from the United States, England, and Canada that derided woman suffrage in Wyoming and Utah). The claim that women were the "catspaw" of the priesthood is from John W. Kingman, testifying before the Joint Special Committee on Woman Suffrage of the Massachusetts Legislature, reported in *The Woman's Journal,* 26 January 1876, cited in Lola Van Wagenen, "Sister-Wives and Suffragists: Polygamy and the Politics of Woman Suffrage, 1870–1896" (Ph.D. diss., New York University, 1994), 182. On the Utah experience in general, see Carol Cornwall Madsen, ed., *Battle for the Ballot: Essays on Woman Suffrage in Utah, 1870–1896* (Logan, Utah, 1997).

38. *New York Times,* 5 March 1869, 5. The resolution introduced in 1882 by Senator John Tyler Morgan, Democrat of Alabama, calling for the immediate investigation of female suffrage in Utah and speedy revocation of the woman's vote is typical of such proposed legislation. See U.S. Congress, Senate, *Miscellaneous Documents,* 47 Cong., 1 sess., S. Doc. 34 (11 January 1882).

39. Newman, "Woman Suffrage in Utah," 5.

40. "Polygamy and Woman Suffrage," *Anti-Polygamy Standard* (June 1880): 20, quoted in Petition of Mrs. Angie F. Newman, in Newman, "Woman Suffrage in Utah," 5. Anthony's testimony is reported at Senate Report 70, 49 Cong., 1 sess., 2 February 1886. Suffragists became increasingly vocal in their opposition to polygamy in the late 1870s. See Mary A. Livermore, "Anniversary Meeting," *The Woman's Journal,* 2 June 1877, 172–73, esp. 176, cited in Van Wagenen, "Sister-Wives and Suffragists," 189. Livermore also endorsed the work of Ann Eliza Young, writing a laudatory introduction to her *Wife No. 19; or, The Story of a Life in Bondage, Being a Complete Exposé of Mormonism, and Revealing the Sorrows, Sacrifices and Sufferings of Women in Polygamy, by Brigham Young's Apostate Wife* (Chicago, 1876), 9–10. See also Amanda E. Dickinson, "Polygamy Degrades Womanhood," *The Woman's Journal,* 29 March 1879, 97.

41. The objections of Republican representative John Reed of Massachusetts were typically perfunctory. In debate in the House on the proposed bill, he declared that while he saw "no reason for incorporating [disenfranchisement] into the bill," nonetheless "the advantage of [the proposed legislation as a whole] under the circumstances constrains my vote" (*CR,* 49 Cong., 2 sess., 592 [12 January 1887]). Republican senator George Hoar of Massachusetts, however, voted against the entire bill, based on his opposition to the "abolition of the right of suffrage by women as not merely unjustifiable but as tyrannical" (ibid., 1904 [18 February 1887]). Wilkinson Call, Democrat of Florida, pointed out with satisfaction the fact that "[t]wenty Senators voted here the other day, who

will vote for this bill, to submit an amendment of the Constitution to the people of the United States as to whether there should be discrimination against women in reference to their right to vote" (ibid., 1903; quoted in "Mrs. Pavy Defends Mrs. Newman's Advocacy of the Disfranchisement of the Women of Utah," *The Woman's Tribune*, July 1886). Edmunds's speech appears in *CR*, 49 Cong., 1 sess., 405 (5 January 1887). On the connections of the revocation of woman suffrage in Utah to broader questions of sovereignty and turn-of-the-century imperialism, see Allison Lee Sneider, "Reconstruction, Expansion and Empire: The United States Woman Suffrage Movement and the Re-Making of National Political Community" (Ph.D. diss., University of California at Los Angeles, 1999).

42. To give a well-known example of the perceived importance of marriage to freedom, Harriet Beecher Stowe's *Uncle Tom's Cabin* is in many senses an allegory of the harm to humans caused by the failure to recognize freedom to marry, to have one's sexual relations surrounded by legal rules and protections. On the overlap between employment law, including the law of slavery, and the law of husband and wife, see Amy Dru Stanley, *From Bondage to Contract: Wage Labor, Marriage, and the Market in the Age of Slave Emancipation* (Cambridge, Eng., 1998), 175–98; Peter W. Bardaglio, Reconstructing the Household: Families, Sex, and the Law in the Nineteenth-Century South (Chapel Hill, N.C., 1995), xi–xiv; and Laura F. Edwards, " 'The Marriage Covenant Is at the Foundation of All Our Rights': The Politics of Slave Marriages in North Carolina after Emancipation," *Law and History Review* 14 (Spring 1996): 85, n. 5. See also James Schouler, *A Treatise on the Law of Domestic Relations: Embracing Husband and Wife, Parent and Child, Guardian and Ward, Infancy, and Master and Servant* (Boston, 1870). The conviction of the coercive nature of polygamy had staying power despite Mormon men and women's vocal defense of their voluntary participation in the system. In 1882, in a story titled "Woman's Consent," Jennie Anderson Froiseth made essentially the same charge, arguing that "women have been, and still are, coerced into giving consent for their husbands to take other women" by church leaders and by the utter absence of legal protection for wives under Utah law. See *Women of Mormonism*, 50, 54, and "Mormon Monster," 5, 6, 9. For the claim that all women in Utah lived in "perpetual agony," whether or not their husbands had taken plural wives, see "Mormon Monster," 13–14.

43. On the importance of the will theory of contract in American legal and social life, see Stanley, *From Bondage to Contract*; J. Willard Hurst, *Law and the Conditions of Freedom* (Madison, Wisc., 1950); Lawrence M. Friedman, *Contract Law in America* (Madison, Wisc., 1965); Morton J. Horwitz, *The Transformation of American Law, 1790–1860* (Cambridge, Mass. 1977), 160–210; and Michael Grossberg, *Governing the Hearth: Law and the Family in Nineteenth-Century America* (Chapel Hill, N.C., 1985), 18–21. Henry Sumner Maine famously described the evolution of all of law as "from status to *Contract*" (*Ancient Law: Its Connection with the Early History of Society and its Relation to Modern Ideas*, 10th ed. [1884; reprint, Gloucester, Mass., 1970], 163–65).

44. Consent to marriage should not be construed as implying consent in any full-bodied sense of the term, either. Even if free from the taint attached to the presumptively invalid consent of plural wives to polygamy, spouses (especially

wives) were by no means free to structure the resulting relationship according to their own negotiations. Instead, the legal definitions of husband and wife were essentially "prefabricated" rather than created by the parties to a marriage, or to an employment relationship. See Christopher L. Tomlins, "Subordination, Authority, Law: Subjects in Labor History," *International Labor and Working-Class History* 47 (Spring 1995): 31.

45. *Speech of Hon. Justin S. Morrill, of Vermont, on Utah Territory and Its Law—Polygamy and Its License; Delivered in the House of Representatives, February 23, 1857* (Washington, D.C., 1857), 10, 13; Joseph E. Brown, *Polygamy in Utah and New England Contrasted: Speech of Hon. Joseph E. Brown, of Georgia; Delivered in the Senate of the United States, Tues., May 27, 1884* (Washington, D.C., 1884), 4, 7–9, 22–25, 30–32.

46. Ballard S. Dunn, *The Twin Monsters; and How National Legislation May Help to Solve the Mormon Problem, and Restore to Society, Somewhat of the Sacramental Character of the Rite of Holy Matrimony* (New York, 1884), 2 (emphasis in original); E. P. W. Packard, *Modern Persecution, or Married Women's Liabilities, as Demonstrated by the Actions of the Illinois Legislature*, 2 vols. (Hartford, 1875), 2:396, quoted in Hendrick Hartog, "Mrs. Packard on Dependency," *Yale Journal of Law and the Humanities* 1 (December 1988): 95 n. 53; Cardinal Gibbons, Bishop Henry E. Potter, and Col. Robert G. Ingersoll, "Is Divorce Wrong?" *North American Review* 149 (November 1889): 520.

47. On occasion, prodivorce commentators advocated treating marriage like a private contract. See sources, including John Stuart Mill's *On Liberty*, cited in George Elliott Howard, *A History of Matrimonial Institutions: Chiefly in England and the United States . . .*, 3 vols. (Chicago, 1904), 3:251, 251 nn. 1, 2; and Elizabeth Cady Stanton, "Address on Marriage and Divorce," in Paulina Wright Davis, comp., *A History of the National Woman's Rights Movement* (New York, 1871), 59–83. Even those who favored liberal divorce laws tended, like Howard, to shy away from the privatization of divorce that contract doctrine would dictate, relying instead on the "careful state regulation" evident in "modern legislation" (*Matrimonial Institutions*, 3:251). Employment contracts also came prepackaged and inescapable, especially for freedmen and paupers (see Amy Dru Stanley, " 'Beggars Can't Be Choosers': Compulsion and Contract in the Age of Emancipation," *JAH* 75 [1988]), and even for white women (see Lea S. Vandervelde, "The Gendered Origins of the *Lumley* Doctrine: Binding Men's Consciousness and Women's Fidelity," *Yale Law Journal* 101 [1992]). See also Tomlins, "Subordination, Authority, Law." On antipolygamists' invocation of the sovereignty of the people, see Newman, "Woman Suffrage in Utah," 5.

48. Noah Davis, "Marriage and Divorce," *North American Review* 139 (July 1884): 31, 34. On connections between contractualism and prostitution in early-twentieth-century fiction, see Walter Benn Michaels, "The Contracted Heart," *New Literary History* 21 (Spring 1990): 506–8. On the popularity and explanatory power of antidivorce theory, see Norma Basch, *Framing American Divorce: From the Revolutionary Generation to the Victorians* (Berkeley, Calif., 1999). On the overlap between "white slavery" and prostitution, see David J. Langum, *Crossing over the Line: Legislating Morality and the Mann Act* (Chicago, 1994), 15–47.

49. Stanton made the connections between marriage and slavery, divorce and freedom: "We assert that man can not hold property in man, and reject the whole code of laws that conflicts with the self-evident truth of that assertion. [Yet in marriage a woman is denied] her rights to person, children, property, wages, life, liberty and the pursuit of happiness" (reprinted in Ellen Carol DuBois, "On Labor and Free Love: Two Unpublished Speeches of Elizabeth Cady Stanton," *Signs* 1 [Autumn 1975]: 265, and Alma Lutz, "Elizabeth Cady Stanton," *Notable American Women*, 3:346). For the antisuffragist response, see Catharine Beecher, "An Address on Female Suffrage, Delivered in the Music Hall of Boston, in December, 1870," reprinted in Catharine E. Beecher, *Woman Suffrage and Woman's Profession* (Hartford, Conn., 1871), 57–58. On Stanton's views on contract, divorce, and coercion, see Elizabeth B. Clark, "Matrimonial Bonds: Slavery and Divorce in Nineteenth-Century America," *Law and History Review* 8 (Spring 1990): 35–36, and Aileen S. Kraditor, *The Ideas of the Woman Suffrage Movement, 1890–1920* (New York, 1965), 249–57. George Q. Cannon to Mormon president John Taylor, 14 June 1882, First Presidency File, John Taylor Presidential Papers, Church of Latter-day Saints Archives, quoted in Van Wagenen, "Sister-Wives and Suffragists," 342. Anthony was careful to point out that "I am among those who hate polygamy and all the subjection of women in the Mormon faith" (quoted in Joan Iversen, "The Mormon-Suffrage Relationship: Personal and Political Quandaries," *Frontiers* 11, nos. 2–3 [1990]: 14).

50. A. R. Cauzauran, comp., *The Trial of Daniel McFarland for the Shooting of Albert D. Richardson* (New York, 1870), 28–29, quoted in Basch, *Framing American Divorce*, 70.

51. Theodore D. Woolsey, *Essay on Divorce and Divorce Legislation, with Special Reference to the United States* (New York, 1869). See also Nathan Allen, "Divorces in New England," *North American Review* 130 (June 1880): 563, on the historical effects of divorce on society. On divorce as a reflection, rather than a cause, of failed marriages, see Elizabeth Cady Stanton, "The Need of Liberal Divorce Laws," *North American Review* 139 (September 1884): 236, and Carroll D. Wright, Commissioner of Labor, Bureau of Labor, *A Report on Marriage and Divorce in the United States, 1867 to 1886*, (1889; reprint, Washington, D.C., 1891), 186.

52. Acts in Relation to Bills of Divorce, 1851–70, Utah Territorial Laws, section 2 (approved 6 March 1852), 82–84. Morrill, *Polygamy and Its License*, 10. On divorce in Indiana, see Richard Wires, *The Divorce Issue and Reform in Nineteenth-Century Indiana* (Muncie, Ind., 1967). Nebraska, Idaho, and Nevada had six-month residency requirements, while South Dakota had a mere ninety-day residency requirement. See Howard, *History of Matrimonial Institutions*, 3:131–32, and Roderick Phillips, *Putting Asunder: A History of Divorce in Western Society* (New York, 1988), 455. The relationship between divorce and conversion is discussed by Richard I. Aaron, "Mormon Divorce and the Statute of 1852: Questions for Divorce in the 1980's," *Journal of Contemporary Law* 8 (1982): 21–22. The public perception of the Utah residency requirement is detailed in Howard, *History of Matrimonial Institutions*, 3:131–32.

53. For travelers' reports, see, for example, J. Remy and J. Brenchley, *A Journey to Great Salt Lake City* (London, 1861), 149. For the consent divorce label, see Wright, *Report on Marriage and Divorce*, 138–54. On divorce rates in Utah, see

Bruce Campbell and Eugene E. Campbell, "Divorce among Mormon Polygamists: Extent and Explanations," *UHQ* 46 (Winter 1978): 4–23; Leonard Arrington, *Brigham Young, American Moses* (Chicago, 1986), 318–20; Edwin B.
Firmage and Richard Collin Mangrum, *Zion in the Courts: A Legal History of the
Church of Jesus Christ of Latter-Day Saints, 1830–1900* (Urbana, Ill., 1988), 325–
27; and Daynes, *More Wives than One*, 141–59.

54. Wright, *Report on Marriage and Divorce*, 203–6. Several cases, including
one decided in her home state of Massachusetts shortly before Field began her
lecture tour, involved prosecutions for polygamy, bigamy, and fornication. Convictions in all of the cases were upheld despite the defendants' claims that they
had been divorced in Utah. The supreme court of Indiana, for example, showing just how quickly a jurisdiction could evolve from a divorce haven into a
divorce watchdog, condemned Utah's divorce statute as a "palpable case of the
exercise of extra-territorial jurisdiction," adding that "[marriage] is more than a
contract. It is not a mere matter of pecuniary consideration. It is a great public
institution, giving character to our whole civil polity" (*Hood v. State*, 56 Ind. 263,
270–73 [1877] [quoting *Noel v. Ewing*, 9 Ind. 37]). See also *Hardy v. Smith*, 136
Mass. 328 (1884); *State v. Armington*, 25 Minn. 29 (1878); and *Davis v. Commonwealth*, 13 Bush 318 (Ky. 1877).

55. "Mormon Monster," 12, 14–15.

56. *New York Tribune*, 28 July 1879, 4. On the connection between bigamy
and westward migration, see Lawrence M. Friedman, "Crimes of Mobility,"
Stanford Law Review 43 (February 1991): 638, and Beverly Schwartzberg, "Grass
Widows, Barbarians and Bigamists: Documenting and Describing Marital Irregularity in Nineteenth-Century America" (unpublished manuscript on file
with author). For a description of some of these bigamy cases and their (generally tolerant) treatment in the courts, see Hendrik Hartog, "Marital Exits and
Marital Expectations in Nineteenth-Century America," *Georgetown Law Journal* 80 (October 1991): 95–129. The *New York Tribune* labeled Utah the most
corrupt of all jurisdictions for allowing divorce when the parties cannot "live
together in peace and union." See also Glenda Riley, *Divorce, an American
Tradition* (New York, 1991), 108. Novelists, lawyers, clerics, and politicians condemned the legal diversity that allowed migratory divorce. See Margaret Lee,
Divorce; or, Faithful and Unfaithful (New York, 1881); James H. Barnett, *Divorce
and the American Divorce Novel* (New York, 1968); Samuel W. Dike, "The
National Divorce Reform League," *Our Day*, 1 (January 1889): 49–54; and
Dunn, *Twin Monsters*, 4–5.

57. James D. Richardson, comp., *Messages and Papers of the Presidents, 1789–
1897*, 10 vols. (Washington, D.C., 1897), 5:628, quoted in James M. McPherson,
Battle Cry of Freedom: The Civil War Era (New York, 1988), 246.

58. *Address of Abraham Lincoln before the Illinois State Republican Convention,
June 16, 1858*. *"Lincoln's House Divided Speech"* (reprinted Springfield, Ill., 1958),
3; Lincoln's inaugural, 4 March 1861, reprinted in Roy C. Basler, ed., *The Collected Works of Abraham Lincoln*, 9 vols. (New Brunswick, N.J., 1955), 4:249–71.

59. Catherine E. Beecher, *A Treatise on Domestic Economy*, rev. ed. (Boston,
1862), 26, quoted in Jeanne Boydston, *Home and Work: Housework, Wages, and
the Ideology of Labor in the Early Republic* (New York, 1990), 161. On the emotional content of the decision to marry in the nineteenth century, see Karen

Lystra, *Searching the Heart: Women, Men, and Romantic Love in Nineteenth-Century America* (New York, 1989), 28–57, 157–91. On the romantic rhetoric of reunion, see Kathleen Diffley, *Where My Heart Is Turning Ever: Civil War Stories and Constitutional Reform, 1861–1876* (Athens, Ga., 1992), 63, 71. For a reversal of the classic love story between Northern man and Southern woman after the Civil War, see Henry James, *The Bostonians* (New York, 1886).

60. Tucker, ed., *Blackstone's Commentaries*, 1:441; quote is from Sen. Thomas Bayard, of Delaware, reprinted in Stanton, Anthony, and Gage, eds., *History of Woman Suffrage*, 2:577; Elizabeth Packard, quoted in Hartog, "Mrs. Packard on Dependency," 101. See also Noah Davis, "Marriage and Divorce," 35.

61. Francis Lieber, *Civil Liberty and Self Government*, 2d ed. (Philadelphia, 1872), 4; [Francis Lieber,] "The Mormons: Shall Utah Be Admitted to the Union?" *Putnam's Monthly* 5 (March 1855): 234; Francis Lieber, *Political Ethics*, 2 vols. (Philadelphia, 1838), 2:124–25. The popular minister Horace Bushnell made the connections between woman suffrage and divorce explicit, condemning woman suffrage as tending toward a "relaxation of the just bonds of marriage, and a greatly increased tendency . . . to obtain divorce" (*Women's Suffrage; The Reform against Nature* [New York, 1870], 152).

62. *Deseret Evening News*, 13 January 1887, reprinted in *Journal History*, 13 January 1887, 12. Hartog, "Mrs. Packard on Dependency," 99–103, and Grossberg, *Governing the Hearth*, 300–302, point out that conservative women appealed ostensibly to traditional rights and disabilities for women in marriage, while implicitly creating potentially subversive legal consciousness in married women. For the precarious legal position of plural wives even before their exposure to criminal punishment, see Carol Cornwall Madsen, " 'At Their Peril': Utah Law and the Case of Plural Wives," *Western Historical Quarterly* 21, no. 4 (November 1990): 425.

CHAPTER SIX

1. *CR*, 49 Cong., 1 sess., 456 (6 January 1886). Edmunds was among the most powerful and legally sophisticated of senatorial Republicans in the 1870s and 1880s. He was frequently spoken of as a presidential candidate, and he turned down a Supreme Court justiceship in 1883 (Walter Hill Crockett, *George Franklin Edmunds* [n.p., 1910]; Selig Adler, *The Senatorial Career of George Franklin Edmunds* [Urbana, Ill., 1934]).

2. Edmunds-Tucker Act, 24 Stats. 637 (1887), secs. 13, 14, 16, and 17. In theory, the statute was merely the legislative enforcement of a provision of the Morrill Act of 1862, which "disapproved and annulled" all acts of the territorial legislature, including but not limited to the incorporation of the church, that "establish, support, maintain, shield or countenance polygamy," and imposed a property limitation that went unenforced from 1862 to 1887. The only exception was for property used exclusively for religious worship, parsonages, and burial grounds.

Opposition to the Edmunds-Tucker Act, as to other antipolygamy legislation introduced by Republican congressmen during the 1880s, came primarily from

Southern Democrats, many of whom recognized the resemblance between the reconstruction of Utah through antipolygamy legislation and the Reconstruction of the South. See M. Paul Holsinger, "Senator George Graham Vest and the 'Menace' of Mormonism, 1882–1887," *Missouri Historical Review* 65 (October 1970); M. Paul Holsinger, "Henry M. Teller and the Edmunds-Tucker Act," *Colorado Magazine* 48, no. 1 (1971); and David Buice, " 'A Stench in the Nostrils of Honest Men': Southern Democrats and the Edmunds Act of 1882," *Dialogue* 19 (1982).

3. With virtually the entire Mormon leadership subject to arrest by the mid-1880s, there was plenty for local law enforcement officials to do. Federal marshals, attorneys, and judges filled the local jail with bearded patriarchs and hunted others who had escaped their nets. But the whole process—indictments, arrests, trials, and jail terms—was expensive as well as time consuming. On pressure for supplementary legislation in the 1880s, see E. Leo Lyman, *Political Deliverance: The Mormon Quest for Utah Statehood* (Urbana, Ill., 1986). On the transformation in Americans' understanding of the sources of monopolistic corruption from a focus on government-sponsored inequalities to a focus on private monopolies, which it was the duty of government to dismantle, see James L. Huston, "The American Revolutionaries, the Political Economy of Aristocracy, and the American Concept of the Distribution of Wealth, 1765– 1900," *American Historical Review* 98 (October 1993): 1079–105, 1102–5.

4. "Suppression of Polygamy in Utah," 49 Cong., 1 sess., H. Rept. 2735 (10 June 1886), 7.

5. John Marchmont, *An Appeal to the American Congress: The Bible Law of Marriage against Mormonism* ([Philadelphia?], 1873), 7.

6. "Woman's Rights versus Polygamy," *The Woman's Journal,* 21 June 1879, 196.

7. On the law of equity, see Mary Beard *Woman as a Force in History: A Study in Traditions and Realities* (New York, 1946), 77–105; Norma Basch, *In the Eyes of the Law: Women, Marriage, and Property in Nineteenth-Century New York* (Ithaca, N.Y., 1982), 70–112, 224–32.

8. For the text of the territorial statute incorporating the church, see Dale Morgan, "The State of Deseret," *UHQ* 8 (1940): 223–25.

9. On fraud, and the fear of fraud, in nineteenth-century political and legal culture, see Laura Hanft Korobkin, *Criminal Conversations: Sentimentality and Nineteenth-Century Legal Stories of Adultery* (New York, 1998), 61–91, and Margaret Susan Thompson, *The "Spider Web": Congress and Lobbying in the Age of Grant* (Ithaca, N.Y., 1985). See also Joseph Frazier Wall, *Andrew Carnegie* (New York, 1970), and Thomas C. Cochran, "The Paradox of American Economic Growth," *JAH* 61 (December 1975): 925–42.

10. On railroads, see Gerald Berk, *Alternative Tracks: The Constitution of American Industrial Order, 1856–1917* (Baltimore, Md., 1994), 25–46; Alfred D. Chandler Jr., *The Visible Hand: The Managerial Revolution in American Business* (Cambridge, Mass., 1977), 81–171; Thomas C. Cochran, *Railroad Leaders, 1845– 1890: The Business Mind in Action* (Cambridge, Mass., 1953); A. B. Stickney, *The Railroad Problem* (St. Paul, Minn., 1891); John James, *Money and Capital Markets in Postbellum America* (Princeton, N.J., 1978).

11. Berk, *Alternative Tracks*, 47–72; Gretchen Ritter, *Goldbugs and Green-backs: The Antimonopoly Tradition and the Politics of Finance in America, 1865–1896* (Cambridge, Mass., 1997).

12. William Godwin Moody, *Land and Labor in the United States* (New York, 1883), 59, 76; Arthur Power Dudden, "Antimonopolism, 1865–1890: The Historical Background and Intellectual Origins of the Antitrust Movement in the United States" (Ph.D. diss., University of Michigan, 1950), 88–128.

13. Lyman, *Political Deliverance*, 69–95.

14. Senator Frehlinghuysen of New Jersey, speaking in favor of his anti-polygamy bill, *CR*, 42 Cong., 1 sess., 1782 (26 February 1873). The Reverend John Newman complained in 1882 that "trains laden with converts brought from overseas," rather than the enlightenment of the Mormon people, was the legacy of the railroad (*New York Times*, 30 January 1882).

15. On the actual rate of growth, see Leonard Arrington, *Great Basin Kingdom: An Economic History of the Latter-day Saints, 1830–1900* (Cambridge, Mass., 1956), 382–84.

16. Moody, *Land and Labor in the United States*, 76. *San Francisco Chronicle*, 6 March 1879, quoted in Lucy E. Salyer, *Laws Harsh as Tigers: Chinese Immigrants and the Shaping of Modern Immigration Law* (Chapel Hill, N.C., 1995), 10; Elmer C. Sandmeyer, *The Anti-Chinese Movement in California* (1939; reprint, Urbana, Ill., 1973), 26; *The Nation*, 20 December 1883, 503. See also Christian G. Fritz, "Due Process, Treaty Rights, and Chinese Exclusion," in *Entry Denied: Exlusion and the Chinese Community in America, 1882–1943*, ed. Sucheng Chan (Philadelphia, 1991), 25–56.

17. William Mulder, "Immigration and the 'Mormon Question': An International Episode," *Western Political Quarterly* 9 (1956): 424; Richard L. Jensen, "Steaming Through: Arrangements for Mormon Emigration from Europe, 1869–1887," *JMH* 9 (1982): 3–23.

18. "Diplomatic Correspondence, Circular No. 10, 9 August 1879, Sent to Diplomatic and Consular Officers of the United States," *Papers Relating to the Foreign Relations of the United States, 1879* (Washington, D.C., 1880), 11–12; "Another Crusade against the Saints," *Latter-day Saints Millennial Star*, 18 August 1879, 520. Although no government committed to prevent emigration in response to the circular, several promised to undertake publicity campaigns to enlighten their citizens, thus reducing the effectiveness of "the enticements of the emissaries of Mormonism." See M. J. Cramer to Secretary Evarts, 17 October 1879, *Foreign Relations, 1879*, 345, cited in Mulder, "Immigration and the 'Mormon Question,'" 424; Baron Rosenorn-Lehn to Secretary Evarts, 31 January 1880, *Foreign Relations, 1880*, 936; and John L. Stevens to Secretary Evarts, 23 September 1879, *Foreign Relations, 1879*, 964. On trains bringing convicted converts east, see "Convicts and Converts," *New York Times*, 27 May 1886.

19. "Annual Report of the Governor of Utah," Secretary of the Interior, *Annual Report, 1883*, 48 Cong., 1 sess., H. Exec. Doc. 1, pt. 5:627. The Contract Labor Act is codified at *U.S. Stats. at Large* 23, ch. 164 (26 February 1885): 332. The drive to transfer control over immigration from local governments to the national sovereign affected Chinese immigrants as well as Mormons. See Salyer, *Law Harsh as Tigers*.

20. On the wealth of Mormon leaders, see D. Michael Quinn, "The Mormon

Hierarchy, 1822–1932: An American Elite" (Ph.D. diss., Yale University, 1976), 81–157; and Arrington, *Great Basin Kingdom*, and "The Settlement of the Brigham Young Estate, 1877–1879," *Pacific Historical Review* 21 (1952): 2–10. For the quoted language, see *The Complete Works of Charles F. Browne, Better Known as "Artemus Ward,"* ed. John Camden Hotten (London, 1865), 219. On humorous depictions of polygamy, see Richard H. Cracroft, "Distorting Polygamy for Fun and Profit: Artemus Ward and Mark Twain among the Mormons," *Brigham Young University Studies* 14 (Winter 1984).

21. *CR*, 49 Cong., 1 sess., 456 (6 January 1886). On the overlap between spiritual and temporal leadership in territorial Utah, see, e.g., Klaus Hansen, *Quest for Empire: The Political Kingdom of God and the Council of Fifty in Mormon History* (East Lansing, Mich., 1967), 147–79. For the quoted language, see Jesse T. Peck, *The History of the Great Republic* (New York, 1868), 499.

22. *CR*, 49 Cong., 2 sess., 592 (12 January 1887). See also Howard Lamar, "Political Patterns in New Mexico and Utah," *UHQ* 28 (Summer 1960): 378–79. On similar behavior by Congress, virtually giving away mining and timber rights as well as outright ownership of more than a million and a half acres of public domain to railroads as "land grants," see Alan Trachtenberg, *The Incorporation of America: Culture and Society in the Gilded Age* (New York, 1982), 19–25. On corporate management in the same period, see Chandler, *Visible Hand*.

23. Arrington, *Great Basin Kingdom*, 160. Henry Ward Beecher's speech, "'Plea for Religious Liberty,' a Thanksgiving sermon preached in Plymouth Church, Brooklyn, in 1883," was reprinted in *Plymouth Pulpit Sermons*, 4 vols. (New York, 1888–90). See also his *Evolution and Religion* (New York, 1885), 66.

24. James Bryce, excerpted in John F. Wilson and Donald L. Drakeman, eds., *Church and State in American History: The Burden of Religious Pluralism*, 2d ed. (Boston, 1987), 154–55.

25. On Catholic children in public schools, see Michael Grossberg, "Teaching the Republican Child: Three Antebellum Stories about Law, Schooling, and the Construction of American Families," *Utah Law Review* 1996, no. 2 (1996): 429, 452–58; R. Lawrence Moore, "Bible Reading and Nonsectarian Schooling: The Failure of Religious Instruction in Nineteenth-Century Public Education," *JAH* 86 (March 2000): 1581–99.

26. Stanley S. Ivins, "Free Schools Come to Utah," *UHQ* 24 (1954): 341–42. See the statement of Brigham Young: "I am opposed to free education as much as I am opposed to taking away property from one man and giving it to another who knows not how to take care of it. . . . Would I encourage free schools by taxation? No! That is not in keeping with the nature of our work" (*JD*, 8:357; quoted in C. Merrill Hough, "Two School Systems in Conflict: 1867–1890," *UHQ* 28 [April 1960]: 117). According to one survey, average daily attendance at school "never reached fifty percent until 1893" (Bruce L. Campbell and Eugene E. Campbell, "Early Cultural and Intellectual Development," in *Utah's History*, ed. Richard D. Poll [Provo, 1978], 301). On Cannon, see Davis Bitton, *George Q. Cannon, A Biography* (Salt Lake, 1999), 396.

27. For a similar argument in a distinct but related area, see Michael O'Malley, "Specie and Species: Race and the Money Question in Nineteenth-Century America," *American Historical Review* 99 (April 1994): 369.

28. *The Revolution* 8, no. 4 (27 July 1871): 10.

29. Frederick Engels, *The Origin of the Family, Private Property, and the State, in Light of the Researches of Lewis Henry Morgan* (1884; reprint, New York, 1942), 67, 72, 148.

30. William Graham Sumner, "The Family Monopoly" and "The Family and Property," in *Earth-Hunger and Other Essays*, ed. Albert Galloway Keller (New Haven, Conn., 1914), 254, 255, 258, 264–65, 269.

31. *CR*, 49 Cong., 1 sess., 407 (5 January 1886).

32. Ibid., 509 (Senator Edmunds), 510 (Senator Morgan); "Suppression of Polygamy in Utah," 49 Cong., 1 sess., H. Rept. 2735 (10 June 1886), 3–4.

33. *CR*, 49 Cong., 1 sess., 504 (7 January 1886). On the role of competition in religious life and evangelism in nineteenth-century America, see R. Laurence Moore, *Selling God: American Religion in the Marketplace of Culture* (New York, 1994), 119–71.

34. *Board of Education v. Minor*, 23 Ohio St. 211, 250 (1872).

35. The theory that an endless struggle for existence was the motivating factor for all of history, and that the weak and unfit must be left to perish, seemed to contradict basic Christian ethics, as well as democratic and humanitarian theories. See, for example, Richard Hofstadter's *Social Darwinism in American Thought*, rev. ed. (Boston, 1955), 85–104. According to one historian, the non-capitalist nature of the pre-1890 Mormon Church was its most distinctive feature. See Arrington, *Great Basin Kingdom*, 380–412.

36. On the Dawes Act, see Felix Cohen, *Handbook of Federal Indian Law* (Washington, D.C., 1942), and D. S. Otis, *The Dawes Act and the Allotment of Indian Lands* (1934; reprint, Norman, Okla., 1973). Roosevelt's statement was contained in his first annual message to Congress as president, 3 December 1901. See *The Works of Theodore Roosevelt*, 28 vols. (New York, 1908–26), 15:129. See also Blue Clark, *Lone Wolf v. Hitchcock: Treaty Rights and Indian Law at the End of the Nineteenth Century* (Lincoln, Nebr., 1994). For Tucker's comparison of Mormon and Indian citizenship, see *CR*, 49 Cong., 2 sess., 694 (12 January 1887).

37. *CR*, 49 Cong., 1 sess. (7 January 1886), 504.

38. *CR*, 49 Cong., 2 sess. (12 January 1887), 594. Although no complete study of all state mortmain statutes has yet been undertaken, a brief review reveals that states restricting property ownership in the late nineteenth century included Delaware, Iowa, Illinois, Indiana, Kentucky, Louisiana, Maine, Maryland, Massachusetts, Michigan, Mississippi, Nevada, New Hampshire, New York, North Dakota, Ohio, Rhode Island, and South Carolina. See Paul G. Kauper and Stephen C. Ellis, "Religious Corporations and the Law," *Michigan Law Review* 71 (August 1973): 1545–49; G. Stanley Joslin, " 'Mortmain in Canada and the United States: A Comparative Study," *Canadian Bar Review* 29 (1951): 622–25; and Carl Zollman, *American Civil Church Law* (New York, 1917), 88–102. Testamentary restrictions were also common. Several states retained such limitations into the twentieth century, including California, Florida, Georgia, Idaho, Iowa, Mississippi, Montana, and New York.

39. "California v. American Sugar Refining Co.," *Railway and Corporate Law Journal* 7 (1890): 83; *People v. Chicago Trust Co.*, 130 Ill. 268, 22 N.E. 789 (1887); "Louisiana v. American Cotton-Oil Trust," *Railway and Corporate Law Journal* 1 (1887): 509; *State v. Nebraska Distilling Co.*, 29 Neb. 700, 46 N.W. 155 (1890).

The question whether either state or federal action was even marginally effective is debated in legal scholarship, as it was at the time. See James L. May, "Antitrust Practice and Procedure in the Formative Era: Political and Economic Theory in Constitutional and Antitrust Analysis, 1880–1918," *University of Pennsylvania Law Review* 135 (1987); Gregory A. Mark, "The Court and the Corporation," *Supreme Court Review* (1997): 403; Morton J. Horwitz, *The Transformation of American Law, 1790–1860* (Cambridge, Mass., 1977), ch. 3; and Herbert Hovenkamp, "The Sherman Act and the Classical Theory of Competition," *Iowa Law Review* 74 (1989).

40. On the corporate quality of Mormonism and its relationship to the defense of polygamy, see Jan Shipps, *Mormonism: The Story of a New Religious Tradition* (Urbana, Ill., 1985), 125.

41. *CR*, 49 Cong., 2 sess. (12 January 1887), 594.

42. Lamar, "Political Patterns"; Martin J. Sklar, *The Corporate Reconstruction of American Capitalism, 1890–1916: The Market, the Law, and Politics* (Cambridge, Eng., 1988), 115; Richard E. Welch Jr., "George Edmunds of Vermont: Republican Half-Breed," *Vermont History* 36, no. 2 (1968).

43. *CR*, 51 Cong., 1 sess. (21 March 1890), 2457 (Senator John Sherman). On the drafting and debates leading up to the enactment of the Sherman Act, see Rudolph J. Peritz, *Competition Policy in America, 1888–1992: History, Rhetoric, Law* (New York, 1996), ch. 2. On the unsettled nature of state antimonopoly law in the 1880s, see May, "Antitrust Practice and Procedure," and Sklar, *Corporate Reconstruction of American Capitalism*, 86–105. Many opponents of the Sherman Act are familiar from debates on the Edmunds-Tucker Act. See, e.g., Senator George Graham Vest of Missouri, *CR*, 51 Cong., 1 sess. (21 March 1890), 2463.

44. After Dyer was replaced as receiver in early 1890, he asked the court for $25,000 in compensation but was awarded only $10,000. Mormons, both at the time and more recently, have also accused Dyer of wasting assets during his receivership. See, e.g., Orma Linford, "The Mormons and the Law: The Polygamy Cases," part 2, *Utah Law Review* 9 (1965): 582. Mormons may also have benefited from Dyer's ineptitude. Wilford Woodruff recorded his impressions of Dyer in a letter to a friend: "Well[,] lightning has just struck; Dyer the marshal came and turned us all out. . . . They demand our Money, our Bank Notes, but miss much—as they are on the warpath they must find those if they can" (Wilford Woodruff to William Atkin, 24 November 1887, quoted in Stephen Cresswell, *Mormons, Moonshiners, Cowboys, and Klansmen: Federal Law Enforcement in the South and West, 1870–1893* [Tuscaloosa, Ala., 1991], 104).

45. It is not clear precisely how much property was in the hands of the receiver by the time the case reached the Supreme Court. The government claimed that the church owned at least $2,000,000 in real property and $1,000,000 in personal property. According to one source (Arrington, *Great Basin Kingdom*, 365–79), Dyer managed to locate over $1,000,000 in combined assets. Another source (Kauper and Ellis, "Religious Corporations and the Law," 1517) claims that the government had seized only $381,812, mostly cash on hand. See also John Noonan, *The Believer and the Powers that Are: Cases, History, and other Data Bearing on the Relation of Religion and Government* (New York, 1987), 203–

4. The receiver himself claimed to have confiscated some $750,000 worth of property, in addition to the Temple Block. See *Late Corporation v. United States*, 136 U.S. (1890), 15.

46. *Late Corporation v. United States*, Brief for Appellants, passim.

47. *Late Corporation v. United States*, Brief for the United States. Solicitor General George A. Jenks argued the case. There is no reported transcript of the argument, but according to newspaper accounts, it was entirely derivative of Garland's brief. See *New York Times*, 21 January 1889.

48. *Late Corporation v. United States*, Brief for the United States, 19.

49. Ibid., 32.

50. *Late Corporation v. United States*, Supplemental Brief for Appellants, 95–97, 107–8.

51. Lyman, *Political Deliverance*, 96–114, 124–49; Gustive O. Larson, *The "Americanization" of Utah for Statehood* (San Marino, Calif., 1971), 217–22, 253–60; Orson F. Whitney, *History of Utah*, 4 vols. (Salt Lake, 1892–1904), 3:834–36; Bitton, *George Q. Cannon*, 290–96.

52. Caine's speech was reprinted in pamphlet form: John T. Caine, *Polygamy in Utah—A Dead Issue* (Washington, D.C., 1888). Clawson's sermon is quoted in the introduction to *Prisoner for Polygamy: The Memoirs and Letters of Rudger Clawson at the Utah Territorial Penitentiary, 1884–1887*, ed. Stan Larson (Urbana, Ill., 1993), 16. On the meaning of provisions declaring polygamy a "misdemeanor" in draft constitutions produced in the late 1880s, see Henry J. Wolfinger, "A Re-Examination of the Woodruff Manifest in Light of Utah Constitutional History," *UHQ* 39 (Fall 1971). On reaction outside the territory to the proposed constitution, see *New York Times*, 4 October 1887, and *Chicago Times*, 1 October 1887.

53. On the law of equity in the late nineteenth century, see Berk, *Alternative Tracks*, 48–51, and Daniel R. Ernst, "Law and American Political Development, 1977–1938," *Reviews in American History* 26 (March 1998): 211–14.

54. *Late Corporation v. United States*, 49–50.

55. Ibid., 48, 49.

56. Ibid., 63–64.

57. Ibid., 44, 49, 50.

58. Joseph K. Angell and Samuel Ames, *Corporations*, 11th ed. (Boston, 1882), 862–63; James Kent, *Commentaries on American Law*, ed. O. W. Holmes Jr. (Boston, 1873), 398–99.

59. *Late Corporation v. United States*, 47–50.

60. Ibid., 51; William Robert Augustus Boyle, *A Practical Treatise on the Law of Charities* (London, 1837), 242–80; George Duke, *The Law of Charitable Uses* (London, 1676), 84–85, 466; Joseph Story, *Commentaries on Equity Jurisprudence*, ed. Isaac F. Redfield, 10th ed. (Boston, 1870), 403–11; *DeCosta v. De Pas*, 1 Vern. 251 (1684).

61. *Town of Pawlet v. Clark*, 9 Cranch. 291, 335 (1815).

62. *Late Corporation v. United States*, 49.

63. Ibid., 51.

64. Ibid., 59, 66, quoting Nathan Dane, *A General Abridgment and Digest of American Law*, 8 vols. (Boston, 1823–24), 4:239.

65. *Late Corporation v. United States*, 67–68; Willard L. King, *Melville Weston Fuller, Chief Justice of the United States* (New York, 1950), 149.

66. William E. Forbath, *Law and the Shaping of the American Labor Movement* (Cambridge, Mass., 1991), 59–97; Stephen N. Subrin, "How Equity Conquered the Common Law: The Federal Rules of Civil Procedure in Historical Perspective," *University of Pennsylvania Law Review* 135 (April 1987): 909–1002; Ernst, "Law and American Political Development," 210–13.

67. Thomas G. Alexander, *Things in Heaven and Earth: The Life and Times of Wilford Woodruff, a Mormon Prophet* (Salt Lake, 1991), 266–73; B. Carmon Hardy, *Solemn Covenant: The Mormon Polygamous Passage* (Urbana, Ill., 1992), 134–37, 148–49.

68. See, e.g., *United States v. Tithing Yard and Offices*, 9 Utah 273 (1893); *United States v. Gardo House and Historian's Office*, 9 Utah 285 (1893); and *United States v. Church Coal Lands*, 9 Utah 288 (1893). Eventually Congress intervened, mandating the return of church property (Arrington, *Great Basin Kingdom*, 378; Edwin B. Firmage and Richard Collin Mangrum, *Zion in the Courts: A Legal History of the Church of Jesus Christ of Latter-day Saints, 1830–1900* [Urbana, Ill., 1988], 259). For the pardons, see Proclamation No. 42, U.S. Stats. at Large 27 (4 January 1893): 1058; Proclamation No. 14, U.S. Stats. at Large 28 (25 September 1894): 1257.

EPILOGUE

1. See, for example, D. Michael Quinn, "LDS Church Authority and the New Plural Marriages, 1890–1904," *Dialogue* 18 (Spring 1985): 9–105, and Kenneth L. Cannon II, "Beyond the Manifesto: Polygamous Cohabitation among LDS General Authorities after 1890," *UHQ* 46 (January 1978): 24–36.

2. Leo Lyman (*Political Deliverance*, 2–6) argues that not only was polygamy the main issue, it was the only issue—that is, church-state relations were far less objectionable to government officials of both parties than polygamy.

3. Gustive O. Larson, *The "Americanization" of Utah for Statehood* (San Marino, Calif., 1971); Orson F. Whitney, *History of Utah*, 4 vols. (Salt Lake, 1892–1904); Brigham H. Roberts, *A Comprehensive History of the Church of Jesus Christ of Latter-day Saints, Century I*, 6 vols. (Provo, Utah, 1965), 5:539–57, 595–619.

4. *Davis v. Beason*, 133 U.S. 333, 341 (1890).

5. Section 501, Rev. Stats. Idaho, reprinted in *Davis v. Beason*, 334. For an account of the introduction, passage, and enforcement of the territorial statute restricting the franchise to non-Mormon voters, see Merle W. Wells, *Anti-Mormonism in Idaho, 1872–1892* (Provo, Utah, 1978). Such test oaths had been hotly debated in American law and politics. Justice Field himself had taken a leading role in two important Supreme Court cases decided on the same day in 1867, *Cummings v. Missouri*, 71 U.S. (4 Wall.) 277 (1867), and *Ex parte Garland*, 71 U.S. (4 Wall.) 333 (1867). Both cases resulted in 5–4 opinions written by Field for a majority comprised exclusively of Democrats, over the vigorous dissents of Republican Lincoln appointees. The Court struck down state and federal oaths of loyalty imposed on Southerners after the war. At the Supreme Court in the

Davis case, Mormon lawyers relied upon the test oath cases of the 1860s, arguing that the Court's own jurisprudence precluded such an invasive inquiry into the institutional memberships of voters ("Argument for Appellant," *Davis v. Beason,* 338–40).

6. *Davis v. Beason,* 342–43, 348.

7. On allegations of Mormon deviousness and perjury, see P. T. Van Zile, "The Twin Relic of Barbarism," in Mrs. Jennie Anderson Froiseth, ed., *The Women of Mormonism; or, The Story of Polygamy as Told by the Victims Themselves* (Detroit, 1882). For the quotation from the Pennsylvania court, see *Updegraph v. Commonwealth,* 11 Serge. & Rawl., 399 (Pa., 1824). See also *People v. Ruggles,* 8 John., 297–98 (1811).

8. *State v. Chandler* 2 Harr. 553, 567 (Del., 1837).

9. The Supreme Court's polygamy jurisprudence is in some measure an answer to those activists (including Supreme Court justice William Strong) who attempted, after the Civil War, to amend the Constitution by including an explicit reference to God's guidance of the nation. See Morton Borden, "The Christian Amendment," *Civil War History* 25 (March 1979): 156, and Jon C. Teaford, "Toward a Christian Nation: Religion, Law and Justice Strong," *Journal of Presbyterian History* 54 (Winter 1976): 422. The amendment was unnecessary, one might say, when the principles of general Christianity had already been incorporated into the jurisprudence of the religion clauses. The quotation is from Phillip Schaff, *America: A Sketch of the Political, Social, and Religious Character of the United States of North America* (New York, 1855), 200–201. Christopher Tomlins argues that the reconfiguration of "private" authority in markets and households extended rather than contracted the power of husbands and employers, challenging the liberal historiography of the movement from "status to contract" ("Subordination, Authority, Law: Subjects in Labor History," *International Labor and Working-Class History* 47 [Spring 1995]: 56).

10. Frances Willard, introduction to Froiseth, ed., *Women of Mormonism,* 18.

11. Ibid., xv, xviii.

12. One disappointed Baptist missionary lamented, "The combined efforts of all evangelical denominations have made no perceptible impression on the Mormon Church as to numbers" (R. Maude Ditmars, "A History of Baptist Missions in Utah, 1871–1931" [master's thesis, University of Colorado, 1931], 82). For a theory of how Mormonism retained and even increased "market share" in Utah after the Manifesto, see Rick Phillips, "The 'Secularization' of Utah and Religious Competition," *Journal for the Scientific Study of Religion* 38, no. 1 (1999): 72–82.

13. The meeting is described in T. Edgar Lyon, "Evangelical Protestant Missionary Activities in Mormon Dominated Areas: 1865–1900" (Ph.D. diss., University of Utah, 1962), 243–44, and by Maude Ditmars ("History of Baptist Missions," 90), who apparently attended the original session that organized the Home Missions Council.

14. The charter and bylaws of the Home Missions Council are reprinted in Henry M. Merkel, *History of Methodism in Utah* (Colorado Springs, 1938), 257–61. The quoted language is from Lyons, "Evangelical Protestant Missionary Activities in Mormon Dominated Areas," 244.

15. For a summary of changes in law and society, see John Noonan and

Edward Gaffney, *Religious Freedom*, 2d ed. (New York, 2001). On Vermont, see "Vermont Gives Final Approval to Same-Sex Unions," *New York Times*, 26 April 2000, p. 14, col. 1.

16. On conservative Christians' tensions with the government, see, e.g., Kenneth F. Craycroft Jr., *The American Myth of Religious Freedom* (Dallas, 1999). On the Mormon Church's opposition to the Equal Rights Amendment, see D. Michael Quinn, "The LDS Church's Campaign against the Equal Rights Amendment," *JMH* 20 (Fall 1994): 85–155, and Sonia Johnson, *From Housewife to Heretic* (Garden City, N.Y., 1983). On continuity amid change, see Leonard J. Arrington and David Bitton, *The Mormon Experience: A History of the Church of Jesus Christ of Latter-day Saints* (New York, 1978), 243–61, and Jan Shipps, *Mormonism: The Story of a New Religious Tradition* (Urbana, Ill., 1985), 131–49.

17. D. Michael Quinn, *Same-Sex Dynamics among Nineteenth-Century Americans: A Mormon Example* (Urbana, Ill., 1996). The *Defense of Marriage Act*, Public Law 104–99, 21 September 1996, 104 Cong., 2 sess., is codified at 1 U.S.C.S. section 1.

18. George Will, widely quoted among Mormons. For an example of the detente, see Craig L. Blomberg and Stephen E. Robinson, *How Wide the Divide? A Mormon and an Evangelical in Conversation* (Downers Grove, Ill., 1997). On the durability of monogamy in American culture, see Robert T. Michael, John H. Gagnon, Edward O. Laumann, and Gina Kolana, *Sex in America: A Definitive Survey* (Boston, 1994), 28, 195, 198.

19. Hardy, *Solemn Covenant*, 365. On theories of denial as an appropriate strategy for dissociating Mormon practice from free love, see, for example, the work of the eroticist Richard Burton, *The City of the Saints*, ed. Fawn Brodie (1861; reprint, New York, 1963), 463–65.

20. Davis Bitton, "The B. H. Roberts Case of 1898–1900," *UHQ* 27 (January 1957); William Griffin White Jr., "The Feminist Campaign for the Exclusion of Brigham Henry Roberts from the Fifty-sixth Congress," *Journal of the West* 17 (January 1978): 45; Shelby M. Cullom, "The Reed Smoot Decision," *North American Review* 184 (15 March 1907): 572–76; M. Paul Holsinger, "For God and the American Home: The Attempt to Unseat Senator Reed Smoot, 1903–1907," *Pacific Northwest Quarterly* 60 (July 1969).

21. Since the second decade of the twentieth century, the church itself took a leading role in the campaign against polygamy. See Martha Sonntag Bradley, *Kidnapped from That Land: The Government Raid on Short Creek Polygamists* (Salt Lake, 1993), 64–67, 86–88, 125–26, 192–95. In some respects, the situation of stubborn pockets of polygamists in Utah resembles the position of Mormon Utah in relation to the nation as a whole in the late nineteenth century (conversation with Edwin Firmage, November 1998, Salt Lake City). Yet the treatment of polygamists in modern Utah is primarily of concern to Utahns and receives only infrequent national attention. Until recently, polygamy was more of a humorous or voyeuristic diversion for the likes of *People* magazine or Oprah Winfrey than a seriously debated alternative form of marital structure that could reform and invigorate (or degrade and debase) the nation as a whole. The conviction of two men in 1999 for abuse and incest, and the conviction of polygamist Tom Green on four counts of bigamy in 2001, as well as the formation of the group "Tapestry of Polygamy," an organization of former plural

wives dedicated to opposing polygamy and publicizing the abuse of women they claim is endemic in polygamous communities, may once again draw sustained attention to the role of women in plural marriage. See Timothy Egan, "The Persistence of Polygamy," *New York Times*, 28 February 1999, p. 51, col. 1. See also Tom Gorman, "Utah Drags Polygamy out of Shadows and into Court," *Los Angeles Times*, 16 May 2001, p. 14, col. 1. On the Smoot hearings, and changes in church doctrine and practice that resulted, see Kathleen Flake, "Mr. Smoot Goes to Washington: The Politics of American Religious Identity, 1900–1920" (unpublished manuscript on file with the author).

22. Laurence Tribe is the most prominent figure among a group of legal scholars who argue on libertarian grounds that polygamy should be constitutionally protected. Tribe has predicted for the last two decades that the leading Supreme Court decision on polygamy, *Reynolds v. United States*, 98 U.S. 145 (1879), would soon be overruled. See his *American Constitutional Law*, 2d ed. (Mineola, N.Y., 1988), 521–28. See also Edwin B. Firmage, "Religion and the Law: The Mormon Experience in the Nineteenth Century," *Cardozo Law Review* 12 (1991): 764–803; Jeremy M. Miller, "A Critique of the *Reynolds* Decision," *Western State University Law Review* 11 (1984): 165–98; G. Keith Nedrow, "Polygamy and the Right to Marry: New Life for an Old Lifestyle," *Memphis State University Law Review* 11 (1981): 323–49; Henry Mark Holzer, "The True *Reynolds v. United States*," *Harvard Journal of Law and Public Policy* 10 (1987): 43–46; Penelope W. Saltzman, "Another Interpretation of Polygamy and the First Amendment," *Utah Law Review* (1986): 345–71; James L. Clayton, "The Supreme Court and the Enforcement of Morals in Nineteenth-Century America: An Analysis of *Reynolds v. United States*," *Dialogue* 12 (Winter 1979): 46–61; Ray Jay Davis, "The Polygamous Prelude," *American Journal of Legal History* 6 (1962): 1–23, and "Plural Marriage and Religious Freedom: The Impact of *Reynolds v. United States*," *Arizona Law Review* 15 (1973): 287–306; and Stephen Pepper, "*Reynolds, Yoder*, and Beyond: Alternatives for the Free Exercise Clause," *Utah Law Review* (1981): 309–78. But see Douglas Parker, "Victory in Defeat—Polygamy and the Mormon Legal Encounter with the Federal Government," *Cardozo Law Review* 12 (1991): 805–19.

23. *Cleveland v. United States*, 329 U.S. 14 (1946), is a case in which the cooperation of the LDS church in supplying information to law enforcement officials was essential. The majority opinion quoted the condemnations of polygamy in *Reynolds* and *Late Corporation* with approval and held that the Mann Act, targeted at the "white slave business and related vices," applied to polygamists as well as pimps and libertines: "The establishment or maintenance of polygamous households is a notorious example of promiscuity" (ibid., 19). Justice Murphy's dissent, therefore, may have disturbed twentieth-century Mormons in unexpected ways, given the church's active involvement with the prosecution of the case (329 U.S. at 26 [Murphy, J., dissenting]). For early arguments that the polygamy cases were wrongly decided, see Orma Linford, "The Mormons and the Law: The Polygamy Cases," part 1, *Utah Law Review* 9 (1964): 308–70, 543–91, 589, and Harrop A. Freeman, "A Remonstrance for Conscience," *University of Pennsylvania Law Review* 106 (1959): 823.

24. 405 U.S. 205 (1972).

25. According to Edwin B. Firmage and Richard Collin Mangrum, in *Zion in*

the Courts: A Legal History of the Church of Jesus Christ of Latter-day Saints, 1830–1900 (Urbana, Ill., 1988), 130: "Imposing conformity on a group of sincerely dedicated dissenters almost inevitably requires a level of force that debases the oppressor. In a sorry cycle, resistance breeds repression that calls forth yet more resistance and yet more savage repression. In the case of polygamy, it may be questioned whether the prize was worth the price."

The federal judiciary adheres to the basic holding of *Reynolds* and its successors. Rejecting a self-styled "fundamentalist" Mormon's argument that the nineteenth-century Mormon cases are no longer good law in today's promiscuous society, the Tenth Circuit Court of Appeals held in 1985 that "monogamy is inextricably woven into the fabric of our society. It is the bedrock upon which our culture is built" (*Potter v. Murray City*, 585 F. Supp. 1126 [D. Utah, 1984], *aff'd*, 760 F.2d 1065 [10th Cir.], *cert. denied*, 106 S. Ct. 145 [1985]). And in 1990, in language explicitly drawn from *Reynolds*, Justice Antonin Scalia denied the religious freedom claim of drug users by resurrecting the polygamy cases' distinction between freedom to believe and the validity of punishing actions, placing the distinction once again at the nub of free exercise jurisprudence (*Employment Division v. Smith*, 494 U.S. 872 [1990]). The *Smith* case has been widely criticized. See, for example, Douglas Laycock, "The Remnants of Free Exercise," *Supreme Court Review* (1990): 1–68; Michael W. McConnell, "Free Exercise Revisionism and the *Smith* Decision," *University of Chicago Law Review* (Fall 1990): 1109–53; and *City of Boerne v. Flores* 521 U.S. 507 (1997).

26. Mark S. Lee, "Legislating Morality," *Sunstone* (1985): 8–12; Elizabeth Harmer-Dionne, "Once a Peculiar People: Cognitive Dissonance and the Suppression of Mormon Polygamy as a Case Study," *Stanford Law Review* 50 (April 1998): 1295, 1318–19.

BIBLIOGRAPHY

PRIMARY SOURCES

Government Documents

Congressional Globe
Congressional Record

Court Decisions

Baker v. Fales, 16 Mass. 492 (1820).
Barron v. Mayor and City of Baltimore, 7 Pet. 243 (1833).
Bassett v. United States, 137 U.S. 496 (1890).
Battles v. Board of Education, 904 F. Supp. 471 (D. Md., 1995).
Board of Education v. Minor, 23 Ohio St. 211, 250 (1872).
Bradwell v. Illinois, 83 U.S. (16 Wall.) 36 (1873).
"California v. American Sugar Refining Co.," *Railway & Corporate Law Journal* 7 (1890).
Cantwell v. Connecticut, 310 U.S. 296 (1940).
City of Boerne v. Flores 521 U.S. 507 (1997).
Clawson v. United States, 114 U.S. 55 (1885).
Cleveland v. United States, 329 U.S. 14 (1946).
Clinton v. Engelbrecht, 80 U.S. 434 (1872).
Commonwealth v. Kneeland, 20 Mass. 206 (1838).
Crowley v. Smithsonian Institution, 462 F. Supp. 725 (D.D.C., 1978)
Cummings v. Missouri, 71 U.S. (4 Wall.) 277 (1867).
Davis v. Beason, 133 U.S. 333, 341 (1890).
Davis v. Commonwealth, 13 Bush 318 (Ky. 1877).
Edwards v. Aguillard, 482 U.S. 578 (1987).
Employment Division v. Smith, 494 U.S. 872 (1990).
Everson v. Board of Education, 330 U.S. 1 (1947).
Ex parte Garland, 71 U.S. (4 Wall.) 333 (1867).
Gheta v. Nassau County Community College, 33 F. Supp.2d 179 (E.D.N.Y., 1999).
In re Hans Nielson, 131 U.S. 176 (1889)
Hardy v. Smith, 136 Mass. 328 (1884).
Hood v. State, 56 Ind. 263, 270–73 (1877).
Kalka v. Hawk, 215 F.3d 90 (D.C. Cir., 2000).
Late Corporation v. United States, 136 U.S. 1 (1890).
Lochner v. New York, 198 U.S. 45 (1905).

"Louisiana v. American Cotton-Oil Trust," *Railway and Corporate Law Journal* 1 (1887).

McDaniel v. Paty, 435 U.S. 618 (1978).

Maynard v. Hill, 125 U.S. 190 (1887).

Meister v. Moore, 96 U.S. 76, 78 (1877).

Miles v. United States, 103 U.S. 304 (1880).

Minor v. Happersett, 88 U.S. (21 Wall.) 162 (1875).

Mozert v. Hawkins, 827 F.2d 1058 (6th Cir., 1987).

Murphy v. Ramsey, 114 U.S. 15, 45 (1885).

People v. Chicago Trust Co., 130 Ill. 268 (1887).

People v. Ruggles, 8 Johns. 290 (N.Y., 1811).

Permoli v. First Municipality of New Orleans, 44 U.S. (3 How.) 589 (1845).

Plessy v. Ferguson, 163 U.S. 537 (1896).

Potter v. Murray City, 585 F. Supp. 1126 (D. Utah, 1984), *aff'd*, 760 F.2d 1065 (10th Cir.), *cert. denied*, 106 S. Ct. 145 (1985).

Reynolds v. United States, 98 U.S. 145 (1879).

Robertson v. Bullions, 11 N.Y. 243 (1854).

Scott v. Sandford, 60 U.S. (19 How.) 393 (1857).

The Slaughter-House Cases, 83 U.S. (16 Wall.) 130 (1873).

In re Snow, 120 U.S. 274 (1887).

State v. Armington, 25 Minn. 29 (1878).

State v. Chandler, 2 Harr. 553, 567 (Del., 1837).

State v. Nebraska Distilling Co., 29 Neb. 700 (1890).

Town of Pawlet v. Clark, 9 Cranch. 291, 335 (1815).

United States v. Church Coal Lands, 9 Utah 288 (1893).

United States v. Gardo House and Historian's Office, 9 Utah 285 (1893).

United States v. Reynolds, 1 Utah 226 (1875).

United States v. Reynolds, 1 Utah 319 (1876).

United States v. Tithing Yard and Offices, 9 Utah 273 (1893).

Updegraph v. Commonwealth, 11 Serge. & Rawl. 393 (Pa., 1824).

Wisconsin v. Yoder, 405 U.S. 205 (1972).

Books and Articles

Address of Abraham Lincoln before the Illinois State Republican Convention, June 16, 1858. "Lincoln's House Divided Speech". Reprinted Springfield, Ill., 1958.

Allen, Nathan. "Divorces in New England." *North American Review* 130 (June 1880): 547–65.

Angell, Joseph K., and Samuel Ames. *Corporations*. 11th ed. Boston, 1882.

Baird, Robert. *Religion in America*. Glasgow, 1843.

Bancroft, George. "The Place of Abraham Lincoln in History." *Atlantic Monthly* 25 (June 1865): 757–64.

Baskin, Robert N. *Reminiscences of Early Utah*. N.p. 1914.

Basler, Roy C., ed. *The Collected Works of Abraham Lincoln*. 9 vols. New Brunswick, N.J., 1955.

Beadle, J. H. *Life in Utah; or, The Mysteries and Crimes of Mormonism. Being an Exposé of the Secret Rites and Ceremonies of the Latter-Day Saints, with a*

Full and Authentic History of Polygamy and the Mormon Sect from Its Origin to the Present Time. Philadelphia, 1870.

Beecher, Catharine E. *A Treatise on Domestic Economy.* Rev. ed. Boston, 1862.

——. *Woman Suffrage and Woman's Profession.* Hartford, Conn., 1871.

Beecher, Catharine, and Harriet Beecher Stowe. *The American Woman's Home; or, Principles of Domestic Science.* New York, 1860.

Beecher, Henry Ward. *Evolution and Religion.* New York, 1885.

——. *Plymouth Pulpit Sermons.* 4 vols. New York, 1888–90.

Beecher, Lyman. *Autobiography.* Edited by Barbara M. Cross. 2 vols. Cambridge, Mass., 1961.

——. *Sermons Delivered on Various Occasions.* Boston, 1828.

Belisle, Orvilla. *Mormonism Unveiled; or, A History of Mormonism from Its Rise to the Present Time.* Philadelphia, 1855.

Bell, Alfreda Eva. *Boadicea; The Mormon Wife. Life Scenes in Utah.* Baltimore, Md., 1855.

——. *The Rebel Cousins; or Life in Secession: The Autobiography of the Beautiful Bertha Stephens, the Accomplished Niece of the Hon. Alexander Hamilton Stephens, Vice-President of the Southern Confederacy.* Written by herself, and prepared for Publication by Her Friend, Alfreda Eva Bell. Philadelphia, 1864.

Bennett, John C. *The History of the Saints; or, An Exposé of Joe Smith and Mormonism.* Boston, 1842.

Bishop, Joel Prentiss. *Commentaries on the Criminal Law.* 2 vols. Boston, 1856.

——. *Commentaries on the Law of Marriage and Divorce and Evidence in Matrimonial Suits.* 2 vols. Boston, 1873.

Blomberg, Craig L., and Stephen E. Robinson. *How Wide the Divide? A Mormon and an Evangelical in Conversation.* Downers Grove, Ill., 1997.

The Book of Mormon, Another Testament of Jesus Christ. 1830. Reprint, Salt Lake, 1989.

Boreman, Jacob Smith. *Curiosities of Early Utah Legislation.* Ogden, Utah, [1895?].

Bowles, Samuel. *Across the Continent: A Summer's Journey to the Rocky Mountains, the Mormons, and the Pacific States.* Springfield, Mass., 1865.

Boyle, William Robert Augustus. *A Practical Treatise on the Law of Charities.* London, 1837.

Brown, Joseph E. *Polygamy in Utah and New England Contrasted: Speech of Hon. Joseph E. Brown, of Georgia; Delivered in the Senate of the United States, Tues., May 27, 1884.* Washington, D.C., 1884.

Burton, Richard. *The City of the Saints.* Edited by Fawn Brodie. 1861. Reprint, New York, 1963.

Bushnell, Horace. *Women's Suffrage; the Reform against Nature.* New York, 1870.

Caine, John T. *Polygamy in Utah—A Dead Issue.* Washington, D.C., 1888.

Cannon, Frank J., and Harvey J. O'Higgins. *Under the Prophet in Utah: The National Menace of a Political Priest Craft.* Boston, 1911.

Cannon, George Q. *A Review of the Decision of the Supreme Court of the United States, in the Case of George Reynolds vs. United States.* Salt Lake, 1879.

Cauzauran, A. R., comp. *The Trial of Daniel McFarland for the Shooting of Albert D. Richardson.* New York, 1870.

Channing, William Ellery. *Works.* Boston, 1841.

Church of Jesus Christ of Latter-day Saints. *History of the Church of Jesus Christ of Latter-day Saints.* 2d. ed. 7 vols. Salt Lake, 1963.

Clawson, Rudger. *Prisoner for Polygamy: The Memoirs and Letters of Rudger Clawson at the Utah Territorial Penitentiary, 1884–1887.* Edited by Stan Larson. Urbana, Ill., 1993.

The Complete Works of Charles F. Browne, Better Known as "Artemus Ward." Edited by John Camden Hotten. London, 1865.

Cooley, Thomas M. *A Treatise on the Constitutional Limitations Which Rest Upon the Legislative Power of the States of the American Union.* Boston, 1868.

Cullom, Shelby M. "The Reed Smoot Decision." *North American Review* 184 (15 March 1907): 572–76.

Curtis, T. W. *The Mormon Problem. The Nation's Dilemma: New Data, New Methods Involving Leading Questions of the Day.* New Haven, Conn., 1885.

Dane, Nathan. *A General Abridgment and Digest of American Law.* 9 vols. Boston, 1823–29.

Davis, Noah. "Marriage and Divorce." *North American Review* 139 (July 1884): 49–54.

Davis, Paulina Wright, comp. *A History of the National Woman's Rights Movement.* New York, 1871.

Dike, Samuel W. "The National Divorce Reform League." *Our Day* 1 (January 1889).

Discourses on Celestial Marriage, delivered in the New Tabernacle, Salt Lake City, October 7, 8 and 9, 1869, delivered by Orson Pratt, George A. Smith and George Q. Cannon. Salt Lake, 1869.

Douglas, Stephen A. *Kansas, Utah, and the Dred Scott Decision. Remarks of Hon. Stephen A. Douglas, Delivered in the State House at Springfield, Ill., on 12th of June, 1857.* [Springfield, Ill.?], 1857.

Doyle, Arthur Conan. *A Study in Scarlet.* London, 1887.

Duke, George. *The Law of Charitable Uses.* London, 1676.

Dunn, Ballard S. *The Twin Monsters; and How National Legislation May Help to Solve the Mormon Problem, and Restore to Society, Somewhat of the Sacramental Character of the Rite of Holy Matrimony.* New York, 1884.

Dwight, Timothy. *The Triumph of Infidelity.* N.p., 1815.

Edmunds, George F. "Political Aspects of Mormonism." *Harper's Magazine* 64 (January 1882): 285–88.

Engels, Frederick. *The Origin of the Family, Private Property, and the State, in Light of the Researches of Lewis Henry Morgan.* 1884. Reprint, New York, 1942.

Ferry, Jeannette H. *The Industrial Christian Home Association.* Salt Lake, 1903.

Field, Kate. "The Mormon Monster" Lecture, delivered by Kate Field, in the Congregational Church, corner of 10th and G Streets, Washington, D.C., Wednesday evening, Dec. 15, 1886, reported by John Irvine. MS 3111, Historical Department, Church of Jesus Christ of Latter-day Saints, Salt Lake City.

———. "Mormon Blood Atonement." *North American Review* 143 (September 1886): 262–68.

Finney, Charles Grandison. *Lectures on Revivals of Religion.* New York, 1835.

Fitzpatrick, John C., ed. *The Writings of George Washington.* 39 vols. Washington, D.C., 1931–44.

Flaherty, J. T. *Glimpses of the Life of Rev. A. E. Phelps and His Co-Laborers.* Cincinnati, 1878.

Froiseth, Mrs. Jennie Anderson, ed. *The Women of Mormonism; or, The Story of Polygamy as Told by the Victims Themselves.* Detroit, 1882.

Gibbons, Cardinal, Bishop Henry E. Potter, and Col. Robert G. Ingersoll. "Is Divorce Wrong?" *North American Review* 149 (November 1889): 513–39.

[Gilchrist, Mrs. Rosetta Luce.] *Apples of Sodom: A Story of Mormon Life.* Cleveland, 1885.

Godkin, E. L. "Woman in the Lyceum." *The Nation* 51, no. 21 (13 May 1869): 371–72.

Gooch, David W. *Polygamy in Utah: Speech of Daniel W. Gooch, of Massachusetts, House of Representatives, April 4, 1860.* Washington, D.C., 1860.

Gunnison, John. *The Mormons, or, Latter-day Saints in the Valley of the Great Salt Lake.* Philadelphia, 1852.

Howard, George Elliott. *A History of Matrimonial Institutions: Chiefly in England and the United States . . ..* 3 vols. Chicago, 1904.

Howe, M. A. DeWolfe, ed. *Life and Letters of George Bancroft.* 2 vols. New York, 1908.

Howe, Samuel Gridley. "Atheism in New England." *New England Magazine* 7 (1834): 500–509; 8 (1835): 53–62.

Jefferson's Virginia Reports. Charlottesville, 1829.

Johnson, Sonia. *From Housewife to Heretic.* Garden City, N.Y., 1983.

Kearney, Scott, ed. *Wilford Woodruff's Journals, 1833–1898.* 9 vols. Midvale, Utah, 1983–84.

Kent, James. *Commentaries on American Law.* 12th ed. 2 vols. Edited by Oliver Wendell Holmes Jr. Boston, 1873.

Lee, John D. *Mormonism Unveiled; or, The Life and Confessions of the Late Mormon Bishop, John D. Lee.* St. Louis, 1877.

Lee, Margaret. *Divorce; or, Faithful and Unfaithful.* New York, 1881.

Lipscomb, Andrew A., ed. *The Writings of Thomas Jefferson.* 26 vols. Washington, D.C., 1904.

Lieber, Francis. *Political Ethics.* 2 vols. Philadelphia, 1838.

[Lieber, Francis]. "The Mormons: Shall Utah Be Admitted to the Union?" *Putnam's Monthly* 5 (March 1855): 225–36.

McKean, John B. "Brigham Young Must Pay Alimony to Ann Eliza. Opinion of Chief Justice McKean." N.p., 1875.

Maine, Henry Sumner. *Ancient Law: Its Connection with the Early History of Society and Its Relation to Modern Ideas.* 10th ed. 1884. Reprint, Gloucester, Mass., 1970.

Marchmont, John. *An Appeal to the American Congress: The Bible Law of Marriage against Mormonism.* [Philadelphia?], 1873.

Merkel, Henry M. *History of Methodism in Utah.* Colorado Springs, 1938.

Moody, William Godwin. *Land and Labor in the United States.* New York, 1883.

Nelson, Thomas A. R. *Polygamy in the Territories of the United States, to Accompany Bill H.R. No 7, March 14, 1860.* Washington, D.C., 1860.

Newman, Angelina French. "Woman Suffrage in Utah." *Miscellaneous Documents.* 49 Cong., 1 sess., S. Doc. 122 (8 June 1886).

Packard, E. P. W. *Modern Persecution, or Married Women's Liabilities, as Demonstrated by the Actions of the Illinois Legislature.* 2 vols. Hartford, 1875.

Paddock, Cornelia. *The Fate of Madame LaTour.* Detroit, 1882.

——. *In the Toils; or, Martyrs of the Latter Days.* Chicago, 1879.

Parker, Theodore. "The Destination of America." In *The Slave Power.* Boston, n.d.

Peck, Jesse T. *The History of the Great Republic.* New York, 1868.

Pond, Major James Burton. *Eccentricities of Genius: Memories of Famous Men and Women of the Platform and Stage.* New York, 1900.

Porter, Kirk H., comp. *National Party Platforms.* New York, 1924.

Pratt, Parley P. *Marriage and Morals in Utah.* Liverpool, 1856.

Reed, Henry. *Bigamy and Polygamy: Review of Reynolds v. U.S.* New York, 1879.

Reed, W. B. "Life and Character of Thomas Paine." *The North American Review* 57 (July 1843): 1–58.

Remy, J., and J. Brenchley. *A Journey to Great Salt Lake City.* London, 1861.

Reynolds, George. Journal. Vols. 1, 3–6. Historical Department, Church of Jesus Christ of Latter-day Saints, Salt Lake, Utah.

Richardson, James D., comp. *Messages and Papers of the Presidents, 1789–1897.* 10 vols. Washington, D.C., 1897.

Roberts, B. H. *A Comprehensive History of the Church of Jesus Christ of Latter-day Saints: Century I.* 6 vols. Provo, Utah, 1965.

Ropes, John Codman. "Introductory Memoir." In *Orations and Addresses on Various Occasions Civil and Military,* by Charles Devens. Boston, 1891.

Rossi, Alice S., ed. *The Feminist Papers: From Adams to de Beauvoir.* New York, 1973.

Schaff, Phillip. *America: A Sketch of the Political, Social, and Religious Character of the United States of North America.* New York, 1855.

Schouler, James. *A Treatise on the Law of the Domestic Relations: Embracing Husband and Wife, Parent and Child, Guardian and Ward, Infancy, and Master and Servant.* Boston, 1870.

Smith, George A. *The Rise, Progress, and Travels of the Church of Jesus Christ of Latter-day Saints.* Salt Lake, 1872.

Speech of Hon. Justin S. Morrill, of Vermont, on Utah Territory and Its Law— Polygamy and Its License; Delivered in the House of Representatives, February 23, 1857. Washington, D.C., 1857.

Stanton, Elizabeth Cady. "The Need of Liberal Divorce Laws." *North American Review* 139 (September 1884): 234–46.

Stanton, Elizabeth Cady, Susan B. Anthony, and Matilda Joslyn Gage, eds., *History of Woman Suffrage.* 6 vols. Rochester, N.Y. 1881–1922.

Stenhouse, Fanny. *A Lady's Life among the Mormons.* New York, 1872.

Stenhouse, T. B. H. *The Rocky Mountain Saints.* New York, 1873.

Stickney, A. B. *The Railroad Problem.* St. Paul, Minn., 1891.

Story, Joseph. *Commentaries on the Constitution.* 3 vols. Boston, 1833.
———. *Commentaries on Equity Jurisprudence.* Edited by Isaac F. Redfield. 10th ed. Boston, 1870.
Story, William W., ed. *Life and Letters of Joseph Story, Associate Justice of the Supreme Court of the United States, and Dane Professor of Law at Harvard University.* 3 vols. Boston, 1851.
———. *Miscellaneous Writings of Joseph Story.* Boston, 1852.
Strong, Josiah. *Our Country.* Philadelphia, 1885.
Sumner, Charles. *The Barbarism of Slavery: Speech of Hon. Charles Sumner, on the Admission of Kansas as a Free State, in the United States Senate, June 4, 1860.* Washington, D.C., 1860.
Sumner, William Graham. *Earth-Hunger and Other Essays.* Edited by Albert Galloway Keller. New Haven, Conn., 1914.
Tanner, Annie Clark. *A Mormon Mother: The Autobiography of Annie Clark Tanner.* Edited by Obert Tanner. 1941. Reprint, Salt Lake, 1973.
Thayer, James Russell. *The Life, Character, and Writings of Francis Lieber, A Discourse Delivered before the Historical Society of Pennsylvania, January 13, 1873.* Philadelphia, 1873.
Tiedeman, Christopher G. *State and Federal Control of Persons and Property in the United States.* 2 vols. St. Louis, 1886.
Tocqueville, Alexis de. *Democracy in America.* Translated by Henry Reeve. 2 vols. 1840. Reprint, New York, 1990.
Tucker, St. George, ed. *Blackstone's Commentaries.* 5 vols. Philadelphia, 1803.
Tullidge, Edward W. *The Women of Mormondom.* New York, 1877.
Victor, Metta Victoria Fuller. *Mormon Wives, A Narrative of Facts Stranger than Fiction.* New York, 1856.
Ward, Maria. *Female Life among the Mormons.* New York, 1855.
Wells, S. R. "William H. Hooper, The Utah Delegate and Woman Suffrage Advocate." *Phrenological Journal* 51 (November 1870): 328–33.
Whitney, Orson F. *History of Utah.* 4 vols. Salt Lake, 1892–1904.
Wilson, James. *Works.* Edited by Robert G. McCloskey. Cambridge, Mass., 1967.
Wilson, John F., and Donald L. Drakeman, eds. *Church and State in American History: The Burden of Religious Pluralism.* 2d ed. Boston, 1987.
Woolsey, Theodore D. *Essay on Divorce and Divorce Legislation, with Special Reference to the United States.* New York, 1869.
The Works of Theodore Roosevelt. 28 vols. New York, 1908–26.
Wright, Carroll D. Commissioner of Labor, Bureau of Labor, *A Report on Marriage and Divorce in the United States, 1867 to 1886.* 1889. Reprint, Washington, D.C., 1891.
Young, Ann Eliza. *Wife No. 19; or, The Story of a Life in Bondage, Being a Complete Exposé of Mormonism, and Revealing the Sorrows, Sacrifices and Sufferings of Women in Polygamy, by Brigham Young's Apostate Wife.* Chicago, 1876.
Zane, Charles S. "The Death of Polygamy in Utah." *Forum* 12 (1891–92).
Zane, John M. "A Rare Judicial Service; Charles S. Zane." *Transactions of the Illinois State Historical Society,* publication no. 33 (1926): 89–101.

Constitutional Conventions, Statutes, and Legal Records

Convention of the State of New York. New York, 1821.
Proceedings of the First Three Republican National Conventions. Minneapolis, Minn., n.d.
Records of the Territorial Courts of Utah, 1870–96. National Archives, Rocky Mountain West Division, Denver, Colo.
Reorganized Church of Jesus Christ of Latter Day Saints, Complainant, vs. Church of Christ at Independence, Missouri; . . . Complainant's Abstract. Lamoni, Iowa, 1893.
Thorpe, Francis N. *The Federal and State Constitutions,* 9 vols. Washington, D.C., 1909.
Utah Territory. *Acts, Resolutions, and Memorials Passed by . . . the Legislative Assembly.* Salt Lake, 1852.
Laws of Utah. Salt Lake, 1853–54.

Newspapers and Periodicals

Anti-Polygamy Standard
Chicago Tribune
Deseret News
Doctrine and Covenants
Journal of Discourses
Journal History
Juvenile Instructor
Latter-day Saints Millennial Star
The Nation
New York Times
New York Tribune
The Revolution
Salt Lake Tribune
San Francisco Examiner
The Seer
Woman's Exponent
The Woman's Journal

SECONDARY SOURCES

Books

Abzug, Robert H. *Cosmos Crumbling: American Reform and the Religious Imagination.* New York, 1994.
Adams, Arlin M., and Charles J. Emmerich. *A Nation Dedicated to Religious Liberty: The Constitutional Heritage of the Religion Clauses.* Philadelphia, 1990.
Adler, Selig. *The Senatorial Career of George Franklin Edmunds.* Urbana, Ill., 1934.
Alexander, Thomas G. *Things in Heaven and Earth: The Life and Times of Wilford Woodruff, a Mormon Prophet.* Salt Lake, 1991.

Arrington, Leonard. *Brigham Young, American Moses.* Chicago, 1986.

———. *Charles C. Rich—Mormon General and Western Frontiersman.* Provo, Utah, 1974.

———. *Great Basin Kingdom: An Economic History of the Latter-day Saints, 1830–1900.* Cambridge, Mass., 1956.

Arrington, Leonard, and Davis Bitton. *The Mormon Experience: A History of the Church of Jesus Christ of Latter-day Saints.* New York, 1978.

Bailey, Paul. *The Armies of God.* New York, 1968.

Baker, Jean Harvey. *Affairs of Party: The Political Culture of Northern Democrats in the Mid-Nineteenth Century.* New York, 1998.

Bardaglio, Peter W. *Reconstructing the Household: Families, Sex, and the Law in the Nineteenth-Century South.* Chapel Hill, N.C., 1995.

Barnett, James H. *Divorce and the American Divorce Novel.* New York, 1968.

Basch, Norma. *Framing American Divorce: From the Revolutionary Generation to the Victorians.* Berkeley, Calif., 1999.

———. *In the Eyes of the Law: Women, Marriage, and Property in Nineteenth-Century New York.* Ithaca, N.Y., 1982.

Beard, Mary. *Woman as a Force in History: A Study in Traditions and Realities.* New York, 1946.

Beecher, Maureen Ursenbach, and Lavina Fielding Anderson, eds. *Sisters in Spirit: Mormon Women in Historical and Cultural Perspective.* Urbana, Ill., 1987.

Berk, Gerald. *Alternative Tracks: The Constitution of American Industrial Order, 1856–1917.* Baltimore, Md., 1994.

Berkhofer, Robert J., Jr. *Salvation and the Savage: An Analysis of Protestant Missions and American Indian Response, 1787–1862.* Lexington, Ky., 1965.

Bigler, David L. *Forgotten Kingdom: The Mormon Theocracy in the American West, 1847–1896.* Spokane, Wash., 1998.

Bitton, Davis. *George Q. Cannon, A Biography.* Salt Lake, 1999.

———. *The Ritualization of Mormon History.* Urbana, Ill., 1994.

Blomberg, Craig L., and Stephen E. Robinson. *How Wide the Divide? A Mormon and an Evangelical in Conversation.* Downers Grove, Ill., 1997.

Bloom, Harold. *The American Religion.* New York, 1992.

Boydston, Jeanne. *Home and Work: Housework, Wages, and the Ideology of Labor in the Early Republic.* New York, 1990.

Boyer, Paul, and Stephen Nissenbaum. *Salem Possessed: The Social Origins of Witchcraft.* Cambridge, Mass., 1974.

Bradley, Martha Sonntag. *Kidnapped from That Land: The Government Raid on Short Creek Polygamists.* Salt Lake, 1993.

Brandwein, Paula. *Reconstructing Reconstruction: The Supreme Court and the Production of Historical Truth.* Durham, N.C., 1999.

Braude, Ann. *Radical Spirits: Spiritualism and Women's Rights in Nineteenth-Century America.* Boston, 1989.

Brodie, Fawn M. *No Man Knows My History: The Life of Joseph Smith, the Mormon Prophet.* New York, 1945.

———. *Thomas Jefferson, An Intimate Biography.* New York, 1974.

Brooke, John L. *The Refiner's Fire: The Making of Mormon Cosmology, 1644–1844.* Cambridge, Eng., 1994.

Brooks, Juanita. *The Mountain Meadows Massacre.* Rev. ed. Norman, Okla., 1962.

Bushman, Richard. *Joseph Smith and the Beginnings of Mormonism.* Urbana, Ill., 1984.

Cairncross, John. *After Polygamy Was Made a Sin: The Social History of Christian Polygamy.* London, 1974.

Carwardine, Richard J. *Evangelicals and Politics in Antebellum America.* New Haven, Conn., 1993.

Chandler, Alfred D., Jr. *The Visible Hand: The Managerial Revolution in American Business.* Cambridge, Mass., 1977.

Clark, Blue. *Lone Wolf v. Hitchcock: Treaty Rights and Indian Law at the End of the Nineteenth Century.* Lincoln, Nebr., 1994.

Cobb, Sanford. *The Rise of Religious Liberty.* New York, 1905.

Cochran, Thomas C. *Railroad Leaders, 1845–1890: The Business Mind in Action.* Cambridge, Mass., 1953.

Cohen, Daniel A. *Pillars of Salt, Monuments of Grace: New England Crime Literature and the Origins of American Popular Culture, 1764–1860.* New York, 1993.

Cohen, Felix. *Handbook of Federal Indian Law.* Washington, D.C., 1942.

Compton, Todd. *In Sacred Loneliness: The Plural Wives of Joseph Smith.* Salt Lake, 1997.

Cott, Nancy F. *Public Vows: A History of Marriage and the Nation.* Cambridge, Mass., 2000.

Cott, Nancy F., and Elizabeth Pleck, eds. *A Heritage of Her Own.* New York, 1979.

Craycroft, Kenneth F., Jr. *The American Myth of Religious Freedom.* Dallas, 1999.

Cresswell, Stephen. *Mormons, Moonshiners, Cowboys, and Klansmen: Federal Law Enforcement in the South and West, 1870–1893.* Tuscaloosa, Ala., 1991.

Crockett, Walter Hill. *George Franklin Edmunds.* N.p., 1910.

Cross, Whitney R. *The Burned-Over District: The Social and Intellectual History of Enthusiastic Religion in Western New York, 1800–1850.* Ithaca, N.Y., 1950.

Cowley, Matthias F. *Wilford Woodruff.* Salt Lake, 1909.

Curry, Thomas J. *First Freedoms: Church and State in America to the Passage of the First Amendment.* New York, 1986.

Daynes, Kathryn M. *More Wives than One: Transformation of the Mormon Marriage System, 1840–1910.* Urbana, Ill., forthcoming.

Degler, Carl N. *At Odds: Women and Family in America from the Revolution to the Present.* New York, 1980.

Demos, John Putnam. *Entertaining Satan: Witchcraft and the Culture of Early New England.* New York, 1982.

Diffley, Kathleen. *Where My Heart Is Turning Ever: Civil War Stories and Constitutional Reform, 1861–1876.* Athens, Ga., 1992.

Douglas, Ann. *The Feminization of American Culture.* New York, 1977.

Eckhardt, Celia Morris. *Fanny Wright: Rebel in America.* Cambridge, Mass., 1984.

Edwards, Laura F. *Gendered Strife and Confusion: The Political Culture of Reconstruction.* Urbana, Ill., 1997.

Embry, Jessie L. *Mormon Polygamous Families: Life in the Principle.* Salt Lake, 1987.

Feldberg, Michael. *The Turbulent Era: Riot and Disorder in Jacksonian America.* New York, 1980.

Firmage, Edwin B., and Richard Collin Mangrum. *Zion in the Courts: A Legal History of the Church of Jesus Christ of Latter-day Saints, 1830–1900.* Urbana, Ill., 1988.

Fisher, Philip. *Hard Facts: Setting and Form in the American Novel.* New York, 1985.

Flake, Chad. *A Mormon Bibliography, 1830–1930: Books, Pamphlets, Periodicals, and Broadsides Relating to the First Century of Mormonism.* Salt Lake, 1978.

———. *A Mormon Bibliography: Ten Year Supplement.* Salt Lake, 1989.

Foner, Eric. *Free Soil, Free Labor, Free Men: The Ideology of the Republican Party before the Civil War.* London, 1970.

———. *Reconstruction: America's Unfinished Revolution, 1863–1877.* New York, 1988.

———. *The Story of American Freedom.* New York, 1998.

Forbath, William E. *Law and the Shaping of the American Labor Movement.* Cambridge, Mass., 1991.

Foster, Lawrence. *Religion and Sexuality: Three American Communal Experiences of the Nineteenth Century.* New York, 1981.

———. *Women, Family, and Utopia: Communal Experiments of the Shakers, the Oneida Community, and the Mormons.* Syracuse, N.Y., 1991.

Fredrickson, George M. *The Inner Civil War: Northern Intellectuals and the Crisis of the Union.* New York, 1965.

Friedman, Lawrence M. *Contract Law in America.* Madison, Wisc., 1965.

Furniss, Norman. *The Mormon Conflict, 1850–1859.* New Haven, Conn., 1966.

Genovese, Eugene D. *Roll, Jordan, Roll: The World the Slaves Made.* New York, 1976.

Givens, Terryl L. *The Viper on the Hearth: Mormons, Myths, and the Construction of Heresy.* New York, 1997.

Godfrey, Kenneth W., Audrey M. Godfrey, and Jill Mulvay Derr. *Women's Voices: An Untold History of the Latter-day Saints.* Salt Lake, 1982.

Greenstone, David J. *The Lincoln Persuasion: Remaking American Liberalism.* Princeton, N.J., 1993.

Grimes, Alan P. *The Puritan Ethic and Woman Suffrage.* New York, 1967.

Grossberg, Michael. *Governing the Hearth: Law and the Family in Nineteenth-Century America.* Chapel Hill, N.C., 1985.

Gurstein, Rochelle. *The Repeal of Reticence: A History of America's Cultural and Legal Struggles over Free Speech, Obscenity, Sexual Liberation, and Modern Art.* New York, 1996.

Halttunen, Karen. *Murder Most Foul: The Killer and the American Gothic Imagination.* Cambridge, Mass., 1998.

Hansen, Klaus J. *Quest for Empire: The Political Kingdom of God and the Council of Fifty in Mormon History.* East Lansing, Mich., 1967.

Hardy, B. Carmon. *Solemn Covenant: The Mormon Polygamous Passage.* Urbana, Ill., 1992.

Hartog, Hendrik. *Man and Wife in America, a History.* Cambridge, Mass., 2000.

Hatch, Nathan O. *The Democratization of American Christianity.* New Haven, Conn., 1989.

Hersch, Blanche Glassman. *The Slavery of Sex: Feminist-Abolitionists in America.* Urbana, Ill., 1978.

Hill, Marvin S. *Quest for Refuge: The Mormon Flight from American Pluralism.* Salt Lake, 1989.

Hofstadter, Richard. *The Progressive Historians: Turner, Beard, Parrington.* New York, 1968.

——. *Social Darwinism in American Thought.* Rev. ed. Boston, 1955.

Horwitz, Morton J. *The Transformation of American Law, 1790–1860.* Cambridge, Mass., 1977.

——. *The Transformation of American Law, 1879–1960: The Crisis of Orthodoxy.* New York, 1992.

Howe, Daniel Walker. *The Unitarian Conscience: Harvard Moral Philosophy, 1805–1861.* Cambridge, Mass., 1970.

Howe, Mark DeWolfe. *The Garden and the Wilderness.* Chicago, 1965.

Hurst, J. Willard. *Law and the Conditions of Freedom.* Madison, Wisc., 1950.

Isaac, Rhys. *The Transformation of Virginia, 1740–1790.* New York, 1982.

Isenberg, Nancy. *Sex and Citizenship in Antebellum America.* Chapel Hill, N.C., 1998.

Iversen, Joan Smyth. *The Anti-Polygamy Controversy in United States Women's Movements, 1880–1925.* New York, 1997.

Jacobs, Clyde E. *Law Writers and the Courts: The Influence of Thomas M. Cooley, Christopher G. Tiedeman, and John F. Dillon upon American Constitutional Law.* Berkeley, Calif., 1954.

James, John. *Money and Capital Markets in Postbellum America.* Princeton, N.J., 1978.

Jameson, John Franklin. *The History of Historical Writing in America.* Boston, 1891.

Johanssen, Robert W. *Stephen A. Douglas.* New York, 1973.

Johnson, Paul, and Sean Wilentz. *The Kingdom of Matthias.* New York, 1994.

Kantrowitz, Stephen. *Ben Tillman and the Reconstruction of White Supremacy.* Chapel Hill, N.C., 2000.

Karlsen, Carol F. *The Devil in the Shape of a Woman: Witchcraft in Colonial New England.* New York, 1987.

Kerber, Linda K. *No Constitutional Right to Be Ladies: Women and the Obligations of Citizenship.* New York, 1999.

Kern, Louis. *An Ordered Love: Sex Roles and Sexuality in Victorian Utopias: The Shakers, the Mormons, and the Oneida Community.* Chapel Hill, N.C., 1981.

Kimball, Stanley B. *Heber C. Kimball, Mormon Patriarch and Pioneer.* Urbana, Ill., 1981.

King, Willard L. *Melville Weston Fuller, Chief Justice of the United States.* New York, 1950.

Konig, David Thomas. *Law and Society in Puritan Massachusetts, 1629–1692.* Chapel Hill, N.C., 1979.

Korobkin, Laura Hanft. *Criminal Conversations: Sentimentality and Nineteenth-Century Legal Stories of Adultery.* New York, 1998.

Kraditor, Aileen S. *The Ideas of the Woman Suffrage Movement, 1890–1920.* New York, 1965.

———. *Means and Ends in American Abolitionism: Garrison and His Critics on Strategy and Tactics, 1834–1850.* Berkeley, Calif., 1981.

Lamar, Howard Roberts. *The Far Southwest, 1846–1912: A Territorial History.* New Haven, Conn., 1966.

Langum, David J. *Crossing over the Line: Legislating Morality and the Mann Act.* Chicago, 1994.

Larson, Gustive O. *The "Americanization" of Utah for Statehood.* San Marino, Calif., 1971.

Launius, Roger D. *Joseph Smith III: Pragmatic Prophet.* Urbana, Ill., 1988.

Launius, Roger D., and Linda Thatcher, eds. *Differing Visions: Dissenters in Mormon History.* Urbana, Ill., 1994.

LeSeuer, Stephen C. *The 1838 Mormon War in Missouri.* Columbia, Mo., 1987.

Levy, Leonard, ed. *Blasphemy in Massachusetts: Freedom of Conscience and the Abner Kneeland Case.* New York, 1973.

Lovejoy, David S. *Religious Enthusiasm in the New World: Heresy to Revolution.* Cambridge, Mass., 1985.

Lyman, E. Leo. *Political Deliverance: The Mormon Quest for Utah Statehood.* Urbana, Ill., 1986.

Lystra, Karen. *Searching the Heart: Women, Men, and Romantic Love in Nineteenth-Century America.* New York, 1989.

McDannell, Colleen. *The Christian Home in Victorian America, 1840–1940.* Bloomington, Ind., 1986.

McClellan, James. *Joseph Story and the American Constitution: A Study in Political and Legal Thought.* Norman, Okla., 1971.

McHenry, Robert, ed. *Liberty's Women.* Springfield, Mass., 1980.

McLoughlin, William G. *New England Dissent, 1630–1833: The Baptists and the Separation of Church and State.* 2 vols. Cambridge, Mass., 1971.

McPherson, James M. *The Abolitionist Legacy: From Reconstruction to the NAACP.* Princeton, N.J., 1975.

———. *Battle Cry of Freedom: The Civil War Era.* New York, 1988.

Madsen, Carol Cornwall, ed. *Battle for the Ballot: Essays on Woman Suffrage in Utah, 1870–1896.* Logan, Utah, 1997.

Miller, Leo. *John Milton among the Polygamophiles.* New York, 1984.

Miller, Perry. *The Life of the Mind in America: From the Revolution to the Civil War.* New York, 1965.

Miller, William L. *The First Liberty: Religion and the American Republic.* New York, 1986.

Moore, R. Laurence. *Religious Outsiders and the Making of Americans.* New York, 1986.

———. *Selling God: American Religion in the Marketplace of Culture.* New York, 1994.

Morgan, Edmund S. *American Slavery, American Freedom: The Ordeal of Colonial Virginia.* New York, 1975.

Mulder, William, and A. Russell Mortensen, eds. *Among the Mormons: Historic Accounts by Contemporary Observers.* New York, 1958.

Mullan, John. *Sentiment and Sociability: The Language of Feeling in the Eighteenth Century.* New York, 1988.

Nelson, William E. *The Americanization of the Common Law: The Impact of Legal Change on Massachusetts Society, 1760–1830.* Cambridge, Mass. 1975.

——. *The Fourteenth Amendment: From Political Principle to Judicial Doctrine.* Cambridge, Mass., 1988.

——. *Roots of American Bureaucracy, 1830–1900.* Cambridge, Mass., 1982.

Nevins, Allan. *Ordeal of the Union.* 2 vols. New York, 1947.

Newell, Linda King, and Valeen Tippets Avery. *Mormon Enigma: Emma Hale Smith.* 2d ed. Urbana, Ill., 1994.

Noonan, John. *The Believer and the Powers That Are: Cases, History, and other Data Bearing on the Relation of Religion and Government.* New York, 1987.

Noonan, John, and Edward Gaffney. *Religious Freedom.* 2d ed. New York, 2001.

Novak, William J. *The People's Welfare: Law and Regulation in Nineteenth-Century America.* Chapel Hill, N.C., 1996.

Nye, Russell B. *George Bancroft: Brahmin Rebel.* New York, 1945.

O'Brien, Conor Cruise. *The Long Affair: Thomas Jefferson and the French Revolution, 1785–1800.* Chicago, 1996.

Otis, D.S. *The Dawes Act and the Allotment of Indian Lands.* 1934. Reprint, Norman, Okla., 1973.

Parker, William Belmont. *The Life and Public Services of Justin Smith Morrill.* New York, 1924.

Pascoe, Peggy. *Relations of Rescue: The Search for Female Moral Authority in the American West, 1874–1939.* New York, 1990.

Paul, Arnold M. *Conservative Crisis and the Rule of Law: Attitudes of Bar and Bench, 1887–1895.* Gloucester, Mass., 1960.

Paulson, Ross Evans. *Woman's Suffrage and Prohibition: A Comparative Study of Equality and Social Control.* Glenview, Ill., 1973.

Pearce, Roy Harvey. *Savagism and Civilization: A Study of the Indian and the American Mind.* Baltimore, Md., 1953.

Peritz, Rudolph J. *Competition Policy in America, 1888–1992: History, Rhetoric, Law.* New York, 1996.

Perry, Lewis. *Radical Abolitionism: Anarchy and the Government of God in Antislavery Thought.* Ithaca, N.Y., 1973.

Peterson, Merrill D. *The Jefferson Image in the American Mind.* New York, 1960.

Pfeffer, Leo. *Church, State, and Freedom.* Boston, 1953.

Phelps, Anson Stokes. *Church and State in the Unites States.* 3 vols. New York, 1950.

Phillips, Roderick. *Putting Asunder: A History of Divorce in Western Society.* New York, 1988.

Pleck, Elizabeth. *Domestic Tyranny: The Making of Social Policy against Family Violence from Colonial Times to the Present.* New York, 1987.

Pomeroy, Earl S. *The Pacific Slope: A History of California, Oregon, Washington, Idaho, Utah, and Nevada.* New York, 1965.

———. *The Territories and the United States, 1861–1890.* Philadelphia, 1947.

Post, Albert. *Popular Freethought in America.* New York, 1943.

Quinn, D. Michael. *Early Mormonism and the Magic World View.* Salt Lake, 1987.

———. *The Mormon Hierarchy: Origins of Power.* Salt Lake, 1994.

———. *Same-Sex Dynamics among Nineteenth-Century Americans: A Mormon Example.* Urbana, Ill., 1996.

Reynolds, David S. *Faith in Fiction: The Emergence of Religious Literature in America.* Cambridge, Mass., 1981.

Ritter, Gretchen. *Goldbugs and Greenbacks: The Antimonopoly Tradition and the Politics of Finance in America, 1865–1896.* Cambridge, Mass., 1997.

Rodgers, Daniel T. *Atlantic Crossings: Social Politics in a Progressive Age.* Cambridge, Mass., 1998.

———. *Contested Truths: Keywords in American Politics Since Independence.* New York, 1987.

Ryan, Mary P. *Cradle of the Middle Class: The Family in Oneida County, New York, 1790–1865.* Cambridge, Mass., 1981.

Salmon, MaryLynn. *Women and the Law of Property in Early America.* Chapel Hill, N.C., 1986.

Salyer, Lucy E. *Laws Harsh as Tigers: Chinese Immigrants and the Shaping of Modern Immigration Law.* Chapel Hill, N.C., 1995.

Samuels, Shirley, ed. *The Culture of Sentiment: Race, Gender, and Sentimentality in Nineteenth-Century America.* New York, 1992.

Sandmeyer, Elmer C. *The Anti-Chinese Movement in California.* 1939. Reprint, Urbana, Ill., 1973.

Scott, Arthur P. *Criminal Law in Colonial Virginia.* Chicago, 1930.

Sellers, Charles C. *The Market Revolution: Jacksonian America, 1814–1846.* New York, 1991.

Shipps, Jan. *Mormonism: The Story of a New Religious Tradition.* Urbana, Ill., 1985.

———. *Sojourner in the Promised Land: Forty Years among the Mormons.* Urbana, Ill., 2000.

Sizer, Sandra S. *Gospel Hymns and Social Religion: The Rhetoric of Nineteenth-Century Revivalism.* Philadelphia, 1978.

Sklar, Martin J. *The Corporate Reconstruction of American Capitalism, 1890–1916: The Market, the Law, and Politics.* Cambridge, Eng., 1988.

Stanley, Amy Dru. *From Bondage to Contract: Wage Labor, Marriage, and the Market in the Age of Slave Emancipation.* Cambridge, Eng., 1998.

Thomas, George M. *Revivalism and Cultural Change: Christianity, Nation Building, and the Market in the Nineteenth-Century United States.* Chicago, 1989.

Thompson, Margaret Susan. *The "Spider Web": Congress and Lobbying in the Age of Grant.* Ithaca, N.Y., 1985.

Tompkins, Jane. *Sensational Designs: The Cultural Work of American Fiction, 1790–1860.* New York, 1985.

Trachtenberg, Alan. *The Incorporation of America: Culture and Society in the Gilded Age.* New York, 1982.

Tracy, Jack. *Conan Doyle and the Latter-day Saints.* Bloomington, Ind., 1978.

Tribe, Lawrence. *American Constitutional Law.* 2d ed. Mineola, N.Y., 1988.

Turner, James. *Without God, without Creed: The Origins of Unbelief in America.* Baltimore, Md., 1985.

Twiss, Benjamin R. *Lawyers and the Constitution: How Laissez Faire Came to the Supreme Court.* Princeton, N.J., 1942.

Van Orden, Bruce A. *Prisoner for Conscience' Sake: The Life of George Reynolds.* Salt Lake, 1992.

Van Wagoner, Richard. *Mormon Polygamy: A History.* 2d ed. Salt Lake, 1989.

Walker, Ronald W. *Wayward Saints: The Godbeites and Brigham Young.* Urbana, Ill., 1998.

Wall, Joseph Frazier. *Andrew Carnegie.* New York, 1970.

Wallace, Irving. *The Twenty-Seventh Wife.* New York, 1961.

Walters, Ronald G. *The Antislavery Appeal: American Abolitionism after 1830.* New York, 1978.

Warhol, Robyn R. *Gendered Interventions: Narrative Discourse in the Victorian Novel.* New Brunswick, 1989.

Warren, Charles. *The Supreme Court in American History.* 3 vols. Boston, 1923.

Watson, Harry L. *Liberty and Power: The Politics of Jacksonian America.* New York, 1990.

Weisbrod, Carol. *The Boundaries of Utopia.* New York, 1980.

Wells, Merle W. *Anti-Mormonism in Idaho, 1872–1892.* Provo, Utah, 1978.

Whiting, Lilian. *Kate Field, a Record . . ..* New York, 1909.

Wires, Richard. *The Divorce Issue and Reform in Nineteenth-Century Indiana.* Muncie, Ind., 1967.

Wood, Gordon S. *The Radicalism of the American Revolution: How a Revolution Transformed a Monarchical Society into a Democratic One Unlike Any That Had Ever Existed.* New York, 1992.

Woodward, Helen Beal. *The Bold Women.* New York, 1953.

Yellin, Jean Fagin. *Women and Sisters: The Antislavery Feminists in American Culture.* New Haven, Conn., 1989.

Young, Kimball. *Isn't One Wife Enough?* New York, 1954.

Zobell, Albert L. Jr. *Sentinel in the East: A Biography of Thomas L. Kane.* Salt Lake, 1965.

Zollman, Carl. *American Civil Church Law.* New York, 1917.

Articles

Aaron, Richard I. "Mormon Divorce and the Statute of 1852: Questions for Divorce in the 1980's." *Journal of Contemporary Law* 8 (1982): 5–45.

Alexander, Thomas G. "Charles S. Zane . . . Apostle of the New Era." *Utah Historical Quarterly* 34, no. 2 (Summer 1966): 121–37.

———. "Federal Authority versus Polygamic Theocracy: James B. McKean and the Mormons, 1870–1875." *Dialogue* 1, no. 3 (Autumn 1966): 85–100.

Allen, James B. " 'Good Guys' vs. 'Good Guys': Rudger Clawson, John Sharp and Civil Disobedience in Nineteenth-Century Utah." *Utah Historical Quarterly* 48, no. 2 (Summer 1980): 148–74.

———. "The Unusual Jurisdiction of the County Probate Courts in the Territory of Utah." *Utah Historical Quarterly* 36, no. 2 (1968): 132–42.

Arrington, Leonard J. "Crusade Against Theocracy: The Reminiscences of Jacob Smith Boreman, 1872–1877." *Huntington Library Quarterly* 24, no. 1 (November 1960): 1–45.

———. " 'In Honorable Remembrance': Thomas L. Kane's Service to the Mormons." Task Papers in Latter-day Saints History, No. 22, Salt Lake, 1978.

Arrington, Leonard J., and Jon Haupt. "Intolerable Zion: The Image of Mormonism in Nineteenth-Century American Literature." *Western Humanities Review* 22, no. 3 (Summer 1968): 243–60.

———. "The Settlement of the Brigham Young Estate, 1877–1879." *Pacific Historical Review* 21, no. 1 (February 1952): 1–20.

Bashore, Melvin L. "Life Behind Bars: Mormon Cohabs of the 1880s." *Utah Historical Quarterly* 47, no. 1 (1979): 22–41.

Baugh, Alexander L. "Missouri Governor Lilburn W. Boggs and the Mormons." *John Whitmer Historical Association Journal* 18 (1998): 111–32.

Bederman, Gail. " 'Civilization,' the Decline of Middle-Class Manliness, and Ida B. Wells's Anti-Lynching Campaign (1892–94)." *Radical History Review* 52 (1992): 5–30.

Beecher, Maureen Ursenbach. "The 'Leading Sisters': A Female Hierarchy in Nineteenth-Century Mormon Society." *Journal of Mormon History* 9 (1982): 25–39.

Bellah, Robert N. "Civil Religion in America." *Daedalus* 96 (Winter 1967): 1–21.

Benedict, Michael Les. "Laissez-faire and Liberty: A Re-evaluation of the Meaning and Origins of Laissez-faire Capitalism." *Law and History Review* 3 (Fall 1985): 293–331.

Bitton, Davis. "Mormon Polygamy: A Review Article." *Journal of Mormon History* 4 (1977): 101–18.

———. "The B. H. Roberts Case of 1898–1900." *Utah Historical Quarterly* 25, no. 1 (January 1957): 27–46.

Bloomfield, Maxwell. "The Supreme Court in American Popular Culture." *Journal of American Culture* 4 (1982): 1–13.

Borden, Morton. "The Christian Amendment." *Civil War History* 25 (March 1979): 156–67.

Bowling, Kenneth R. "A Tub to the Whale: The Founding Fathers and the Adoption of the Federal Bill of Rights." *Journal of the Early Republic* 8, no.3 (1988): 223–51.

Buckley, Thomas E. "After Disestablishment: Thomas Jefferson's Wall of Separation in Antebellum Virginia." *Journal of Southern History* 61 (August 1995): 445–80.

Buice, David. " 'A Stench in the Nostrils of Honest Men': Southern Democrats and the Edmunds Act of 1882." *Dialogue* 21 (Autumn 1988): 100–113.

Bullough, Vern L. "Polygamy: An Issue in the Election of 1860?" *Utah Historical Quarterly* 29 (Spring 1961): 119–28.

Campbell, Bruce L., and Eugene E. Campbell. "Divorce among Mormon

Polygamists: Extent and Explanations." *Utah Historical Quarterly* 46 (Winter 1978): 4–23.

———. "Early Cultural and Intellectual Development." In *Utah's History*, edited by Richard D. Poll, 295–316. Provo, Utah, 1978.

Cannon, Charles A. "The Awesome Power of Sex: The Polemical Campaign against Mormon Polygamy." *Pacific Historical Review* 43 (February 1974): 61–68.

Cannon, Kenneth L., II. "Beyond the Manifesto: Polygamous Cohabitation among LDS General Authorities after 1890." *Utah Historical Quarterly* 46, no. 1 (January 1978): 24–36.

Cannon, M. Hamlin, ed. "The Prison Diary of a Mormon Apostle." *Pacific Historical Quarterly* 16 (November 1947): 393–409.

Chused, Richard. "Married Women's Property Law: 1800–1850." *Georgetown Law Journal* 71, no. 5 (June 1983): 1359–1425.

Clark, Elizabeth B. "Matrimonial Bonds: Slavery and Divorce in Nineteenth-Century America." *Law and History Review* 8, no. 1 (Spring 1990): 25–54.

———. "Self-Ownership and the Political Theory of Elizabeth Cady Stanton." *Connecticut Law Review* 21, no. 4 (Summer 1989): 905–41.

Clayton, James L. "The Supreme Court, Polygamy, and the Enforcement of Morals in Nineteenth-Century America: An Analysis of *Reynolds v. United States*." *Dialogue* 12 (Winter 1979): 46–61.

Cochran, Thomas C. "The Paradox of American Economic Growth." *Journal of American History* 61 (December 1975): 925–42.

Commager, Henry Steele. "The Blasphemy of Abner Kneeland." *New England Quarterly* 8 (March 1935): 29–41.

Cott, Nancy F. "Giving Character to Our Whole Civil Polity: Marriage and the Public Order in the Late Nineteenth Century." In *U.S. History as Women's History: New Feminist Essays*, edited by Linda K. Kerber, Alice Kessler-Harris, and Kathryn Kish Sklar, 107–21. Chapel Hill, N.C. 1995.

———. "Marriage and Women's Citizenship in the United States, 1830–1934." *American Historical Review* 103 (December 1998): 1440–74.

Cracroft, Richard H. "Distorting Polygamy for Fun and Profit: Artemus Ward and Mark Twain among the Mormons." *Brigham Young University Studies* 24, no. 2 (Winter 1984): 272–88.

Cushman, Barry. "Intestate Succession in a Polygamous Society." *Connecticut Law Review* 23, no. 2 (Winter 1991): 281–332.

Davis, David Brion. "The New England Origins of Mormonism." *New England Quarterly* 26 (June 1953): 147–68.

———. "Some Themes of Countersubversion: An Analysis of Anti-Masonic, Anti-Catholic, and Anti-Mormon Literature." *Mississippi Valley Historical Review* 47 (September 1960): 205–24.

Davis, Ray Jay. "The Polygamous Prelude." *American Journal of Legal History* 6 (1962): 1–27.

———. "Plural Marriage and Religious Freedom: The Impact of *Reynolds v. United States*." *Arizona Law Review* 15, no. 2 (1973): 287–306.

Derr, Jill Mulvay. " 'Strength in Our Union': The Making of Mormon Sisterhood." In *Sisters in Spirit: Mormon Women in Historical and Cultural*

Perspective, edited by Maureen Ursenbach Beecher and Lavina Fielding Anderson, 153–207. Urbana, Ill. 1987.

Dewey, Frank L. "Thomas Jefferson's Notes on Divorce." *William & Mary Quarterly* 39 (1982): 212–23.

Driggs, Ken. "Lorenzo Snow's Appellate Court Victory." *Utah Historical Quarterly* 58 (1990): 81–93.

DuBois, Ellen Carol. "On Labor and Free Love: Two Unpublished Speeches of Elizabeth Cady Stanton." *Signs* 1 (Autumn 1975): 257–68.

Durham, G. Homer. "The Development of Political Parties in Utah: The First Phase." *Utah Humanities Review* 1 (January 1947): 122–33.

Edwards, Laura F. " 'The Marriage Covenant Is at the Foundation of All Our Rights': The Politics of Slave Marriages in North Carolina after Emancipation." *Law and History Review* 14, no. 1 (Spring 1996): 81–124.

Egan, Timothy. "Persistence of Polygamy." *New York Times*, 28 February 1999, 51–54.

Embry, Jessie L., and Martha Sonntag Bradley. "Mothers and Daughters in Polygamy." *Dialogue* 18 (Fall 1985): 98–107.

Ernst, Daniel R. "Law and American Political Development, 1977–1938." *Reviews in American History* 26, no. 1 (March 1998): 205–19.

Ferguson, Robert A. "Story and Transcription in the Trial of John Brown." *Yale Journal of Law and the Humanities* 6, no. 1 (Winter 1994): 37–73.

Firmage, Edwin B. "Religion and the Law: The Mormon Experience in the Nineteenth Century." *Cardozo Law Review* 12 (February 1991): 765–803.

Flaherty, David. "Law and the Enforcement of Morals in Early America." In *American Law and the Constitutional Order: Historical Perspectives*, edited by Lawrence M. Friedman and Harry Scheiber, 53–66. Cambridge, Mass., 1988.

Fleek, Sherman L. "Thomas L. Kane: Friend of the Saints." *Mormon Heritage* 1 (May–June 1994): 36–42.

Friedman, Lawrence M. "Crimes of Mobility." *Stanford Law Review* 43 (February 1991): 637–58.

Fritz, Christian G. "Due Process, Treaty Rights, and Chinese Exclusion." In *Entry Denied: Exlusion and the Chinese Community in America, 1882–1943*, edited by Sucheng Chan, 25–56. Philadelphia, 1991.

Gee, Elizabeth C. "Justice for All or for the 'Elect'? The Utah County Probate Court, 1855–1872." *Utah Historical Quarterly* 48 (Spring 1980): 129–47.

Gentry, Leland H. "The Danite Band of 1838." *Brigham Young University Studies* 14, no. 4 (Summer 1974): 421–50.

Ginzberg, Lori D. " 'The Hearts of Your Readers Will Shudder': Fanny Wright, Infidelity, and American Freethought." *American Quarterly* 46, no. 2 (June 1994): 195–226.

Gordon, Robert W. "Legal Thought and Legal Practice in the Age of American Enterprise." In *Professions and Professional Ideologies in America*, edited by Gerald L. Geison, 70–110. Chapel Hill, N.C. 1983.

Gordon, Sarah Barringer. "Blasphemy and the Law of Religious Liberty in Nineteenth-Century America." *American Quarterly* 52, no. 4 (December 2000): 682–720.

———. "The Liberty of Self-Degradation": Polygamy, Woman Suffrage, and Consent in Nineteenth-Century America." *Journal of American History* 83 (December 1996): 815–47.

Griswold, Robert L. "Law, Sex, Cruelty and Divorce in Victorian America, 1840–1900." *American Quarterly* 38 (Winter 1986): 721–45.

Grossberg, Michael. "Teaching the Republican Child: Three Antebellum Stories about Law, Schooling, and the Construction of American Families." *Utah Law Review* 1996, no. 2 (1996): 429–60.

Gutjahr, Paul. "The Golden Bible in the Bible's Golden Age: *The Book of Mormon* and Antebellum Print Culture." *American Transcendental Quarterly: Nineteenth-Century American Literature and Culture* 12 (December 1998).

Hallwas, John E. "Mormon Nauvoo from a Non-Mormon Perspective." *Journal of Mormon History* 16 (1990): 53–69.

Hammett, Theodore M. "Two Mobs of Jacksonian Boston: Ideology and Interest." *Journal of American History* 62 (December 1976): 845–68.

Hardy, B. Carmon. "Lords of Creation: Polygamy, the Abrahamic Household, and Mormon Patriarchy." *Journal of Mormon History* 20 (Spring 1994): 119–52.

Harmer-Dionne, Elizabeth. "Once a Peculiar People: Cognitive Dissonance and the Suppression of Mormon Polygamy as a Case Study." *Stanford Law Review* 50 (April 1998): 1295–1347.

Hartog, Hendrik. "The Constitution of Aspiration and the Rights that Belong to Us All." In *The Constitution in American Life*, edited by David Thelen, 353–74. New York, 1987.

———. "Lawyering, Husbands' Rights and the 'Unwritten Law' in Nineteenth-Century America." *Journal of American History* 84 (June 1997): 67–96.

———. "Marital Exits and Marital Expectations in Nineteenth-Century America." *Georgetown Law Journal* 80 (October 1991): 95–129.

———. "Mrs. Packard on Dependency." *Yale Journal of Law and the Humanities* 1 (December 1988): 79–103.

Hasday, Jill Elaine. "Federalism and the Family Reconstructed." *University of California at Los Angeles Law Review* 45 (June 1998): 1297–1400.

Haskell, Thomas G. "Capitalism and the Origins of the Humanitarian Sensibility." Part 1. *American Historical Review* 90, no. 2 (1985): 339–61.

Holsinger, M. Paul. "For God and the American Home: The Attempt to Unseat Senator Reed Smoot, 1903–1907." *Pacific Northwest Quarterly* 60 (July 1969): 154–60.

Holzer, Henry Mark. "The True *Reynolds v. United States.*" *Harvard Journal of Law and Public Policy* 10 (Winter 1987): 43–46.

Homer, Michael W. "The Judiciary and the Common Law in Utah Territory, 1850–1861." *Dialogue* 21 (Spring 1988): 97–108.

———. "Sir Arthur Conan Doyle: Spiritualism and 'New Religions.'" *Dialogue* 23, no. 4 (Spring 1990): 97–121.

Hough, C. Merrill. "Two School Systems in Conflict: 1867–1890." *Utah Historical Quarterly* 28 (April 1960): 113–30.

Hovenkamp, Herbert. "The Sherman Act and the Classical Theory of Competition." *Iowa Law Review* 74 (July 1989): 1019–65.

Howe, Daniel Walker. "American Victorianism as a Culture." *American Quarterly* 27, no. 5 (December 1975): 507–32.

———. "The Evangelical Movement and Political Culture in the North during the Second Party System." *Journal of American History* 77 (March 1991): 1216–39.

Huston, James L. "The American Revolutionaries, the Political Economy of Aristocracy, and the American Concept of the Distribution of Wealth, 1765–1900." *American Historical Review* 98 (October 1993): 1079–105.

———. "Thomas Jefferson's Letter to the Danbury Baptists: A Controversy Rejoined." *William & Mary Quarterly*, 3d ser., 66 (October 1999): 775–90.

Isaac, Rhys. " 'The Rage of Malice of the Old Serpent Devil': The Dissenters and the Making and Remaking of the Virginia Statute for Religious Freedom." In *The Virginia Statute for Religious Freedom: Its Evolution and Consequences in American History*, edited by Merrill D. Peterson and Robert C. Vaughan, 139–69. Cambridge, Eng., 1988.

Iversen, Joan. "Feminist Implications of Mormon Polygyny." *Feminist Studies* 10, no. 3 (Fall 1984): 505–22.

———. "The Mormon-Suffrage Relationship: Personal and Political Quandaries." *Frontiers* 11, nos. 2–3 (1990): 8–16.

Ivins, Stanley S. "Free Schools Come to Utah." *Utah Historical Quarterly* 24 (1954): 321–42.

———. "Notes on Mormon Polygamy." *Western Humanities Review* 10, no. 3 (Summer 1956): 229–39.

Jensen, Richard L. "Steaming Through: Arrangements for Mormon Emigration from Europe, 1869–1887." *Journal of Mormon History* 9 (1982): 3–23.

John, Richard R. "Taking Sabbatarianism Seriously: The Postal System, the Sabbath, and the Transformation of American Political Culture." *Journal of the Early Republic* 10, no. 4 (Winter 1990): 516–67.

Jones, Alan. "Thomas M. Cooley and the Michigan Supreme Court." *American Journal of Legal History* 10, no. 2 (April 1966): 119–38.

Joslin, G. Stanley. "Mortmain in Canada and the United States: A Comparative Study." *Canadian Bar Review* 29, no. 5 (May 1951): 621–30.

Kauper, Paul G., and Stephen C. Ellis. "Religious Corporations and the Law." *Michigan Law Review* 71, no. 8 (August 1973): 1499–1574.

Kern, Louis J. "Sectarian Perfectionism and Universal Reform: The Radical Social and Political Theory of William Lloyd Garrison." In *Religious and Secular Reform in America: Ideas, Beliefs and Social Change*, edited by David K. Adams and Cornelis A. van Minnen, 91–120. New York, 1999.

King, Andrew J. "Sunday Law in the Nineteenth Century." *Albany Law Review* 64 (2000): 675–772.

Korobkin, Laura Hanft. "The Maintenance of Mutual Confidence: Sentimental Strategies at the Adultery Trial of Henry Ward Beecher." *Yale Journal of Law and the Humanities* 7, no. 1 (January 1995): 1–48.

Lamar, Howard. "Political Patterns in New Mexico and Utah." *Utah Historical Quarterly* 28 (Summer 1960).

Laycock, Douglas. "The Remnants of Free Exercise." *Supreme Court Review* (1990): 1–68.

Lee, Mark S. "Legislating Morality." *Sunstone* 10, no. 4 (April 1985): 11–12.

Lee, R. W. "The Law of Blasphemy." *Michigan Law Review* 16 (January 1918): 149–57.

Linford, Orma. "The Mormons and the Law." Parts 1 and 2. *Utah Law Review* 9 (Winter 1964): 308–70; (Summer 1965): 543–91.

Lynn, Karen. "Sensational Virtue: Nineteenth-Century Mormon Fiction and American Popular Taste." *Dialogue* 14 (Fall 1981): 101–12.

McConnell, Michael W. "Free Exercise Revisionism and the *Smith* Decision." *University of Chicago Law Review* (Fall 1990): 1109–53.

McCurdy, Charles W. "Justice Field and the Jurisprudence of Government-Business Relations." *Journal of American History* 61 (December 1975): 970–1005.

Madsen, Carol Cornwall. " 'At Their Peril': Utah Law and the Case of Plural Wives." *Western Historical Quarterly* 21, no. 4 (November 1990): 425–43.

———. "Emmeline B. Wells: A Voice for Mormon Women." *John Whitmer Historical Association Journal* 2 (1982): 11–21.

Magrath, Peter. "Chief Justice Waite and the Twin Relic." *Vanderbilt Law Review* 18, no. 3 (1965): 507–43.

Marcuse, Herbert. "Repressive Tolerance." In *A Critique of Pure Tolerance*, by Robert T. Paul Wolff, Barrington Moore Jr., and Herbert Marcuse, 81–123. Boston, 1969.

Mark, Gregory A. "The Court and the Corporation." *Supreme Court Review* (1997), 403–57.

Mathews, Donald G. "The Second Great Awakening as an Organizing Process, 1780–1820: An Hypothesis." *American Quarterly* 21, no. 1 (1969): 23–43.

May, James L. "Antitrust Practice and Procedure in the Formative Era: Political and Economic Theory in Constitutional and Antitrust Analysis, 1880–1918." *University of Pennsylvania Law Review* 135 (March 1987): 495–593.

Mehr, Kahlile. "Women's Response to Plural Marriage." *Dialogue* 18 (Fall 1985): 84–97.

Michaels, Walter Benn. "The Contracted Heart." *New Literary History* 21, no. 3 (Spring 1990): 495–531.

Miller, Jeremy M. "A Critique of the *Reynolds* Decision." *Western State University Law Review* 11 (Spring 1984): 181–201.

Moore, Lawrence. "Bible Reading and Nonsectarian Schooling: The Failure of Religious Instruction in Nineteenth-Century Public Education." *Journal of American History* 86 (March 2000): 1581–1699.

Morgan, Dale. "The State of Deseret." *Utah Historical Quarterly* 8, nos. 2, 3, 4 (1940): 65–240.

Mulder, William. "Immigration and the 'Mormon Question': An International Episode." *Western Political Quarterly* 9, no. 2 (June 1956): 416–33.

———. "Prisoners for Conscience' Sake." In *Lore of Faith and Folly*, edited by Thomas E. Cheney, 135–44. Salt Lake, 1971.

Murdock, George Peter. "World Ethnographic Sample." *American Anthropologist* 59, no. 4 (August 1957): 664–87.

Nedrow, G. Keith. "Polygamy and the Right to Marry: New Life for an Old Lifestyle." *Memphis State University Law Review* 11 (1981): 303–49.

Nelson, Marie H. "Anti-Mormon Violence and the Rhetoric of Law and Order in Early Mormon History." *Legal Studies Forum* 21, no. 2 (1997): 353–88.

Oaks, Dallin H. "The Suppression of the Nauvoo Expositor." *Utah Law Review* 9, no. 4 (Winter 1965): 862–903.

O'Malley, Michael. "Specie and Species: Race and the Money Question in Nineteenth-Century America." *American Historical Review* 99 (April 1994): 369–95.

Parker, Douglas. "Victory in Defeat—Polygamy and the Mormon Legal Encounter with the Federal Government." *Cardozo Law Review* 12 (1991): 805–19.

Pascoe, Peggy. "Miscegenation Law, Court Cases, and Ideologies of 'Race' in Twentieth-Century America." *Journal of American History* 83, no. 1 (June 1996): 44–69.

Pepper, Stephen. "*Reynolds, Yoder,* and Beyond: Alternatives for the Free Exercise Clause." *Utah Law Review* (1981): 309–78.

Peterson, Paul H. "The Mormon Reformation of 1856–1857: The Rhetoric and the Reality." *Journal of Mormon History* 15 (1989): 59–87.

Phillips, Rick. "The 'Secularization' of Utah and Religious Competition." *Journal for the Scientific Study of Religion* 38, no. 1 (1999): 72–82.

Poll, Richard D. "The Mormon Question Enters National Politics." *UHQ* 25, no. 2 (April 1957): 117–31.

Poll, Richard D., and William P. MacKinnon. "Causes of the Utah War Reconsidered." *Journal of Mormon History* 20 (Fall 1994): 16–44.

Post, Robert. "Cultural Heterogeneity and Law: Pornography, Blasphemy and the First Amendment." *California Law Review* 76 (1988): 297–335.

Quinn, D. Michael. "LDS Church Authority and the New Plural Marriages, 1890–1904." *Dialogue* 18, no. 1 (Spring 1985): 9–105.

——. "The LDS Church's Campaign against the Equal Rights Amendment." *Journal of Mormon History* 20 (Fall 1994): 85–155.

Rohrer, James R. "Sunday Mails and the Church-State Theme in Jacksonian America." *Journal of the Early Republic* 7, no. 1 (Spring 1987): 53–74.

Rosenblum, Nancy L. "Democratic Sex: *Reynolds v. U.S.,* Sexual Relations, and Community." In *Sex, Preference, and Family: Essays on Law and Nature,* 63–85. New York, 1997.

Saltzman, Penelope W. "Another Interpretation of Polygamy and the First Amendment." *Utah Law Review* (1986): 345–71.

Scott, Patricia Lyn. "Mormon Polygamy: A Bibliography, 1977–1992." *Journal of Mormon History* 19 (Spring 1993): 133–55.

Siegel, Reva B. "The Modernization of Marital Status Law: Adjudicating Wives' Rights to Earnings, 1860–1930." *Georgetown Law Journal* 82 (1994): 2125–211.

Smith, Timothy L. "The Book of Mormon in a Biblical Culture." *Journal of Mormon History* 7 (1980): 3–21.

Smith-Rosenberg, Carroll. "Beauty, the Beast and the Militant Woman: A Case Study in Sex Roles and Social Stress in Jacksonian America." *American Quarterly* 23, no. 4 (October 1971): 562–84.

Subrin, Stephen N. "How Equity Conquered the Common Law: The Federal Rules of Civil Procedure in Historical Perspective." *University of Pennsylvania Law Review* 135 (April 1987): 909–1002.

Teaford, Jon C. "Toward a Christian Nation: Religion, Law and Justice Strong." *Journal of Presbyterian History* 54 (Winter 1976): 422–37.

Tomlins, Christopher L. "Subordination, Authority, Law: Subjects in Labor History." *International Labor and Working-Class History* 47 (Spring 1995): 56–90.

Vandervelde, Lea S. "The Gendered Origins of the *Lumley* Doctrine: Binding Men's Consciousness and Women's Fidelity." *Yale Law Journal* 101 (1992): 775–852.

Van Wagenen, Lola. "In Their Own Behalf: The Politicization of Mormon Women and the 1870 Franchise." *Dialogue* 24, no. 4 (Winter 1991): 31–43.

Walker, Ronald W. "The Stenhouses and the Making of a Mormon Image." *Journal of Mormon History* 1 (1974): 51–72.

Weisbrod, Carol, and Pamela Sheingorn. "Reynolds v. United States: Nineteenth-Century Forms of Marriage and the Status of Women." *Connecticut Law Review* 10 (1978): 828–58.

Welch, Richard E., Jr. "George Edmunds of Vermont: Republican Half-Breed." *Vermont History* 36, no. 2 (1968): 64–73.

White, William Griffin, Jr. "The Feminist Campaign for the Exclusion of Brigham Henry Roberts from the Fifty-sixth Congress." *Journal of the West* 17, no. 1 (January 1978): 45–52.

Whittaker, David J. "The Bone in the Throat: Orson Pratt and the Public Announcement of Plural Marriage." *Western Historical Quarterly* 18 (July 1987): 293–314.

———. "Early Mormon Polygamy Defenses." *Journal of Mormon History* 11 (1984): 43–63.

Wolfinger, Henry J. "A Re-examination of the Woodruff Manifest in Light of Utah Constitutional History." *Utah Historical Quarterly* 39 (Fall 1971): 328–49.

Wood, Gordon S. "Evangelical America and Early Mormonism." *New York History* 61 (October 1980): 357–86.

Wyatt-Brown, Bertram. "Prelude to Abolitionism: Sabbatarian Politics and the Rise of the Second Party System." *Journal of American History* 58 (September 1971): 316–41.

Unpublished Manuscripts, Dissertations, Theses

Cannon, Mark W. "The Mormon Issue in Congress, 1872–1882, Drawing on the Experience of Territorial Delegate George Q. Cannon." Ph.D. diss., Harvard University, 1960.

Casterline, Gail Farr. " 'In the Toils' or 'Onward for Zion': Images of Mormon Women, 1852–1890." Master's thesis, Utah State University, 1974.

Clark, Elizabeth B. "Anticlericalism and Antistatism." Unpublished manuscript on file with the author.

Cullen, Jack B. "Ann Eliza Young: A Nineteenth-Century Champion of Women's Rights." Paper presented at the Annual Meeting of the Western Speech Communication Association, Albuquerque, N.M., February 1983.

Ditmars, R. Maude. "A History of Baptist Missions in Utah, 1871–1931." Master's thesis, University of Colorado, 1931.

Dudden, Arthur Power. "Antimonopolism, 1865–1890: The Historical Background and Intellectual Origins of the Antitrust Movement in the United States." Ph.D. diss., University of Michigan, 1950.

Evans, Rosa Mae McClellan. "Judicial Prosecution of Prisoners for LDS Plural Marriage: Prison Sentences, 1884–1895." Master's thesis, Brigham Young University, 1986.

Flake, Kathleen. "Mr. Smoot Goes to Washington: The Politics of American Religious Identity, 1900–1920." Unpublished manuscript on file with the author.

Grow, Stewart L. "A Study of the Utah Commission." Ph.D. diss., University of Utah, 1954.

Haynes, Alan E. "The Federal Government and Its Policies Regarding the Frontier Era of Utah Territory, 1850–1877." Ph.D. diss., Catholic University, 1968.

Ivins, Stanley S. "The Moses Thatcher Case." Typescript [1964?]. Utah State Historical Society, Salt Lake.

Lyon, T. Edgar. "Evangelical Protestant Missionary Activities in Mormon Dominated Areas: 1865–1900." Ph.D. diss., University of Utah, 1962.

Poll, Richard D. "The Twin Relic: A Study of Mormon Polygamy and the Campaign of the U.S. Government for Its Abolition, 1852–1890." Master's thesis, Texas Christian University, 1938.

Quinn, D. Michael. "The Mormon Hierarchy, 1822–1932: An American Elite." Ph.D. diss., Yale University, 1976.

Schwartzberg, Beverly. "Grass Widows, Barbarians and Bigamists: Documenting and Describing Marital Irregularity in Nineteenth-Century America." Unpublished manuscript on file with author.

Sneider, Allison Lee. "Reconstruction, Expansion and Empire: The United States Woman Suffrage Movement and the Re-Making of National Political Community." Ph.D. diss., University of California at Los Angeles, 1999.

Van Wagenen, Lola. "Sister-Wives and Suffragists: Polygamy and the Politics of Woman Suffrage, 1870–1896." Ph.D. diss., New York University, 1994.

ACKNOWLEDGMENTS

Without the opportunity to think and learn from insightful teachers, this intellectual history could not be written. Mary B. Corcoran, Donald Olson, and Elizabeth Clark gave me much support and joy. I miss them all. Margaret Farley and John Mullin at Yale Divinity School; Burke Marshall, Perry Dane, Barbara Black, and Robert Cover at Yale Law School; and David Brion Davis in the history department, all showed me the great moral power of the past. In the history department at Princeton, Daniel Rodgers has been an unflinching friend and rigorous mentor. His example has been one to admire and, when possible, to emulate. Stanley Katz is a true and wise counselor.

Outside Princeton, I received invaluable support from a year as a Golieb Fellow at the Legal History Colloquium at New York University Law School, as well as from a Charlotte Newcombe Fellowship from the Woodrow Wilson Fellowship Foundation, a Littleton-Griswold Travel Grant from the American Historical Association, a Huntington Library Fellowship, a Rockefeller Fellowship at the Center for Human Values at Princeton University, a Pew Fellowship at the Center for the Study of American Religion at Yale University, and a Young Scholar in Ethics and Public Life Fellowship from Cornell University. Last but not least, the University of Pennsylvania Law School allowed me to start with a year's leave as I began the process of turning an unwieldy dissertation into a reasonably short book. Libraries and librarians have also been key to this project, including but not limited to Firestone Library at Princeton University and its curator of Western Americana, Alfred Bush; the Historical Department of the Church of Jesus Christ of Latter-day Saints, especially Ronald Barney and William Slaughter; the Utah State Historical Society; Van Pelt and Biddle Law Libraries at the University of Pennsylvania, and reference librarians Catharine Krieps, Heidi Heller, and Edwin Greenlee; Marriott Library at the University of Utah; the Rocky Mountain West Division of the National Archives; the Library of Congress; Beinecke and Sterling Libraries at Yale University; Widener Library at Harvard University; the New York Public

Library; the Historical Society of Pennsylvania; the Library Company of Philadelphia; the Wisconsin Historical Society; and the Boston Public Library.

Generous friends and scholars have helped me hone, polish, and clarify. They include, but are not limited to, Kathy Abrams, Tom Alexander, Maureen Baron, Norma Basch, Maureen Beecher, Richard Bernstein, Davis Bitton, Kathy Brown, Nancy Cott, Bridget Crawford, Barry Cushman, Bill Deverell, Norman Dorsen, Katherine Franke, Barry Friedman, Lori Ginzberg, Bob Gordon, Jill Hasday, Richard Helmholz, Peter Hoffer, Walter Johnson, Bob Kaczorowski, Larry Kramer, Leo Lyman, Charles McCurdy, Bruce Mann, Bill Nelson, Simon Newman, Bill Novak, Mike Quinn, John Reid, Richard Ross, Jan Shipps, David Skeel, Allison Sneider, Kathy Stone, Susan Sturm, Tom Sugrue, Chris Tomlins, Andrea Tone, Martha Umphrey, Lola Van Wagenen, John Wilson, Kariann Yokota, Henry Yu, and especially Linda Kerber. All of them deserve my thanks. Laura Kalman is a wonderful and generous critic; her support and friendship have helped this book and its author in many ways.

My editors and friends Dirk Hartog and Tom Green have spent many, many hours on this book. Their dedication is widely known among legal historians. Many of us owe them, big time. I thank Dirk and Tom, as many authors have before me, and I understand now why they did. Charles Grench and Ruth Homrighaus at UNC Press have been delightfully supportive and thoughtful. Mary Caviness has been especially astute, editing copy, explaining the production and design process, and even laughing at my jokes.

My husband, Dan, and our children, Patrick and Sophia, are all doubtful that work on this book will ever end. I thank them for their love and patience. My mother, Nancy, missed the publication of this book by only six months, but her joy in books and scholarship sustains me still.

and, 46–47; polygamy and, 192–95, 214, 286 (nn. 18, 19)
Incest, 164, 166
Incorporation doctrine, 77
Indiana, 175, 177, 283 (n. 54), 288 (n. 38)
Industrial Christian Home, 164, 277 (n. 30)
Infidelity, 38, 39, 175. *See also* Free love
In re Hans Nielson (1889), 276 (n. 22)
In re Snow (1887), 276 (n. 22)
Iowa, 256–57 (n. 29), 288 (n. 38)
Ireland, Marshal, 276 (n. 20)

Jefferson, Thomas, 7, 37, 38, 258 (n. 39), 270 (n. 30); George Bancroft on, 133; on judicial usurpation of legislative power, 74–75; Morrison Remick Waite's citation of, 132–35
Jenks, George, 212
Johnson, Richard, 248–49 (n. 37)
Journal of Mormon History, 239–40 (n. 1)
Judicial power, 73–74; equity, 209, 213, 218–19; vs. legislative power, 74–75, 210, 218
Jury service, 111–12, 115–16, 151–54, 157

Kane, Thomas L., 255 (n. 12), 268 (n. 2)
Kansas, 60
Keitt, Lawrence, 58
Kent, James, 66, 68, 71–73, 140–41, 257 (n. 36)
Kentucky, 256–57 (n. 29), 288 (n. 38)
Kimball, Heber, 106–7, 261–62 (n. 13)
Kimball, Sarah, 102
Kingdom of God (Mormon doctrine), 26–27, 28, 86, 90, 96, 108, 244 (n. 17), 260 (n. 2), 261 (n. 9), 287 (n. 21)
Kingman, John W., 279 (n. 37)
Kneeland, Abner, 39, 71, 76

Labor injunctions, 218. *See also* Equity
Lamar, Lucius Quintius Cincinnatus, 213, 218
Late Corporation v. United States (1890), 186–87, 209–19, 235. *See also* Charity
Latham, Milton, 259 (n. 55)
Latter-day Saints. *See* Mormons/Mormonism
Law, William, 261 (n. 7)
LDS church. *See* Mormons/Mormonism
Lee, John D., 127
Legislation, antipolygamy, 57–58, 184, 222, 251–53 (nn. 63, 70); Democrats and, 58, 60, 62, 151, 203; higher-law concept and, 80; Mormon view of, 91–92, 111, 113; post-*Reynolds* acts, 149–54, 164–66, 171, 180, 278 (n. 32); Republicans and, 62–65, 69, 70, 78–83, 149–54, 208, 284–85 (n. 2)
"Letter to the Danbury Baptists" (Jefferson), 132–33
Libertarianism, 236, 237, 294 (n. 22)
Liberty, 5, 28, 29, 30, 35, 37, 38, 40, 62, 78, 87, 124, 133, 145, 224, 225, 230, 231, 232, 238. *See also* Religious liberty
Lieber, Francis, 66, 81, 140–41, 272 (n. 47)
Lincoln, Abraham, 51, 62, 79, 80, 82, 133, 178
Linford, Orma, 237
Literature. *See* Novels, antipolygamy
Local sovereignty. *See* Popular sovereignty
Lockwood, Belva, 175
Louisiana, 288 (n. 38)
Love, 88–89; monogamous marriage and, 67–68, 89; polygamous marriage and, 100, 101
Loveridge, Ledru, 277 (n. 28)
Loveridge, Marintha, 162–63, 277 (n. 28)

atonement doctrine, 59, 127, 254 (n. 8); contemporary defense of traditional marriage, 233–34; contemporary polygamy, 236, 237; corporate status, 26, 69–70, 81, 185–98, 202–11, 213–19, 221, 233; divorce and, 173, 175–77; founding and early years, 6, 19–27, 107–9; fundamentalist, 236; legal and political power of, 26–27, 33–35, 69, 93–94, 111–12, 150, 168, 183–89, 195, 196, 202–6, 209, 210, 266 (n. 48); Mann Act support, 294 (n. 23); marital economy, 185–211, 221; marriage legal authority claim, 22–23, 26, 28, 34, 40, 69, 94, 139, 196, 210, 221 (*see also* Polygamy); missionaries, 23, 110, 192–95, 214, 244 (n. 12); monogamous marriages, 244 (n. 16); Morrill Act's impact on, 81–83, 87, 97, 115; New Movement, 89; as new religion, 11–12; non-Mormon terminology, 239 (n. 1); novel-reading condemnation, 30, 254 (n. 5); polygamy disavowal, 1, 211–13, 220, 221, 234–36; property holdings, 26, 69–70, 81, 185, 187–89, 196–97, 203–4, 206–11, 215–20, 284–85 (n. 2), 289–90 (n. 45); public education opposition, 198–200, 206, 287 (n. 26); Raid and, 155–57, 164, 183, 188, 200; Reformation movement, 58–60, 127; resistance to antipolygamy movement by, 85–116, 147–63, 186–87, 285 (n. 3) (see also *Late Corporation v. United States*; *Reynolds v. United States*); "Revelation on Celestial Marriage," 22–24, 96, 236; term origin, 239 (n. 1); tithing mandate, 189, 196, 197, 206, 215; Underground, 158–61, 187, 276 (nn. 20, 23); woman suffrage and, 97, 169. *See also* Utah; Young, Brigham

Mormon War of 1857, 60–62, 273 (n. 5)

Mormon Wives (Victor), 29, 31–32, 42, 45, 245–46 (n. 26), 251 (n. 62)

Morrill, Justin, 63–65, 68–69, 79, 80, 82, 144

Morrill Anti-Bigamy Act (1862), 87, 97, 154, 210, 259 (n. 55), 274 (n. 14); Mormon legal power and, 81–83; property issues, 81, 188, 284–85 (n. 2); Reynolds conviction under, 115–16, 123, 126

Mortmain laws, 69–70, 187, 206

Mountain Meadows massacre, 126–27, 128

Murphy, Frank, 236–37, 294 (n. 23)

National Woman Suffrage Association, 278–79 (n. 36)

Native Americans, 56, 72, 127, 204, 205

Nativism, 8, 192–93

Nauvoo, Illinois, 23, 25, 89, 108, 109

Nauvoo Legion, 108

Nebraska, 282 (n. 52)

Nelson, Sarah, 156

Nelson, Thomas, 57, 68, 80

Nevada, 282 (n. 52), 288 (n. 38)

New Deal, 219

New Dispensation, 4, 21, 22, 26, 29, 85, 88, 89, 93, 95, 110, 119, 147. *See also* Mormons/Mormonism

New Hampshire, 288 (n. 38)

New Jersey, 256–57 (n. 29)

Newman, Angelina French, 171

Newman, John, 286 (n. 14)

New Mexico, 192

New Movement, 89

New York, 71–73, 256–57 (nn. 29, 36), 288 (n. 38)

New York Times, 169

New York Tribune, 177, 283 (n. 56)

North Dakota, 288 (n. 38)

Northwest Ordinance, 270 (n. 30)

Novels, antipolygamy, 29–54, 89, 254 (n. 5)

Ohio, 24, 107, 256–57 (n. 29), 288 (n. 38)

Old Order Amish Church, 237

Old Testament. *See* Bible

210; unlawful cohabitation ruling, 160, 276 (n. 22); *Wisconsin v. Yoder* case, 237

Taney, Roger Brooke, 123–24, 125, 183
"Tapestry of Polygamy," 293–94 (n. 21)
Taylor, John, 95, 211, 276 (nn. 20, 23)
Temperance movement, 230
Territories: antipolygamist views on, 49, 55; domestic relations issues in, 57–58, 65, 139, 151; *Late Corporation* case issues in, 210; local sovereignty issues in, 9–10, 116, 123, 125–26, 132, 134, 224–25; and Poland Act of 1874, 111–12; polygamy criminalization in, 81–82, 87; Taney opinion on status of, 123–24. *See also* Utah
Test oaths, 225, 226–28
Thatcher, Moses, 106
Thayer, James Bradley, 245 (n. 22)
Theocracy, 34, 35, 90, 142, 206
Theodemocracy, 95–96. *See also* Democracy: Mormon view of
Third-party system, 55, 253–54 (n. 2)
Thirteenth Amendment, 124
Tiedeman, Christopher, 138
Tilden, Samuel, 149
Tithing, 189, 196, 197, 206, 215
Tocqueville, Alexis de, 70, 257 (n. 30)
Tomlins, Christopher, 292 (n. 9)
Tompkins, Jane, 250 (n. 46)
Transcontinental railroad, 85, 97, 176. *See also* Railroads
Tribe, Laurence, 294 (n. 22)
Trustees-in-trust, 197
Tucker, John Randolph, 180, 197, 204, 207
Tullidge, Edward, 101
Turner, James, 38–39

Uncle Tom's Cabin (Stowe), 32, 49, 250 (n. 46), 280 (n. 42)
Underground, Mormon, 158–61, 187, 276 (nn. 20, 23)
Unitarians, 71

United States v. Reynolds (Utah, 1875, 1876), 267–68 (n. 59)
Unlawful cohabitation, 152–54, 157, 159–61, 213, 233, 266 (n. 50), 273 (n. 2), 276 (n. 22). *See also* Edmunds Act of 1882
Utah: church-state relations in, 63, 65, 81–82, 195–98, 231–32; common law rejection by, 74; Compromise of 1850 and, 110; divorce law in, 175–77, 283 (nn. 54, 56); and federal vs. local law conflicts, 4, 5, 9–10, 14, 49, 52–54, 58, 60, 65, 111–12, 254 (n. 8); immigrants to, 46–47, 193–95, 214, 286 (nn. 18, 19); legal reform efforts in, 63; Mormon economic influence in, 27, 187–92, 195–98, 200–211, 221; Mormon settlement of, 25–27, 50, 109–10; Mormon War of 1857, 60–62, 273 (n. 5); polygamy prosecutions in, 115, 147, 155–62, 220, 267 (n. 56), 273 (n. 2), 275 (n. 16), 277 (n. 28); probate courts in, 94–95, 111–12; Protestant missions in, 198, 203, 231–32, 292 (n. 12); public education in, 198–200, 204–7, 215–18, 232, 287 (n. 26); *Reynolds* decision impact on, 147, 149; statehood, 62, 86, 109–11, 213, 221, 265 (n. 42); woman suffrage in, 97, 164, 166, 167–71, 180, 278–80 (nn. 36–38, 41). *See also* Mormons/Mormonism; Popular sovereignty

Van Buren, Martin, 107–8
Van Zile, P. T., 276 (n. 19)
Vermont, 216, 217, 233
Vest, George Graham, 268–69 (n. 9)
Victor, Metta, 29–32, 35, 37, 38, 40, 43, 45, 47, 49, 51, 52, 230, 246–47 (n. 28), 250–52 (nn. 46, 63, 64)
Violence, 47, 108, 156, 161
Virginia, 7, 132–34, 135, 197, 274–75 (n. 15)
Voluntarism, 57, 63, 96, 172, 203, 222, 232